Oracle Press™

Hudson Continuous Integration in Practice

Ed Burns and Winston Prakash

New York Chicago San Francisco
Athens London Madrid Mexico City
Milan New Delhi Singapore Sydney Toronto

Cataloging-in-Publication Data is on file with the Library of Congress

Hudson Continuous Integration in Practice

1 2 3 4 5 6 7 8 9 0 DOC DOC 1 0 9 8 7 6 5 4 3

ISBN 978-0-07-180428-8
MHID 0-07-180428-5

Sponsoring Editor
Brandi Shailer

Editorial Supervisor
Janet Walden

Project Manager
Sheena Uprety, Cenveo® Publisher Services

Acquisitions Coordinator
Amanda Russell

Technical Editors
Steve Christou and Bob Foster

Copy Editor
Margaret Berson

Proofreader
Bev Weiler

Indexer
Ted Laux

Production Supervisor
James Kussow

Composition
Cenveo Publisher Services

Illustration
Cenveo Publisher Services

Art Director, Cover
Jeff Weeks

To my wife, Amy, whose boundless patience and dedication inspire me in everything I do.

—Ed Burns

I dedicate this book to my wife, Dora, who never stops encouraging me to take on new endeavors.

—Winston Prakash

About the Authors

Ed Burns is currently a consulting engineer at Oracle America, Inc., where he leads a team of Web experts from across the industry in developing JavaServer Faces Technology through the Java Community Process and in open source. He is the author of three other books for McGraw-Hill: *Secrets of the Rock Star Programmers* (2008), *JavaServer Faces: The Complete Reference* (coauthored with Chris Schalk, 2006), and *JavaServer Faces 2.0: The Complete Reference* (coauthored with Chris Schalk and Neil Griffin, 2009).

Dr. Winston Prakash is currently an architect at Oracle Corporation. He has extensive experience in object-oriented design and development of large-scale applications. At present, his main focus is on developing data-driven, enterprise Web applications using advanced Java EE technologies. He leads the open source project, Hudson CI Server, at Eclipse Foundation.

About the Technical Editors

Steve Christou is a software developer with a focus on Continuous Integration. His experience with programming started with QBasic in high school and moved to Java and C++ in college. Steven currently has six years of progressive computer programming experience. He is now the lead designer of Cobertura, an open-source code coverage tool for Java, and continues to provide support for Hudson.

Bob Foster is a Consulting Developer at Oracle and an active Hudson committer. He designed and led implementation of the CPU/Memory Profiler in JDeveloper 11*g*. Prior to joining Oracle, he was an Eclipse contributor and author of the XMLBuddy XML Editor. He worked on several Integrated Development Environments (IDEs) for C++ and Java that are no longer in use, beginning 20 years ago, when he wrote the Classy C++ visual editor, which was purchased by Symantec and released as Visual Architect for Macintosh.

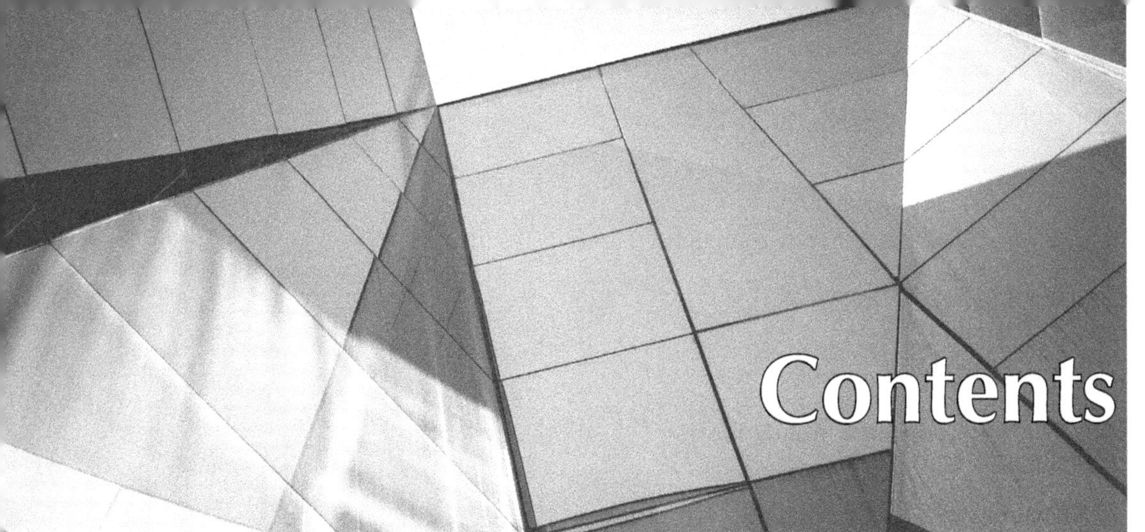

Contents

Foreword

Years ago, Tim O'Reilly coined the phrase "architecture of participation." His insight was that successful open source projects all shared one common trait: the ability for developers outside of the core team to easily extend the code to meet their needs. Examples of this successful pattern include the Linux kernel, the Apache Web server, Firefox extensions, and Eclipse plugins. Hudson was one of the first open source Continuous Integration tools to embrace this notion. It provided an extensible platform and, in turn, created an ecosystem of plugins that allowed it to support a myriad of repository, build, and analysis tools in many different workflows. Kohsuke Kawaguchi, Hudson's original author, worked hard to create a vibrant and engaged community around the Hudson project, and that has been a big part of its success.

In many ways, Hudson changed the face of software development. By making it significantly easier to implement Continuous Integration for a development team—or even an entire software organization—it moved what was considered a best practice to common practice. By allowing developers to more easily automate their builds, it helped make software production a repeatable process. By lowering the developer cost of builds, it helped make Continuous Integration mainstream. It is a rare open source project that can claim to have advanced the state of the art in software development.

The Eclipse Foundation itself is a great example of a large, distributed organization that relies on Hudson. At the time of writing, we have over 150 separate open source projects using Hudson as their Continuous Integration server. Our 2013 simultaneous release, Eclipse Kepler, consisted of 71 projects and 58 million lines of code. It was built by 420 Eclipse committers from over 50 companies around the world, as well as hundreds of individual contributors. And it was entirely built with Hudson. In fact, it is hard to imagine how we could operate without the automation and Continuous Integration provided by Hudson.

Winston Prakash is the leader of the Eclipse Hudson project, and is intimately aware of its internal architecture and implementation. I know that he has worked tenaciously over the past couple of years to improve the reliability, code quality, and scalability of Hudson. Ed Burns is the leader of JavaServer Faces, and has used Hudson extensively in managing the complexity of that project. Together the coauthors bring a wealth of experience and insight to the topic. I am sure that you will find their book a valuable resource as you embrace the "Hudson Lifestyle."

—*Mike Milinkovich*
Executive Director, Eclipse Foundation
June 2013

Acknowledgments

Hudson is a software tool that can help increase team productivity, but productivity lives or dies at the hands of the team wielding that tool. The same can be said for authoring a book. Neither Winston nor I could have been productive in writing this book without the team from McGraw-Hill Education. Sponsoring editor Brandi Shailer provided firm and experienced guidance through all phases of the authoring process. I especially appreciated her understanding as Winston and I juggled our day jobs with the task of writing this book. Acquisitions coordinator Amanda Russell weathered several episodes of chapter renumbering and reallocation and managed to keep track of all the moving parts of this book, entirely using e-mail attachments. Thanks to the illustrators at Cenveo Publisher Services for turning the rough art from Winston and me into professional images. Steve Christou and Bob Foster provided timely, in-depth, and above all, frank technical editing that served both as an advocate for the reader, and an oversight on cohesiveness. In a world where more and more information is available only online, and much of that information is coming from self-published individuals, I continue to believe that curated information from a traditional publishing team is the best way to deliver high-quality technical content in a portable and easily digestible way.

My personal support team also deserves a huge thank you. My wife, Amy, has supported me through four books now. With two small kids growing up, each one has been a different kind of sacrifice for her to pick up the slack I leave due to the spare-time nature of my technical book authoring arrangement. Thanks to my sons Owen and Logan as well, for understanding that it doesn't really take forever to finish a book; it just seems that way.

Thanks to Dad and Mom, Edward M. and Kathy Burns. Your solid support of my family has made it much easier to get this book done. Thanks also to my brother, Brendan Burns; as an avid reader, I appreciate your contribution to the book publishing ecosystem and, more importantly, I appreciate your personal support.

I'd like to give a special thanks to my long-time friends from Vienna, Austria: Erich Ruetz and Regina Preslmair, their two sons Christoph and Jakob, and Eric Sr. and Hedwig Ruetz. I look forward to the annual JSF conference in Vienna that I have been blessed to attend since 2008, and our traditional visits after that conference.

Finally, and above and under all, I give thanks to my Lord and Savior Jesus Christ, whose blessings make all things possible, including this book.

—Ed Burns
Florida, U.S.A.

First I want to thank Ed Burns for inviting me to write this book with him and giving me an opportunity to experience, first hand, writing a book. Writing the initial manuscripts may be easy, but taking them through the editing process and making them worthy chapters is an involved process. Many thanks go to Brandi Shailer and Amanda Russell for making the process easy for us. Special thanks go to Bob Foster and Steven Christou for taking time from their busy schedule to do a thorough technical review of the chapters. I also want to thank Jim Clark for the many helpful brainstorming sessions we had about Hudson. Finally, thanks to my wife and son for letting me work during weekends, sacrificing fun outdoor activities.

—Winston Prakash
California, U.S.A.

In the ever-evolving practice of software development, the only constant is that complexity keeps increasing. In his work on JavaServer Faces at Oracle, coauthor Ed Burns has found that Hudson is the single most valuable software tool to enable keeping a lid on that complexity, though it must be carefully applied, lest even more complexity is created. This book places the Hudson Continuous Integration product in the context of the larger software development lifecycle as a means to achieve higher productivity and contain complexity. The reader will learn how to install Hudson in a way that suits their particular environment. Hands-on examples, in Java, will be used to explain the depth and breadth of using Hudson. This approach will lead the reader from novice, to apprentice, to mastery. The Hudson plugin ecosystem will be examined in detail, and the software architecture that enables that ecosystem will be fully explained, with code examples leading the reader to writing their own plugin. The book closes with a thorough treatment of how to effectively live the Hudson lifestyle, which can be summed up as "automate everything."

This book is divided into four parts and contains ten chapters and three appendixes.

Part I: Essential Knowledge

Reading Part I will give you everything you need to know to be completely effective using Hudson for the tasks for which it is most commonly used.

Chapter 1: Getting Started

This chapter introduces Hudson and its fundamental concept of "job" and defines the characteristics of a production-ready Hudson server. You'll learn how to install Hudson and get it running for the most basic kinds of jobs.

Chapter 2: Hudson Precondition Primer

This chapter acknowledges the unique position of Hudson as a tool of tools. As a consequence of this fact, mastery of Hudson implies mastery of, or at least solid familiarity with, all of the tools being managed by Hudson. This chapter introduces the reader to the main classes of tools that you will encounter as you learn to use Hudson in practice.

Chapter 3: Basic Concepts

This chapter rounds out the essential knowledge for using Hudson in most enterprise environments. After reading the first three chapters, you will have everything you need to know to be effective using Hudson for most common tasks. More importantly, you will have the foundation for learning more.

This chapter introduces Software Configuration Management (SCM) and shows how to add it to a job. The reader is walked through the process of creating jobs for a Java application and Java Servlet. The concept of Hudson plugins is introduced via the Plugin Center and the JobConfig plugin. The sample Hudson instance is configured for security. Finally, you are introduced to software quality assurance tools and the most common build notifiers.

Part II: Applying Hudson

Part II builds on the knowledge from Part I and covers usage appropriate for those who are committed to moving toward Continuous Delivery as their primary approach for developing and delivering software.

Chapter 4: Hudson as Continuous Integration Server

Continuous Integration is the main task performed by most Hudson instances. This chapter defines the term with examples and shows how to achieve practical continuous integration with Hudson. It also introduces the concept of Continuous Delivery and how to approach it with Hudson.

Chapter 5: Hudson and Automated Testing

Automated testing is essential to Continuous Integration. This chapter provides an overview of the kinds of automated testing one can perform with Hudson, with code examples of current testing technologies such as HtmlUnit and Arquillian.

Chapter 6: Hudson as Part of Your Tool Suite

Because Hudson is a tool of tools, it's important to examine how Hudson fits into the wider tool suite used by software developers. This chapter surveys IDE integration and issue tracker integration, and closes with some popular ways to stay informed on Hudson job status in browsers and on mobile devices.

Chapter 7: Distributed Building Using Hudson

Even though significant value can be achieved using a single Hudson instance, many production environments need more than what a single instance can provide. This chapter explains when you would need a distributed Hudson system, and how to set one up. The Matrix Build feature is explained in detail.

Chapter 8: Basic Plugin Development

You can't get very far in using Hudson without having to install plugins. Similarly, you can't get very far in mastering Hudson without learning how to write your own Hudson plugin. This chapter is tutorial content on only the essential aspects of writing Hudson plugins.

Part III: The Hudson Lifestyle

Part III stands alone from the preceding two parts but is essential to maximizing the benefit of using Hudson in a software development team.

Chapter 9: Advanced Plugin Development

This chapter expands on the knowledge in the previous chapter to cover less common, but still important, aspects of plugin development such as integrating with various dashboards, accessing SCM information from your plugin, custom notifiers, and the Jelly UI technology.

Chapter 10: Hudson Best Practices

System administration tasks are an important aspect of Hudson management. This chapter treats such topics as memory and disk requirements, JVM options, Web proxy concerns, server redundancy, and upgrading Hudson.

Part IV: Appendixes

The appendixes supplement content in Part III for important areas that do not warrant an independent chapter.

Appendix A: Widely Used Hudson Plugins

This appendix gives insight into the process used by Oracle for curating the plugins in the Hudson Plugin Manager, as well as providing an overview of the most important plugins available there.

Appendix B: Personal Hudson Instance

This appendix delivers on the promise of showing how to live the Hudson lifestyle by examining several approaches to using a personal Hudson instance (Hudson-as-valet) to achieve higher individual developer productivity.

Appendix C: Hudson for Windows Developers

In a nod to the fact that Hudson is used in non-Java development as well as Java development, this appendix introduces several plugins that make it possible to use Hudson effectively for Windows-based software development projects.

Intended Audience

Code quality is something that everyone passionately admits is essential, but when it comes time to pay the cost to achieve it, the passion often dries up, leaving only the best efforts of the software developers writing the code. As such, software quality books tend to be seen as a longer-term investment than books on practical programming skills. In the face of this business reality, the saving grace of Hudson is that it admits this tendency of people to skimp on quality. Hudson endeavors to lower the cost of quality to the point where people will actually pay for it (mostly in terms of developer effort).

The major audience for this book is anyone working in software development. The Hudson product is clearly a system administration tool, but it is important to note that most developers *are not* sysadmins. In fact, developers often see sysadmin work as taking time away from their primary responsibility of programming. This book is aimed squarely at developers who want to spend less time on operations tasks and more time programming, and maintain higher code quality while doing so.

The secondary audience for this book is system administrators who work closely with programmers. These highly valued team members are often referred to as "buildmeisters." In practice, one of the developers often assumes this role, in addition to their normal programming responsibilities, but if the team is fortunate enough to have a dedicated buildmeister, this book is for them too.

Retrieving the Examples

Some of the source files used in this book can be downloaded from the Oracle Press website at www.OraclePressBooks.com. The files are contained in a ZIP file.

PART I

Essential Knowledge

CHAPTER 1

Getting Started

This book will explain what Hudson is, and how to use it to increase the quality and improve the productivity of your software development team through the practice of Continuous Integration. Teams that practice Continuous Integration can move faster, and with consistently higher-quality code, than teams that do not. This first chapter is a tutorial that takes you through the process of downloading, installing, and configuring a working, resilient Hudson installation. Such an installation has the following characteristics.

- It runs on a master machine whose primary purpose is to run Hudson.
- It automatically starts when the master operating system starts up.
- It has at least one job that runs regularly. "Job"[1] is the term Hudson uses to describe a unit of work that Hudson can perform. For example, a Hudson server could have a job that compiles the code in a project, runs tests on the compiled code, and produces a report with the results.
- Its configuration is set to back up automatically so that the value provided by the Hudson installation can quickly be restored in the event of failure of the host machine.

The ability to create a Hudson installation with these characteristics forms the basis of the skills necessary to apply the techniques in the rest of this book.

Installing Hudson

Hudson is the kind of software that does most of its work when no one is looking. It differs from other kinds of software such as word processors, spreadsheets, debuggers, and diagramming programs. For most of the time that Hudson is running, no one is sitting in front of a user interface telling it what to do. In fact, in most cases Hudson is installed on a master machine without a dedicated keyboard, mouse, and monitor. Such a master machine is colloquially called a "server," and Hudson is essentially server software. When using Hudson in practice, it is strongly recommended to have a dedicated server for the sole purpose of running Hudson. Installation instructions for server software are very platform-dependent, but Hudson does provide an easy-to-run, cross-platform installation method whose only precondition is a sufficiently recent Java Development Kit installation. This installation method is only intended to allow quick and easy evaluation of Hudson and will be described next. The following sections will cover the more robust and platform-dependent installation methods.

[1] The Hudson user interface is inconsistent in the term it uses for "job." Sometimes the user interface refers to this concept as "project." Other times the term "build" is used. This book will always use the term "job" to mean the unit of work performed by Hudson.

Trying Hudson with the Easy Installation Method

Hudson is written in Java, and thus you must install a Java Development Kit on the host operating system that is to run Hudson. It's important that you get the Java Development Kit (JDK) and not just the Java Runtime Environment (JRE). The JDK includes development tools such as the Java compiler and the jar tool, whereas the JRE does not. The latest JDK downloads for all operating systems may be found at www.oracle.com/java/. Older releases of the JDK are available at that address as well, except for JDK 6 and earlier on Mac OS X. For JDK 6 and earlier on Mac Os X, Apple distributes its own JDK releases and these are available through the Software Update feature accessible from the Apple menu. The examples in this book require at least JDK 6 to be installed.

Once the JDK is installed, the easy installation method of running Hudson is to download the Hudson Web Application Archive (war) file. This kind of file is a JavaEE Web Application Archive suitable for running in a JavaEE application server or similar software such as Apache Tomcat or Jetty. The Hudson war file provides a built-in server, which will be used in this section. The Hudson war file may be downloaded from http://eclipse.org/hudson/download.php.

The simplest syntax for starting Hudson using the easy installation method is to invoke **java -jar hudson-<*version*>.war**, where **<*version*>** is the version number of the Hudson server you downloaded, such as 3.0.0 or 2.2.1. There is one argument to the Java executable here, something like **-jar hudson-3.0.0.war**. This syntax will start Hudson with default values of 8080 for server port and ~/.hudson for the Hudson home directory. To avoid conflict with existing ports and directories you may have on your host, let's pass two additional command-line arguments to the Java executable. The ordering of arguments to the Java executable is significant: all arguments that are intended directly for the Java executable must precede all arguments that are intended for the Hudson program itself. This example has one of each kind of argument.

- **-DHUDSON_HOME=<*fully qualified path to the directory to use as Hudson home*>**
  This argument is intended for the Java executable and is an example of a Java "system property." All such arguments must start with "-D" and be immediately followed by a string of the format name=value. This string is case sensitive, there must be no spaces between the -D and name, and the name itself must have no spaces. Also, if the value has spaces, the entire value must be in quotes.

  Hudson needs to write out lots of configuration information when it runs, and this is the place where it does so. If this argument is not specified, the easy installation method will use the value .hudson in the current user's home directory as the value. To simplify backing up the Hudson configuration, specify this option explicitly. If the named directory does not exist, Hudson will create it and populate it with the configuration information.

- **--httpPort=<*some number, usually between 7000 and 9000*>**
  This argument is intended for the Hudson program itself. If this option is not specified, Hudson will use 8080. In practice, this port is often occupied, so for this example, a much less likely number is chosen. While HUDSON_HOME was an argument to the Java executable, httpPort is an argument to the Hudson main class itself.

With these additional two arguments, the complete invocation syntax to start Hudson using the easy installation method is shown here:

```
F:\>java
-DHUDSON_HOME=F:\HUDSON_HOME
-jar E:\hudson-3.0.0.war
--httpPort=7214
```

The Java executable should immediately begin producing output similar to the following:

```
Running from: E:\hudson-3.0.0.war
/E:/hudson-3.0.0-RC2.war
2012-09-07 14:56:49.062:INFO::Logging to STDERR via org.mortbay.log.
StdErrLog
War - /E:/hudson-3.0.0-RC2.war
2012-09-07 14:56:49.109:INFO::jetty-6.1.26
2012-09-07 14:56:49.203:INFO::Extract file:/E:/hudson-3.0.0-RC2.war to
F:\HUDSON_HOME\war\webapp
2012-09-07 14:57:04.984:INFO::NO JSP Support for /, did not find org.
apache.jasper.servlet.JspServlet
2012-09-07 14:57:05.031:WARN::Unknown realm: default
Sep 7, 2012 2:57:05 PM org.eclipse.hudson.HudsonServletContextListener
contextInitialized
INFO: Home directory: F:\HUDSON_HOME
Sep 7, 2012 2:57:07 PM org.eclipse.hudson.HudsonServletContextListener
contextInitialized
INFO:
================>
Initial setup required. Please go to the Hudson Dashboard and complete
the setup
.
<================
```

Because Hudson is server software, the most effective way to make the graphical user interface available is via a Web browser. Therefore, most of the configuration you must do in Hudson is done by visiting the Hudson server in a Web browser. Because you started the server with a specific value for httpPort, that value must be included in the URL. For example, you may type either **http://localhost:7214/** or **http://127.0.0.1:7214/** into a browser on the same host where the Hudson command was invoked. If the host where the Hudson command was invoked is different from the host where the browser is running, the hostname or IP address of that host must be used, but the port number would stay the same. For example, http://192.168.2.105:7214/ is the IP address in a local area network.

With Hudson 3.0.0, the first time the Hudson console is visited, you are presented with a configuration screen that allows you to install some optional plugins. A subsequent example will illustrate this optional installation step. For now, just click the Finish button at the bottom of the page. A working connection to the public Internet is required the first time you start it. After installing some basic required plugins, Hudson will present the message, "Please wait while Hudson is getting ready to work." When the initialization is complete, the Hudson main dashboard will appear, as shown here.

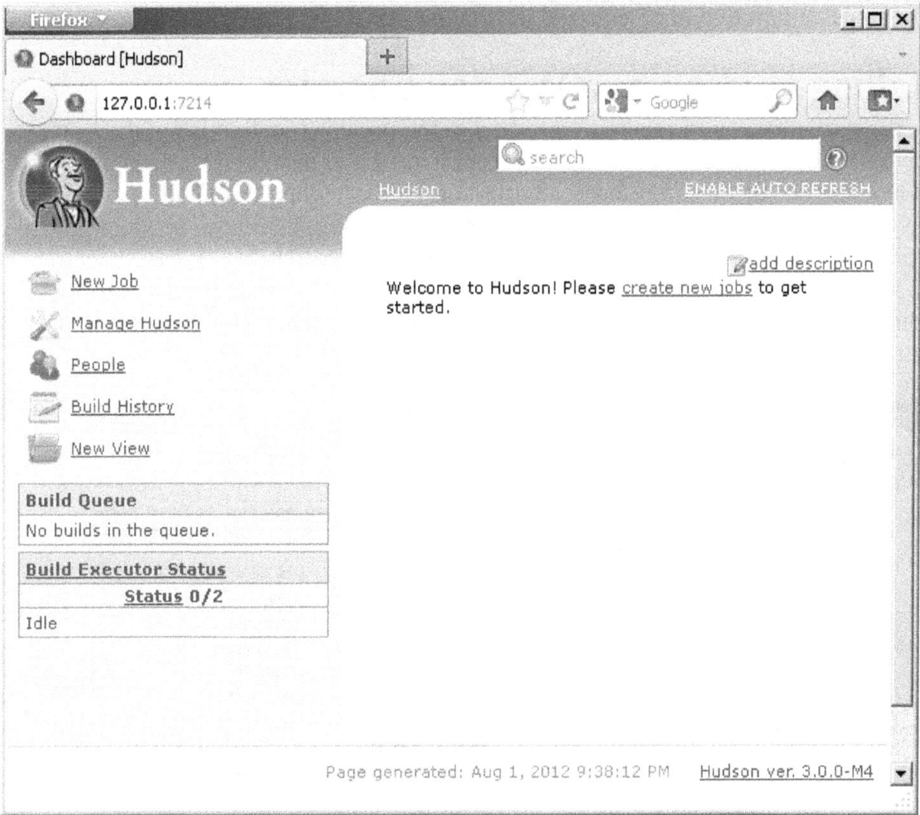

To conclude this example, we will shut down the Hudson instance correctly. Click Manage Hudson in the navigation list on the left. This view is the gateway for all Hudson settings not specific to any one Hudson job. At the bottom of this list is a link titled Prepare for Shutdown. It is a good idea to get in the habit of always clicking this link and waiting for any currently running jobs to complete before shutting down Hudson completely. Clicking this link should show a message similar to "Hudson is preparing to shut down." In this case, we haven't created any jobs yet, so we can proceed immediately to the command line from which the Java executable was invoked and press CTRL-C. Instead of this command immediately causing Java to exit, it causes Hudson to shut down gracefully. You should see a message similar to the following in the command-line window.

```
2012-12-28 07:27:21.204:INFO:oejsh.ContextHandler:stopped
o.e.j.w.WebAppContext{/,file:/C:/.hudson/war/webapp/},file:/E:/hudson-3.0.0.war
2012-12-28 07:27:21.257:INFO:oejut.ShutdownThread:shutdown already commenced
```

As a precaution to avoid contaminating future exercises, delete the directory that was specified as HUDSON_HOME.

Hudson offers numerous command-line options to optimize its performance. Such settings and more will be covered in Chapter 10.

Installing Hudson as a Windows Service

While the easy installation method described in the previous section is not the best choice for production use, it is useful as a steppingstone to installing Hudson as a Windows service. This will automatically start up Hudson when Windows starts, one of the four properties of a resilient Hudson installation. Windows services are controlled using the Services dialog. There are several ways to bring up the Services panel, but one way that works on Windows XP, Vista, and 7 is to run the services.msc executable from the Windows command prompt. The Windows XP Services panel, without Hudson installed, is shown here.

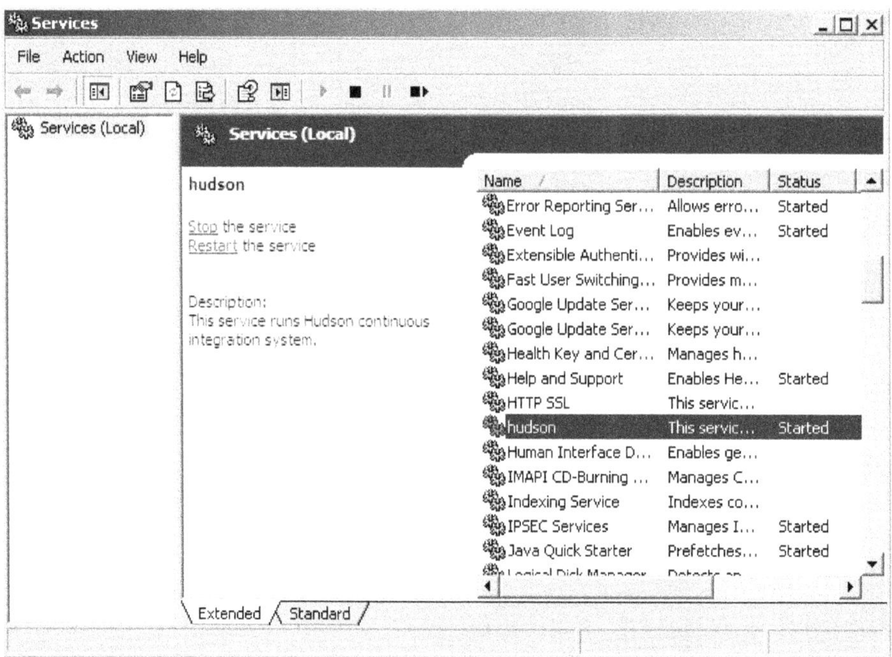

1. Make a fresh directory with an easy path, for example, F:\HUDSON_SERVICE. Go through the steps to start Hudson with the easy installation method again.
2. Once Hudson is running, click the Manage Hudson link in the list of links in the upper left of the main Hudson dashboard.
3. Click the next-to-last link, titled Install as Windows Service, on the Manage Hudson page.
4. In the text field labeled Installation Directory, enter the fully qualified path to the directory you just created and click Install. You should see a message stating that installation successfully completed and asking if you want to start the newly installed Windows service. Click Yes. Eventually the Hudson instance running on port 7214 will stop and the new, Windows service-based instance will be started on port 8080 by default.
5. To verify that the new service is running, open the Windows Services panel and in the Action menu, choose Refresh.
6. Click the Name column in the table to sort the services by name and scroll to the letter H.
7. You should now see a row with the name hudson, with a lower case h.
8. The last step is to change the port back to 7214.

Visit the Hudson dashboard, now at http://localhost:8080/, and go through the initial setup steps as with the easy installation method. Prepare Hudson for shutdown, as in the previous section. Then, go into the Windows Services panel, click on the name hudson, and in the Action menu, select Stop. Within the directory you created at the beginning of this exercise, open the hudson.xml file in a text editor. Locate the line that starts with <arguments>. This is an XML element that contains the arguments to pass to the Java VM when starting Hudson. If there is an httpPort option, change its value to **7214**. If not, add one, **--httpPort=7281**, just before the closing </arguments> tag. Now, go back into the Services panel, click on the name hudson, and choose Start in the Action menu. Now Hudson will automatically start when Windows starts.

The final step will be to clean up by uninstalling the Hudson Windows Service. Prepare Hudson for shutdown and then perform the shutdown using the Windows Services panel. At a command prompt, type

```
sc delete Hudson
```

Refresh the Windows Services panel and the hudson row should disappear. Finally, delete the directory created at the beginning of this exercise to leave your machine clean for further exercises.

Installing Hudson to Start When a User Logs in to Mac OS X

This tutorial demonstrates how to make it so Hudson starts up automatically when a specific user logs in to Mac OS X. The Hudson-specific part of this tutorial is identical to the preceding section about trying Hudson with the easy installation method. The Mac OS X–specific part uses the Automator utility built into OS X. Automator is a powerful utility for getting work done on Mac OS X. Its purpose is similar to Hudson itself: workflow automation. However, because this is an Apple program, the creation of the workflows can be done visually in a drag-and-drop fashion. In the Finder, navigate to Applications and launch Automator. In the pop-up modal dialog that appears when Automator is launched, select Application and click the Choose button. Automator opens up in the application creation mode. The basic Automator user interface is shown here.

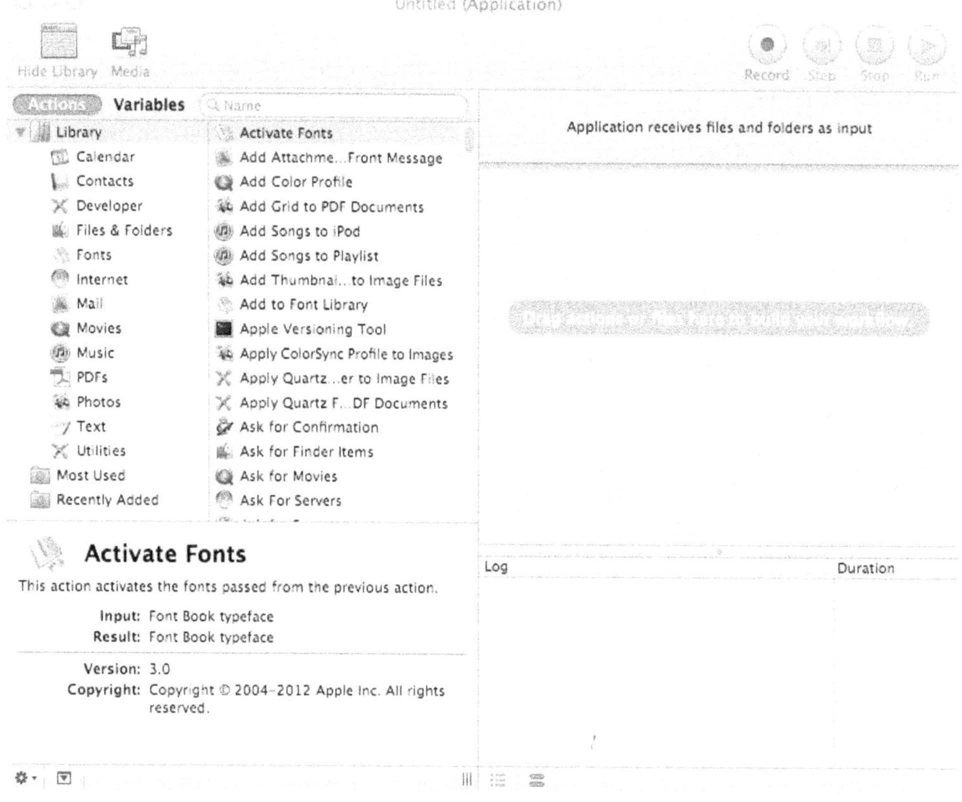

The left part of the panel shows all the available actions that can make up a workflow, or application. The leftmost part of the panel lists the categories of actions.

1. Select Utilities in this list.
2. Scroll to the right of this panel to expose the Run Shell Script action.
3. Drag this action from the panel into the area that says "Drag actions or files here to build your workflow." The Run Shell Script action comes prepopulated to invoke the UNIX program cat to delete this text and replace it with the Java invocation from the easy installation section. Make sure to use fully qualified paths for the HUDSON_HOME system property, and the argument to the -jar option, pointing to the Hudson war file.
4. Save the application by choosing Save in the File menu. Name it Start Hudson and save it to Applications.
5. Since this is a Mac, we need a proper icon. Show the Start Hudson application in the Finder, right-click it, and choose Get Info.
6. Open up a Web browser and visit http://eclipse.org/hudson/. Arrange the windows so that both the browser and the info window for Start Hudson are showing.
7. Drag the image of Hudson the butler from the browser onto the small robot icon at the top of the info window. Close the info window.
8. The final step is to run the Start Hudson application from the finder and make it so that it starts at login.

Once the Hudson application has started, verify that it's running by visiting http://localhost:7214/ in the browser. If HUDSON_HOME was previously an empty directory, you have to do the initial install again. Prepare Hudson for shutdown as before and find the Java icon in the dock that represents the running Hudson instance. Right-click it and choose Quit. You may have to wait a bit for Hudson to completely shut down. The running status of Hudson can be queried from the command line with the command **ps -e | grep hudson**. If the only output shown is a line containing **grep hudson**, you can rest assured that Hudson has stopped. Locate the Start Hudson application in the Finder and drag it to the dock. Once the script has been dragged into the dock, its icon will appear as shown here.

Right-click the icon and mouse over the word Options. Select Open at Login in the pop-up menu. Now Hudson will start whenever this user logs in to Mac OS X.

Installing Hudson Within Tomcat

Application containers are a class of server-side software that provides a platform for running arbitrary server-side software, including Hudson. Apache Tomcat is a very popular lightweight Java application container. There are many application containers to choose from, each with its strengths and weaknesses. Finding the right application container for the job at hand is beyond the scope of this book, but for most purposes, Tomcat is perfectly suitable for a departmental Hudson installation. This section will cover just the basics to get Hudson running in Tomcat. This tutorial will use a Tomcat 7.0 series release, the single binary for which can be downloaded from http://tomcat.apache.org/. Download one of the bundles from the Core section and unpack it into an empty directory. Once you've downloaded the bundle, getting Hudson working in Tomcat is really as easy as one-two-three:

1. Enable the manager Web app.
2. Pass the HUDSON_HOME environment variable to Tomcat.
3. Deploy the war file.

Enable the Manager Web App

The most fundamental skill in using an application container is called *deployment*. This process describes the practice of making a unit of server-side software, such as Hudson, available for use. To provide a base level of security, the ability to deploy software is disabled by default in Tomcat. Enabling it is a simple matter of editing the tomcat-users.xml file, located in the conf directory of the Tomcat distribution.

Make it so the following XML elements appear within the <tomcat-users> element.

```
<role rolename="tomcat"/>
<user username="tomcat" password="tomcat" roles="tomcat,manager-gui"/>
<role rolename="manager-gui" />
```

The preceding lines must not be duplicated in the tomcat-users.xml file. After ensuring that the tomcat-users.xml file is correctly configured, we need to ensure that HUDSON_HOME is passed to Tomcat as an environment variable. One reliable way to accomplish this is to set the value in the catalina.sh or catalina.bat file, on non-Windows and Windows platforms, respectively. These files are located in the bin directory. To illustrate a tip regarding the use of Windows directory names with spaces, the following example uses "F:\My Hudson Home" as the HUDSON_HOME environment variable. At the Windows command prompt, use the **dir /x** command to output the special syntax to display an alternate name for a directory with spaces in the directory name. In this case, the value would be F:\MYHUDS~1. With this value in hand, edit the catalina.bat file and insert the following lines after the initial list of lines starting with rem.

```
...
rem
rem
rem $Id: catalina.bat 1344732 2012-05-31 14:08:02Z kkolinko $
rem ---------------------------------------------------------------------------

set HUDSON_HOME=F:\MYHUDS~1

rem Suppress Terminate batch job on CTRL+C
if not ""%1"" == ""run"" goto mainEntry
...
```

This script should be invoked from the bin directory and the argument **start** must be passed to the script, like this.

```
.\catalina.bat start
```

The analogous edit for the catalina.sh looks like this.

```
#
# $Id: catalina.sh 1202062 2011-11-15 06:50:02Z mturk $
# -----------------------------------------------------------------------------

HUDSON_HOME=/Users/edburns/HUDSON_HOME

# OS specific support.  $var _must_ be set to either true or false.
```

By default, tomcat starts on port 8080. After startup, the manager app, which will be used to deploy Hudson, may be found at this URL, http://localhost:8080/manager. Visit this URL in your browser and find the Deploy section. Find the WAR file to deploy within the Deploy section. Click Browse and use the file chooser to navigate to the Hudson WAR file, in this case, hudson-3.0.0.war. The manager app is shown here.

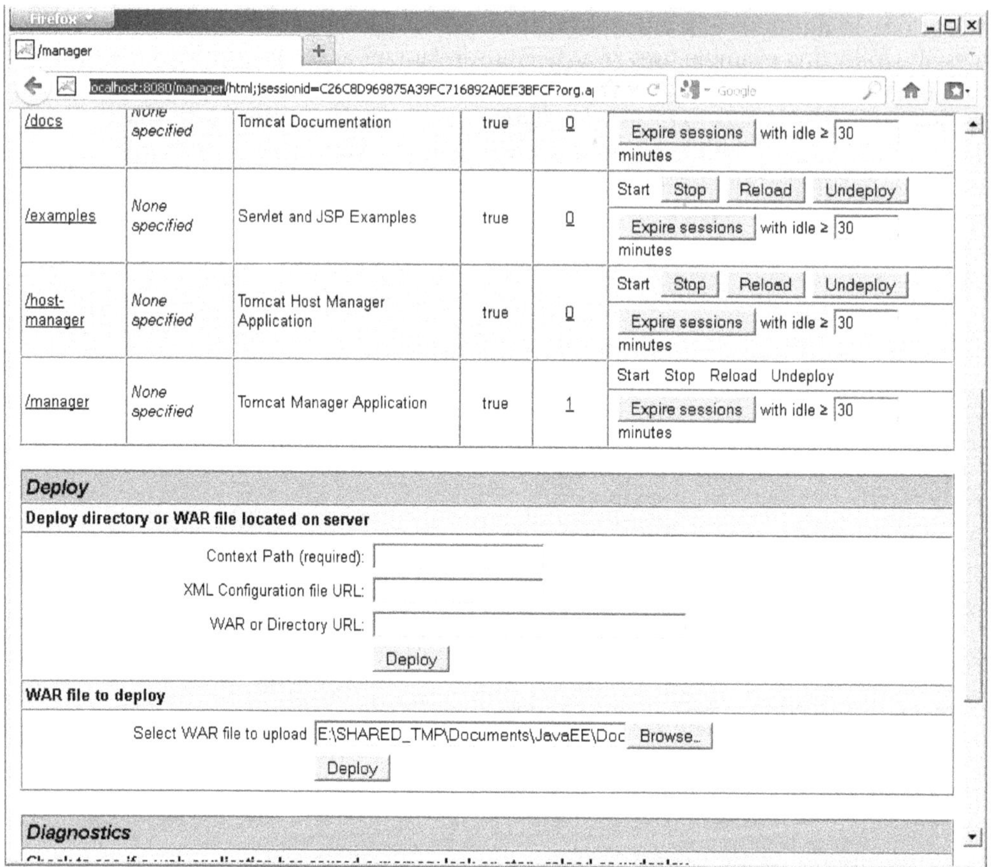

Click the Deploy button and wait for Tomcat to deploy the app. If the deployment is successful, a new row will appear in the Applications section. Click on the entry in the Path column in this table. If the browser shows an HTTP Status 404 message, append a / (slash) to the URL and reload the page. This should show the Hudson installation screen as in the other examples. Tomcat can be shut down by invoking the catalina.bat or catalina.sh script and passing **stop** as the argument.

We will revisit Tomcat in Chapter 10 in the context of proxying Tomcat using Apache Server for the purpose of better security.

Installing Hudson on GNU/Linux

The last of the big three operating systems on which the installation of Hudson will be demonstrated is GNU/Linux. To be fair, calling GNU/Linux a single operating system is an oversimplification, and a complete treatment of all the many variants of GNU/Linux is beyond the scope of this book. This section will use Oracle Enterprise Linux, which is a variant of Red Hat Enterprise Linux. All of the steps in this section apply to any variant of GNU/Linux and most variants of UNIX. Furthermore, because UNIX is really the best choice for running a dedicated Hudson server, a few other steps are included as recommendations.

Preparing the Host Operating System

More depth on the topic of preparing the host OS for running Hudson can be found in Chapter 10, but for now, the most basic preparation is to create a UNIX user and group under which the Hudson server will run. It will be very important to use the exact same user (and corresponding UNIX uid and gid) to run Hudson on every server in the case of a distributed build system. This is also important when using UNIX file sharing (usually Network File System or NFS) to share files between the servers. For this reason, it is recommended that you manually specify UNIX id and group information when creating the UNIX user to run Hudson. By convention, the name of this user and group is hudson. Each UNIX distribution has its own way of creating users and groups, but the syntax for Oracle Enterprise Linux is as follows. Open a terminal, log in as root on the system, and type the following three commands.

```
# groupadd --gid 7213 hudson
# useradd --gid 7213 --uid 7214 --create-home --shell /bin/bash Hudson
# passwd hudson
```

These commands enable creating the hudson user and group with an arbitrary uid and gid.

Alternatively, Hudson is available as a convenient RedHat .rpm file that creates the hudson userid and a hudson UNIX group, as well as a readymade startup script in /etc/init.d/hudson upon install. There are many ways to install an .rpm file, but the GNU/Linux yum installer is the easiest way to install the .rpm for Hudson. Before installing with this approach, verify that the system does not have a hudson user or group because the install scripts may not complete successfully if these exist. Make sure the system is connected to the public Internet and is not behind any proxy servers.

```
# cd /etc/yum.repos.d
# wget http://hudson-ci.org/redhat/hudson.repo
# sudo yum check-update
# sudo yum install hudson
```

You may be prompted to continue the installation after being shown the size of the download. In this case, answer **y**. If the installation proceeds successfully, the output should look like the following.

```
Loaded plugins: downloadonly, refresh-packagekit, security
Setting up Install Process
Resolving Dependencies
--> Running transaction check
---> Package hudson.noarch 0:3.0.1.b2-1.1 will be installed
--> Finished Dependency Resolution
...
Downloading Packages:
...
  Installing : hudson-3.0.1.b2-
1.1.noarch                                             1/1
  Verifying  : hudson-3.0.1.b2-
1.1.noarch                                             1/1
Installed:
  hudson.noarch 0:3.0.1.b2-1.1
Complete!
```

If the uid and gid numbers for the newly created hudson user and group need to be changed, the /etc/passwd and /etc/group files can be edited, respectively. This must be done before running Hudson because any files created before making this change will become inaccessible afterward. It is best to start with the /etc/group file. Once again, as root, edit the /etc/group file and find the line that starts with hudson. Change the number at the end of the line to be the desired group number, as shown here.

```
hudson:x:7213:
```

Next the hudson userid is changed. As root, edit the /etc/passwd file and locate the line starting with hudson. Make the line look like the following.

```
hudson:x:7214:7213:Hudson Continuous Build server:/var/lib/hudson:/bin/bash
```

The first number in this line must be the UNIX uid, in this case 7214. The next number must be the UNIX gid, in this case 7213. Finally, change the text after the final ":" to be /bin/bash. The Hudson RPM creates the hudson user so that one cannot log in as that user. This is desirable for security, but a hindrance for easy configuration.

To complete enabling the hudson userid for login, change the password by running the following command as root.

```
# passwd hudson
```

Some UNIX distributions will place restrictions on the quality of the password before allowing the new password to be created.

Starting Hudson and Configuring Basic Settings

After you've installed the RPM package, the next reboot will automatically start Hudson. Alternatively, Hudson can be manually started and stopped using the script placed by the installer at /etc/init.d/hudson. Pass the **start** argument to this script to start Hudson.

The version of the startup script installed by the RPM defers to the /etc/sysconfig/hudson file for most of the settings that need to be customized at startup time, such as HUDSON_HOME and HUDSON_PORT. If using a different HUDSON_HOME, make sure it is owned by the hudson user and group. In UNIX, use the **su** command to switch users, as shown here.

```
# su - hudson
```

A good strategy for creating a new HUDSON_HOME is to create the directory as root and then change its ownership and group to be hudson as shown here:

```
# mkdir /MyHudsonHome
# chown hudson /MyHudsonHome
# chgrp hudson /MyHudsonHome
```

Now the /etc/sysconfig/hudson file can be edited to change the HUDSON_HOME and HUDSON_PORT values. As root, edit the file and locate the HUDSON_HOME line. Make it look like this:

```
HUDSON_HOME= "/MyHudsonHome "
```

And do the same for the HUDSON_PORT.

```
HUDSON_PORT= "7214 "
```

Start Hudson with the command **/etc/init.d/hudson start**. Visit Hudson in your browser at the URL http://<hostname>:7214/. Depending on the version of Hudson installed by the RPM, the initial configuration may still need to be performed.

TIP

While using a nonstandard value for HUDSON_HOME does let you easily back up just the configuration information for the Hudson server, important configuration information still "leaks" out into the UNIX home directory of the user running Hudson. For example, the hudson userid will have its own Maven settings file. These and other "dot files," in UNIX parlance, crop up in the UNIX home directory. Therefore, a better strategy is to let HUDSON_HOME be the same as the UNIX home directory. In this way, all the settings, including those unknown to HUDSON, can be backed up.

At this point you have learned how to install Hudson on Windows, Mac OS X, and GNU/Linux, including how to set an alternate HUDSON_HOME and HUDSON_PORT and automatic startup capability on each platform. We have also covered how to install Hudson inside Apache Tomcat. We will build on these capabilities in the remaining sections on further configuring Hudson and building your first job.

Basic Hudson Configuration

The next chapter will provide more details on each of the technologies touched on in this section. For now, we just introduce the basics for the purpose of completing the resilient Hudson installation described at the beginning of this chapter. We've already covered how to achieve the first two points: running Hudson on a dedicated machine, and making it so Hudson starts up automatically when the host operating system starts. The remainder of the chapter will cover the minimum practical Hudson configuration and how to configure your first Hudson job. This job will simply back up the Hudson configuration to a separate location on the filesystem available to the host OS running Hudson.

Java Installations Within Hudson

While Hudson 3.0.0 requires Java 6.0 to run, it is important to make a distinction between the installation of Java used to run Hudson itself and the versions of Java Hudson uses to execute jobs and build software. This exercise will demonstrate configuring Hudson with a number of JDK instances so that when the time comes to create jobs, several choices are available.

1. Visit the Hudson dashboard in your browser and click on the second link in the upper left-hand corner of the page. This link is titled Manage Hudson. Clicking this link will take you to a page where you can access nearly all of the settings

that are not specific to any one Hudson job. Other chapters will cover all of the links on the Manage Hudson page, but at this point just click on the "Configure system" link. The System Configurations page is shown here.

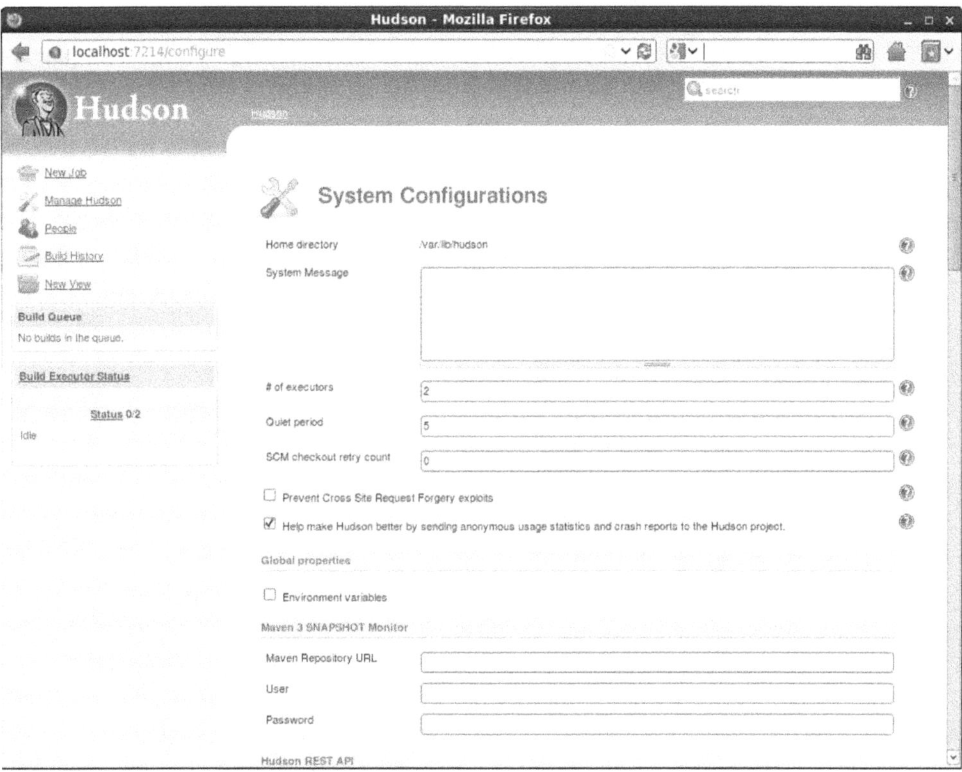

2. Scroll down to the subsection titled JDK.
3. Click the Add JDK button.
4. Uncheck the "Install automatically" check box. This will cause Hudson to change the UI to allow manually entering the JAVA_HOME.
5. While the automatic installation feature is a nice convenience, in practice it is best to install the software manually.
6. In a separate terminal window, become the hudson user.

By way of best practices, all software used by Hudson should be saved to the Downloads directory of the Hudson user. Another useful convention is to install software to a common directory, also within the home directory of the hudson user.

For this book, we will install such software into the "files" subdirectory of the hudson home directory. The JDK may be downloaded from www.oracle.com/java/. Make sure to save the downloaded files so they show up as being owned by the hudson userid. The process of designating the installation directory for Java varies from platform to platform, but at the end of the installation you will have a fully qualified path to the Java installation. This value must be entered into the JAVA_HOME box. The filled-out values for JDK 1.6.0_35 and JDK 1.7.0_07 are shown here.

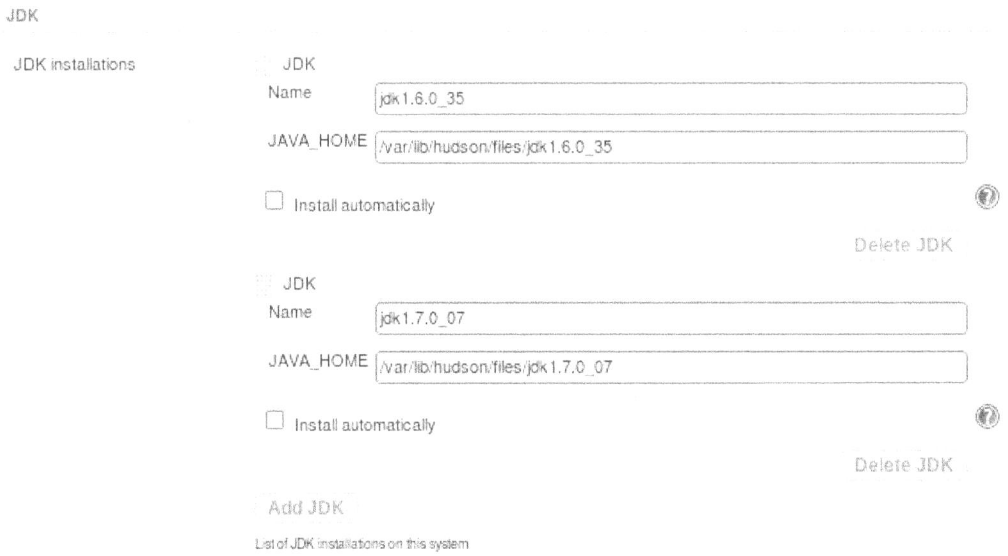

JDK

JDK installations

JDK
Name: jdk1.6.0_35
JAVA_HOME: /var/lib/hudson/files/jdk1.6.0_35
Install automatically
Delete JDK

JDK
Name: jdk1.7.0_07
JAVA_HOME: /var/lib/hudson/files/jdk1.7.0_07
Install automatically
Delete JDK

Add JDK
List of JDK installations on this system

After filling in the values for Name and JAVA_HOME for at least two JDK installations, scroll down to the bottom of the page and click Save. The reason you must put at least two different JDK installations is that Hudson will only offer the choice of JDK version in the job configuration if there is more than one JDK installation to choose from.

Ant

Apache Ant will be introduced in the next chapter, but for now it is sufficient to know that Ant is a tool for compiling collections of Java source files. As with the JDK installations, Hudson offers an automatic installation option, but we will also decline to use it here. Unselecting the "Install automatically" check box gives you the option to manually enter a value for Name and ANT_HOME. Apache Ant may be downloaded from http://ant.apache.org/. Download at least two versions of Ant so that Hudson explicitly provides a choice of which version to use in the Hudson job configuration screen. A completed Ant configuration is shown next.

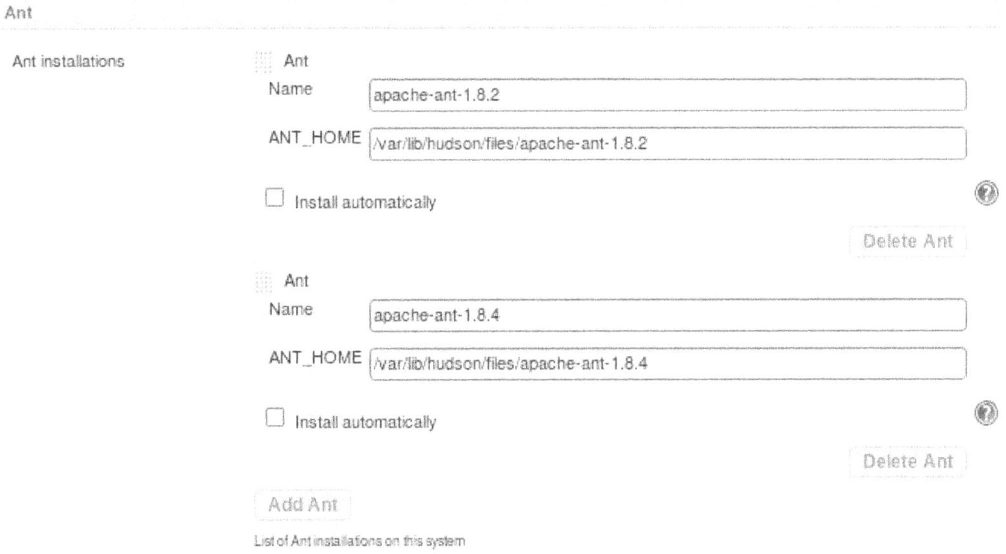

Ant

Ant installations

Ant

Name apache-ant-1.8.2

ANT_HOME /var/lib/hudson/files/apache-ant-1.8.2

Install automatically

Delete Ant

Ant

Name apache-ant-1.8.4

ANT_HOME /var/lib/hudson/files/apache-ant-1.8.4

Install automatically

Delete Ant

Add Ant

List of Ant installations on this system

Make sure to scroll down to the bottom of the page and click Save before continuing on to the next step.

Maven

Apache Maven will be introduced in the next chapter, but for now it is sufficient to know that Maven is a tool that does everything Ant does, but adds a large number of other features especially useful with Hudson. Hudson 3.0.0 has separate installation sections on the System Configurations screen for Maven 3 and earlier versions of Maven, but the procedure for declaring Maven installations is the same as for Java and Ant. Follow the same procedure as in the preceding sections. The reason for the two Maven sections is for conceptual backward compatibility with earlier versions of Hudson. A completed Maven configuration section is shown in the illustration that follows.

1. Scroll to the bottom of the page and click Save.
2. Return to the System Configurations screen and locate the section titled Maven 3 Builder Defaults.
3. In the Maven 3 item, select the drop-down and change the value from (Bundled) to be the version you just manually installed.
4. Scroll to the bottom of the page and click Save.

Maven

Maven installations

Maven

Name apache-maven-2.2.1

MAVEN_HOME /var/lib/hudson/files/apache-maven-2.2.1

Install automatically

Delete Maven

Add Maven

List of Maven installations on this system

Maven 3

Maven 3 installations

Maven 3

Name apache-maven-3.0.4

MAVEN_HOME /var/lib/hudson/files/apache-maven-3.0.4

Install automatically

Delete Maven 3

Add Maven 3

List of Maven 3 installations on this system

E-mail Notification

Hudson has many means of sending notifications on the status of jobs, but the most basic and important means of notification is e-mail. The E-mail Notification section in the System Configurations screen allows you to configure the e-mail settings. These settings will always be specific to your particular enterprise, but the following settings have been tested and are known to work with Google's gmail service. If you are going to use gmail to send Hudson notifications, it is strongly advised that you configure Google's two-step verification service, as well as create an application-specific password for Hudson. This process will give you a new password, separate from your regular gmail password, just for the purpose of Hudson sending e-mails. Doing this step allows you to easily revoke access should the Hudson security become compromised. In the absence of doing this step, you can use your regular gmail password. The following values have been tested and are known to work with Hudson 3.0.0.

Setting Name	Setting Value
SMTP server	smtp.gmail.com
Default User E-mail Suffix	blank
System Admin E-mail Address	Hudson <yourGmail@gmail.com>

Setting Name	Setting Value
Hudson URL	http://<hostname>:<port> (This value will be prepended to Hudson job URLs so they will be clickable from within the e-mail.)
Use SMTP Authentication	checked
User Name	Your gmail address
Password	Your gmail password or application-specific password.
SMTP Port	465
Charset	UTF-8

After filling in values, click Save, then return to the System Configurations page and click the "Test configuration by sending e-mail to System Admin Address" button.

More advanced e-mail settings will be covered in Chapter 3.

Your First Job: Back Everything Up

In the practice of enterprise software development, the configuration settings one must define while developing the software are nearly as important as the software itself. Erroneous or incompletely understood configuration settings can lead to puzzling problems. For example, a far too common class of problem is where the software works correctly on one developer's machine, but not on another's. These sorts of problems are nearly always caused by erroneous or incompletely understood configuration settings. Hudson's core function is to store a large and arbitrarily complex collection of configuration settings to enable the reliable and repeatable production of quality assured software. Because software and settings grow organically, it's very important to have everything backed up from the beginning of the effort. The preceding section generated a large enough number of configuration settings that having to re-enter them all would be more hassle than the effort involved in setting up an automated backup. That is the core value proposition of Hudson: make the cost of automating so low that it's faster to automate than to re-enter, even once. In this final section of the chapter, we will complete the minimal configuration for a resilient Hudson server: having one job that runs regularly and having the system back itself up every night.

It must be mentioned that there are several Hudson plugins dedicated to the task of backing up Hudson. The use of those plugins is beyond the scope of this chapter, but it's very likely that using one of them would yield a more robust and maintainable backup solution than the simple approach described here. One such plugin is the JobConfigHistory plugin, which will be covered in Chapter 3. Nonetheless, this section is primarily an example, and secondarily a useful job.

In a Web browser, return to Hudson's main page and click on the first link in the upper-left corner of the page, titled New Job.

In the "Job name" field, type **Nightly HUDSON_HOME backup**. Click OK. This takes you to the Job Configurations screen. Most of the configuration will be left with default values for this job, but rest assured that every field will be touched upon somewhere in this book.

The first check box is titled Discard Old Builds. Enter the value **1** into the "Max # of builds to keep" field. This field tells Hudson how many builds to save. This value has no impact on the number of backups that will be saved. It only controls how many build logs (and other job execution—specific records) to keep.

Find the Build Triggers section. Check the "Build periodically" check box. This reveals a text area into which a value is entered that tells Hudson to run this job every so often. Clicking on the "?" icon next to the text area will bring up context-sensitive help, which is particularly useful in this case. For now, just enter the value **@midnight** to indicate that the job should be run every day at midnight.

Locate the Build section. Click the "Add build step" button. For simplicity, we will choose "Execute shell." Note that, by definition, what you enter here will be OS specific. On UNIX, the following commands will work. Assume that the path /mnt/HudsonBackup is owned by the hudson userid and group and is a directory on a separate physical hard disk from the one that holds the hudson home directory. The following commands will back up the hudson home directory to a file in /mnt/HudsonHome.

```
export BACKUP_ROOT=/mnt/HudsonBackup
cd ${BACKUP_ROOT}
cp -r ${HUDSON_HOME} HUDSON_HOME-${BUILD_ID}-backup
tar -cf HUDSON_HOME-${BUILD_ID}-backup.tar HUDSON_HOME-${BUILD_ID}-backup
gzip HUDSON_HOME-${BUILD_ID}-backup.tar
rm -rf HUDSON_HOME-${BUILD_ID}-backup
(ls -t|head -n 5;ls)|sort|uniq -u|xargs rm -rf
```

The last line in the shell input removes all but the last five entries from the backup directory.[2]

Summary

This chapter introduced Hudson and its fundamental concept of "job" and defined the characteristics of a resilient Hudson server. The next chapter will explain the technologies and concepts introduced in this chapter in greater detail, setting up the remainder of the first part of the book.

---

[2] Thanks to @thelsdj on Twitter for the script, via StackOverflow.

CHAPTER 2

Hudson Precondition Primer

The previous chapter introduced Hudson and explained the process of setting up a working Hudson instance and creating a simple job. One thing that is immediately apparent after completing that first job is the unique nature of Hudson: it's a product that is only useful in combination with other products. For this reason, skill in using Hudson is only valuable when combined with skill in using the other products with which Hudson integrates. This chapter introduces the tools most commonly used with Hudson, and introduces the software development concepts in which Hudson can play a central role. It is beyond the scope of this book to provide full coverage of all these tools, but references are provided where full coverage can be found.

Hudson in the Software Development Lifecycle

It is difficult to understate the importance of software in history and in today's economy. Even though software is an extremely recent development in history, it is only the fifth knowledge storage medium in history. Philip G. Armour, in his 2003 book *The Laws of Software Process*, identifies five knowledge storage media in history: DNA, brains, tools, printed media, and software. The pervasiveness of software and its impact on everyone's life means that software should be as high quality as possible. To achieve high-quality software, the processes for creating, testing, documenting, delivering, and maintaining software should be as good as possible. This is the purpose of the software development lifecycle.

Though the sole purpose of the software development lifecycle is to make software, many ways have been devised over the years to partition the required tasks, with various names such as "waterfall," "spiral," and "agile." Such topics are well beyond the scope of this book, but all of these approaches are made more successful when automation can be brought to bear in their execution. This is where Hudson comes in. Regardless of the process used for software development, or the number of people involved, Hudson can be used to achieve higher-quality software.

The most basic and common usage of Hudson in the software development lifecycle looks like what's shown in Figure 2-1.

In this simple usage example, the only role represented is the developer. Several developers are simultaneously producing software and using Hudson to verify the correctness of their work.

Let's take a look at some of the different roles one finds in a software development effort and examine how they might use Hudson. There are many other ways of breaking down the roles, and not all of them are covered here. Only those roles that typically interact directly with Hudson are discussed. Each role has different tasks to perform at different times during the lifecycle. Also, it is very common for individuals to take on different roles at different times depending on the size and nature of the project.

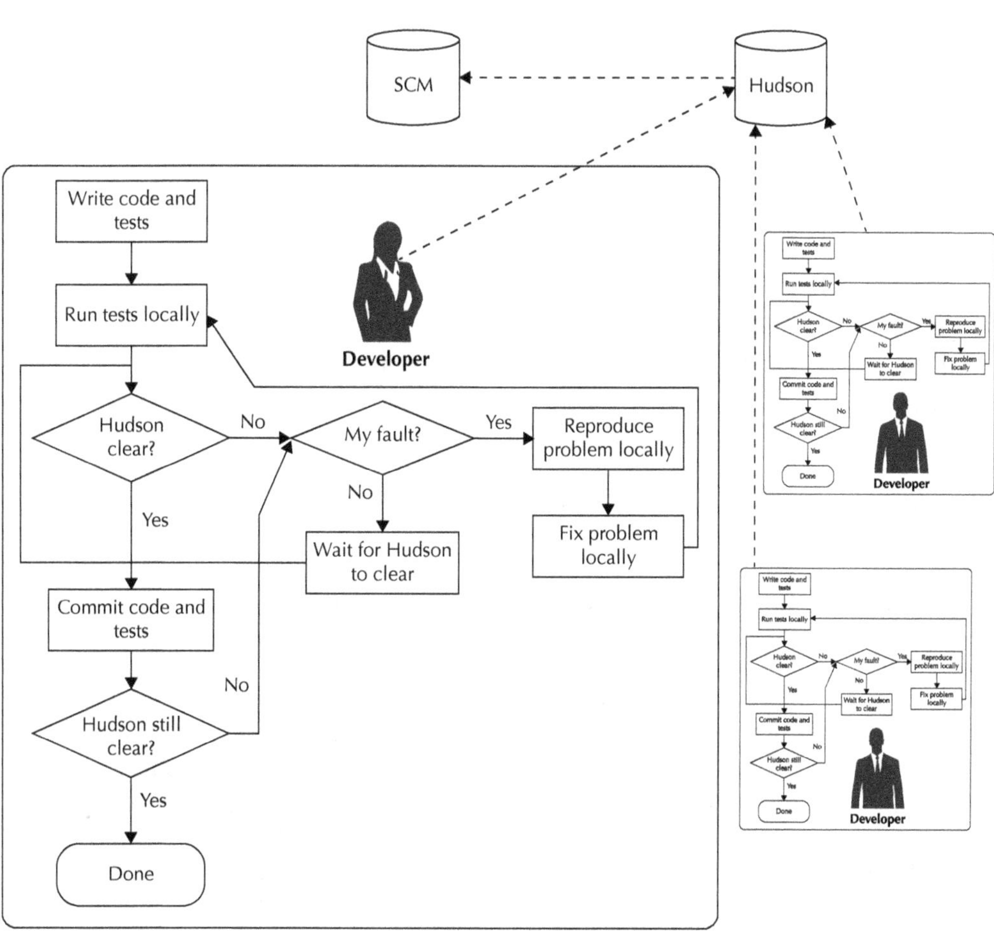

FIGURE 2-1. *Basic Hudson usage*

In the smallest possible project, one person can perform all the roles, and in larger enterprises each role is performed by a different person. Figure 2-2 illustrates some roles and their shared dependency on Hudson.

Developer

The developer is the most obvious role in the software development lifecycle. The developers are the ones who write the code and the accompanying tests that prove its basic correctness. Developers typically work on small chunks of functionality over small chunks of time, saving their work frequently using a class of tool called

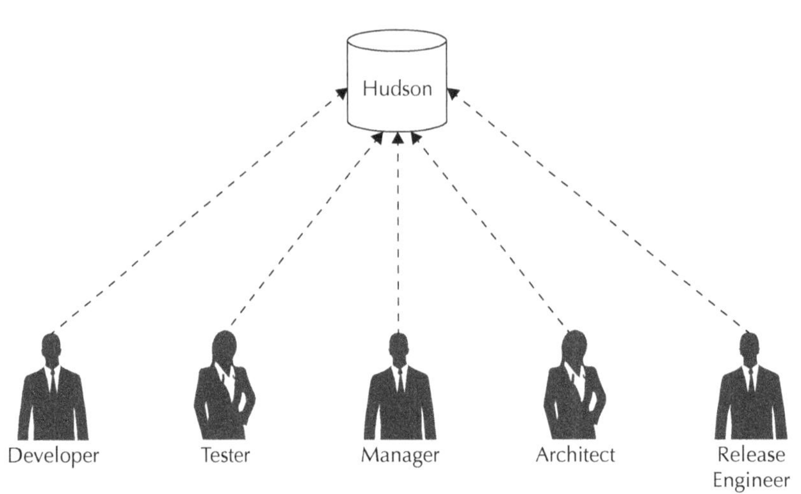

FIGURE 2-2. *All of the roles in the software development lifecycle depend on Hudson.*

Software Configuration Management (SCM). SCM helps developers collaborate on a software project by minimizing the chances that the saved work from multiple developers will conflict. The act of saving work to SCM is known by various names, depending on the SCM in use. Common names are "commit," "push," "put back," "revert," and "check-in." It is common practice for a commit to include both the source code of the product being developed and the unit tests that demonstrate the correctness of this code. Hudson comes into play by continuously running the collected automated tests and producing a report of the test results. Developers must refrain from committing code unless all of the tests are running successfully.

Tester

Although common best practice dictates that the developers write their own tests at the same time they write production code, the formal role of the tester is still essential. The tester role produces different kinds of tests than those written by the developer, but generally, all the tests produced by the tester role are broader in scope than developer-written tests. Chapter 5 provides more details on the different kinds of tests in the software development lifecycle. Like the developer, the testers commit their tests to an SCM, which is similarly used by the Hudson instance. There may be separate Hudson jobs for developer tests than for tester tests, and in this case, the testers will pay particular attention to those jobs running their tests, and the reports generated from their results.

Manager

Though the manager role doesn't usually write code or tests, managers still have a very important function in helping those who do. The manager uses Hudson to keep track of trends as milestones are approached and achieved. As explained in Chapter 3, the kinds of reports a manager cares about include the test result trend reports produced by the developer and tester, and also the higher-level reports regarding code quality, system performance, and even bug count and resolution rates. The managers may also create their own Hudson jobs that aggregate reports from the jobs maintained by the developer and tester, creating a "dashboard" that simplifies their task of reporting project status to key stakeholders.

Architect

In this context, the architect role is responsible for defining the modules of the software being produced and how they interact with each other. In projects using Hudson, the architect applies that responsibility to the stewardship of the Hudson jobs created and maintained by the developer. The most important ingredient of success with Continuous Integration is responsiveness: The production of report results from the Hudson jobs looked at by the developer role must take at most ten minutes. The architect must ensure that the system is decomposed into modules (buildable units) and corresponding Hudson jobs to achieve and maintain that ten-minute maximum goal. The architect is often responsible for knowing the universe of possible Hudson plugins and how they can best be used to give useful feedback to the developer, tester, and manager. In this capacity the architect works with the release engineer to make sure the desired set of plugins is installed and working correctly.

Release Engineer

Traditionally the role of release engineer has the most to gain when the other roles have bought into the value of Continuous Integration. The release engineer can be thought of as the gatekeeper who sends the packaged output of the work from all the other roles out into the larger world. They are often the ones responsible for the technical aspects of the build system and may help ensure that everyone's builds, both individually and on Hudson instances, are running as efficiently as possible. Release engineers use Hudson to collect artifacts produced by other roles and bundle them into a larger product. Release engineers usually span multiple projects and need to be able to cope with process differences between those projects, including adjusting for varying levels of process maturity and use of Continuous Delivery tools such as Hudson.

Example: Orchestration of Roles Around Hudson

Figure 2-2 illustrated the fact that all of the roles in the software development lifecycle may leverage Hudson. The following example illustrates this in greater detail.

The Acme Company has an in-house system for ordering office supplies. The system conforms to the three-tier architecture, with each tier (presentation, business logic, and persistence) having a three-person *developer* team. One of the developers on the business logic team is the *architect*. A single *tester* and *release engineer* are allocated. All of them report to one *manager*. This arrangement is shown here.

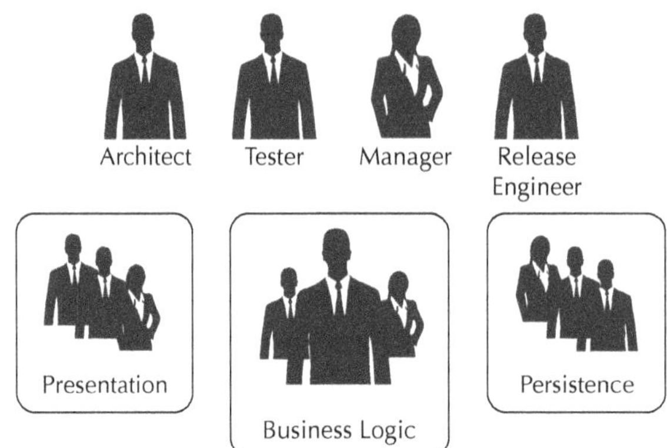

Office Supply System Development Team

The architect has decided that three Hudson instances will be used by the team. The presentation team maintains its own Hudson instance for its developer and integration tests, with the tester role helping to write the latter. They prefer to have their own Hudson instance to accommodate the unique testing requirements inherent in presentation technologies, for example, accommodating different browsers running on different operating systems. The release engineer helps the presentation team configure and maintain this Hudson instance. The business logic and persistence teams share a Hudson instance because their testing requirements overlap in the area of database requirements. Finally, the release engineer maintains the official Hudson instance for the whole team, which is carefully watched by the manager, and the reports displayed on this Hudson instance often find their way into presentations given by the manager to the larger company.

In addition to the Hudson instance architecture, the architect works with each team to define module boundaries and the contracts that exist between each module. This helps the architect achieve the all-important ten-minute responsiveness goal so that developers can maintain maximum velocity.

Software Development as Marionette Theatre Production

It is helpful to use the analogy of a marionette theatre to explain the many different entities one encounters when using Hudson. The software development lifecycle can be thought of as a theatre production. The roles of developer, tester, architect, manager, and release engineer can be thought of as marionette manipulators, the many tools and technologies used in the production as the marionettes, and Hudson as the stage where it all comes together. Of course, it's a special kind of stage, where the manipulators encode the knowledge of how to manipulate their marionettes so that the show can go on without the manipulators having to do the work every time the show is performed.

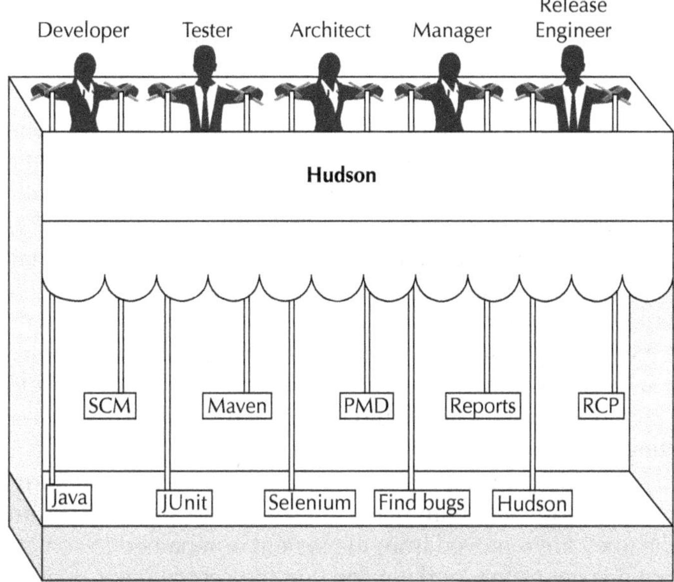

In this section we introduce the tools you must understand to effectively use Hudson: the characters in the Hudson show. After introducing the characters, an example is provided that shows how Hudson uses each in the context of the software development lifecycle. All of the tools in this section must be installed both on the developer's local workstation, and also in the Hudson instance.

Development Platforms

The first choice in many modern software development endeavors is the development platform. Hudson is primarily used in software development endeavors that use the Java platform. As such, this book focuses mainly on this usage. However, there is significant and productive use of Hudson in non-Java platforms, most notably Windows .NET and Ruby. (Appendix C covers Hudson for Windows Developers.) Of course, Hudson is very frequently used for non–software development tasks, such as system administration and monitoring. These usages will be covered in the book. The choice of platform is sometimes tied to the operating system that will be used as the runtime for the finished software product. For example, .NET projects most commonly run only on Windows and Apple AppKit Objective-C projects only ever run on Mac OS. Hudson can be useful in many different platforms and environments.

One very important usage of Hudson that applies to platforms and operating systems is the concept of "matrix build." This is a Hudson feature specifically designed for software development endeavors whose product needs to work on a variety of operating systems and runtimes. The matrix build feature lets the product be tested in a wide variety of environments with a minimum amount of work and maintenance. This feature is covered in detail in Chapter 7.

Software Configuration Management

Most software professionals are familiar with some form of software configuration management (SCM), but it wasn't that long ago when a shared hard disk where everyone agreed not to edit the same file at the same time was not uncommon. Thankfully, the pervasiveness of the network has made SCM the norm. In all forms of SCM, there is the notion of the *repository*. The repository is the place where the source files for all aspects of the project are stored. It's important to note that when it comes to Continuous Delivery, *all* source files: configuration, settings, build scripts, tests, XML, properties files, and, of course, source code—absolutely everything—must be stored in the SCM system. A good rule of thumb to tell if something should be maintained in SCM is this: can this file be automatically generated by a tool in some way? If the answer is no, the file should probably be in SCM. Obviously, this excludes committing binary files to SCM. The other key notion with SCM is *versions*. All the files stored in the SCM system are subject to a lifetime: they are born (initially committed), they get older (changes are made and committed to the repository), and sometimes they die (they are removed from the system or renamed to something else). These two notions, repository and version, are the central ideas of all SCM.

SCM systems can be classified based on how they present the notion of repository. There are two cases. The basic case is a *distributed SCM*. In this kind of SCM, there are actually as many copies of the entire repository as there are individuals using the instance of the SCM. Changes can be fluidly copied between repositories using commands such as *push* and *pull*. In distributed SCM, one repository is commonly designated as the most important one, and the individual who manages that repository is very careful about what changes get pulled in. The two most popular SCM systems used with Hudson are Git and mercurial. The latter, which is a degenerate case of the former, is a *non-distributed SCM*. In this kind of SCM, there is one repository and all individuals using it must commit and check out their changes from it. This form of SCM is much older and less agile than distributed SCM, but, due to its age, non-distributed SCM is currently in more widespread use. The two most popular non-distributed SCM systems are Subversion and CVS.

Regardless of the type of SCM, most Hudson jobs begin by doing a pull or a checkout from some repository.

Builders

Once you have some source code, you're going to want to compile it, and this is where builders come in. "Builder" is the term Hudson uses for a software tool that uses other tools, such as dependency managers, compilers, and linkers, to process multiple source files and create a binary artifact that can be executed in some way. Some executable artifacts can be executed directly by an operating system, such as .exe files on Windows. Some executable artifacts require an intermediate tool, itself running directly on the operating system, such as a .jar or .class file running in a Java Virtual Machine. There are many different kinds of builders and most of them can be directly used with Hudson. When the builder is done doing its job, some code is ready to execute.

The two most common builders in use with Hudson are both open source projects from the Apache Software Foundation: Maven and Ant. Both of these builders have built-in support with Hudson, but many other builders, such as Gradle, Rake, Make, and MSBuild, are available as external plugins. Windows-based builders are covered in Appendix C.

Apache Ant

Apache Ant was the first widely popular build system for the Java platform, emerging four years after Java itself, in 2000. The input to Ant is a build script, named build.xml by default. In most cases, this file consists of <property> and <target> elements. Within a <target> element, a variety of "tasks" are used to perform actions relating to the compilation, assembly, and other build-related tasks for Java programs. Ant does not impose any structure on how you arrange your source files, nor does it have any built-in mechanism for managing compilation classpaths and intramodule dependencies, though the Apache Ivy project has grown up to fill this need. Ivy makes the Internet-accessible software repository feature of Maven available to Ant build files, automatically adding the requested software to the compilation classpath. Absent the use of Ivy, developers are on their own to use Ant primitives to satisfy the requirements of compilation classpaths and intramodule dependencies.

Here is a simple build.xml file that compiles a Java class and produces a jar when the **ant** command line is invoked from the same directory that contains the build.xml file. This jar can be executed by the Java runtime interpreter with the command **java -jar target/helloant.jar**, producing the familiar "Hello Ant!" on the command line.

```
<?xml version='1.0' encoding='UTF-8'?>
  <project name="01_ant" default="main" basedir=".">
  <target name="main">
    <mkdir dir="target/classes" />
    <javac srcdir="src/main/java" destdir="target/classes"
           includeAntRuntime="false"/>
    <jar destfile="target/helloant.jar" basedir="target/classes">
      <manifest>
        <attribute name="Main-Class"
                   value="net.hudsonlifestyle.HelloAnt" />
      </manifest>
    </jar>
  </target>
```

```
  <target name="clean">
    <delete dir="target"/>
  </target>

</project>
```

The directory structure for this project follows the format of a Maven project, which will be explained in the next section. Ant does not impose any restrictions on where files are placed. The directory structure is shown here.

```
build.xml
src/main/java/net/hudsonlifestyle/HelloAnt.java
```

To complete the example, here is the Java source file.

```
package net.hudsonlifestyle;

public class HelloAnt {

    public static void main(String args[]) {
        System.out.println("Hello Ant!");
    }
}
```

For complete coverage of Ant, see the self-contained and very informative Ant Manual, at http://ant.apache.org/manual. For complete coverage of Apache Ivy, start with http://ant.apache.org/ivy/history/latest-milestone/tutorial/start.html.

Apache Maven

For a very long time, Apache Ant was the only game in town for building Java projects. By 2005, a viable contender had emerged in the form of Apache Maven 2.0. The 1.0 version of Maven, which is largely incompatible with the 2.0 version, was not very widely adopted and is seen mainly as a steppingstone to the more enterprise-ready 2.0. Maven is similar to Ant in that they both use XML as the format for their input files. They also both use an arrangement of elements within those XML files to perform actions relating to the compilation, assembly, and other build-related tasks for Java programs. There the similarities end.

The most important difference between Ant and Maven is a philosophical one. With Ant, the build script tells Ant exactly what to do. Ant won't do anything without explicitly being told to do it in a build script. With Maven, the input file, pom.xml by default, provides hints to Maven so that it can perform any number of built-in actions. Maven makes extremely heavy use of conventions for all aspects of its functionality. In order to use Maven effectively, you have to understand these conventions very well. Failure to fully understand the conventions of Maven can lead to what feels like fighting with the software to get it to do what you want. The thing to keep in mind with Maven is this: Maven is going to do what it wants; you just have to give it hints so that what it wants happens to be the same as what you want. This philosophy is commonly known as "convention over configuration." Rather than the software requiring all configuration to be explicitly declared, naming conventions are used to reduce or eliminate the configuration entirely.

Mastery of Apache Maven is a topic for a book in itself, and indeed there are several of those. A very solid introduction is found in the Web site/book "Maven by Example," from Sonatype, the company that created Maven and continues to sponsor its development at Apache. The entire content of the book may be found at www.sonatype.com/resources/books/maven-by-example/. To round out the appropriate level of coverage of Maven here, we will simply touch on a few of the main concepts: the Dependency Management System, the Project Object Model, and plugins.[1]

Maven Dependency Management Much of the power in Maven comes from its built-in dependency management system. This system is built around the concept of the Java jar file. Every piece of reusable Java code ever written is distributed in jar files. Maven honors this fact by defining elaborate structure and infrastructure for identifying, transferring, packaging, and otherwise making jar files available for use in creating Java programs. The dependency management system in Maven has the concept of an "artifact repository." This is simply a Web site where jar files are available, with the vitally important caveat that the arrangement of the directories in the Web site conforms exactly to the conventions expected by Maven. This convention is built around the answers to the two most pressing questions a build system might have about a piece of reusable software: "What is it called?" and "what is its version number?" Maven introduces a two-level name to answer the first question. The first level is the groupId. This usually corresponds to the name of the organization that creates and maintains the artifact, and sometimes contains project-specific names as well. By convention a groupId looks like a Java package name, for example: org.glassfish or net.sourceforge. The second level is the artifactId. This always corresponds to the concrete name by which the reusable software is known.

The second question, "what is the version number?" is sensibly answered with the familiar N.N or N.N.N (major.minor.patch-build) syntax. For example 2.0, and 1.3.5 are valid version numbers. Maven also allows non-numeric characters in version numbers, such as 2.2.0-m04. One particular non-numeric sequence in version numbers is the suffix -SNAPSHOT. If a version number ends with –SNAPSHOT, Maven treats it specially and always tries to download the latest

[1] For further information on Maven, the authors suggest http://www.sonatype.com/Support/Books/Maven-The-Complete-Reference or http://www.sonatype.com/Support/Books/Maven-By-Example

timestamped instance of that artifact it can find. SNAPSHOT builds represent development in progress. Finally, the 3-tuple of groupId, artifactId, and version are known as *GAV coordinates* and expressed like this: javax.faces:javax.faces-api:2.2, where javax.faces is the groupId, faces-api is the artifactId, and 2.2 is the version.

Project Object Model While Ant imposes no structure on how source files are arranged in the file system, Maven imposes a very strict and complete structure. It is true that in most cases Maven provides ways to customize this arrangement, but most often people just choose to do things the Maven way. While this may sound draconian, the truth is that conforming to this arrangement has been a huge productivity boost for the entire community of Java developers using Maven. Once one learns the Maven Project Object Model, one immediately knows where everything is in any project that uses Maven. Maven follows the old adage, "Have a place for every thing and keep every thing in its proper place." This adage applies to both aspects of the Project Object Model: the arrangement of files in the file system, and the structure of the Project Object Model descriptor: the pom.xml file.

Where Ant has the build.xml file, Maven has the pom.xml file. Pom files conform to an XML schema, and as such you must be very careful to conform exactly to that schema. A simple pom.xml file analogous to the previous Ant example follows.

```
<?xml version="1.0" encoding="UTF-8"?>
<project xmlns="http://maven.apache.org/POM/4.0.0" xmlns:xsi="http://
www.w3.org/2001/XMLSchema-instance" xsi:schemaLocation="http://maven.
apache.org/POM/4.0.0 http://maven.apache.org/xsd/maven-4.0.0.xsd">
  <modelVersion>4.0.0</modelVersion>
  <groupId>net.hudsonlifestyle</groupId>
  <artifactId>hellomvn</artifactId>
  <version>1.0</version>
  <packaging>jar</packaging>
  <build>
    <plugins>
      <plugin>
        <groupId>org.apache.maven.plugins</groupId>
        <artifactId>maven-jar-plugin</artifactId>
        <version>2.4</version>
        <configuration>
          <archive>
            <manifest>
              <mainClass>net.hudsonlifestyle.HelloMvn</mainClass>
            </manifest>
```

```
          </archive>
        </configuration>
      </plugin>
    </plugins>
  </build>
</project>
```

The most important line here is <packaging>jar</packaging>. This tells Maven that the files for which this pom.xml has responsibility are intended to add up to a Java jar file. The XML within the <plugin> element for the maven-jar-plugin gives advice to Maven to ensure that the generated jar file is executable. Note the groupId, artifactId, and version (GAV) elements within the <plugin> element. This GAV uniquely identifies the library providing the behavior of generating the jar file. The Java source code is exactly the same as in the Ant example except that the class name is HelloMvn and the message printed out is "Hello Maven!"

It's also important to note that nowhere in the pom.xml is the location of the Java source file mentioned. This is because Maven first checks src/main/java as the source root for source files. If the directory src/test/java existed, it would be assumed to contain automated tests and these would automatically be invoked at build time. The command-line invocation to cause Maven to inspect the pom.xml file, compile the Java source file, and build the executable jar is a simple **mvn install**. This actually puts the jar file in two places, the "target" directory and the "local repository." This is a special area on your local hard disk where Maven stores artifacts after they are built, and also after they are downloaded from a remote repository. The resultant jar can be invoked with **java -jar target/hellomvn-1.0.jar**. The jar file name is simply the artifactId, a dash, the version, and ".jar".

Maven is notorious for producing verbose build output, even without running the build with the -X argument to **mvn**, which instructs the system to produce more verbose output. Two elements of this output are interesting now: the test output and the build result. The test output section looks like this:

```
[surefire:test]
No tests to run.
Surefire report directory: E:\02_mvn\target\surefire-reports
-------------------------------------------------------
 T E S T S
-------------------------------------------------------
Results :
Tests run: 0, Failures: 0, Errors: 0, Skipped: 0
```

This section of the output is where the output of running the tests located in src/test/java is first reported. Hudson ultimately culls this data into reports that provide much of the value-add that motivates people in the manager and architect roles to want to use Hudson in the first place. Even in the simple "Hello Maven!" example, Test Driven Development is assumed. This assumption is part of the philosophy of Maven being a software layer designed to fit the software development lifecycle. Chapter 5 will cover Test Driven Development in more detail.

The build result section looks like this:

```
[install:install]
Installing E:\02_mvn\target\hellomvn-1.0.jar to
E:\SHARED_TMP\Documents\JavaEE\workareas\mvnrepository\net\hudsonlifestyle\
hellomvn\1.0\hellomvn-1.0.jar
Installing E:\02_mvn\pom.xml to E:\mvnrepository\net\hudsonlifestyle\hellomvn\
1.0\hellomvn-1.0.pom
------------------------------------------------------------------------
BUILD SUCCESS
------------------------------------------------------------------------
Total time: 11.515s
Finished at: Sat Jul 14 09:37:13 EDT 2012
Final Memory: 7M/17M
------------------------------------------------------------------------
```

The BUILD SUCCESS message is your quick visual indicator that everything went as expected. If anything went wrong with the build, including test failures, the message would be BUILD FAILURE.

Maven Plugins and the Maven Build Lifecycle Absolutely everything of interest done by Maven is done by a plugin in the context of the Maven build lifecycle. For example, even though the preceding pom.xml didn't explicitly state it, the maven-compiler-plugin was used during the compile lifecycle phase to compile the Java source files. The command-line arguments to the Maven executable, mvn, are called "goals." These provide advice to the build lifecycle to achieve the desired outcome when invoking Maven. The main reason to explicitly mention a plugin in a pom.xml is when specific configuration information needs to be provided. In this case, the maven-jar-plugin must be told what to put as the value of the Main-Class entry in the MANIFEST.MF file so that the Java interpreter knows what class to run first. Most of the work in using Maven comes from poring over the documentation for its many and varied plugins to find out what special incantations to put inside the <configuration> section. Any Maven plugins that pertain specifically to Hudson will be explained in the context of their usage with Hudson.

This section introduced some of the characters in the Hudson show. While an Integrated Development Environment (IDE) is one of the rare tools that is *not* invoked by Hudson, it is important to introduce this tool because, in many ways, it is the interface developers use to interact with many parts of the Software Development Lifecycle, including managing Hudson.

Integrated Development Environments

Most enterprise software development is now done in specialized programs called Integrated Development Environments (IDEs). These tools are referred to as such because they bring together many different, but related, tools under one unified user interface. All IDEs have some notion of a "project" that groups together source files, build instructions, and anything else necessary to produce a software module. A "project" is to an IDE what a document is to a word processor. The IDEs mentioned in this book each have their own proprietary project formats, but all of them have at least basic support for Maven. Special attention will be given to using Maven in each IDE because Maven is a great choice as a common tool between developers who use IDEs to interact with the code, and the Hudson server, which can only use command-line tools to interact with the code. It's very important that nearly everything done to the code, except actually developing it, be capable of automation, and thus accessible entirely on the command line.

In addition to a concept of "project," all IDEs include at least a source code editor, source-level debugger, and build system, but developers expect much more than that these days. There have been many different Java IDEs over the course of that platform's lifetime, but the most popular ones, in no particular order, are Eclipse, IntelliJ IDEA, NetBeans, and JDeveloper. Each of these IDEs has various levels of support for Hudson, and will be treated individually in Chapter 6. For now, the basics of each IDE will be covered, including references for further study.

Eclipse

The Eclipse brand is much bigger than just the IDE, but for most intents and purposes, when one says "Eclipse" one means the Eclipse IDE. Other than the IDE, though, Eclipse is also a rich client platform for building desktop applications, a server platform for building server applications, and a project foundry that hosts a number of other open source projects, including Hudson itself. Eclipse is also the foundation for a number of other products, such as JBoss Developer Studio and SpringSource Tools Suite. The gateway to the Eclipse ecosystem is www.eclipse.org/.

The most important thing to know about Eclipse is its plugin-heavy nature. It's not as bad as Maven in that regard, because there really is a significant amount of functionality built into the base Eclipse, but, as with Maven, there are literally thousands of plugins available. In fact, there is even a startup option (–clean) that is recommended to try if the IDE installation becomes corrupted by a particular collection of plugins. In practice, once people find a core set of plugins that work for them, they tend to stick with them and upgrade very carefully.

Installing Eclipse

The Eclipse IDE may be downloaded from www.eclipse.org/downloads/. There are many different download bundles on that page. Most developers will want to grab the "Eclipse IDE for Java EE Developers" because this one has the most commonly used tools for enterprise development. This will give you a zip file on your local system containing an eclipse directory. Within that directory, launch eclipse.exe (not the eclipcsec.exe) or equivalent application for your operating system.

The first time you start Eclipse, you will be presented with a Workspace Launcher dialog. Choose a directory on a fast local disk, preferably without spaces in the path. This dialog is shown here.

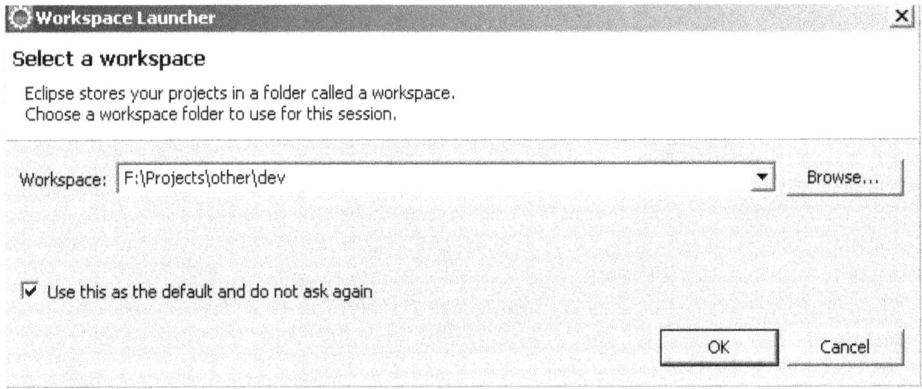

Installing the M2E Plugin to Get Maven Support

Because working with Maven is essential for many Hudson projects, we will install the m2eclipse plugin.

1. Select the Help menu and choose Install New Software.
2. Find the "Work with" drop-down menu and click the Add button next to the drop-down. In the Add Repository dialog, fill in **m2e** as the Name and http://download.eclipse.org/m2e/releases as the Location, as shown next.

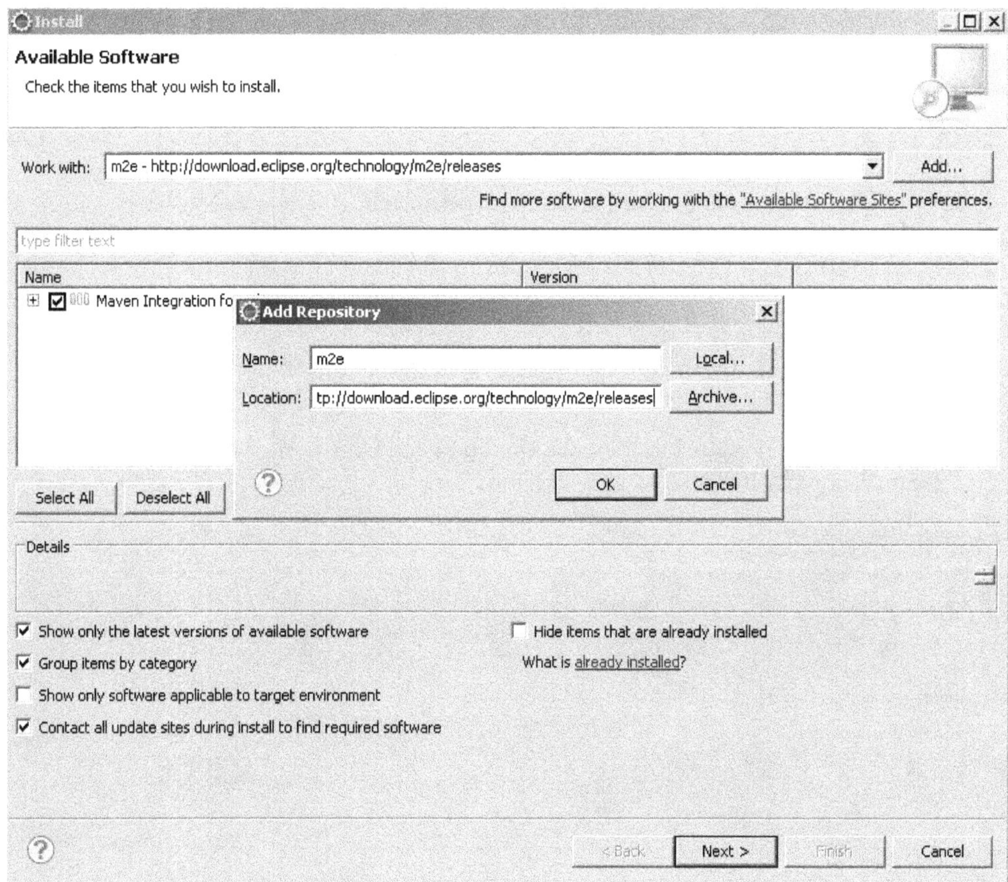

Make sure the box next to Maven Integration for Eclipse is checked.

3. Click Next and you will be shown a page that details what is going to be installed.

4. Click Next again and accept the terms of the license agreement. Then click Finish. You will be prompted to restart your IDE, which you must do to continue.

Building a Simple Maven Project from Eclipse

To conclude the introduction to Eclipse, we will build the Maven project from the preceding section about Maven. To open a Maven project in Eclipse, you must first import the project. Once a project is imported into Eclipse, it remains in the Project

Explorer until deleted from there. Note that deleting the project from the Project Explorer does not delete it from the file system, unless the corresponding UI checkbox is checked.

1. In the File menu, choose Import.
2. In the "Select an input source" text field, type **maven**. This will expand the Maven folder.
3. Select Existing Maven Project and click Next.
4. Click the Browse button next to the select menu next to the Root Directory label. Navigate to the folder that contains the pom.xml from the preceding example and click OK.
5. Click the check box next to the pom.xml and click Finish. After importing the project, your IDE should look like this.

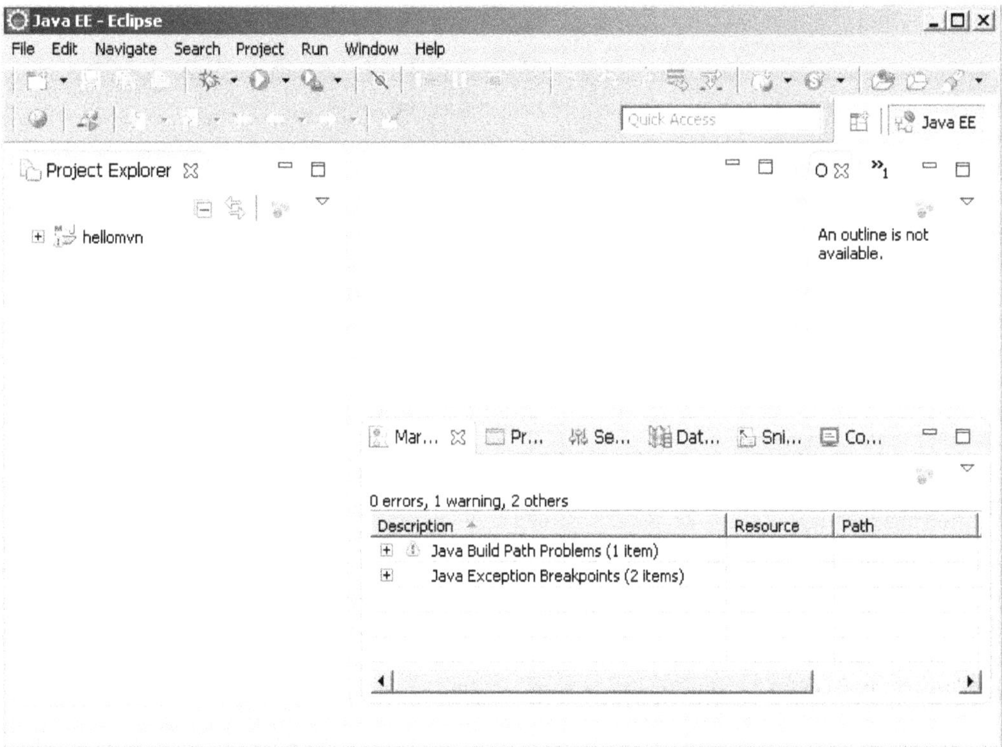

Before building the project, it is good practice to have the Maven console showing. To do this:

1. Select the Window menu and choose Show View | Console.
2. In the row of icons in the Console tab, which is normally in the lower right-hand corner of the main IDE window, locate the rightmost icon that has a downward triangle on it. Click that little triangle and choose the Maven Console item.
3. Back in the Project Explorer area, which is normally in the lower-left corner of the main IDE window, select the hellomvn item.
4. In the Run menu, choose Run As | maven install. In the Maven Console you should see a lot of build output scroll by, ending with the ever-so-satisfying [INFO] BUILD SUCCESS.

The final exercise is to run the project jar:

1. Click the + icon next to the hellomvn in the Project Explorer, click the + icon next to the target folder, and select the hellomvn-1.0.jar.
2. In the Run menu, select Run.

The Java Application console should appear and show the familiar "Hello Maven!" response.

Oracle JDeveloper

Oracle JDeveloper is a full featured enterprise development environment that is engineered to maximize developer productivity, especially when used as the front end to Oracle's Fusion software stack. This powerful tool will get more coverage in Chapter 6. In that chapter, the Oracle Team Productivity Center, which is built on JDeveloper, will also be covered. In this chapter, JDeveloper is introduced and the simple hellomvn project is built.

Installing JDeveloper

Aware of the need for a quick installation process, Oracle provides two installation bundles of JDeveloper on the main download page, www.oracle.com/technetwork/developer-tools/jdev/downloads/. The Generic Release is much smaller than the full-featured release and is perfect for the purposes of a quick evaluation. Downloading the Generic Release will result in a zip file on your local disk. Unpacking the zip file

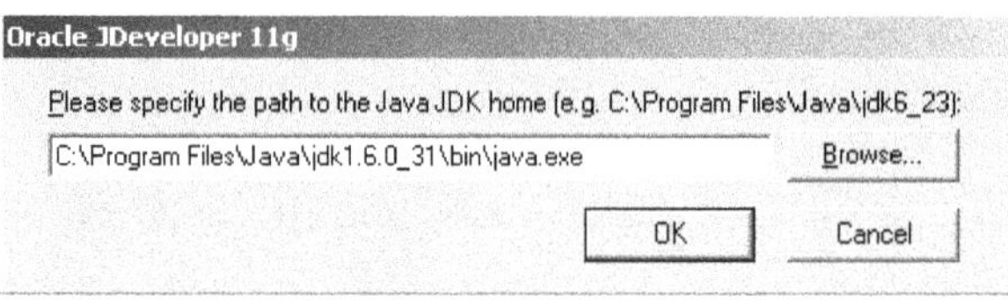

reveals a jdeveloper directory, in which a JDeveloper executable resides. Launching this executable may prompt for a JDK installation. If so, navigate to the install location of the Java interpreter, as shown here.

It is also possible to start JDeveloper from the command line, and the script to do so is located in the jdeveloper/jdev/bin directory and is called jdev for GNU/Linux and Mac OS and jdev.exe on Windows.

Using JDeveloper with Maven

JDeveloper 11*g* Release 2 includes built-in support for Maven, with no need to download an additional plugin. To open a Maven project:

1. Select the File menu and choose New.
2. In the New Gallery dialog, expand the General tree item on the left and select Applications.
3. Select Maven Application on the right and click OK. This dialog is shown here.

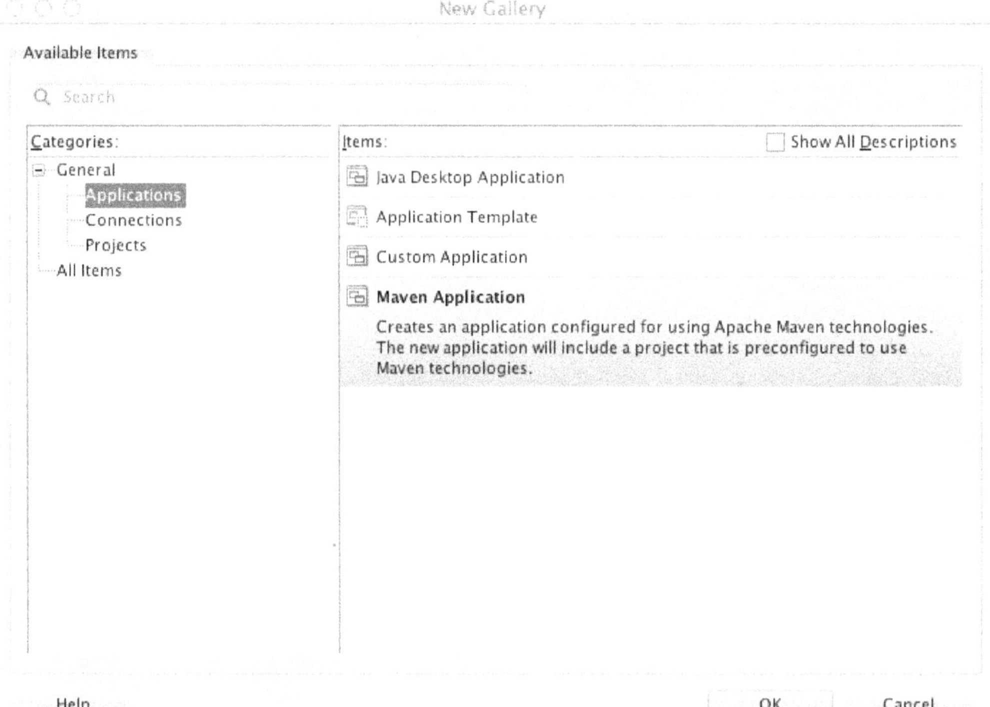

4. JDeveloper maintains its own project format, even when working with Maven projects. Enter **hellomvn** as the value of the Application Name field, leave the Application Package Prefix blank, and click Next.

5. On the next page of the wizard, Step 2 of 3, enter **hellomvn** as the Project Name.

6. Click the Browse button next to the Directory field and browse to the parent directory of the pom.xml from earlier in the chapter. Click Next.

7. Enter **net.hudsonlifestyle** as the Group ID, **hellomvn** as the Artifact ID, and **1.0** as the version. Make sure the two check boxes at the bottom of the wizard, labeled Generate Default Application POM If No Application POM Exists and Modify Normal Project Structure To Match The Default Maven Structure, are *not* checked. Click Finish.

At this point, you may work with the project as a JDeveloper application using the native techniques of that IDE, or you may work with the project using Maven techniques. For conceptual portability with other IDEs, the latter will be explained next.

Building and Running Maven Projects from JDeveloper

The Application Navigator pane is how one interacts with open applications in JDeveloper. Expand the mavenProj node, and the Resources node within it to reveal the pom.xml.

1. Right-click on pom.xml and choose Run Maven Goal(s) and then Manage Goals. This dialog lets you populate the context menu with an arbitrary set of Maven goals. For this example, a new entry will be added that executes both the clean and the install Maven goals.

2. Type **clean install** into the text field to the left of the Add Goal button and click that button. Add any other necessary goals from the Available Goals list on the left by selecting them and clicking the right chevron button. (This dialog can be called up at any time when using Jdeveloper, so don't worry about not making all the necessary choices now.)

3. Click OK to dismiss the dialog.

4. Now, right-click on the pom.xml entry again, choose Run Maven Goal(s), and select the newly added clean install item. This will build the project and show the familiar BUILD SUCCESSFUL text in the Apache Maven Log pane in the lower right of the JDeveloper window.

To complete the exercise, we will run the executable jar.

1. In the Run menu, choose "Run mavenProj.jpr". The first time you take this action in an application, you must tell the system what to run.
2. In the Choose Default Run Target dialog, click the Browse button and navigate to the target directory of the directory that you selected when opening the project.

NOTE
Maven always places the target directory in the same directory as the pom.xml file.

3. Within the target directory, choose the hellomvn-1.0.jar file (*not* the identically named folder).
4. Click OK to dismiss the file chooser, and OK again to dismiss the Choose Default Run Target dialog.

In the same pane in which you saw the BUILD SUCCESSFUL message, you should see the "Hello Maven!" message.

IntelliJ IDEA

JetBRAINS is an independent software company whose flagship product is its IntelliJ IDEA IDE. In addition to IntelliJ IDEA, JetBRAINS has several other useful products for working in the software development lifecycle, including its own Continuous Integration product, TeamCity. As such, the support for Hudson is minimal, but still worth covering. Therefore, this chapter covers the basics of installing IntelliJ IDEA and running the basic Maven project.

Installing IntelliJ IDEA

JetBRAINS offers two editions of IntelliJ IDEA, called Ultimate and Community, both of which are available for download from www.jetbrains.com/idea/download/. These instructions cover the Ultimate edition, which offers a free trial. The Community edition is similar. The install bundle is very easy to use and has been optimized for Windows, Mac, and GNU/Linux. On the last page of the installer, please make sure the Run IntelliJ IDEA box is checked before clicking Finish. When IntelliJ IDEA starts, you will be prompted for license information.

1. Select the "Evaluate for free for 30 days" radio button and click OK.
2. Under Select VCS Integration Plugins, choose the version control systems to activate. Because this book deals only with Git, Subversion, and CVS, you may want to only check those boxes. Naturally, these options can be changed at any time. Leave the defaults and click Next.

3. Under Select Web/JavaEE Technology Plugins, leave the defaults and click Next.
4. Under Select HTML/JavaScript Development Plugins, leave the defaults and click Next.
5. Under Select Other Plugins, leave the list unchanged and click Finish.

Using IntelliJ IDEA with Maven

IntelliJ IDEA has very good Maven support. Unlike Eclipse and JDeveloper, IntelliJ IDEA can open Maven projects directly, but like those two IDEs, it does create additional private settings based on information derived from the Maven project.

1. In the File menu, choose Open Project.
2. Browse to the parent directory of the pom.xml file and click OK.

The first time IntelliJ IDEA opens a Maven project, there is some delay while the IDE inspects the pom.xml and configures its internal data structures.

3. After opening the project, in the View menu, select Tool Windows, then Maven Projects.
4. Expand the hellomvn node and then the Lifecycle node in the tree viewer within the Maven Projects pane. This shows you the common Maven goals available for this project. The IDE window is shown here.

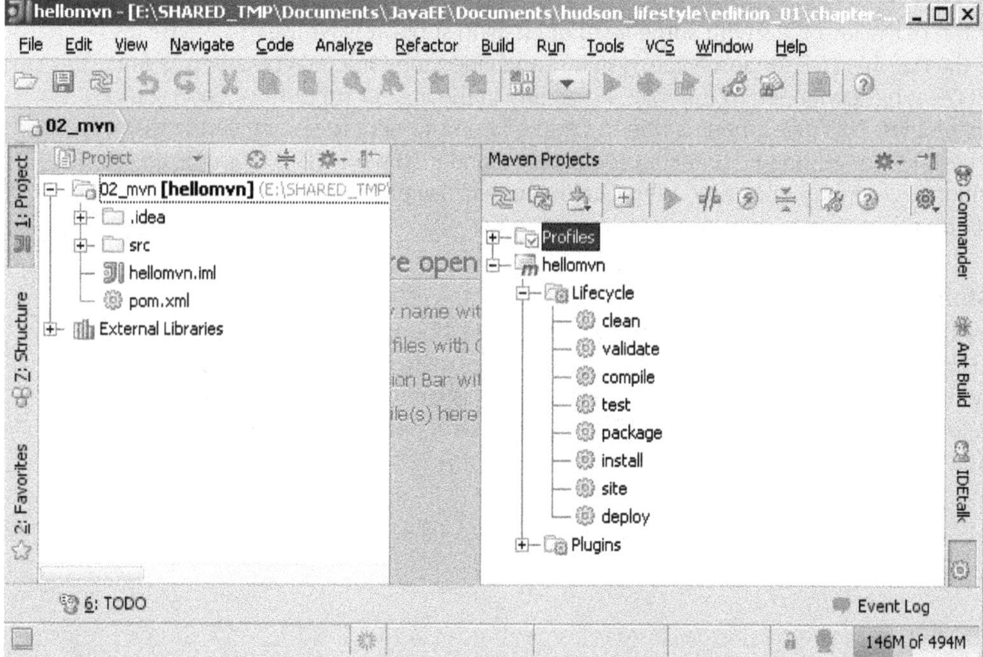

5. Double-click the clean goal, and wait for it to complete. Then double-click the install goal. Look for the BUILD SUCCESSFUL message in the log window.

To run the project we must create a run configuration:

1. Select the pom.xml node in the upper-left pane of the IDE window.
2. In the Run menu, choose Edit Configurations. This brings up the Run/Debug Configurations dialog.
3. Click the tan-colored plus icon and choose Application in the pop-up menu. The right side of the dialog now shows a form allowing you to identify the main class.
4. At the top, type a name for the configuration, run.
5. Click on the … button to the right of the Main class field. The system should automatically discover the HelloMvn class.
6. Click OK to dismiss the Choose Main Class dialog.
7. Click OK to dismiss the Run/Debug Configurations dialog.
8. In the Run menu choose "Run 'run'". The log window should show the familiar "Hello Maven!" output.

NetBeans

The last of the Java IDEs with some level of Hudson support is NetBeans. NetBeans was the flagship IDE for Sun Microsystems, and since the Oracle acquisition of Sun in 2009, it has continued to improve, especially in the area of support for open source technologies. This investment is due to Oracle's commitment to having NetBeans be the best IDE for cutting-edge technologies and standards, while JDeveloper is being positioned as tightly integrated with Oracle's enterprise products as a rock-solid platform for corporate development.

Installing NetBeans

As with every other IDE, there are several choices of bundles to download. Visiting http://netbeans.org/downloads/ allows you to choose from five different varieties. Downloading either the JavaSE or JavaEE versions is sufficient for most of what one would do with Hudson. The NetBeans installer is very solid and nearly always results in a clean install.

Using NetBeans with Maven

NetBeans was an early leader in supporting Maven in all of its distributions. Its support for Maven is, in the author's opinion, the most intuitive and closely aligned with using Maven from the command line. There is no "import" step, as with Eclipse. Simply use File | Open Project and navigate to the preceding example. The NetBeans IDE with the Maven project opened is shown here.

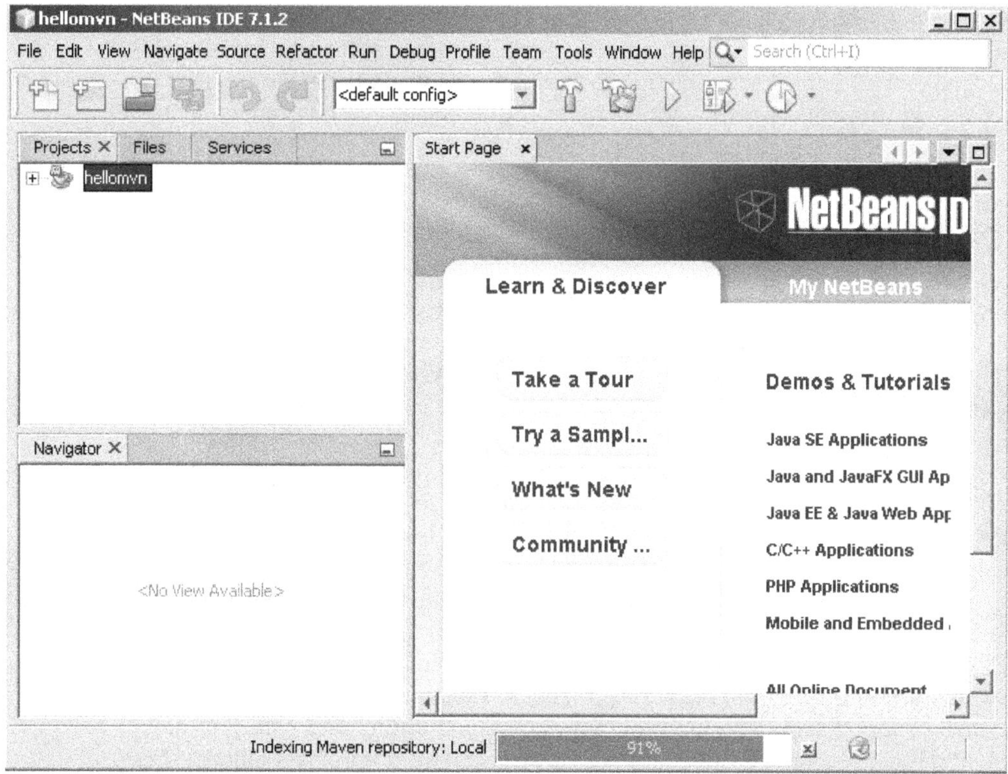

In the Run menu, select Clean and Build Project (hellomvn). The familiar BUILD SUCCESS output soon appears in the Output pane in the lower right of the NetBeans window.

In the Run menu, select Run Project (hellomvn). Because NetBeans hasn't yet been told what the main class is, the Select Main Class for Execution dialog comes up, with the net.hudsonlifestyle.HelloMvn class helpfully preselected. Your choice in this dialog may be recorded just for this IDE session, or you may choose to save it so that when you open this particular Maven project in the future, this choice is remembered. Choose Remember in Current IDE Session for now and click the Select Main Class button.

In another demonstration of NetBeans' deep Maven integration, this choice is actually used to configure the maven-exec-plugin, the execution of which is appended to the build steps performed by Maven. Because the Run action in NetBeans needs to ensure that the project is built before it is run, you will see the build output before the "Hello Maven!" message, again in the Output pane in the lower-right corner of the NetBeans IDE window.

The previous section introduced some of the characters in the Hudson show. This section introduced IDEs, which take action behind the scenes. We have covered the basics of Maven and demonstrated its use in Eclipse, JDeveloper, IntelliJ IDEA, and NetBeans. The next section will round out the main characters in Hudson by introducing some of the testing tools one encounters in common practice when using Hudson.

Testing Tools

Returning to our example of the marionette theatre production, the various testing tools can be thought of as marionettes that perform a role in the software development lifecycle. They perform a role alongside the other tools, and their role is every bit as vital to the show as the compiler and the build tool. While these testing tools will be covered in greater detail on in Chapter 5, it is useful to introduce the concept in broad terms now.

Testing tools are all about asserting correctness. They can be classified based on the kind of correctness they assert. It is useful to define two classes of correctness: hard and soft. Failures in hard correctness cannot be tolerated; the system cannot proceed with failures in hard correctness. Compilation failures are the most basic form of hard correctness failure. Another example is a test case that examines program output for the presence of a specific string. If that string is not present in the output, the test fails, usually failing the entire build as a result. On the other hand, failures in soft correctness are subjective. The architect typically sets the parameters that determine which soft correctness failures may be safely ignored, and which cause a failure of equal magnitude to a hard correctness failure. These failures are discovered through some kind of inspection and analysis of the source code or how a module performs under load. Examples of soft correctness failures include a method having too many lines, a class having too many methods, or an application taking unacceptably long to start up. Soft correctness failures usually don't halt the build, and usually are compiled into reports that are viewed and acted on by someone serving in the architect role. Each kind of correctness assertion has its own tools, each of which is useful with Hudson. The remainder of the chapter introduces the most common tools for asserting hard and soft correctness outside the context of Hudson so that they may be safely treated for use inside Hudson, as described in Chapter 5.

Hard Correctness Testing Tools

The two most common testing tools for asserting hard correctness in Java are JUnit and TestNG. Version 3.8.1 of JUnit was the de facto standard testing tool in Java until TestNG arrived on the scene in 2006. The main advantage TestNG brought over JUnit was its heavy usage of the Java language annotations introduced in JavaSE 5. This approach made it unnecessary to subclass JUnit's TestCase class, which is a requirement for JUnit 3.8.1. However, JUnit 4.0, released shortly after, also added annotation-style test cases. At this point in the development of both frameworks, either one will do a fine job in filling the role of asserting hard correctness. JUnit has the added legitimacy that several other very popular testing frameworks have been built on top of it.

This exercise will add a JUnit test case to the HelloMvn example. The most obvious challenge one faces in writing automated tests is how to interact with the production code whose correctness is being asserted. The depth of this interaction depends on the kind of testing being performed. One kind of testing is called "black box testing" because the code being tested is like an opaque black box as far as the test is concerned. This exercise shows a black box test: the test case knows that the string "Hello Maven!" will be written to standard out, but it doesn't have any knowledge about the internals of the code being tested. To contrast with the term "black box testing," the term "white box testing" is a kind of testing where the test case *does* have knowledge about the internals. These and other different kind of tests will be covered in greater detail in Chapter 5.

Here is the simple JUnit test case. This source file resides in the directory src/test/java/net/hudsonlifestyle. The practice of putting the test case into the Java package as the code being tested is very handy for white box tests because the test case can access package private data. Because this test is a black box test, it need not be in the same package.

```
package net.hudsonlifestyle;

import java.io.ByteArrayOutputStream;
import java.io.PrintStream;
import static org.junit.Assert.assertTrue;
import org.junit.Test;

public class TestHelloMvn {
    @Test
    public void testMain() throws Exception {
        ByteArrayOutputStream capture = new ByteArrayOutputStream();
        PrintStream newOut = new PrintStream(capture);
        System.setOut(newOut);
        HelloMvn.main(null);
        assertTrue(capture.toString().contains("Hello Maven!"));
    }
}
```

Note that this class does not extend any special base class, and the only imports it has from JUnit are the @Test annotation, which is placed on the method to be treated as a test, and the static import of the method Assert.assertTrue(). One trivial novelty of the test class is its use of System.setOut() to overwrite what the production code writes to when it calls System.out().

The point when tests are added to a Maven project is when the "convention-over-configuration" approach taken by Maven really shines. The only change we need to make to the pom.xml file is to add a dependency on the JUnit library. Dependencies are indicated by adding a <dependencies> section to the pom.xml, like this:

```
<dependencies>
  <dependency>
    <groupId>junit</groupId>
    <artifactId>junit</artifactId>
    <version>4.10</version>
    <scope>test</scope>
  </dependency>
</dependencies>
```

Dependencies are simply an expression of the groupId, artifactId, and version of the software library whose behavior must be made available to the primary code of the project, or, in the case of dependencies that indicate <scope>test</scope>, the test.

Depending on the version of maven and JDK being used, the compiler may need to be configured to use a version of Java that supports annotations. With Maven, this is done by introducing a <plugin> element, next to the existing entry for maven-jar-plugin, that alters the default values passed to the Java compiler. This configuration is shown here.

```
<plugin>
  <groupId>org.apache.maven.plugins</groupId>
  <artifactId>maven-compiler-plugin</artifactId>
  <version>2.4</version>
  <configuration>
    <source>1.5</source>
    <target>1.5</target>
    <showWarnings>true</showWarnings>
  </configuration>
</plugin>
```

Now, when the Maven build is run, the test section, which formerly stated "No tests to run," now states the following.

```
-------------------------------------------------------
 T E S T S
-------------------------------------------------------
Running net.hudsonlifestyle.TestHelloMvn
Tests run: 1, Failures:
0, Errors: 0, Skipped: 0, Time elapsed: 0.453 sec
```

Soft Correctness Testing Tools

There is a much greater variety of tools for asserting soft correctness than for asserting hard correctness; this is due to the nature of the problem. For the class of soft correctness testing tools that rely on static analysis of source code, the bulk of the work in applying the tool centers on configuring the parameters so that the desired coding standards are met. Part of this work involves facing up to the reality that no project consists entirely of perfect code, and exceptions must be made where necessary.

This section will apply the FindBugs plugin to the HelloMvn class. FindBugs was the first open-source Java static analysis tool to achieve widespread industry adoption, and it came out shortly after JUnit started gaining popularity. Because the HelloMvn class is so trivial, something must be added to cause FindBugs to complain. An intentionally incorrect implementation of boolean equals(Object) does the trick.

```
@Override
public boolean equals(Object obj) {
  return false;
}
```

Now that there is a correctness violation to assert, all that remains is advising Maven to run the FindBugs plugin. This is achieved by adding a <reporting> section to the pom.xml, as shown here.

```
<reporting>
  <plugins>
        <plugin>
          <groupId>org.codehaus.mojo</groupId>
          <artifactId>findbugs-maven-plugin</artifactId>
          <version>2.4.0</version>
        </plugin>
  </plugins>
</reporting>
```

Maven offers a very rich set of report generation capabilities, all of which are configured in the <reporting> section. The configuration in this section takes action when the Maven "site" goal is invoked, like this: **mvn clean package site**. This excerpt of the build output shows the report generation, including the FindBugs analysis:

```
[INFO] [site:site {execution: default-site}]
[WARNING] No URL defined for the project - decoration links will not be resolved
[INFO] artifact org.apache.maven.skins:maven-default-skin: checking for up-
dates from central
[INFO] Generating "Project Team" report.
[INFO] Generating "Issue Tracking" report.
[INFO] Generating "Continuous Integration" report.
[INFO] Generating "Project Plugins" report.
[INFO] Generating "Dependencies" report.
```

```
[INFO] Generating "Plugin Management" report.
[INFO] Generating "Mailing Lists" report.
[INFO] Generating "Source Repository" report.
[INFO] Generating "Project Summary" report.
[INFO] Generating "FindBugs Report" report.
[WARNING] Deprecated API called - not org.apache.maven.doxia.sink.Sink in-
stance and no SinkFactory available. Please update this plugin.
[INFO] Locale is en
[INFO] Fork Value is true
     [java] Warnings generated: 1
[INFO] Done FindBugs Analysis....
[INFO] Generating "About" report.
[INFO] Generating "Project License" report.
[INFO] ------------------------------------------------------------------------
[INFO] BUILD SUCCESSFUL
[INFO] ------------------------------------------------------------------------
[INFO] Total time: 18 seconds
[INFO] Finished at: Tue Jul 17 09:53:24 EDT 2012
[INFO] Final Memory: 55M/554M
[INFO] ------------------------------------------------------------------------
```

The FindBugs report ends up in the file target/site/findbugs.html. Viewing this report in a Web browser shows the following table.

Bug	Category	Details	Line	Priority
net.hudsonlifestyle.HelloMvn.equals(Object) always returns false.	CORRECTNESS	EQ_ALWAYS_FALSE	11	High

Summary

This chapter acknowledges the unique position of Hudson as a tool of tools. As a consequence of this fact, mastery of Hudson implies mastery, or at least solid familiarity, with all of the tools being managed by Hudson. After reading this chapter, you have been introduced to the main classes of tools that you will encounter as you learn to use Hudson in practice. Other chapters in the book will provide greater depth of coverage on the kinds of tools mentioned here.

CHAPTER 3

Basic Concepts

Now that we have introduced Hudson and defined the most foundational technologies commonly employed in the course of its everyday use, it is time to round out the fundamentals of Hudson by covering the rest of the common configuration for an industrial-strength Hudson installation. This chapter contains tutorial content covering how to configure your jobs for version control, quality assurance, and build notifiers. There will also be tutorial content covering installation of new plugins, and adding security to your Hudson server.

Intermediate Hudson Configuration

This section goes beyond the minimal configuration introduced in the first chapter. After completing this section, your Hudson instance can reasonably be considered an industrial-strength Hudson instance. One general note about Hudson configuration: the user interface for configuration seldom, if ever, offers a Cancel button. Instead, you need to navigate away to a different page, such as by clicking the Back to Dashboard link, to effectively cancel any changes that have not been saved, and need not be saved.

Adding Source Code Management (SCM) to Your Jobs

SCM serves two purposes for Hudson. The first and obvious one is to allow Hudson to obtain the code to build. The second is to give Hudson a way to tell if the code has changed so it can decide whether to start a new build or not. A change in the source code is one way that a build can be "triggered." Hudson jobs can be configured to poll the SCM system periodically. If the poll concludes that the code has changed, the build is triggered. Other build triggers that will be covered later in the chapter include making the job depend on the completion of other jobs, or when the Maven dependencies of the job have changed.

True to its form as an integration technology, Hudson has built-in support for the most popular Source Code Management (SCM) technologies, but the exact manner of their configuration varies. A job may only have one choice for SCM but may have several different repositories of that sort from which the job obtains code.

Git

Git has been around since 2005, but the introduction of the GitHub service and its competitors, such as BitBucket, has built Git into the overwhelming favorite for source code management for new projects. The design of Git makes it very easy for distributed teams to collaborate, while minimizing the occurrences of developers inadvertently interfering with each other's code. For more information, you can refer to *Version Control with Git, Second Ed.* by Jon Loeliger and Matthew McCullough.

Adding Git to a Hudson job is easy once the particulars are known. At a minimum, one needs the username and password under which the code is checked out and the URL of the repository. Most URLs start with http or http:// or https://, but Git URLs can also start with ssh:// or even git://. All of these are examples of "protocols," and they define how communication between the client and server must proceed. All Git hosting services offer the full set of choices for accessing the repository; generally, one can just copy the repository URL from the Git hosting service into the Hudson UI. Let's walk through the process with a new job.

From the main Hudson dashboard, click New Job. Leave the default selection of "Build a free-style software project" in place, and enter a value for the "Job name" such as **git-01**. In the Source Code Management section, select Git and observe the options panel appear. Once you choose a particular SCM for a job, it is possible to change it, but in practice it is often easier to create a new job instead. Paste the value from the Git hosting service into the "URL of repository" text field. At this point, the notion of username and password must be addressed. For open source projects, it is normally sufficient to allow the Hudson server to check out the source code anonymously, because there is no reason for the Hudson server to have the capability to check code in. Git hosting services are optimized for this case. For projects where a username and password are required to access the source code, it is necessary to encode that information in the repository URL. This requires putting the username and password in clear text in the URL. Hudson instances that have such information must be protected, and this is covered later in the chapter. The following syntax can be used when username and password must be included so that Hudson can check out the code.

```
https://username:password@hostname/repository/path.git
```

The remainder of the fields can be left blank. There are other techniques for specifying the username and password, but this one is the simplest and easiest to configure.

The Advanced button immediately beneath the "URL of repository" text field allows you to specify less common parameters pertinent to the repository:

- The name of the repository, "origin" by default
- The refspec, an advanced Git concept
- The local subdirectory within the job's workspace to use for the code being checked out

Branching and merging are at the heart of the popularity of Git. Hudson makes it easy to specify which branch to pull with a simple text field where you can enter the branch specifier. If left blank, this field will default to **master**.

Beneath the branch specifier text field, the Add button allows additional Git repositories to be specified. If configured for polling, all of the repositories for the job will be polled and any of them that have a change will cause the build to trigger.

The Advanced panel reveals many additional options specific to configuring Git. These options generally correspond to options that are passed to the Git executable when performing the checkout.

Beneath the Advanced button, the Repository browser drop-down menu allows you to configure what repository browser service will be used in the links to easily inspect what source code changes triggered the build. These links will appear on the result pages of the job. It is generally safe to leave this set to (Auto), which will cause Hudson to inspect the repository URL to determine which service to use. Several popular services are supported, including GitHub's browsing service, githubweb. Other services may require additional configuration so that the service is aware of your code. This approach essentially adds another client to the source code repository.

Subversion

Another popular SCM is Subversion, though its use is waning in favor of Git. The non-distributed nature of Subversion makes it less suitable to distributed teams because merging is more difficult. When creating a new job, choose Subversion in the Source Code Management list. Enter the repository URL and save the configuration. This is necessary to cause Hudson to offer the ability to set the username and password. From the main page for the job, click the Configure link in the left-hand navigation panel. You will now see a link named "Update credentials" under the Repository URL text field. In this panel, you can set the username and password or use several other authentication options.

The "Local module directory" text field lets you choose a directory within the job's workspace that will contain the checked-out code. The remaining options in the Subversion section correspond to command-line options passed to the underlying **svn** executable.

The Check-out Strategy drop-down menu offers several options.

- Use **svn update** as much as possible. This option will just use the normal **svn update** command to get only the changes since the last time the code was updated. This is faster because there are usually only a small number of changes in the code in the normal interval that jobs tend to be polling (daily or hourly).

- Emulate clean checkout by first deleting unversioned/ignored files, then using **svn update**. This option will cause all files in the workspace not known by **svn** to be deleted, and then **svn update** is used. This option is unadvisable because the act of selectively deleting files is best left to the build system.

- Clean workspace and then check out. This option takes more time, but is safe because it is impossible for the workspace to be in a corrupted state from build to build. For jobs that run overnight, this is a great choice.
- Use **svn update** as much as possible, with **svn revert** before **update**. This option is also unadvisable since the Hudson job should never have modified files in its workspace.

As with Git, there is a Repository browser drop-down menu, but the choices are specific to Subversion.

CVS

CVS (Concurrent Versioning System) is the old man of SCM. Hudson includes it because many legacy projects still use it, and these projects could benefit from using Hudson. The following options are available when configuring a job to use CVS:

- The Cvsroot value is analogous to the Repository URL in Git and Subversion. As with Git, the username and password can be specified in the Cvsroot. If the repository requires a password and it is not specified in the Cvsroot text field, it is taken from the .cvspass file in the home directory of the user that runs Hudson. The easiest way to generate the .cvspass is to simply check out the code with CVS from the command line and throw away the checked-out code.
- Module(s) is a CVS concept that can be used to organize code within a CVS repository. Multiple modules can be separated by whitespace.
- Branch is a CVS concept that enables isolating related changes to the repository so that they are only visible within that branch.
- Local directory is the local subdirectory within the job's workspace to use for the code being checked out.

The Advanced button reveals options that are passed to the underlying **cvs** executable. Interestingly, the Repository browser drop-down menu is hidden within the Advanced button, whereas with the other SCM choices it is available at the top level.

Your Second Job: A Simple Java Program

Chapter 1 walked through the simplest possible Hudson job that could actually be useful, a job that backs up the Hudson configuration itself nightly. This section walks through a job that builds a simple Java program using Maven: the HelloMvn program from the preceding chapter.

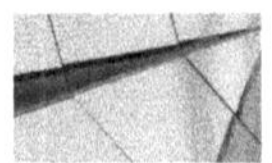

TIP

One particularly vexing class of bug is the case when an automated test works just fine when run on the engineer's workstation, but the same test fails when run by Hudson. Adding testing to a job will be covered later in the chapter, but the practice of minimizing the chance of this kind of bug begins right now. The best preventative is to have Hudson's environment be exactly the same as the engineer's workstation. One way to achieve this is to have the complete development stack be stored in SCM. There could be a Hudson job that runs daily that checks out from SCM to update the set of tools used by the Hudson instance itself. This job could run once per day, and before any of the other jobs run by that Hudson instance.

The preceding chapter covered how to build the simple program outside Hudson. Now we will create a job that builds it inside Hudson. Assuming the source code of HelloMvn has been committed to a Git repository, follow the steps from the previous section to create a new job called 01_mvn, and pull the source code from Git. From the dashboard of the 01_mvn job, click the Build Now link to run the job once to verify that the source code is successfully pulled.

Configuring the Build Trigger

This job will use SCM polling to trigger the execution of the job. From the dashboard for the job, choose Configure. This brings up the configuration page for the job.

From the Configure page for the job, locate the Build Triggers section and choose Poll SCM. This expands a text area into which you can type a compact representation of when the job should poll SCM to see if there were changes in the code. In this text area, you can see the remnant of the most basic precursor to Hudson, the UNIX **cron(1M)** command. Clicking the **?** icon next to the text area will bring up some help for the text you can enter into this box. Briefly, the text in the Poll SCM text area must contain five fields, separated by whitespace, which represent the minute of the hour (0–59), the hour of the day (0–24), the day of the month (1–31), the month of the year (1–12), and the day of the week (0–7). Interestingly, both 0 and 7 in the last field represent Sunday. A value of * for any field means that field will take any value. For example, the value "30 * * * *" means "at 30 minutes after the hour, every hour of the day, every day of the month, every month of the year, every day of the week."

Configure Links in the Hudson UI

There are two panels, both labeled Configure, within a job, and it's important to avoid confusion between them. The first Configure link is on the main dashboard for the job, as shown in this illustration. This Configure link is the most important one for the rest of this chapter. Nearly all of the configuration options for a job are made via this link.

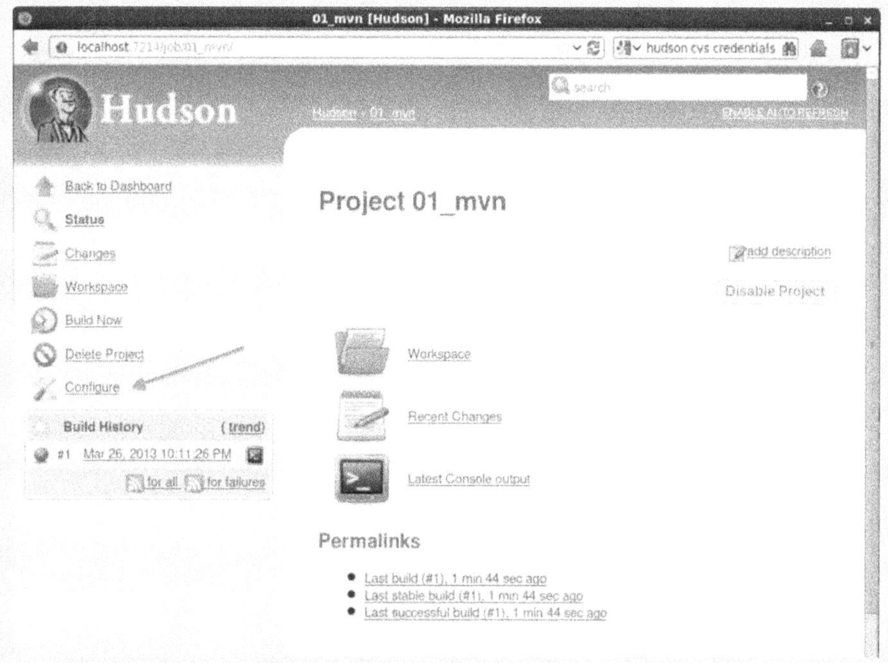

The second Configure link is only shown on the page when viewing a particular build of a job. This page is reached by clicking on a link in the Build

(*Continued*)

History section of the main dashboard for the job. As the following illustration shows, the two pages are very similar looking, but the result of clicking the Configure link is very different.

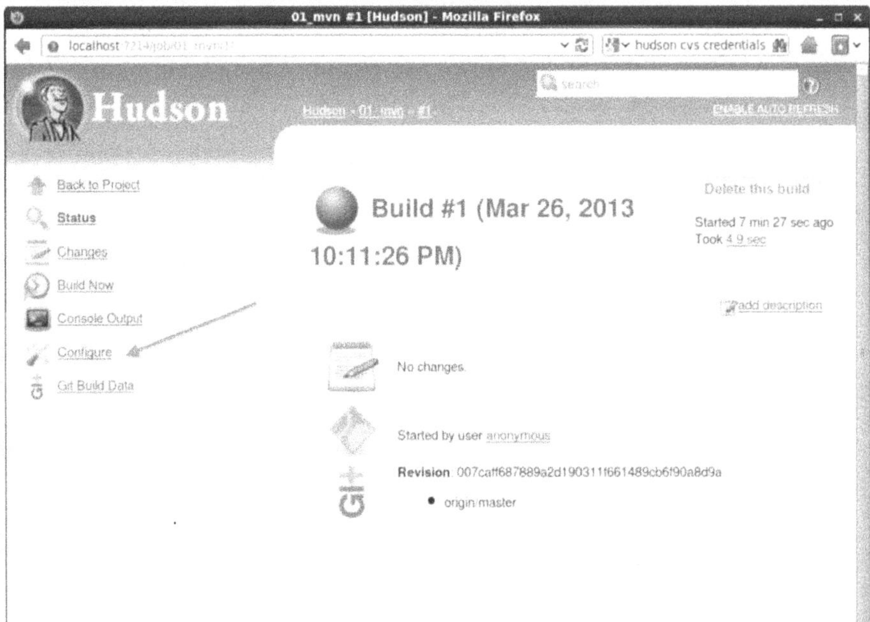

The only settings that can be configured from this second Configure link pertain specifically to the execution of this specific job. This can be useful for adding descriptive notes. In practice, this feature is seldom used. If you find yourself on this second Configure page, just click on the job name in the list of links starting with Hudson at the top of the page. This is 01_mvn in the following illustration. This list of links is known as a *breadcrumbs list* in user interface parlance because every element in the list indicates a step in a workflow. In this case, the list looks like Hudson » 01_mvn » #1. If you find yourself on a Hudson page you don't want to be on, such as this configuration page, the breadcrumbs links can get you back to where you want to be. In this case, clicking on 01_mvn will take you back to the main dashboard.

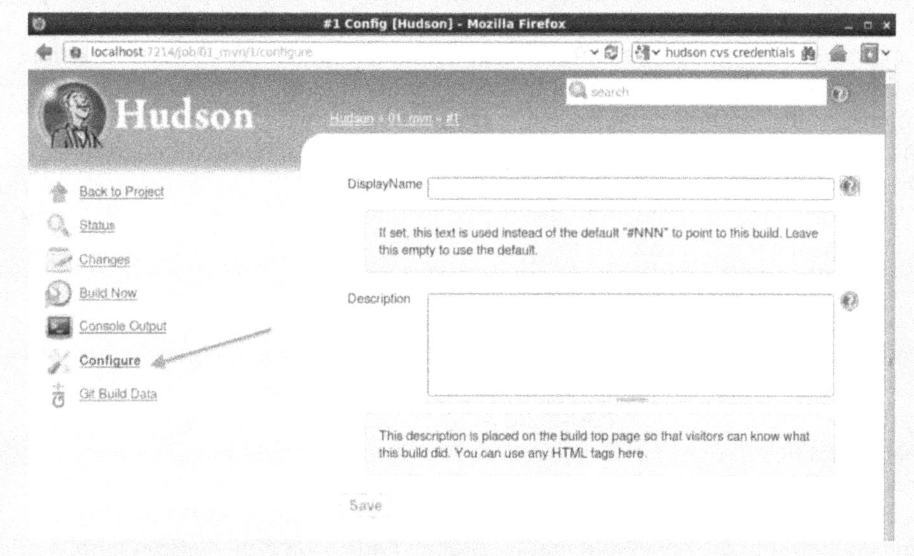

The text area can accommodate comments, which must be prefixed by the # character. More advanced configuration options can be provided as documented in the help box.

Industrial-strength Hudson installations tend to only use the Poll SCM feature for jobs that trigger other jobs. It is better to set up a cascade of job dependencies than to maintain a large number of individual job trigger times. However, for this simple example, you can use the simple @hourly shorthand, which causes the job to poll every hour on the hour. Click Save at the bottom of the configuration page to continue.

Adding a Maven Build Step

Return to the configuration page for the job and find the Build section. The "Add build step" button opens a drop-down menu. From the menu, choose Invoke Maven 3. This will expand the UI to show the default Maven options. Leaving the default values will cause Hudson to invoke **mvn clean install** in the top level of the source code checked out from SCM. Recall from the preceding chapter that **mvn install** was used to build the example from the command line. The additional clean step is necessary because Hudson wants to clear out whatever was left over from the previous invocation of the job. The clean may not be necessary if the SCM options elected to clean the entire workspace before checkout. In the common case of using **update** from the SCM options, the clean is necessary, however.

Because this particular example will only build the single 01_mvn example from the Basic Concepts chapter, Hudson must be configured to invoke Maven in the appropriate directory. Click the Advanced button in the Invoke Maven 3 section. This brings up a large number of configuration options, most of which correspond to command-line options to be passed to **mvn**, and all of which are documented with help via the **?** icon. In this case, the POM File box must be modified to refer to the path to the 01_mvn pom.xml, as shown in Figure 3-1.

After identifying the pom.xml, save the configuration and choose the Build Now link from the main dashboard for the job.

Archiving the Artifacts

To round out this simple example, the job will be configured to archive the output of the build: the hellomvn jar file. From the configuration page, find the "Archive the artifacts" check box in the Post-build Actions section. Clicking the check box reveals a text field into which the path of any artifacts that should be archived can be entered. The helpful Validate button will execute the path expression and show a warning if the file is not found. In this case, enter **BasicConcepts/01_mvn/target/hellomvn-*.jar** into the box. Note that we are not hard-coding the version number, as this can easily change as the project evolves. In practice, it's good to find a balance between specificity and generality with this field because the artifacts that get archived do consume disk space. The Advanced panel enables exclusions relative to the files found by the "Files to archive" link. To save disk space, the "Discard all but the last successful/stable artifact to save disk space" option can be

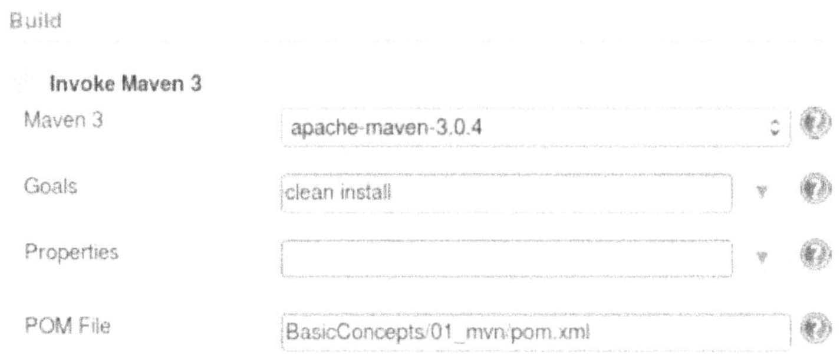

FIGURE 3-1. *Selecting the right pom.xml*

checked. If this option is checked, Hudson will only save the artifacts from the last successful build. Click Save and rerun the job. The successful execution of the job is shown next. Hudson provides a link to the artifact that enables it to be downloaded directly from Hudson. When using Hudson with Maven, this is usually not necessary, because the Maven build process always publishes the artifacts to the local Maven repository and can be configured to publish them to a remote repository as well.

Your Third Job: A Simple Servlet

Hudson is most commonly used in enterprise software environments, and one aspect of enterprise software that is common to all environments is the concept of middleware. *Middleware* is software that plugs into other enterprise software environments such as application servers, load balancers, and the like. A very self-contained example of middleware is a Java servlet. Java servlets have been around since the late 1990s and are Java's answer to the Common Gateway Interface (CGI) concept pioneered by Rob and Mike McCool at the University of Illinois at Urbana-Champaign in 1994. CGI is a way to let a program that is running on a Web server interact with the Web browser to provide interactivity beyond simple static Web pages. Servlets do the same thing, but with a nicer API and in Java. All Java servlets extend from the Java class javax.servlet.Servlet or (much more commonly) its subclass javax.servlet.http.HttpServlet. This section creates a Hudson job that builds a simple servlet to illustrate how Hudson is used with middleware.

The pom.xml

The pom.xml is very similar to the one from the HelloMvn example in the preceding chapter. The new elements are shown in **boldface**.

```
<?xml version="1.0" encoding="UTF-8"?>
<project xmlns="http://maven.apache.org/POM/4.0.0" xmlns:xsi="http://
www.w3.org/2001/XMLSchema-instance" xsi:schemaLocation="http://maven.
apache.org/POM/4.0.0 http://maven.apache.org/xsd/maven-4.0.0.xsd">
  <modelVersion>4.0.0</modelVersion>

  <groupId>net.hudsonlifestyle</groupId>
  <artifactId>simpleservlet</artifactId>
  <version>1.0</version>
  <packaging>war</packaging>

  <build>
    <plugins>
      <plugin>
        <groupId>org.apache.maven.plugins</groupId>
        <artifactId>maven-war-plugin</artifactId>
        <version>2.3</version>
```

```
        <configuration>
          <failOnMissingWebXml>false</failOnMissingWebXml>
        </configuration>
      </plugin>
      <plugin>
        <groupId>org.apache.maven.plugins</groupId>
        <artifactId>maven-compiler-plugin</artifactId>
        <inherited>true</inherited>
        <configuration>
          <source>1.6</source>
          <target>1.6</target>
          <encoding>${project.build.sourceEncoding}</encoding>
        </configuration>
      </plugin>
    </plugins>
  </build>

  <dependencies>
    <dependency>
      <groupId>javax.servlet</groupId>
      <artifactId>javax.servlet-api</artifactId>
      <version>3.0.1</version>
       <scope>provided</scope>
    </dependency>
  </dependencies>
</project>
```

This project uses Maven war packaging, as shown in the <packaging>war</packaging> declaration. This declaration tells Maven that the project should be assumed to conform to the Maven war project layout and that the final artifact is a Java Web Application Archive (war) file, rather than a jar file. The war project layout can be thought of as an extension of the Maven jar project layout shown in the preceding chapter. In addition to having Java packages in the src/main/java directory, the Web application root is assumed to be in the directory src/main/webapp. This directory will hold any Web pages needed to be shown by the servlet. This simple example has no such need. The src/main/webapp directory also can hold the Web app deployment descriptor, which must be located in the src/main/webapp/WEB-INF directory and contained in the file web.xml. Because this servlet uses annotations to convey the information that would otherwise be in the web.xml file, it doesn't need a src/main/webapp/WEB-INF/web.xml file.

Any project that uses war packaging will automatically use the maven-war-plugin. Due to a historical setting in this plugin, we must provide explicit configuration of the plugin to enable the project to successfully build, even though there is no web.xml file. This is the purpose of the <failOnMissingWebXml>false</failOnMissingWebXml> configuration.

Another historical setting whose default value must be overridden is the Java version. We use the value of 1.6 in the <source> and <target> elements.

The <encoding> element prevents a warning from maven regarding the platform encoding to be passed to the Java compiler.

The final difference between this pom and the simple example from the preceding chapter is the dependency on the servlet API. The declaration here states that this project depends on version 3.0.1 of the servlet API. The <scope>provided</scope> declaration tells the Maven war plugin to *not* bundle the servlet API jar into the completed war file.

The Servlet Class

The servlet class has even fewer lines than the pom.xml, and is arguably simpler because it is more self-contained. Here is the code listing for the servlet, which is located in the src/main/java/net/hudsonlifestyle/SimpleServlet01.java file.

```
package net.hudsonlifestyle;

import java.io.IOException;
import java.io.PrintWriter;
import javax.servlet.ServletException;
import javax.servlet.annotation.WebServlet;
import javax.servlet.http.HttpServlet;
import javax.servlet.http.HttpServletRequest;
import javax.servlet.http.HttpServletResponse;

@WebServlet(name = "SimpleServlet01", urlPatterns = {"/SimpleServlet01"})
public class SimpleServlet01 extends HttpServlet {

    @Override
    protected void service(HttpServletRequest request, HttpServletRe-
sponse response) throws ServletException, IOException {
        response.setContentType("text/html;charset=UTF-8");
        PrintWriter out = response.getWriter();
        try {
            out.println("<html>");
            out.println("<head>");
            out.println("<title>Servlet SimpleServlet01</title>");
            out.println("</head>");
            out.println("<body>");
            out.println("<h1>Servlet SimpleServlet01 at " + request.getCon-
textPath () + "</h1>");
            out.println("</body>");
            out.println("</html>");
        } finally {
            out.close();
        }
    }
}
```

The only method from the superclass that must be overridden is the service() method. This method is called whenever the application server in which the war file is deployed receives a Web request with a path /SimpleServlet01. For example, simply deploying the war file to the GlassFish application server makes the URL http://localhost:8080/simpleservlet-1.0/SimpleServlet01 be handled by the servlet, resulting in the Web page being served as shown in the code listing.

Creating a Job and Using Views to Organize Jobs

Follow the steps from the preceding section, "Your Second Job," to create a job to build the simple servlet. The only differences lie in the location of the POM file, which is BasicConcepts/02_mvn/pom.xml, and the artifact to archive, which is captured by the path expression BasicConcepts/02_mvn/target/*.war.

Now that you have three jobs on your Hudson instance, we can demonstrate the Views feature. Views let you group related jobs together so that complexity can be better managed as the number of jobs on a server grows. On the main Hudson dashboard under the words "Jobs Status," you will see a tab with a "+" sign. Clicking the "+" sign brings up the New View page. We will create two views: "Administrative" and "Product." Enter the value **Administrative** into the Name field that appears after clicking the "+" sign, as shown in Figure 3-2.

Choose the jobs to be included in the view by checking the check box next to the job name. In the Columns section, you can drag and drop the columns to be displayed in the view, deleting the ones that are not desired. The meaning of the various columns is described in the following list:

- **Status** The outcome of the most recent build of this job.
- **Weather** An indication of the trend of the status of several previous builds of the job. This is useful to get a quick idea of the stability of the job. If a job has been having trouble getting a clean build, this will show up as an icon of a cloud with rain. If the job has been free of failures lately, it will show up as a sun icon.
- **Job** The name of the job.
- **Last Success** The timestamp of the last successful build of the job.
- **Last Failure** The timestamp of the last failed build of the job.
- **Last Duration** The time it took for the last build of the job to complete.
- **Console** A link to view the build console for the most recent build of the job.
- **Build button** A button that manually starts a build.

The "Add column" drop-down menu lets you re-add any columns that were deleted. A good list of columns is Status, Weather, Job, Last Success, and Console.

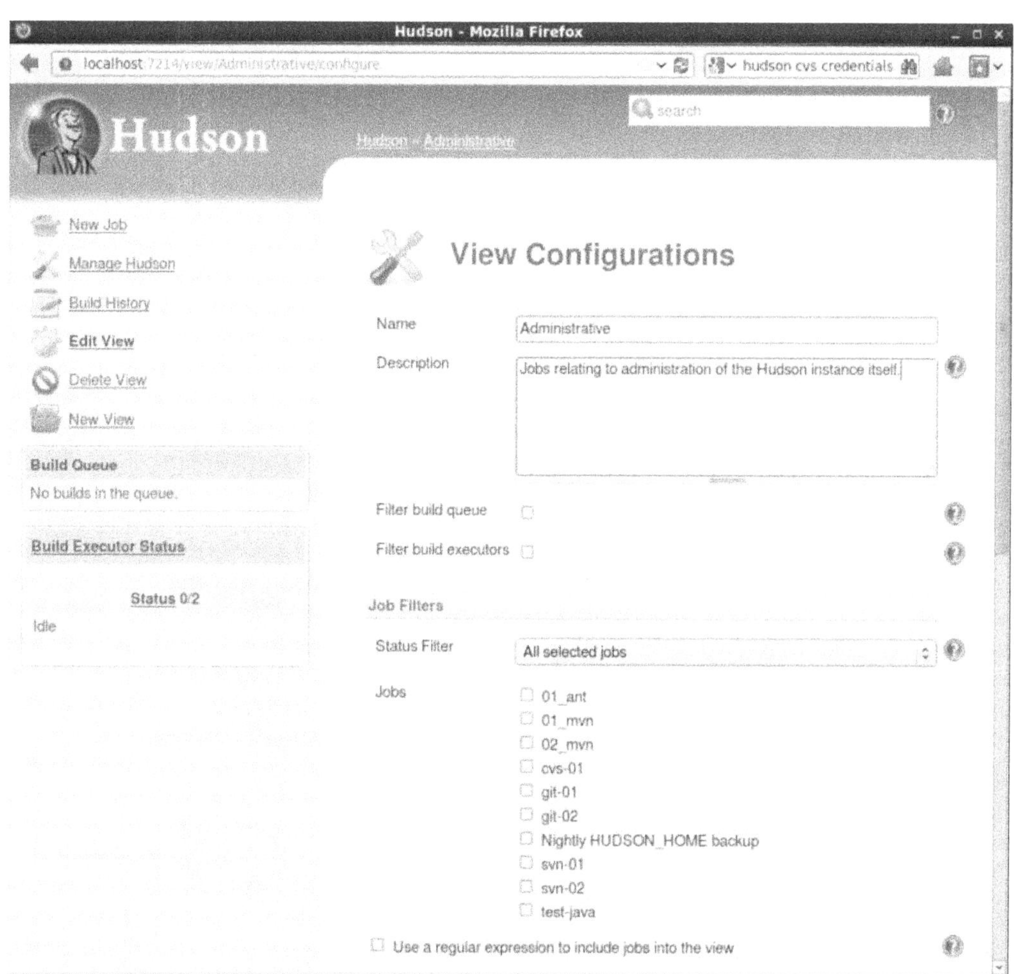

FIGURE 3-2. *View Configurations page*

Follow the same steps to create the Product view, but include the two Java-related jobs. Views can be very helpful when the number of jobs on a Hudson instance becomes too great to show on a single screen.

Using the Plugin Center

The integration software nature of Hudson means that plugins are important. The Hudson Plugin Center is where you can manage the installation of Hudson's many plugins. Similar to an app store for a smart phone, the Plugin Center lets you see what plugins are currently installed (allowing updating them if necessary) and what plugins are available to install (allowing installing them if desired).

The Plugin Center Tab Panel

The Plugin Center can be reached from the main dashboard by clicking Manage Hudson and then clicking Manage Plugins. Note that the browser URL bar shows "pluginCenter/" but the label of the panel is "Hudson Plugin Manager." This panel will be referred to as the Plugin Center for discussion.

TIP

Note that the Manage Hudson page also has a link titled "Manage Plugins using Classic Plugin Manager." This feature is provided for compatibility with versions of Hudson prior to 3.0. All of the necessary functionality for managing plugins has been reimplemented in Hudson 3.0 within the Manage Plugins link. The classic plugin manager will not be discussed further in this book.

Proxy Concerns (the Advanced Tab) When using Hudson behind an HTTP firewall, it is necessary to configure the proxy settings so that Hudson itself can become aware of the available plugins and install them if necessary. This may be done from the Advanced tab within the Plugin Center. The values entered here must be exactly the same as whatever values enable you to browse the external Internet.

Updates Tab The Updates tab shows which of the currently installed plugins are not the most recent versions available for that particular plugin. Only plugins for which the currently installed version is not the most recent version are shown in this panel. This panel provides an easy way to keep your plugins up to date. However, it is advisable to read the release notes for each plugin before conducting an update to see if the new version introduced any problems with respect to the current version of Hudson you are running. For this reason, make sure your Hudson backup story is in good shape so you can easily revert to a previous version in the event a new plugin causes problems. Figure 3-3 shows the Updates tab with three pending updates.

Available Tab The Available tab is the gateway to all available Hudson plugins that can be installed using the Plugin Center. Subtabs in this panel include: Featured, Recommended, Others, and Search. Starting with Featured and moving through to Search, the plugins are listed in decreasing order of the amount of quality assurance (QA) that is done by the Hudson development community. Plugins in the Featured tab are known to be the highest quality and least likely to cause trouble, while those

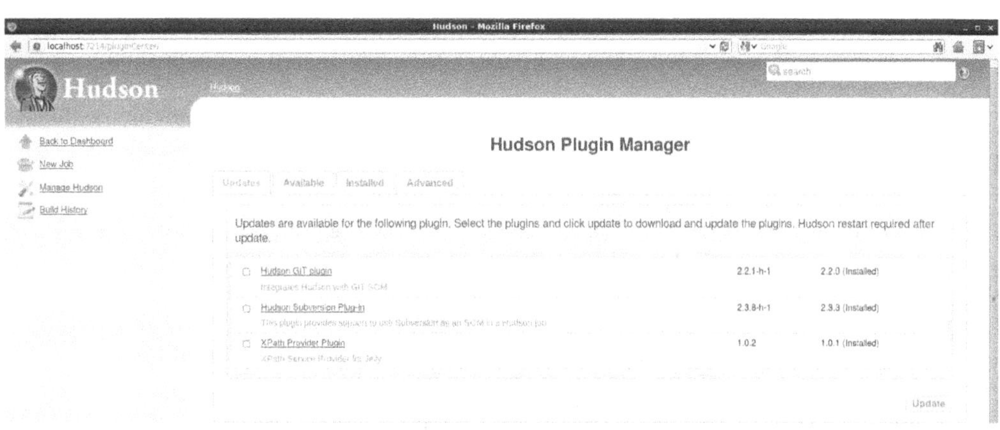

FIGURE 3-3. *Updates tab with three pending updates*

found in the Search tab could be unstable. Each of the tabs, except the Search tab, are grouped functionally. For ease of browsing, all of the functional groups are open by default, but they can be collapsed by clicking the "-" box next to the functional group heading.

The Featured subtab shows only plugins that are designated as featured by the Hudson project administrators. All of the plugins in this panel are tested and certified by the Hudson QA team. As such, they have a higher level of quality assurance than any random Hudson plugin available on the Internet.

Every plugin in the Recommended subtab is looked after by the Hudson project administrators, but they are not subject to the same QA constraints as those in the Featured subtab. Generally, it is a safe strategy to limit yourself to the Featured and Recommended subtabs until you have become comfortable with rebuilding your Hudson instance from backup; these plugins will meet 99 percent of your needs.

The Others subtab shows only plugins that are known by the Hudson project administrators, but not given very much scrutiny with respect to quality. Plugins here should be researched before installing.

The Search subtab allows open text search for any kind of plugin. No guarantee of quality is made of the plugins found in this manner, though naturally every plugin that can be found in any of the other subtabs is also available from this tab. Generally, it's only a good idea to use the search subtab if the desired plugin cannot be found in any of the other subtabs.

Installed The Installed tab shows the installed plugins and lets you enable or disable each one, including plugins fundamental to the operation of Hudson. Therefore, exercise great care when using this panel. It is best to only take action on plugins that you have installed yourself.

Updating an Installed Plugin

As shown in Figure 3-3, the Plugin Center allows discovery of the need to update installed plugins, as well as performing the update. Continuing with the smartphone analogy, a familiar complaint with smartphone apps is the occasional experience of losing functionality in an important app as a consequence of updating that app from the app store. In such instances, one would like to be able to downgrade to the earlier version. Unfortunately, this is not as easy with smartphones as it could be. The story is similar for Hudson, though downgrading is not as difficult. This section will explain how to save aside the current XPath Plugin Provider before using the Plugin Center to update the plugin. After successfully demonstrating the installation of the updated plugin, the previously installed version will be reinstalled, restoring the prior functionality.

Saving Aside the Current Version of the Plugin Note the HUDSON_HOME directory being used by your Hudson instance. In the command shell, change to that directory and then to the plugins subdirectory. There you will find files ending in .hpi, which stands for Hudson Plugin. These are zip files containing the expected file layout for a Hudson plugin. Alongside each .hpi file you will see a directory that is the result of unzipping that .hpi file. For this example, there would be an xpath-provider.hpi file and an xpath-provider directory. To verify that the Hudson instance is, in fact, running the version of the plugin in the plugins directory, you can compare the value of the Plugin-Version attribute in the META-INF/MANIFEST.MF file in the unzipped plugin directory with that shown in the Plugin Center's Updates tab. Note this version number so you can verify that the update succeeded. To save aside the currently installed version, simply copy the .hpi file to another directory outside of the plugins directory, taking care to note where you saved it.

Performing the Update Before doing any updates, it's a good idea to wait for any existing jobs to complete, then put the Hudson instance in shutdown mode. This prevents any new jobs from executing until Hudson is restarted, which must be done after installing or updating a plugin. To put Hudson in shutdown mode, visit the Manage Hudson page from the main dashboard and find the Prepare for Shutdown link. After you click this link, a red banner containing the text "Hudson is preparing to shutdown" appears on every Hudson page.

Performing the update is a simple matter of checking the check box next to the plugin to be updated and clicking the Update button. Doing so will cause the Hudson UI to present a progress notification while the update is being performed. When the update completes, Hudson must be restarted.

After Hudson restarts, visit the Plugin Center's Installed Plugins tab and search for the plugin that you updated. Note that the version number has increased to the new version.

Performing the Downgrade Using the Downgrade Button Hudson helpfully provides a Downgrade to N button, where N is the previously installed version of the plugin. Click the Downgrade to N button and you will be presented with this dialog.

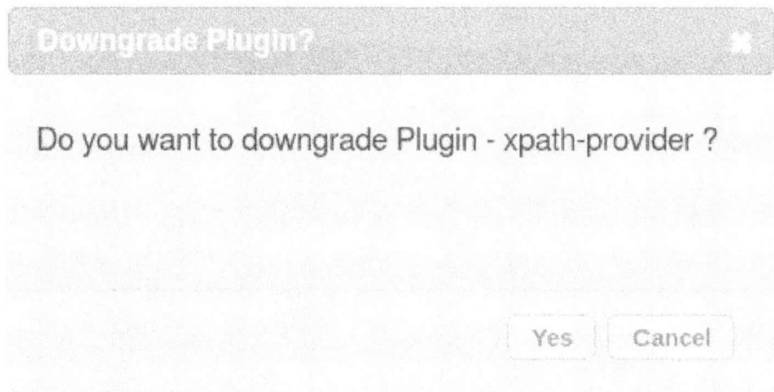

Accept the dialog and shut down Hudson. After restarting Hudson, visit the Updates tab of the Plugin Center and verify that the downgrade was successful.

Performing the Downgrade Using the Manual Method As an added measure of security, it is possible to perform the downgrade without using the Downgrade button. This technique can be useful if there is a specific version of the plugin that was known to work with your environment, but which is not available via the "Downgrade to N" button. Ensure that Hudson is shut down and use the command prompt to change to the plugins directory within the HUDSON_HOME directory. Find the .hpi file and corresponding directory for the plugin in question. Verify that your saved-aside .hpi file is valid using a zip utility, such as unzip -t. Delete the .hpi file and corresponding directory from within the plugins directory, and copy the saved-aside .hpi file into the plugins directory. When you restart Hudson, the .hpi file is automatically unzipped, and you should see that the plugin shows up in the Updates tab of the Plugin Center as being eligible for update.

Installing a New Plugin

This section walks through the installation of the JobConfigHistory plugin. This useful plugin can record any changes to your configuration, both systemwide changes and per-job changes. The usage of the JobConfigHistory plugin will be further explored later in the chapter. From the Plugin Center tab panel, click on the Available tab and then on the Recommended subtab. Use your browser's "find in page" feature to locate the text "JobConfigHistory" in the page. Click the check box next to the plugin, scroll down to the bottom of the page, and click the Install button. Hudson will display a progress indicator while the plugin is being downloaded. The amount of time this progress indicator will display depends on your environment. When the progress indicator disappears, restart Hudson. After the restart, you should see a new link on the main Hudson dashboard: Job Config History. This is your indication that the plugin installed successfully.

Disabling and Re-enabling an Installed Plugin

Now that the Job Config History plugin has been successfully installed, we will describe the act of disabling an installed plugin. Disabling a plugin makes the plugin effectively disconnected from the system, except for the fact that it can easily be re-enabled. It is one step short of fully removing the plugin from the system, which is explained in the next section. To disable an installed plugin, visit the Plugin Center and the Installed tab within the tab panel. In this case, search for the text "JobConfigHistory" in the list. Click the Disable button, and you will be presented with a dialog confirming that you want to disable the plugin. Accept the dialog. Note that there is no need to click any kind of save button. You must restart Hudson immediately in order for the changes to take effect. Do not delay in restarting after making configuration changes that require a restart, so as to minimize the chance of disrupting the system. After Hudson completes restarting, visit the main dashboard and note that the Job Config History link is missing. To re-enable the plugin, visit the Plugin Center's Installed tab, find the entry for JobConfigHistory, and click the Enable button. By now, the practice of restarting Hudson should be very familiar.

Removing a Plugin Entirely

The Hudson management console does not offer a way to remove a plugin entirely from the system, but it can be done from the command line. When removing a plugin in this way, care must be taken to remove all the files installed by the plugin, a process which varies from plugin to plugin. Failure to completely remove a plugin from the system can lead to unpredictable results when reinstalling the same plugin later. The process has two broad steps, both of which must take place while Hudson is shut down. First, remove the .hpi file and corresponding directory from the plugins directory. Second, remove any extra files created by the plugin itself. Restart Hudson and verify that the plugin has been removed.

These skills provide the basis for all manner of plugin management in Hudson. The next section explores the JobConfigHistory plugin as a means to expand on the backup job from the Chapter 1.

Your Fourth Job: Advanced Backup Options

As with any enterprise software, maintaining backups of critical infrastructure is essential for smooth operation of the business. Due to Hudson's special place in the software environment and the tendency of Hudson to encapsulate complexity so that those working in the environment can safely forget about many of the configuration options once they are built into a working state, it is especially important to exercise good backup hygiene with Hudson. Recall the "Back Everything Up" section from Chapter 1. This job runs nightly and saves the last five runs worth of the HUDSON_HOME directory. Because this would include all of the jobs on the entire Hudson instance, this might prove to consume too much disk space. This section explores the JobConfigHistory plugin installed in the preceding section, and uses that plugin to enable a more fine-grained approach that uses far less disk space by saving only the job configurations.

Upgrading the JobConfigHistory Plugin

The steps in this section assume version 2.3 or later of the JobConfigHistory plugin. As of this writing, the version of JobConfigHistory plugin available via the Plugin Center was only 1.9. The steps in this section will allow you to upgrade to a more recent version of the JobConfigHistory plugin.

As with all command-line Hudson maintenance, shut down Hudson first. For those plugins not available in the Plugin Center, but which are known to work with Hudson, you can download the .hpi file and place it in the plugins directory in HUDSON_HOME. Make sure to delete the old .hpi and corresponding directory first before putting the new plugin in place. In this case, the latest version of the JobConfigHistory plugin can be found at http://dl.aragost.com/hudson/plugins/jobConfigHistory. Restart Hudson and verify that the version shows up as expected in the Installed tab in the Plugin Center.

Exploring the JobConfigHistory Plugin

Visit the main Hudson dashboard and click on the Job Config History link. Immediately after installing the plugin, there is no config history to show. To cause this page to show some data, we will make a change to an existing job. Visit the configuration page for an existing job, such as the servlet example earlier in this chapter. Any change made to the job will be captured by the JobConfigHistory plugin. For this example, simply change the text in the "Description" text area, such as by adding the text **Test the JobConfigHistory Plugin**. Scroll down to the bottom of the configuration page and click Save. Now visit the main dashboard and click on the Job Config History link. You will see more data in this page. Now, go back to the job configuration page and make another change to the "Description" text area, saving the change. Return to the main dashboard and click the Job Config History link. This page displays links that let you filter the kind of configuration history to display:

- **Show system configs only** This shows changes to the Hudson configuration outside of those made to individual jobs.
- **Show job configs only** This shows changes to individual jobs.
- **Show deleted jobs only** This shows jobs that have been deleted.
- **Show all configs** Shows all kinds of configs.

To view the changes just made, click the "Show job configs only" link and click on the most recently changed job. You can compare the differences between any two incarnations of the selected job by selecting the appropriate File A and File B radio buttons and clicking the Show Diffs button.

Saving and Restoring a Previous Job Configuration

The JobConfigHistory plugin automatically starts saving all changes to all jobs as soon as it is running. Restoring a previous job config can be as easy as clicking a button or as hard as copying in an XML file to the job's directory, depending on the version of the JobHistoryConfig plugin that is running.

The config changes for a job can be viewed from the main Job Config History link, or from the Job Config History link for an individual job. The latter is more convenient because it takes you straight to the relevant history without any extra navigation. When viewing the Job Configuration History for a job, the "Restore old config" button should automatically reset the current state of the job config to be equal to that of the saved job config. Unfortunately, this may not work due to divergence between Hudson and Jenkins. If the button does not work, you can achieve the same effect by saving aside the RAW link to an XML file and then overwriting the job's config.xml file with the saved-aside file. When making such command-line changes, you must stop Hudson before copying in the file. The jobs are located in the jobs directory of the HUDSON_HOME directory. For example, if the Simple Servlet example was 02_mvn, and HUDSON_HOME is /var/lib/hudson, the file to replace is /var/lib/hudson/jobs/02_mvn/config.xml.

Saving and Restoring System Configuration

Because tracking all system changes can be more resource-consuming, the plugin comes with this option disabled by default. To enable it, visit the Manage Hudson link from the main dashboard, then the Configure System link. This takes you to the System Configurations page. Find the Job Config History section, which only appears if the plugin is installed and enabled. Click the Advanced button. Check the box next to the text "Save system configuration changes." If desired, fill in values for the other fields. In practice, the most useful field is "Max number of history entries to keep," which should be set to around 5. After making these changes and saving them, go back to the System Configurations page and make a change in the "System Message" text area. Save the change. Return to the main dashboard and click the "Show system configs only" link. You will see a list with lots of entries for all the different kinds of system configurations. The entry pertaining to the System Message change is labeled "config (system)." Click this entry and you will see the same kind of Diff UI as with the job config, enabling you to inspect the differences between versions of the system config over time. Unlike the job config, there is no "restore" button, so you must use the same practice of saving aside the raw XML and overwriting the appropriate file after shutting down Hudson. In the case of the System Message change, the appropriate file is config.xml within the HUDSON_HOME directory. Copying in the saved-aside file and restarting Hudson should show the system message as it was prior to changing it.

Using a Hudson Job to Save the Output of JobConfigHistory

Find the backup job from the first chapter. We will use this as the basis for this new job. If you haven't already created that job, do it now. For discussion, the job is called "Nightly HUDSON_HOME backup." Create a new job by clicking on the New Job link from the main dashboard. Type in a new name, such as **Nightly JobConfig backup**. Select the radio button next to the "Copy existing job" option and fill in N**ightly HUDSON_HOME backup** in the "Copy from" text field. The system will auto-complete based on the set of existing jobs. Leave all fields the same except for the Command text area in the Execute shell entry in the Build section. Replace the existing text with the following, which is similar to the existing text, but with the differences shown in bold.

```
export BACKUP_ROOT=/mnt/JobConfigBackup
cd ${BACKUP_ROOT}
cp -r ${HUDSON_HOME}/config-history JOB_CONFIG-${BUILD_ID}-backup
tar -cf JOB_CONFIG-${BUILD_ID}-backup.tar JOB_CONFIG-${BUILD_ID}-backup
gzip JOB_CONFIG-${BUILD_ID}-backup.tar
rm -rf JOB_CONFIG-${BUILD_ID}-backup
(ls -t|head -n 5;ls)|sort|uniq -u|xargs rm -rf
```

As before, the last line ensures that only the last five entries are saved. Make sure the /mnt/JobConfigBackup is writable by the user id under which Hudson is running.

Hudson Authentication Security

This section covers how to configure Hudson using its existing security settings. A full treatment of Internet security, especially as it applies to securing a host that is running on the open public Internet, is well beyond the scope of this book. If your Hudson instance is running on the public Internet, you will need to do more than just what the standard Hudson security settings provide. Much of this configuration can be done using the administrative features of the container in which you are running Hudson. Even in a trusted environment such as a corporate intranet, which is the most common place to run Hudson, enabling the authentication system is useful because it provides accountability for the person who has the ability to make changes to the configurations. For example, the JobConfigHistory plugin shows who made each change to the configuration. If everyone is logged in as the same user, then this information is lost. We will walk through the most common authentication and authorization.

Standard Security Configuration

This section will create two accounts, one named Alice, intended to be an administrator account, and another named Bob, intended to have fewer privileges, but enough to be productive. Before proceeding, some terms must be established.

Hudson Security Terms Hudson security can be broken down into two aspects:

- **Authentication** Proving to the system that a user's identity is authentic. In other words, "you are who you say you are." Hudson calls this aspect "Security Realm" for historical reasons due to Hudson's origins inside the Application Server group at Sun Microsystems.
- **Authorization** Granting access to certain parts of the system based on the user's identity. This is sometimes referred to as *role-based access control* because each user is associated with one or more roles, and the roles dictate what actions the user may take. In other words, "we know who you are; now, what are you allowed to do?"

There are a few steps to take for each aspect.

Authentication From the main Hudson dashboard, choose Manage Hudson and then Configure Security. Click the Enable Security check box, which is unchecked by default. This reveals the basic security configuration panel. In the Security Realm section, choose "Hudson's own user database" and ensure that the "Allow users to sign up" and "Notify user of account creation" check boxes are checked. These will be unchecked later after the two accounts are created. This approach places the burden on the Hudson administrator for creating accounts. This is more work for the admin, but it ends up being more secure.

In the Authorization section, select the "Logged-in users can do anything" radio button and click Save. The first time these steps are followed, the act of clicking Save will effectively introduce a login policy where there was none before. Naturally, this means you are now effectively logged out, but don't worry. Because we kept the "Allow users to sign up" check box checked, and selected the "Logged-in users can do anything" option, we will now use the Hudson UI to create the accounts for Alice and Bob and then assign them privileges accordingly.

Click the Sign up link in the upper-right corner of the screen. This link appeared when Save was clicked. Hudson will show this UI for creating an account.

Sign up

Username: alice
Password: •••••
Confirm password: •••••
Full name: Alice Admin
E-mail address: alice@example.com
Sign up

Fill in the UI as shown for Alice and click the Sign up button. This will log you in as that user. Log out of Alice's account by clicking on the "log out" link at the top right of the Hudson UI. Follow the same steps to create an account for Bob (with bob as the username), logging Bob out and logging back in as Alice again.

Authorization Visit Manage Hudson, then Configure Security. In the Security Realm section, uncheck the "Allow users to sign up" and "Notify user of Hudson account creation" check boxes. In the Authorization section, choose the "Matrix-based security" radio button. This reveals a UI for configuring access control lists (ACLs) for the existing users that have been created using the Hudson UI. It is not possible to create users from the "Matrix-based security" UI. Creating users is easiest to do as shown in the preceding section. Type **alice** into the "User/group to add" box and click Add. Note that only existing usernames may be typed here. Do the same for **bob**. Make sure all of the check boxes are checked for Alice and all but the Administer check box (in the Overall section) and Slave check box are checked for Bob. The divisions between the columns in the access control list UI are not very clear. For reference, the first column in the Job section is "Create." Figure 3-4 shows the configured ACL panel.

Click Save and then log out Alice. Log back in as Bob and note that the Manage Hudson link is simply not present. Logging back in as Alice will reveal this link again.

User/group	Overall		Slave		Job						Run		View		
	Administer	Read	Configure	Delete	Create	Delete	Configure	Read	Build	Workspace	Delete	Update	Create	Delete	Configure
alice	✓	✓	✓	✓	✓	✓	✓	✓	✓	✓	✓	✓	✓	✓	✓
bob		✓			✓	✓	✓	✓	✓	✓	✓	✓	✓	✓	✓
Anonymous															

User/group to add: Add

FIGURE 3-4. *The ACL panel*

Because Hudson jobs can contain sensitive information such as passwords, it is best to always apply at least these security steps to any enterprise-level Hudson instance.

Adding Quality Assurance Systems

Arguably the most valuable function Hudson can perform is to increase the quality of the world's software (and therefore the world itself). Software Quality Assurance is the broad term applied to all such worthy efforts. Obviously, a detailed treatment of this topic is beyond the scope of this book. This section introduces tools for testing, inspection, coverage, and reporting. For each of these aspects of software quality assurance, there are many tools that are able to work well with Hudson. The most popular of each aspect will be explored in turn. The topic of testing will be examined in more detail in the chapter on Hudson and automated testing.

Testing

With respect to Hudson, testing refers to the act of including the running of automated tests in a Hudson job. If any of the tests fail, the job fails just as badly as if there were a syntax error in the source code. Once your organization is committed to keeping the Hudson jobs clean (that is, no failures), the simple step of adding testing as a precondition for job success is the last hurdle to achieving significant return on the time invested in Hudson thus far.

The exact manner in which testing can be included in your Hudson jobs can vary greatly depending on what build system is being used and what kind of test (unit, system, integration, acceptance, and so on) is being executed. In general, it is best to minimize the amount of configuration relating to testing kept in the job itself. Rather, strive to keep such configuration entirely in the build configuration, which is kept under SCM.

The Simplest Test That Could Possibly Work This section adds a unit test to the HelloMvn example. Maven assumes that the software is composed of loosely coupled modules, each of which is self-contained and reasonably small. It is challenging to keep the software organized in this way over time, but it is very important to keep disciplined about doing so. One part of "self-contained" means the code and the tests are kept closely together. At a minimum, this means the unit tests are kept very close to the code. Other kinds of tests may reasonably be allowed to live in their own modules, separate from the code.

As shown previously, Maven assumes the source code is kept in subdirectories of src/main/java. A similar assumption is made about tests: they reside in src/test/java. Placing your tests in this directory allows Maven to automatically execute them as part of the build lifecycle. The following listing is src/test/java/net/hudsonlifestyle/HelloMvnTest.java. This test uses JUnit, but another popular and mostly equivalent technology is TestNG.

```
package net.hudsonlifestyle;

import org.junit.Test;
import static org.junit.Assert.*;

public class HelloMvnTest {

    @Test
    public void testHelloMvn() throws Exception {
        assertTrue(false);
    }
}
```

Note that the package of this class is identical to the HelloMvn class. This trick allows the test to access package private code. This test imports two things from JUnit: the Test annotation and the assertion static functions. The former is placed on every method that is to be called by the Maven plugin that will be running the test. The latter are used to assert the correctness of the code. These assertions are the way in which the outcome of the test is determined. A single failed assertion will cause the test to be considered failed. Consequently, a single failed test will cause the job to be considered failed. For this reason, assertions are really important. The assertion in this test: assertTrue(false) will always fail. This is done to illustrate the reporting feature of Hudson. After running the job with the failed test, it will be corrected and rerun.

Some additional configuration is necessary in the pom.xml. Because JUnit uses annotations, the compiler plugin must be told to use a version of Java that supports annotations. This was shown in the preceding example regarding servlets. Because we are using JUnit, we must include a dependency on it. This goes in the <dependencies> section.

```
<dependency>
  <groupId>junit</groupId>
  <artifactId>junit</artifactId>
  <version>4.11</version>
  <scope>test</scope>
</dependency>
```

Note the <scope>test</scope>. This is necessary to prevent Maven from adding the dependency to the classpath on build lifecycle phases other than test. This prevents accidentally introducing test dependencies in the main code, since such code would fail to compile.

Rerunning the Hudson job for this code will automatically cause this test to be executed. As shown in this output, the test will fail.

```
-------------------------------------------------------
 T E S T S
-------------------------------------------------------
Running net.hudsonlifestyle.HelloMvnTest
Tests run: 1, Failures: 1, Errors: 0, Skipped: 0, Time elapsed: 0.047 sec <<< FAILURE!

Results :

Failed tests:   testHelloMvn(net.hudsonlifestyle.HelloMvnTest)

Tests run: 1, Failures: 1, Errors: 0, Skipped: 0

[INFO] ------------------------------------------------------------------------
[INFO] BUILD FAILURE
[INFO] ------------------------------------------------------------------------
[INFO] Total time: 2.764s
[INFO] Finished at: Sat Apr 06 03:03:09 EDT 2013
[INFO] Final Memory: 13M/151M
[INFO] ------------------------------------------------------------------------
[INFO] o.h.m.e.h.MavenExecutionResultHandler - Build failed with exception(s)
[INFO] o.h.m.e.h.MavenExecutionResultHandler - [1] org.apache.maven.lifecycle.Lifecy-
cleExecutionException: Failed to execute goal org.apache.maven.plugins:maven-surefire-
plugin:2.10:test (default-test) on project hellomvn: There are test failures.

Please refer to /var/lib/hudson/jobs/03_mvn/workspace/BasicConcepts/03_mvn/target/
surefire-reports for the individual test results.
[DEBUG] Closing connection to remote
[ERROR] Failed to execute goal org.apache.maven.plugins:maven-surefire-
plugin:2.10:test (default-test) on project hellomvn: There are test failures.
[ERROR]
[ERROR] Please refer to /var/lib/hudson/jobs/03_mvn/workspace/BasicConcepts/03_mvn/
target/surefire-reports for the individual test results.
[ERROR] -> [Help 1]
[ERROR]
[ERROR] To see the full stack trace of the errors, re-run Maven with the -e switch.
[ERROR] Re-run Maven using the -X switch to enable full debug logging.
[ERROR]
[ERROR] For more information about the errors and possi-
ble solutions, please read the following articles:
[ERROR] [Help 1] http://cwiki.apache.org/confluence/display/MAVEN/MojoFailureException
[DEBUG] Waiting for process to finish
[DEBUG] Result: 1
Archiving artifacts
Recording test results
[DEBUG] Skipping watched dependency update for build: 03_mvn #7 due to result: FAILURE
Finished: FAILURE


Page generated: Apr 6, 2013 3:04:35 AM Hudson ver. 3.0.0
```

In addition to the test output, the Hudson UI provides numerous cues to indicate the failure of the job.

Now that the test is being run by Hudson, we must take the additional step of configuring Hudson to know about the test results. From the main page for the job, click the Configure link and find the Post-build Actions section. Click the check box labeled "Publish JUnit test result report." This will reveal a text field into which you would enter a file path similar to the one in the "Archiving the Artifacts" exercise earlier in the chapter. The value in this field is validated against the latest job workspace when the cursor is moved out of the field. If the value did not match any files, a helpful error message is displayed. In this case, enter the value **BasicConcepts/03_mvn/surefire-reports/TEST-*.xml** (or similar). Rerun the job and you should see something similar to the following.

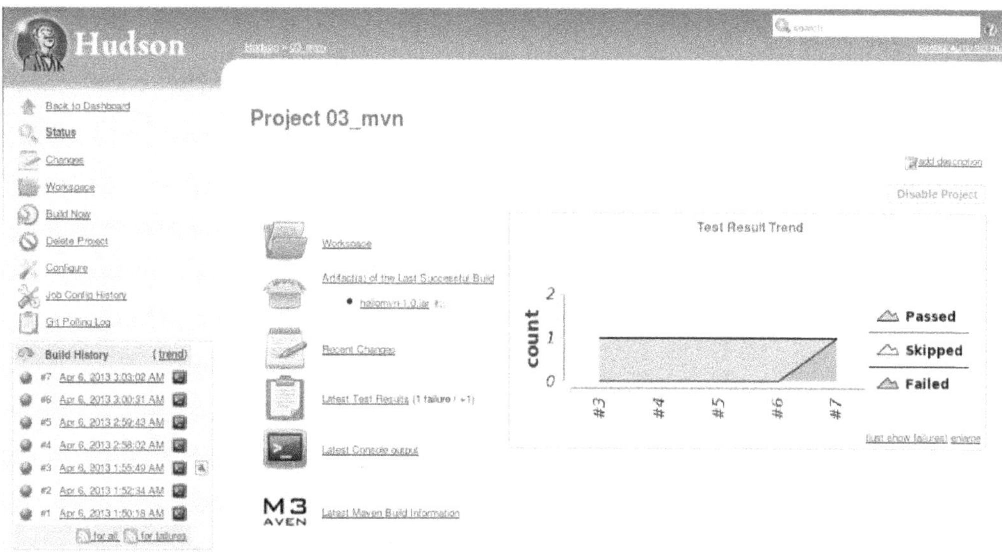

Click on the link Latest Test Results. This brings you to a collection of pages that allow quick discovery of the failed test(s) and, more importantly, start to discover the cause of the failure(s). Given that the goal is Continuous Delivery and the software cannot be delivered if there are failing tests, making it as easy as possible to fix problems is very important. The All Failed Tests section has links to pages that contain information that may be helpful in determining the cause of the failure. By default this is the stack trace to the failed assertion. In this case, the stack trace looks like this.

```
java.lang.AssertionError
        at org.junit.Assert.fail(Assert.java:86)
        at org.junit.Assert.assertTrue(Assert.java:41)
        at org.junit.Assert.assertTrue(Assert.java:52)
        at net.hudsonlifestyle.HelloMvnTest.testHelloMvn(HelloMvnTest.java:12)
```

```
      at sun.reflect.NativeMethodAccessorImpl.invoke0(Native Method)
      at sun.reflect.NativeMethodAccessorImpl.
invoke(NativeMethodAccessorImpl.java:57)
      at sun.reflect.DelegatingMethodAccessorImpl.invoke(DelegatingMethodAcc
essorImpl.java:43)
      at java.lang.reflect.Method.invoke(Method.java:616)
```

The remaining frames of the stack trace have been omitted because they pertain only to the mechanics of Maven invoking the test.

To fix the test, replace the assertion with this code.

```
HelloMvn.main(null)
```

This is the only method we have on HelloMvn. In its present form, the main() method does nothing with the argument String array, but perhaps a future change will do so. In any case, this test could be considered a "fuzz test": a test that intentionally passes invalid input to the code to assert that it behaves correctly even in such cases. In this case, because the test method declares **throws Exception**, the expected behavior is that the null input is silently ignored. Rerun the job and the failed test will start to pass, allowing the job to pass.

```
-------------------------------------------------------
 T E S T S
-------------------------------------------------------
Running net.hudsonlifestyle.HelloMvnTest
Hello Maven!
Tests run: 1, Failures: 0, Errors: 0, Skipped: 0, Time elapsed: 0.543 sec

Results :

Tests run: 1, Failures: 0, Errors: 0, Skipped: 0

[INFO]
[INFO] --- maven-jar-plugin:2.4:jar (default-jar) @ hellomvn ---
[INFO] Building jar: /var/lib/hudson/jobs/03_mvn/workspace/BasicConcepts/03_mvn/target/
hellomvn-1.0.jar
[INFO]
[INFO] --- maven-install-plugin:2.3.1:install (default-install) @ hellomvn ---
[INFO] Installing /var/lib/hudson/jobs/03_mvn/workspace/BasicConcepts/03_mvn/target/
hellomvn-1.0.jar to /var/lib/hudson/.m2/repository/net/hudsonlifestyle/hellomvn/1.0/
hellomvn-1.0.jar
[INFO] Installing /var/lib/hudson/jobs/03_mvn/workspace/BasicConcepts/03_mvn/pom.
xml to /var/lib/hudson/.m2/repository/net/hudsonlifestyle/hellomvn/1.0/hellomvn-1.0.pom
[INFO] ------------------------------------------------------------------------
[INFO] BUILD SUCCESS
[INFO] ------------------------------------------------------------------------
[INFO] Total time: 41.403s
[INFO] Finished at: Sat Apr 06 09:38:40 EDT 2013
[INFO] Final Memory: 13M/153M
[INFO] ------------------------------------------------------------------------
[DEBUG] Closing connection to remote
[DEBUG] Waiting for process to finish
[DEBUG] Result: 0
```

```
Archiving artifacts
Recording test results
[DEBUG] Skipping watched dependency update; build not configured with trigger: 03_mvn #8
Finished: SUCCESS
```

Adding Inspection or Analysis Another important class of software quality assurance tool is the inspection or analysis tool. Generally there are two subclasses of inspection tool, named for the manner in which the inspection is performed. Static analysis tools look at the source code without running it, comparing it to a set of best practices for the kind of source code being examined. The two most popular static analysis tools in use with Hudson are FindBugs and PMD. Dynamic analysis tools look at the code as it is being run. Dynamic analysis tools are less commonly used but should at least be considered when taking a holistic look at software quality. This section adds PMD to the HelloMvn example.

At a high level, there are three steps to introducing any new kind of static analysis tools to your Hudson instance.

1. Identify the code to analyze.
2. Configure the build system to perform the analysis.
3. Configure Hudson to display the results of the analysis in a usable report.

Because the HelloMvn example is trivial, we must introduce a PMD violation in the form of an unused import. Adding this line to the class will suffice:

```
import java.util.List;
```

Because we have been using Maven, we will need to add a <reporting> top-level section to the pom.xml, as shown in the boldfaced text.

```
<project xmlns="http://maven.apache.org/POM/4.0.0" xmlns:xsi="http://
www.w3.org/2001/XMLSchema-instance" xsi:schemaLocation="http://maven.
apache.org/POM/4.0.0 http://maven.apache.org/xsd/maven-4.0.0.xsd">
  <modelVersion>4.0.0</modelVersion>

  <groupId>net.hudsonlifestyle</groupId>
  <artifactId>hellomvn-04</artifactId>
  <version>1.0</version>
  <packaging>jar</packaging>
    <build>
    <plugins>
      <plugin>
        <groupId>org.apache.maven.plugins</groupId>
        <artifactId>maven-jar-plugin</artifactId>
        <version>2.4</version>
        <configuration>
          <archive>
```

```
          <manifest>
            <mainClass>net.hudsonlifestyle.HelloMvn</mainClass>
          </manifest>
        </archive>
      </configuration>
    </plugin>
    <plugin>
      <groupId>org.apache.maven.plugins</groupId>
      <artifactId>maven-compiler-plugin</artifactId>
      <inherited>true</inherited>
      <configuration>
        <source>1.6</source>
        <target>1.6</target>
        <encoding>${project.build.sourceEncoding}</encoding>
      </configuration>
    </plugin>
    <plugin>
      <groupId>org.apache.maven.plugins</groupId>
      <artifactId>maven-pmd-plugin</artifactId>
      <version>2.7.1</version>
      <configuration>
        <targetJdk>1.6</targetJdk>
      </configuration>
      <executions>
        <execution>
          <phase>site</phase>
          <goals>
            <goal>pmd</goal>
          </goals>
        </execution>
      </executions>
    </plugin>
  </plugins>
</build>

<dependencies>
  <dependency>
    <groupId>junit</groupId>
    <artifactId>junit</artifactId>
    <version>4.11</version>
    <scope>test</scope>
  </dependency>
</dependencies>

<reporting>
  <plugins>
    <plugin>
```

```
        <groupId>org.apache.maven.plugins</groupId>
        <artifactId>maven-jxr-plugin</artifactId>
        <version>2.3</version>
      </plugin>
    </plugins>
  </reporting>

</project>
```

There is a huge variety of software available to include in the <reporting> section, ranging from generating a Web site to creating documentation. In fact, the surefire-reports plugin is already being used by virtue of the JUnit example, but the default configuration is sufficient for the purposes of this chapter.

The final step is to configure Hudson. Visit the Plugin Center as described earlier and install the following plugins, all of which are in the Available tab, in the "recommended" subtab.

- Static Analysis Collector plugin
- Static Analysis utilities
- PMD plugin

These plugins can all be installed together, requiring only one Hudson restart. Be prepared to wait a while depending on the speed of your environment. Progress can be watched by tailing the Hudson log file. To verify that the PMD plugin has installed successfully, look for this message in the Hudson log file:

```
INFO: Attained Initializing plugin pmd
```

Restart Hudson and visit the configuration page of the job for HelloMvn. In the Build section, locate the one and only Invoke Maven 3 section and make the text of the Goals section be **clean package site**. Save the configuration and rerun the job. This will cause Maven to download all the necessary dependencies for producing the PMD results report. Once the job has completed successfully, return to the configuration page. In the Post-build Actions section, check the check box next to "Publish PMD analysis results," which only appears when the PMD plugin has successfully been installed. If this check box is not present, try restarting Hudson. As with the JUnit test results, this check box reveals a text field into which a file path expression must be typed. The PMD results file is called pmd.xml, and is placed in the target/site/pmd.xml. Because this job is only building the 04_mvn project, the full path to the pmd.xml file is "BasicConcepts/04_mvn/target/site/pmd.xml". Save the configuration and rerun the job. After the job completes, the job page should look like Figure 3-5.

FIGURE 3-5. *Job page with PMD results*

Because the maven-jxr-plugin was included in the reporting section, HelloMvn.java shows up as a link in the page on the Details tab. Clicking on this link shows the exact error in the offending source file. The maven-pmd-plugin has many configuration options that can be used to cause the build to fail for certain kinds of validations. These options are very project-specific and are beyond the scope of this chapter.

There are numerous other software quality assurance plugins available with Hudson. The most common and essential ones will be visited in the chapter on automated testing.

Build Notifiers

Now that we have a Hudson job that we have seen can pass or fail, the final step before we can declare that we have a minimally functional Hudson instance is to configure a means for Hudson to alert others of the status of a build. Such is the task of the build notifier. As with software quality assurance, there are numerous plugins to fill the job. Thankfully, the task of build notification is a much smaller topic. This section will use the built-in e-mail notification feature. The feature can work with any SMTP e-mail service, such as Google's gmail. As one would expect, it is necessary to enter e-mail credentials so that Hudson can send mail using that SMTP server. This is yet another reason to have Hudson security in place.

Configuring E-mail Server

The E-mail Server is configured on the System Configurations page reached via the Manage Hudson link. Note that if Hudson security is set, you will need admin privileges to use this page. The E-mail Notification section displays the configuration information and fields to modify the configuration as shown in Figure 3-6.

The "SMTP server" field value is either the IP number of the mail server or a fully qualified name including the domain. In Figure 3-6, a freely available Google SMTP server is used to send e-mail. The value of the Default User e-mail Suffix is used to compute the e-mail address of a user. For example, if the user name is jane.doe and the e-mail suffix is @gmail.com, then Hudson will try to send e-mail to jane.doe@gmail.com. This is especially useful if Hudson security setup uses an identity management system like LDAP, all the users have a uniform e-mail domain suffix,

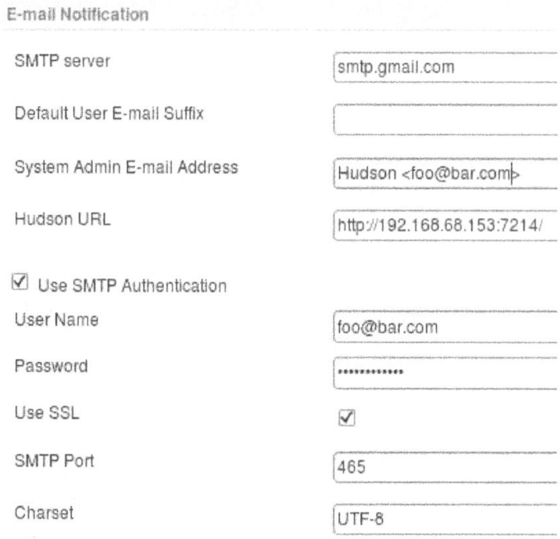

FIGURE 3-6. *Gmail settings*

and the individual user e-mail address is not set. The System Admin E-mail Address is used by Hudson for the "from" header of the e-mail. We recommend using a real e-mail address like notifications@myserver.com. We also recommend filling the Hudson URL field, for example, **http://hudson.myserver.com**.

The generated e-mail will contain a hyperlink to the URL provided in the Hudson URL field. This URL should be easily resolvable by the intended audience of the e-mail, though they may need to access VPN to resolve the URL depending on what e-mail address they use to receive the notification. Hudson provides a very helpful button, labeled "Test configuration by sending e-mail to System Admin Address." Click the button, and verify that the e-mail is received. This may take some time depending on the environment. Once the e-mail is verified to have been received, interested parties can sign up to be notified of the status of builds.

On the job configuration page find the text "E-mail Notification." Fill in the e-mail addresses of the desired recipients and click Save.

Most of the time, if the SMTP server specified is internal to the company, then authentication may not be required, but while using an external SMTP server like Google SMTP server, you may have to provide authentication. If authentication is needed for your SMTP server, then specify the username and password. Unless your SMTP server is running in a nondefault port, the port need not be specified. Hudson assumes the default port as 25 or 465 for SMTP with SSL. To check if all the configuration information is correct, click the "Test configuration by sending e-mail to System Admin Address" button. On success, Hudson would display the message "Email was successfully sent." Be aware that if the server configuration (including any authentication information) is correct and only the System Admin e-mail address is incorrect, Hudson will still display the success message.

Configuring the Job to Send Build Status Message

Once the E-mail Server is successfully configured, the next step is to configure the job to tell Hudson which recipients it should send e-mail to about the success or failure of the build. This is done at the Email Notification check box at the Post-build Actions section of the job configuration. Multiple e-mail addresses can be specified, separated by whitespace. We recommend using a generic mailing list to which the team members are subscribed.

When the e-mail notification is configured:

- Every failed build triggers a new e-mail.
- A successful build after a failed (or unstable) build triggers a new e-mail, indicating that a crisis is over.
- An unstable build after a successful build triggers a new e-mail, indicating that there's a regression.
- If checked, every unstable build triggers a new e-mail, indicating that regression is still there.

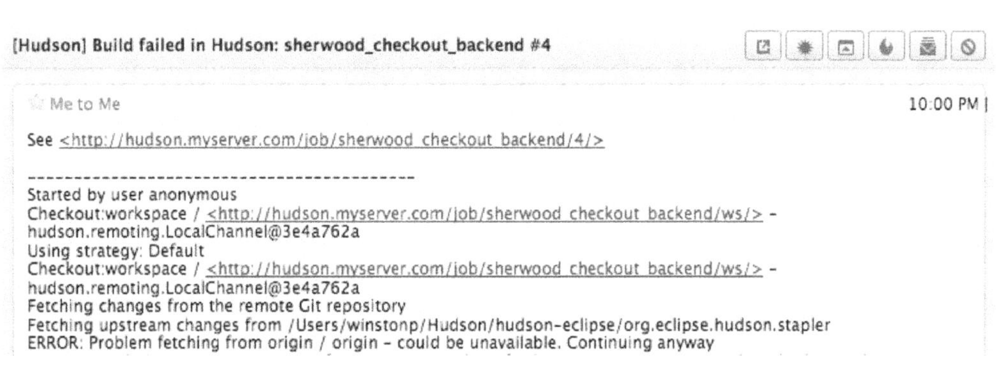
[Hudson] Build failed in Hudson: sherwood_checkout_backend #4

Me to Me 10:00 PM

See <http://hudson.myserver.com/job/sherwood_checkout_backend/4/>

Started by user anonymous
Checkout:workspace / <http://hudson.myserver.com/job/sherwood_checkout_backend/ws/> - hudson.remoting.LocalChannel@3e4a762a
Using strategy: Default
Checkout:workspace / <http://hudson.myserver.com/job/sherwood_checkout_backend/ws/> - hudson.remoting.LocalChannel@3e4a762a
Fetching changes from the remote Git repository
Fetching upstream changes from /Users/winstonp/Hudson/hudson-eclipse/org.eclipse.hudson.stapler
ERROR: Problem fetching from origin / origin - could be unavailable. Continuing anyway

FIGURE 3-7. *Email sent by Hudson via gmail*

A build is unstable, even though it was built successfully, if one or more of the post-build actions (especially publishers) are unstable. For example, if the JUnit publisher is configured and a test fails, then the build will be marked unstable. Unlike a CI build, for some jobs, for example functional tests only job, the "Send e-mail for every unstable build" option could be unchecked.

If the "Send separate e-mails to individuals who broke the build" option is checked, the notification e-mail will be sent to individuals who have committed changes for the broken build. We recommend checking this for every Commit job. The committer e-mail address is inferred from the Change Set information of the SCM configured in the job. Figure 3-7 is a sample failure e-mail sent by Hudson. It includes a complete failure log.

Summary

This chapter rounds out the essential knowledge for using Hudson in most enterprise environments. After reading the first three chapters, you have everything you need to know to be effective when using Hudson for most common tasks. More importantly, you have the foundation for learning more.

We introduced SCM and showed how to add it to your job. We created jobs for a simple Java application and servlet. We introduced the plugin manager, and used the JobConfigHistory plugin to more completely back up the Hudson instance with a nightly job. We showed how to secure a Hudson instance for use on a corporate intranet. Finally, we introduced software quality assurance tools and introduced the common build notifiers.

PART II

Applying Hudson

CHAPTER 4

Hudson as a Continuous Integration Server

Hudson is a full-fledged execution and scheduling engine. To fully utilize it as a real Continuous Integration (CI) build server, rather than merely an execution tool, you must plan and architect the builds to meet the conditions necessary to achieve CI. This chapter will explore the nuances of CI and how to set up Hudson as a true CI build server for your agile team.

What Is Continuous Integration?

The term *Continuous Integration* was originally coined by Kent Beck[1] as part of the Extreme Programming conceptualization in the '90s. Eventually, the three software engineering processes—Test-Driven Development,[2] Continuous Integration,[3] and Continuous Delivery or Deployment[4]—became the solid supporting pillars of a successful agile team. In a Test-Driven Development build pipeline, Continuous Integration is the first step and Continuous Delivery is the end result.

Martin Fowler, in his landmark article titled "Continuous Integration,"[5] described CI as:

> a software development practice where members of a team integrate their work frequently, usually each person integrates at least daily—leading to multiple integrations per day. Each integration is verified by an automated build (including test) to detect integration errors as quickly as possible.

To achieve this goal, Continuous Integration relies on the principles Fowler considers the "ten commandments" of CI:

- Maintain a single-source repository.
- Automate the build.
- Make your build self-testing.
- Everyone commits to the baseline every day.
- Every commit should build the mainline on an integration machine.
- Keep the build fast.
- Test in a clone of the production environment.

---

[1] Kent Beck, *Extreme Programming Explained: Embrace Change*. Addison-Wesley Professional, 2000.
[2] Kent Beck, *Test-Driven Development: By Example*. Addison-Wesley Professional, 2002.
[3] Paul M. Duvall, Steve Matyas, and Andrew Glover, *Continuous Integration: Improving Software Quality and Reducing Risk*. Addison-Wesley Professional, 2007.
[4] Jez Humble and David Farley, *Continuous Delivery: Reliable Software Releases through Build, Test, and Deployment Automation*. Addison-Wesley Professional, 2010.
[5] Martin Fowler, "Continuous Integration."http://martinfowler.com/articles/continuousIntegration.html

- Make it easy for everyone to get the latest executable.
- Everyone can see what is happening.
- Automate deployment.

In this chapter, we will explore how to achieve each of these principles using Hudson CI Server. We assume you already know how to work with Hudson, create a job, manually run a build, and view the build result. If you are not familiar with the Hudson environment, we encourage you to read Chapters 1–3 first.

Setting Up the CI Environment

Once you decide to implement CI for your project, your first step is to establish the following prerequisites:

- **Centralized SCM repositories** A Source Code Management (SCM) system is one of the key components of CI. SCM is a repository where a complete history of every file in a software project is kept. Setting up a single repository that contains everything needed to build a buildable software unit is the first step of a good CI process.
- **Dedicated build servers** If the environment where the CI builds happen is significantly different from a production environment, there is greater risk for failures at production time. While it may not be possible to have an exact replica of the production environment, a scalable version of the actual production in a virtualized environment will greatly alleviate the risks. Principally, same versions of runtime environments such as JDK, database, and operating systems in the build machines will help reduce the risks.
- **Continuous Integration software** To ensure that the main branch of the SCM repository remains healthy, the mainline should be built on every commit to verify that the integration was indeed correct. A common practice is to use an automated CI tool to do the build on a dedicated integration machine. Usually, the CI tool monitors the commits in the SCM system and then automatically runs the build process. Here, we assume you are using Hudson as the CI tool.
- **Unit testing framework** A CI build is not only about catching compilation errors, but also about catching bugs early and efficiently. This is achieved by including automated unit tests in the build process. Once the code is compiled, unit tests should run to confirm that it behaves as the developers expect it to behave or else the build should be marked as a failed build. Hudson supports several unit-testing frameworks. In this chapter we will explore the use of JUnit as a unit-testing framework.

- **Build tool** Automating the build using a single command is an important principle of a CI build. Many build tools—such as Make for the UNIX world, Ant and Maven for the Java community, and Nant and MSBuild for the .NET community—exist to automate the build and are frequently used in CI environments. Automating the build does not mean just compiling the source, but also running unit tests, executing a test harness, generating documentation, and finally deploying the freshly built product. While Hudson supports several popular build tools (including Maven, Gradle, Ivy, and MsBuild) through plugins, we will be highlighting the use of Maven as the build tool in this chapter.
- **Deployment environment** It is easy to incorporate scripts in the build automation process that execute the built product after a build finishes. It is possible to extend this and write scripts to deploy the application to a live test server for the QA team to test periodically or to a semiproduction server where a subset of the user base has subscribed for early adoption testing. Wherever possible, incorporating automated deployment is a good practice. In this chapter, we will use Hudson plugins to automate the deployment of a Java Web application to a Tomcat server.
- **Build dashboard** The primary goal of an agile team is to make sure what they are building is correct. Getting feedback from stakeholders and testers early on can reduce the amount of rework and ensure that the feature they are building indeed meets the requirements. To achieve this, anyone involved with a software project should be able to get the latest build artifacts and test them. Hudson provides an excellent Web UI for getting the latest executable of a build, which we will explore in this chapter.
- **Communication tool** Another important principle of CI is to communicate the state of the build, especially if it is broken. It should be easy to find out whether the build is in progress or complete. If the build is in a complete state, it should be identifiable as successful or broken, and if it's broken, changes relevant to the failure should be easily identifiable as well. In this chapter, we will use customized e-mail to communicate the build status to the team and beyond.

As mentioned in the preceding list, we will use Git, Maven, and JUnit in this chapter to explain how to effectively set up Hudson as your CI server. To learn more about these technologies, refer to Chapter 2.

Sherwood County Library

For the purpose of explaining how Hudson could be used as an agile tool to implement CI, we have invented a fictitious county called Sherwood. This county has a public library, Sherwood County Library, which serves hundreds of people each day. The library council believes the library will provide better service if it automates the lending process for county residents. The entire process of automating the lending process was handed over to a software development team. The team lead is an energetic, forward-thinking engineer who decided the fastest turnaround would be possible if the team followed agile methodologies. They decided to do:

- Continuous Integration
- Test-Driven Development
- Continuous Delivery

Because the library is publicly funded, the budget is limited, so the development team will use freely available goodies to keep the cost at a minimum:

- GitHub for remote repositories
- Git as SCM
- Maven as build tool
- Nexus as artifact repository manager
- MySQL as database
- JUnit and HTMLUnit for test harness
- Hudson as CI Server

Sherwood Library Software Components

The software developed by the Sherwood team has various components (see Figure 4-1). The team has identified the scope of each component required for automation as shown in the following table:

Component	**Scope**
Library Web Application	Back End UI
Persistence	Library REST API
Checkout	Web Interface Back End REST API
Returns	Web Interface Back End REST API

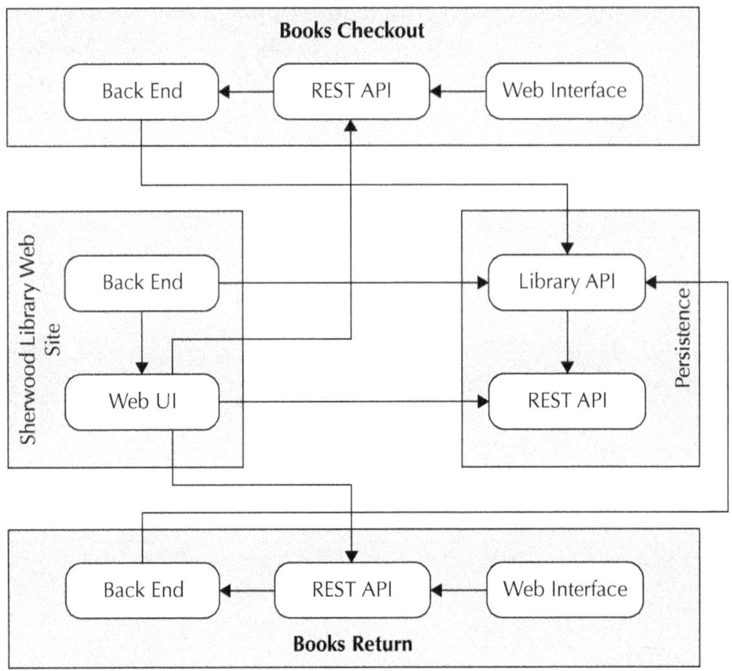

FIGURE 4-1. *Relationship between various components of Sherwood Library software*

Buildable Units

As we saw earlier, one important CI guideline is building fast and giving feedback quickly. To achieve this, rather than building the entire source in one single job, divide the project sources into buildable chunks. Each chunk of software must be able to build independent of each other. The dependent chunks must be built separately and stored in an artifact repository manager for other software chunks to use them as dependencies. Each of the software chunks is a buildable unit and is built by a single Hudson job.

In the Maven world, each of the buildable units can be represented in terms of Maven projects. Though it is possible to create a top-level Maven project and keep the subprojects (for example, Checkout | REST API) as Maven modules, for the sake of better buildable units, it is better to keep each of them as a separate Maven project. When we explore various aspects of CI for our system, this becomes clearer.

Hudson Jobs

If you are not familiar with a Hudson job, refer to Chapter 3 to define Hudson jobs, learn how to create one, and view its build result. Table 4-1 lists the mapping of the Sherwood software buildable chunks to Hudson jobs.

	Buildable Chunk	Hudson Job
1.	Sherwood Library Web App	sherwood_webapp
2.	Sherwood Library Web App | Backend	sherwood_webapp_backend
3.	Sherwood Library Web App | UI	sherwood_webapp_ui
4.	Persistence	sherwood_persistence
5.	Persistence | Library	sherwood_persistence_library
6.	Persistence Layer | REST API	sherwood_persistence_rest
7.	Checkout	sherwood_checkout
8.	Checkout | Web Interface	sherwood_checkout_webapp
9.	Checkout | Backend	sherwood_checkout_backend
10.	Checkout | REST API	sherwood_checkout_rest
11.	Returns	sherwood_returns
12.	Returns | Web Interface	sherwood_returns_webapp
13.	Returns | Backend	sherwood_returns_backend
14.	Returns | REST API	sherwood_returns_rest

TABLE 4-1. *Hudson Jobs for Sherwood Software*

NOTE
As a best practice, several software project teams could share a single Hudson master. Jobs belonging to a particular software project could be grouped into a single Job Status view of the Hudson main dashboard page (refer to Chapter 3 for information on Hudson dashboards and views). In order to facilitate the grouping, it is advisable to use certain conventions for job names. For example, use the project name as prefix. We use sherwood_checkout_* as the prefix for all jobs related to the Sherwood Checkout module, so they can be aggregated into a single view for the team responsible for that module.

There may be additional jobs for functional and integration tests, such as those listed in Table 4-2, but they will be built outside the realm of CI builds.

	Buildable Chunk	Hudson Job
1.	Sherwood Library Web App automated functional tests	sherwood_webapp_func_tests
2.	Books Checkout Web App automated functional tests	sherwood_checkout_webapp_func_test
3.	Book Returns Web App automated functional tests	sherwood_returns_webapp_func_test
4.	Sherwood Library automated integration tests	sherwood_integration_tests

TABLE 4-2. *Additional Hudson Jobs for Sherwood Software*

In the preceding setup, when the top-level jobs are built, their modules are also built. The prefix sherwood in the job name makes it easy to list the jobs corresponding to the Sherwood software project in a single Jobs Status view, as shown in Figure 4-2. (If you want to know how to create a custom Jobs Status view for your project, track back to Chapter 3.)

FIGURE 4-2. *Sherwood Library software, Hudson Jobs Status view*

Source Code Management

The principle, "maintain a single-source repository," encourages the project team to use a centralized Source Configuration Management (SCM) system, also known as Source Code Management tools, to maintain their source code. The SCM system must be accessible to all members of the team. As a rule of thumb, all artifacts required to build the project, including test scripts, properties files, database schema, and install scripts, should be placed in this repository. The convention is that the system should be buildable from a fresh checkout and not require additional dependencies. If you are using more advanced build tools like Maven or Gradle, then you have the option to keep the build dependencies in external repositories such as Nexus or Artifactory rather than in the SCM system itself. A common distinction is that all build artifacts created by the project team are kept in the SCM system, while dependencies such as open source software or, in large organizations, built artifacts created by other teams, are kept in repositories. Refer to Chapter 3 to learn about adding SCM to your Hudson jobs.

Everyone in the project team must commit regularly to the SCM system. By doing so, a committer can easily find out if there are any conflicting changes with another developer. Regular integration effectively communicates changes to other developers in the team and reduces the risk of conflicting with other features developed by other team members. Committing all changes at least once a day is considered a best practice. An important prerequisite for a developer committing to the mainline is that they do a build on their machine after merging with other integrations. Several SCM systems, such as CVS, SVN, and Git, have gained wide acceptance in the industry. Though Hudson provides support for several SCM systems, in this chapter, we will use Git as an SCM system and GitHub as a Remote Hosted Repository.

Though there are various advanced commands (and every system has its own nomenclature), the basic operations of an SCM system are:

- **checkout** This command fetches the latest version of files in a software project.
- **commit** This operation allows you to add, modify, or remove files by checking in your changes.

While performing checkout and commit, the good state of the SCM system is preserved by merging files modified by other members of the developer team.

The Sherwood Library software development team decided to use the freely available, centralized, hosted SCM system called GitHub. The primary SCM system supported by this hosted service is called Git, another freely available tool to do SCM operations, which was briefly introduced in Chapter 2. Each of the components and their subcomponents are kept in separate repositories under a single umbrella called

"SherwoodLibrary organization." GitHub organization is a way to group related repositories. The SherwoodLibrary organization can have various teams with different access to the repositories of the organization. The Sherwood Library development team created the repositories as listed in Table 4-3.

The team kept the repository name closely resembling the Hudson job for easy recognition of the modules as shown in Figure 4-3. Notice that the team could have created only four repositories, combining the subcomponents into a single repository, but the decision to have ten repositories instead of four is a good strategic move to set up a strong CI. This will be further evident when we set up automated builds later in the chapter.

As we mentioned earlier, Hudson supports a variety of well-known SCM systems. This support is provided through plugins, which must be installed through the Plugin Manager. For the exercise in this chapter, we assume you have already installed the Git plugin. If not, refer to Chapter 2. See Appendix A for a list of plugins for popular SCMs.

The Hudson job that builds a CI build must first check out the latest revision from the centralized SCM system. Since each job is associated with a single software component, the checkout must also include everything needed for the build to happen. This means not only the source code, but also build scripts, resources, unit tests, and related resources.

Distributed SCM systems like Git do not support partial checkout, but an entire copy of the repository is pulled into the build machine. This is one of the reasons Sherwood Library developers chose to keep each subcomponent in its own repository. A particular CI build is specific to a subcomponent; they don't want the rest of the code to be pulled into the workspace where the subcomponent is being built.

	Software Component	Git Repository
1.	Sherwood Library Web App | Backend	sherwood_webapp_backend
2.	Sherwood Library Web App | UI	sherwood_webapp_ui
3.	Persistence | Library	sherwood_persistence_library
4.	Persistence Layer | REST API	sherwood_persistence_rest
5.	Checkout | Web Interface	sherwood_checkout_webapp
6.	Checkout | Backend	sherwood_checkout_backend
7.	Checkout | REST API	sherwood_checkout_rest
8.	Returns | Web Interface	sherwood_returns_webapp
9.	Returns | Backend	sherwood_returns_backend
10.	Returns | REST API	sherwood_returns_rest

TABLE 4-3. *GitHub Repositories*

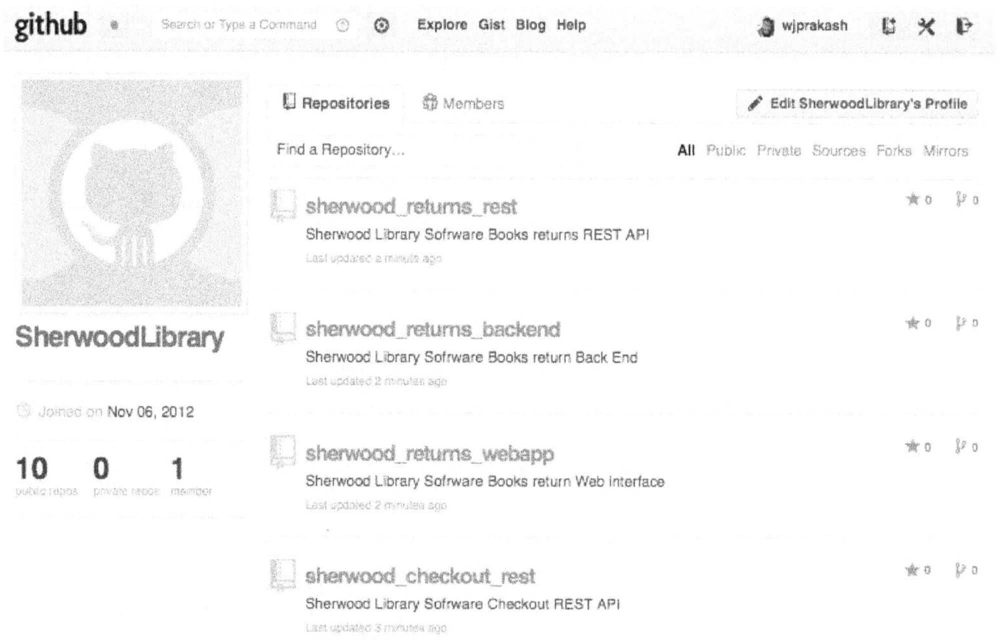

FIGURE 4-3. *Sherwood Library GitHub organization*

This simplifies checking out the source code (and also automating the build, as we see in the next section) by each job. With this setup, specifying the URL of the remote repository from which the sources must be checked out is easy, as shown in Figure 4-4.

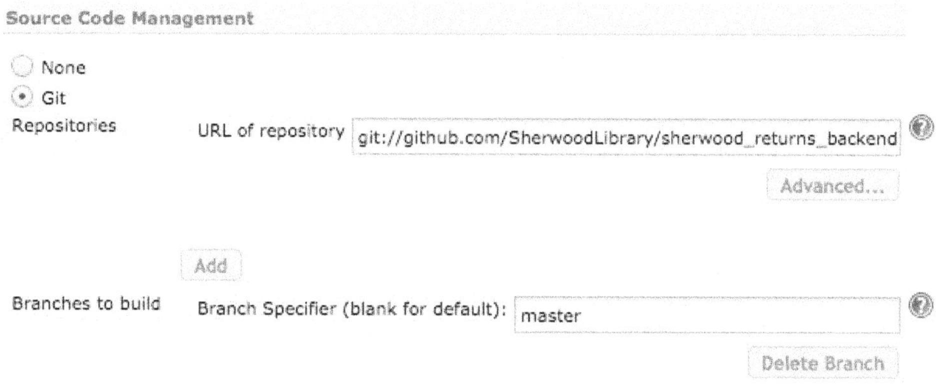

FIGURE 4-4. *Git SCM configuration of a job*

In the preceding example, to build the subcomponent sherwood_returns_backend, the sources are checked out from the repository git://github.com/SherwoodLibrary/sherwood_returns_backend.git.

NOTE
Most of the SCM systems provide read-write mode and read-only mode. Only in read-write mode can a developer do both checkout and commit. Proper authentication is required in this mode. As a best practice, we recommend using a URL corresponding to read-only mode in the SCM configuration. This makes the CI build setup more portable, since no specific authentication setup is required to checkout sources by the build job. See Chapter 3 for more details on Git authentication.

Using an SCM branch to implement a specific feature of a software component is a common practice. Often the build may have to be made on the sources checked out from that branch. In Git terminology, the default branch is called *master* (*trunk* in some other SCM systems). The Hudson Git plugin configuration provides a UI to specify the branch if the build needs to be made from a branch other than the default master branch. The Git plugin also allows you to check out sources from multiple repositories, but unless absolutely necessary, we recommend to use one repository per build unit for your CI builds.

- Build your job and see the result. The only build step that happened is the SCM checkout, as shown in Figure 4-5.
- You can explore the workspace, using Workspace Explorer (see Figure 4-6).

Console Output

```
Started by user wjprakash
Building on master
Checkout:workspace / /usr/opt/hudson/hudson_home/jobs/cobertura-plugin_hr/workspace -
hudson.remoting.LocalChannel@c6891db
Using strategy: Default
Last Built Revision: Revision b1f034d2813a048a3b075559d667eda728f1156d (origin/master)
Checkout:workspace / /usr/opt/hudson/hudson_home/jobs/cobertura-plugin_hr/workspace -
hudson.remoting.LocalChannel@c6891db
Fetching changes from the remote Git repository
Fetching upstream changes from https://github.com/hudson-plugins/cobertura-plugin.git
Commencing build of Revision b1f034d2813a048a3b075559d667eda728f1156d (origin/master)
Checking out Revision b1f034d2813a048a3b075559d667eda728f1156d (origin/master)
```

FIGURE 4-5. *SCM checkout console output*

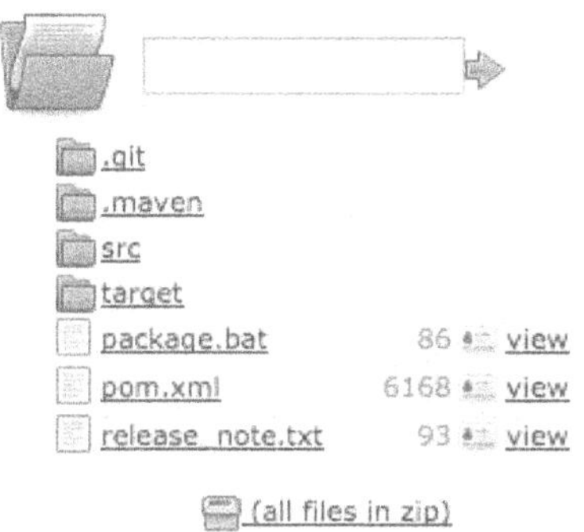

FIGURE 4-6. *Workspace Explorer*

In this section, you saw how to chunk your software project into buildable units, create repositories for those buildable units, create Hudson jobs for the buildable units, and then specify the repository URL in the job configuration. Next, let us see how to automate the jobs to do CI builds.

Build Automation

Build automation is not a new notion in the software industry. For years, scripts have been used to compile a project and automatically produce an executable by linking with the proper libraries. The tool Make in the UNIX world is a fine example. Tools like Ant, Maven, and Gradle are gaining popularity in the Java community. By using these tools, artifacts created from buildable chunks can be stitched together to produce an integrated product.

In this chapter, we will cover how to use Maven, a popular open-source build management tool, to automate the build in Hudson. To do this successfully, you need to do two things first:

- Install Maven on your build machine and configure Hudson to use that Maven installation. Refer back to Chapter 3 for how to set up your tools needed for the build.
- Install the Maven 3 plugin from Plugin Center. This plugin adds the Maven Builder to your job configuration, which you can use to build your software units. Refer to Chapter 3 for how to use Plugin Center.

Maven as an Automated Build Tool

The fundamental unit of work for the Maven build tool is the pom.xml file. This is committed along with other sources into the source repository. The previous build step, SCM checkout, pulled the pom.xml along with other sources from the remote

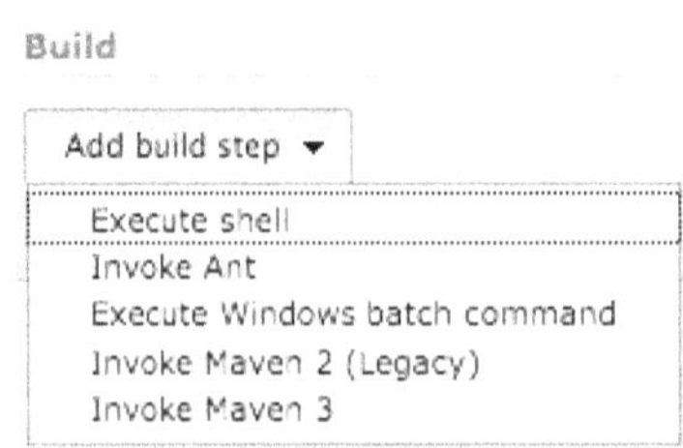

FIGURE 4-7. *Hudson Builders List and Maven Builder*

repository into the workspace (see Figure 4-6). In order for Hudson to build the project source, the Hudson job needs to be configured to use Maven as a build tool. Hudson has support for several build tools via plugins. Some of the popular build tools are listed in Appendix A. Based on the build tool plugins installed, Hudson provides a drop-down list of builders for you to choose to build your project. Choose Invoke Maven 3 from the list as shown in Figure 4-7 to use Maven to build your software unit. This builder knows to find the pom.xml in the workspace where the sources are checked out and invoke the command **mvn** to do the build. The Maven 3 builder has tons of settings to customize. The minimal setting is specifying the Maven goals to invoke. By default, the goal clean install is invoked. We will learn about more advanced use of Maven Builder later in this chapter.

Speeding Up the Build

In a CI environment that has been set up successfully, the build needs to complete rapidly. If there were a problem with integration, it would be quickly identified and fixed. The basic idea of CI is to provide feedback as soon as possible. If a build takes hours, then it cannot be deemed a CI build. As a rule of thumb, CI builds should finish within about 10 minutes. Though 10 minutes is not a hard-and-fast rule, it is advocated by Extreme Programming (XP) guidelines.

In order to achieve this 10-minute guideline, Martin Fowler and other CI gurus advocate *staged builds* (also known as build pipelines). Though it is possible to create a build environment with any number of stages, a simplified example is a two-stage build. The first stage would do the compilation and localized unit tests. The unit tests may be created without any real-time database or server connections, to keep it fast. In the second stage, the extended builds run different suites of tests, often with real-time server and database connections. By doing this, the first stage build (commit build) could finish within 10 minutes so that other developers could confidently pick up the commits without waiting several hours to get a full-fledged build. However, any build failure observed during the extended build must be attended to as quickly as possible. The commit build unit tests should be strengthened to avoid future extended build failure. Let us see how the Sherwood Library developers achieved fast builds in their environment using Hudson and staged builds.

Job Chaining Using the Upstream–Downstream Paradigm

Hudson has the concept of upstream and downstream jobs. Upstream jobs are built before downstream jobs. An upstream job triggers the downstream job. This does not mean the downstream job cannot be built without building the upstream job. For example, SCM triggers can start a downstream job. However, if an upstream job is successfully finished, it always triggers the downstream job. Though it is common to start the downstream job only when the upstream job finishes successfully, it is possible to tell Hudson to start the downstream job even if the upstream job fails. Hudson is smart enough not to schedule a downstream job again if it is already scheduled by another trigger.

The upstream–downstream job build pipeline can be specified in two ways:

- As part of a build trigger, specified as "Build after other projects are built," as shown in Figure 4-8. A comma-separated list of jobs can be specified as upstream jobs. The current job will be triggered when any of the upstream jobs finish successfully. This is useful in situations where you want to trigger a job, which builds an extensive suite of tests when any of the upstream jobs finish building. The example in Figure 4-8 shows that the downstream job sherwood_checkout_test_harness is scheduled for build after one of sherwood_checkout, sherwood_checkout_backend, sherwood_checkout_rest, or sherwood_checkout_webapp is built successfully.
- As part of post-build action, specified as "Build other projects," as shown in Figure 4-9. This is just the opposite of the previous method. In this case, the current job schedules other jobs once it finishes successfully. A comma-separated list of jobs can be specified as downstream jobs. The current job

FIGURE 4-8. *Build trigger to build the current job after other jobs are built*

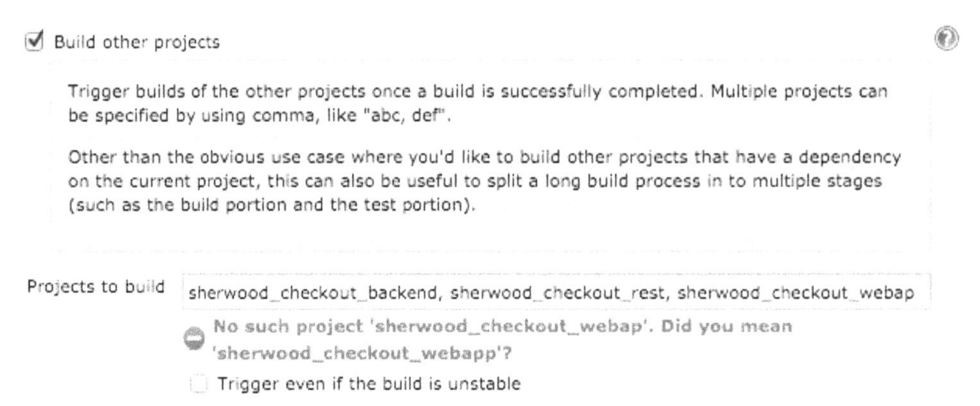

Build other projects
Trigger builds of the other projects once a build is successfully completed. Multiple projects can be specified by using comma, like "abc, def".
Other than the obvious use case where you'd like to build other projects that have a dependency on the current project, this can also be useful to split a long build process in to multiple stages (such as the build portion and the test portion).
Projects to build
sherwood_checkout_backend, sherwood_checkout_rest, sherwood_checkout_webap
No such project 'sherwood_checkout_webap'. Did you mean 'sherwood_checkout_webapp'?
Trigger even if the build is unstable

FIGURE 4-9. *Post-build action of a job that schedules other jobs*

will trigger all the downstream jobs after its successful completion. This is useful when you want to build all other jobs that have a dependency on the current job. The example in Figure 4-9 shows that, when the sherwood_checkout (core module) completes, it schedules sherwood_checkout_backend, sherwood_checkout_rest, and sherwood_checkout_webapp, because all three of these modules depend on the core module.

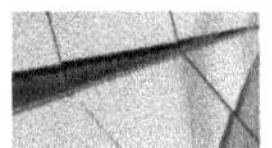

NOTE

Hudson has a nice feature to let you know that a particular job name you typed may not be the correct job name in Hudson. Figure 4-9 shows red text stating that sherwood_checkout_webap may not be the correct name and suggesting a reasonably correct name. Hudson does not store the upstream or downstream job name in the job configuration file if it does not yet exist. Also, be aware that if you delete a job that is defined as a downstream or upstream job in any of the jobs, Hudson does not warn you that it is a required job, either when you delete it or when one of the jobs that require it is built. If you open the configuration for a requiring job, however, you will see the "No such project" error and Save will remove it from the configuration.

The Sherwood Library development team analyzed different approaches to shorten the commit build time. They concluded that multistage builds, thus a faster commit build, could be achieved via the upstream–downstream paradigm in two ways. The first scenario is to split the test suites as multiple Maven modules within a buildable unit. The module structure in Figure 4-10 shows how this is done. Sherwood_checkout is the top-level Maven project with a single pom.xml (which itself is a buildable unit) defining the rest of the buildable subunits as Maven modules. Each of the Maven modules has extended tests as submodules. If a developer commits to the sherwood_checkout Git repository, the Poll SCM trigger triggers a build of the sherwood_checkout job. The purpose of this top-level job is to check out or update the sources

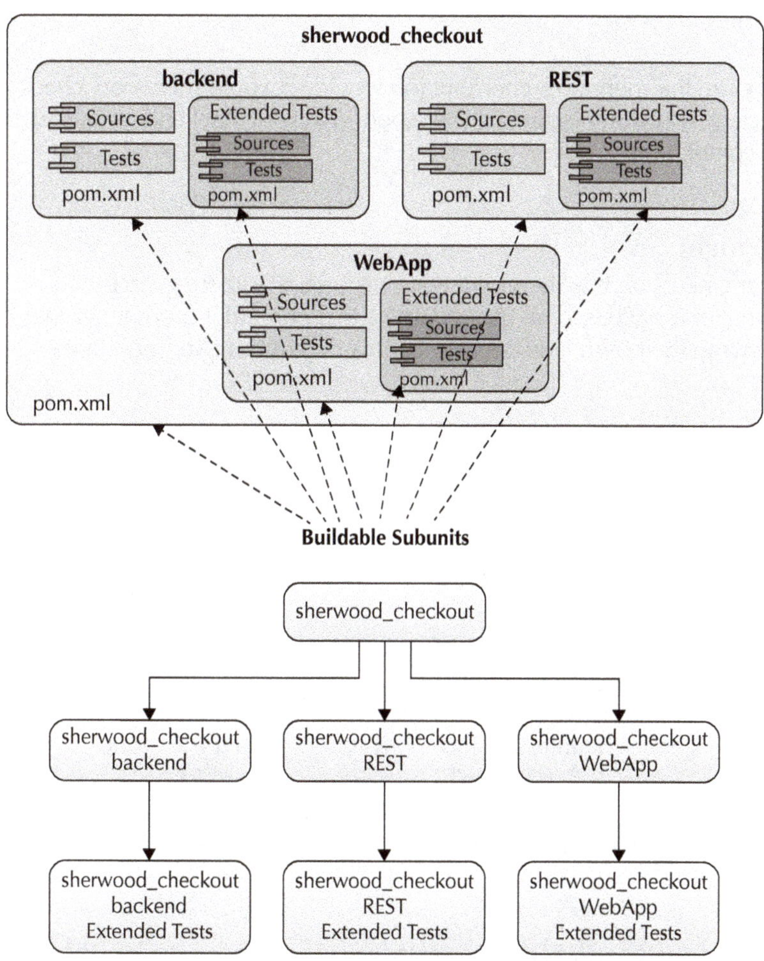

FIGURE 4-10. *Extended unit tests as submodules*

from SCM and trigger the job corresponding to the module(s) where the actual source modification happened. Assume that one of the Sherwood developers modifies some source code in the module sherwood_checkout/backend (yes, the developer is smart enough to write the corresponding unit test also) and commits the code to the central repository. This triggers the build of the sherwood_checkout job. This job build does the following:

- Checks out the commit from the remote repository
- Finds the modules corresponding to the change set (done through a special plugin as explained in the sidebar, "Custom Plugin")
- Schedules the jobs corresponding to the modules where code change happened

In the this case, the sherwood_checkout job would schedule sherwood_checkout_backend, which in turn would schedule sherwood_checkout_backend_extended_tests on successful completion.

Custom Plugin

The smart engineers on the Sherwood team realized that there is no built-in feature to trigger a job based on user commits to a particular module, so they decided to write their own Hudson plugin. This plugin has two important features:

- A build wrapper that analyzes the source base for the Maven module hierarchy using the Maven API[6] and identifies the modules. This wrapper finds the modules corresponding to the ChangeSet obtained from the SCM system, sets the groupId:artifactId of the modules for which a job should be scheduled, and sets the value to a predefined build parameter.
- A post-build action to schedule a job corresponding to the modules where the code changes happened. This post-build action obtains the predefined parameter that contains the groupId:artifactId of the modules and schedules the jobs corresponding to these modules.

They installed the plugin and added the build wrapper to the sherwood_checkout job. They also added the post-build action to the job.

---

[6] Maven Core API. http://maven.apache.org/ref/3.0.4/maven-core/apidocs/

The second scenario they arrived at is to keep all the extensive suites of tests as a single separate Maven module within the buildable unit. As shown in Figure 4-11, all the extensive unit tests are kept in a single top-level module. Each of the jobs corresponding to the top module will invoke the extended unit tests module.

Each approach has its own advantage. The former approach builds the extensive test suite of only the particular module being built. This makes it faster to get the build results of the extended test suite of each module. However, the dashboards displaying the test unit results are fragmented across different jobs. On the other

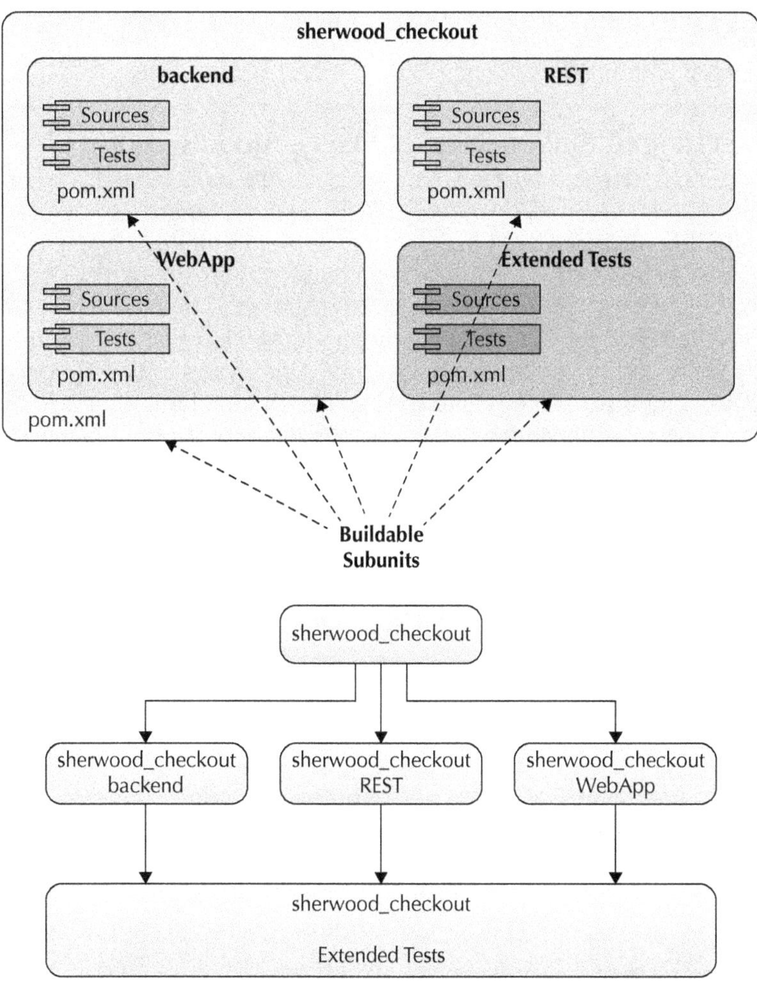

FIGURE 4-11. *Extended unit tests as top-level module*

hand, the second approach keeps the test unit results on one dashboard. However, the single build may be lengthier, and multiple builds may happen if developers do multiple commits to different modules. The Sherwood team was smart enough to experiment with both approaches for various buildable units of their project.

However, in both cases, the XP guideline to keep the commit build within 10 minutes could be achieved if the times to build each of the buildable subunits are kept to the minimum by introducing more Maven modules. When a subunit builds and fails, the commit build failure will be communicated within 10 minutes. Even if the commit build passes, it is possible that the time-consuming extended unit tests and other dependent modules might fail. So it is important to have enough unit test coverage in each of the modules for better confidence on the commit build as well as any build failure in the multistage extended builds and dependency builds that should be dealt with immediately.

Hudson Job Setting to Build a Specific Maven Module

As shown in Figures 4-10 and 4-11, the Sherwood buildable units comprise a top-level Maven project with several Maven modules. These modules are also buildable subunits. Each build unit, along with build subunits, is committed to a single repository. As an SCM build step, the Git plugin checks out the entire repository with all subunits. By default, when a Maven build is started from a top-level Maven project, it builds the entire project including the modules. However, this is not desirable in the Sherwood build scenario because the team wants to build a specific module based on commits to the modules to keep the commit build time within 10 minutes. The Maven Builder added to the job configuration can be configured to build only a specific module (called Maven project) identified by groupId and artifactId. Figure 4-12 shows a portion of Maven Builder Configuration to set up the job to build only the specific Maven module. Note that the Recursive property is unchecked to let the builder know not to build the submodules recursively. It is checked by default. The value sherwood_checkout:backend_extended_tests for the Projects property of Maven Builder specifies to build only the particular subunit.

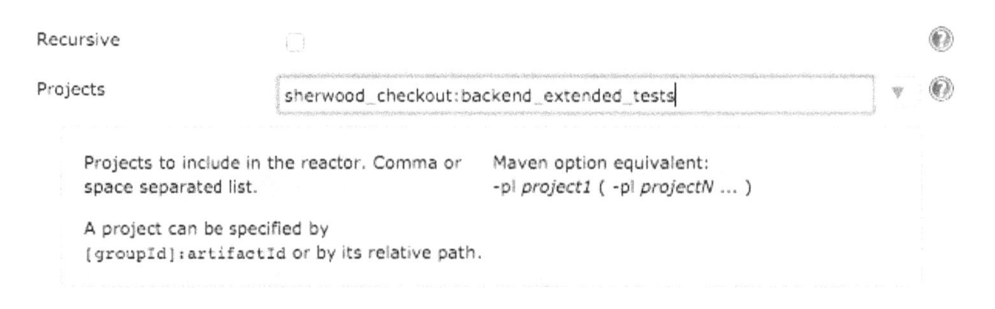

Recursive

Projects sherwood_checkout:backend_extended_tests

Projects to include in the reactor. Comma or space separated list.

A project can be specified by [groupId]:artifactId or by its relative path.

Maven option equivalent:
-pl *project1* (-pl *projectN* ...)

FIGURE 4-12. *Portion of Maven Builder configuration to build a Maven module*

Managing the Upstream–Downstream Jobs Complexity

The upstream–downstream build pipeline soon becomes complicated. Large software projects may have hundreds of such jobs with complicated upstream–downstream scenarios. Several free Hudson plugins exist to alleviate this issue. They can be used to view the build status as graphs of the build chain. Some of these plugins are listed in Appendix A. Figure 4-13 shows one such graphical representation of a build pipeline.

Also, several jobs may have redundant properties and maintaining them can soon become a nightmare. Hudson addresses this issue using Cascading Jobs, as explained next.

Cascading Jobs

Cascading Jobs, appearing in the Hudson UI under the name Cascading Project, allow child jobs to inherit configuration properties of a parent job. In an environment set up for typical agile CI builds, several jobs could share the same configuration properties. This could be solved by using templates or by copying jobs at the time of job creation, but what about further down the road when these properties change? The Cascading Jobs feature allows for the inheritance of properties throughout the life of jobs.

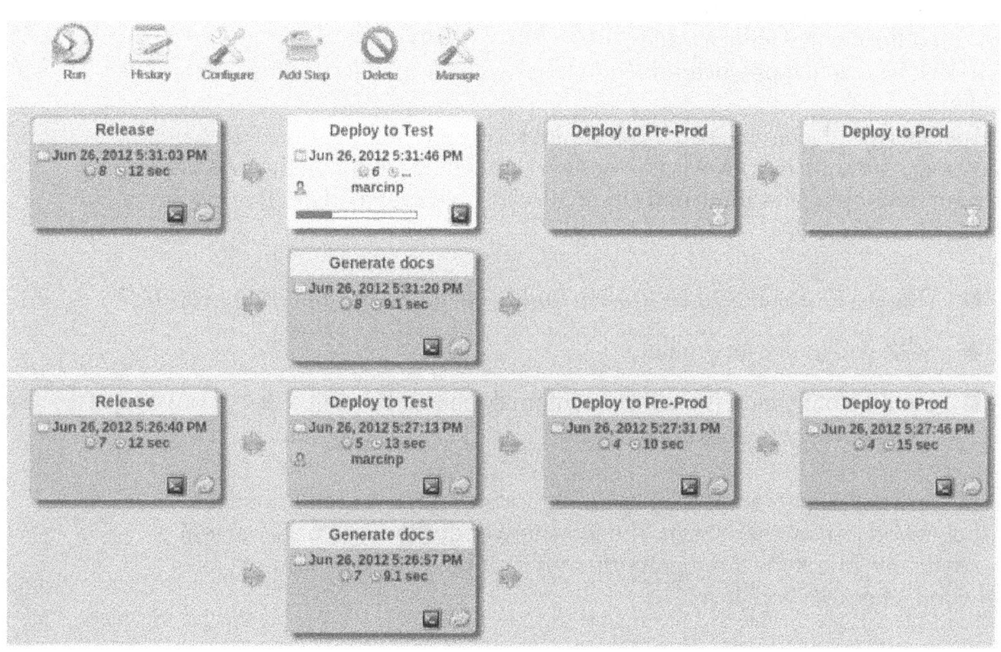

FIGURE 4-13. *Graphical representation of a build pipeline*

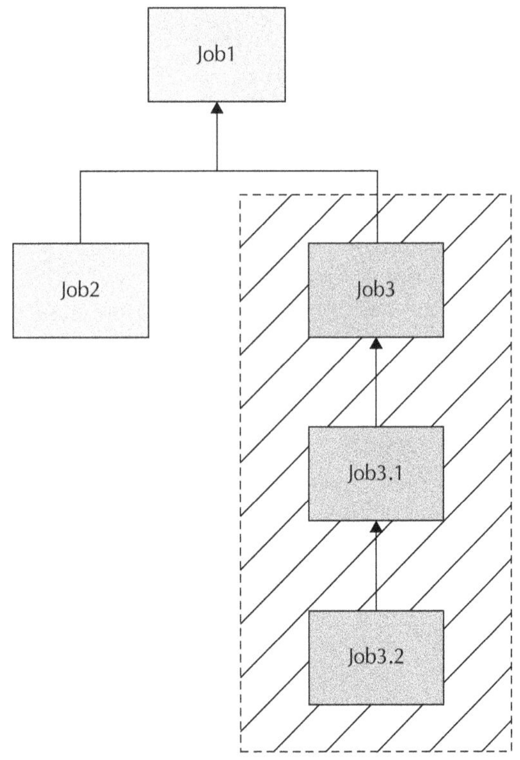

Cascading Jobs is not a template; you can configure a job to inherit properties from its parent, while overriding those that need to be changed or later reverted back to the parent. Any changes you make to the properties in a parent will cascade down through the child jobs that inherit that property.

Cascading Jobs should not be confused with Job Chaining. Job Chaining defines how different jobs are triggered based on the outcome of another job.

Look at the example shown in the illustration. Job3.2 will inherit its properties from Job3.1, which in turn inherits from Job3 and so on. What if you override a property in Job3, which is inherited from Job1? That change will cascade down to Job3.1 and Job3.2. If the same property is subsequently changed in Job1, then the change will cascade down to Job2, but the one overridden in Job3 will stay in place for that job and its children.

The Sherwood team created top-level jobs for each of the teams. For example, sherwood_checkout_top_level is the top-level cascading job for all the jobs used by the team developing the Sherwood Library Books Checkout module. This job primarily defines three properties:

- Discard Old Builds (days to keep builds:10 and max # builds to keep 10)
- SCM Poll (poll every minute)
- E-mail Notification (specifies an internal mailing list called dev_sherwood_checkout@sherwood_library.org)

As shown in Figure 4-14, the Job Configurations page is used to select an existing saved job to inherit from. The job sherwood_checkout_backend will automatically inherit the three properties (in the preceding list) from the job sherwood_checkout_top_level.

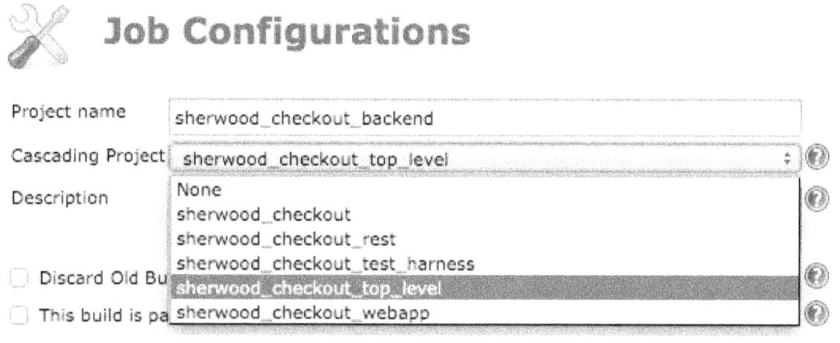

FIGURE 4-14. *Specifying a cascading parent*

Most of the Sherwood Checkout module jobs inherit the properties from sherwood_checkout_top_level. But the job sherwood_checkout_test_harness has a slightly different e-mail notification requirement, because the QA team also wanted to get e-mail notification if this job fails. So the E-mail Notification property is overridden to include both the mailing lists dev_sherwood_checkout@sherwood_library.org and qa_sherwood_checkout@sherwood_library.org (see Figure 4-15). This property is highlighted to show that it has been overridden by this job. You have to save the configuration and reopen it to see the highlight. A left arrow icon also appears near the overridden property, which is used to remove the overridden property and refresh to the value inherited from the parent.

Any job can be used as the parent, but you cannot create a cyclic inheritance. Most of the job properties are cascadable, and if the parent contains Builders, Publishers, or Triggers, they will be merged with the child. A few of the most common examples of job property cascading are e-mail notification lists, project-based security, reports, published locations, and polling the source repository.

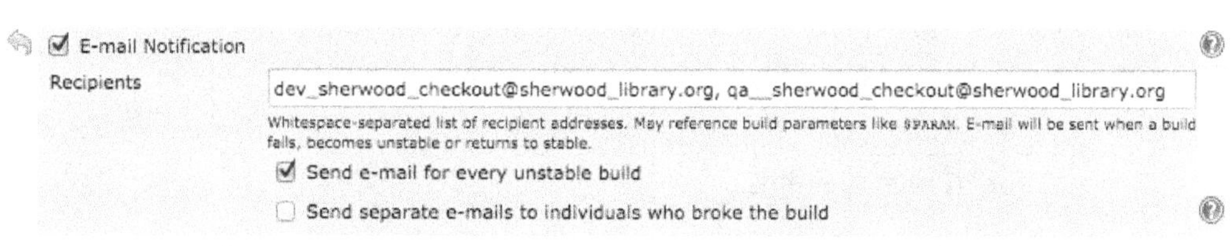

FIGURE 4-15. *Overridden cascading property*

Continuous Testing

As we mentioned earlier, for a CI build, it is not enough to compile the source code and catch compilation errors. The CI build must be set to catch bugs more *quickly* and *efficiently*. This is achieved by including automated unit tests in the build process. Running unit tests whenever source code changes in a version control repository on the CI build machine can help verify problems throughout a development life cycle. Every CI build must run the unit tests (also known as developer tests) to confirm that it behaves as the developers expect it to behave; otherwise, the build should be marked as failed or unstable.

Types of Tests

There are various types of tests you can run to validate each build. It is important to understand what kind of tests should be included in a commit build. The most commonly used tests are:

- *Unit tests* are fast-running tests that typically test individual classes that don't have heavy external dependencies like databases. However, their isolated nature means they only test a portion of the functionality. They must be included as part of your commit build.
- *Component tests* are essentially tests that verify more than one class and may rely on external dependencies such as a database. Component tests are written in much the same way as unit tests, except instead of mocking classes for isolation, it might use other frameworks like DbUnit or HtmlUnit to facilitate working with a database or Servlet Container. As discussed earlier, these tests may be kept as Extended Unit tests and executed immediately after the commit build as a downstream job. Care must be taken to attend immediately to any test failures reported by this build.
- *Functional tests* are typically used to test the presentation layer, if the application provides a user interface. Both sherwood_checkout_webapp and sherwood_returns_webapp provide a browser-based UI to help the librarian to check out or return the book. So the Sherwood team developed lots of functional tests to test the functionality. There are several functional testing frameworks available for functional tests. One of the most popular, and that used by the Sherwood team, is the Selenium suite of tools. Functional tests are typically not part of CI builds, thus not built for every commit. They are typically run as nightly builds.
- *Integration tests* are run as part of the integration build. Any tests that are not unit tests, such as performance tests, system tests, and acceptance tests, can be clustered as integration tests. Integration tests are not part of the CI build.

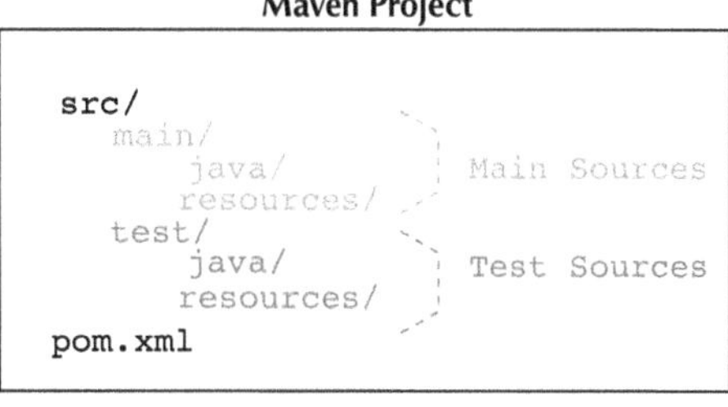

Refer to Chapter 5 for more details on automating various types of tests with Hudson. Hudson has built-in support for displaying JUnit test results and displaying JUnit statistics over various builds. Unless this function is specified specifically (using the –skipTests flag), Maven will run your unit tests automatically. So, if you are using Maven as a build tool, it is easy to run your unit tests and view the results using Hudson. For Hudson to build your sources and then the unit tests using Maven, simply place your sources and test sources in a folder hierarchy as shown in this illustration.

Viewing the Unit Test Results

Hudson has built-in support to understand the XML format of the JUnit test report. Hudson also supports various other test frameworks. They are all supported through plugins (see Appendix A for a list of well-known unit test frameworks supported by Hudson via plugins). In order for Hudson to load the JUnit test results, Hudson must know where the JUnit test report XML files are stored during the build. This is done using the "Publish JUnit test result report" check box in the Post-build Actions section of the build configuration, as shown in Figure 4-16.

Based on how the build happens, the JUnit test report XML may be placed in any folder. Maven specifically places the test results under the folder target/surefire-reports, where the target is the folder where Maven keeps all the build outputs. Each module and submodule will have its own target folder. If you want Hudson to aggregate all the test results of the modules and submodules of the build, then you specify the XML files using the filter pattern ****/target/surefire-reports/*.xml**. Hudson will recursively search all the folders in the job workspace and include all the XML files in subfolders of target/surefire-reports.

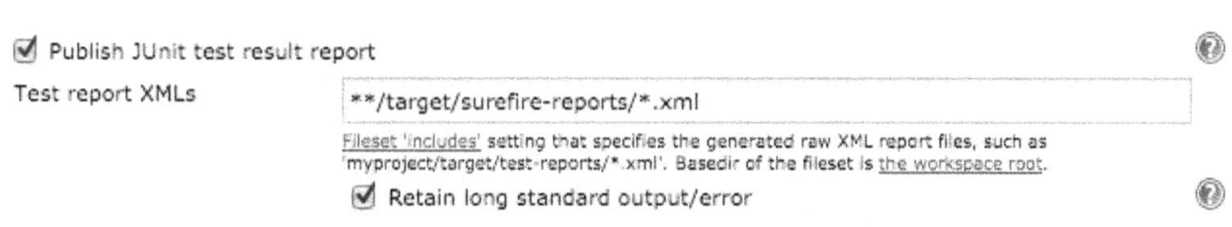

FIGURE 4-16. *Publishing a JUnit Test Results report using Hudson*

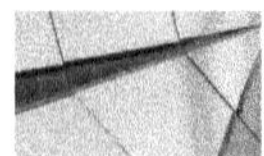

NOTE
*When you specify the filter format for the JUnit Test result XML files, Hudson will immediately try to validate the existence of files. If the XML files don't exist, immediate feedback will be provided by Hudson with an error message similar to "'**/target/surefire-reports/*.xml' doesn't match anything: '**' exists but not '**/target/surefire-reports/*.xml'." If you are creating a new job and specifying the filter pattern, the XML files may not be available yet and you must ignore the error message. Even if it shows an error, the filter will still be retained in the configuration on Save.*

Once the build is complete, it is easy to view the test results. Go to the build dashboard and find the clipboard icon labeled Test Result (see Figure 4-17) on the main section of the dashboard. Alternatively, you can reach the Test Result view page by clicking on the Test Result link on the side panel. If the icon or the action link is absent in the build dashboard, then either the build does not contain any test results or the JUnit Test Result Publisher is not configured correctly.

Test Result Trends

Monitoring the Test Result trends helps to understand the productivity of a team. The main job dashboard displays the Test Result trends on the right-hand side.

FIGURE 4-17. *Test Result icon in the build dashboard*

The Test Trend graph displays failing tests as a red curve, unstable tests as a yellow curve, and passing tests as a blue curve (see bottom graph in Figure 4-18).

This graph should never have yellow or red curves; it should always be blue, as a developer should never commit a code for which a test fails. The top graph shown in Figure 4-18 represents a CI build of a responsible team. Another aspect of monitoring the trend is to increase the number of tests over time. As product development progresses, the amount of code checked in increases. Since a healthy CI environment enforces unit tests when the code base grows, the number of unit tests also grows. Figure 4-18 shows a healthy increase in trend for unit tests.

The bottom graph in Figure 4-18 shows the trend of integration tests. Since integration tests involve several external entities, such as databases and deployment

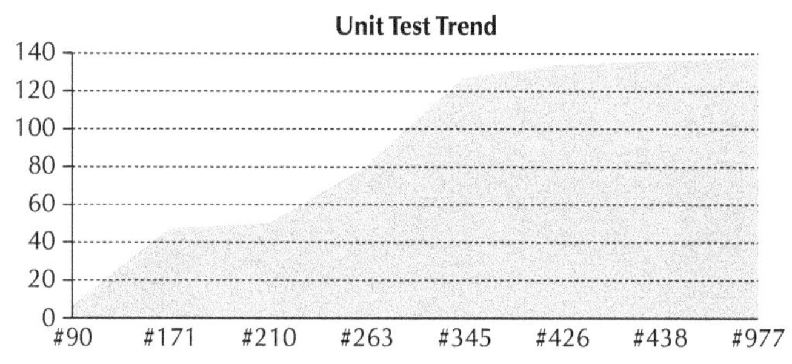

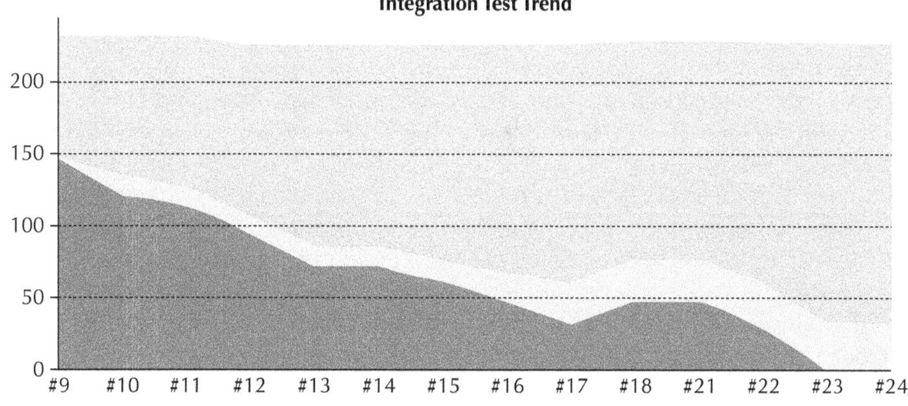

FIGURE 4-18. *Unit and integration test result trends*

servers, it is acceptable to have failed or unstable tests in the initial stage of the product development. However, the team must strive to reduce the number of test failures when the product matures, so the integration trend on the bottom of the figure also shows a healthy trend.

Code Metrics and Code Coverage

Along with test trends, a better way to look at the entire picture is by adding two more trends for Code Metrics and Code Coverage. One of the Code Metrics is counting the Line of Code (LOC). One of the free tools available to measure the LOC is called SLOCCount. For installing and using SLOCCount, see its documentation page.[7] Hudson already has a free plugin for SLOCCount, which plots the Line Count trend over several builds. To get the SLOCCount result, set the plugin configuration and the build step as follows:

- Add an Execute Shell build step in your Hudson job to compute the code metrics.
- Add the following shell command:

```
/usr/bin/sloccount --duplicates --wide --details src >build/sloccount.dat.
```

- In the Post-build Actions section, select the check box "Publish SLOCCount analysis results," and then provide the SLOCCount output file build/sloccount.dat.

There are several tools available for Code Coverage analysis. One of the free tools available for code coverage is Cobertura, which is a free Java tool that calculates the percentage of code accessed by tests.

Figure 4-19 shows the trend charts of Test Results, Code Coverage, and Line Count. Based on the three trend charts, it is possible to get a broad picture of the team's CI effectiveness. Over several builds, the line count of the project increased from 1000 lines of code to 8000 lines of code. The unit tests also increased from 10 to 140. This is good progress. Looking at the Code Coverage trend, there is very good coverage of almost 90 percent of the classes, but 28 percent package and 45 percent lines. Depending on the situation of the code base, this could be improved. It is always a good idea to analyze the trends from various code metrics, and use Code Coverage tools along with unit Test Result trends to understand the effectiveness of CI builds.

---

[7] SLOCCount documentation. www.dwheeler.com/sloccount/sloccount.html

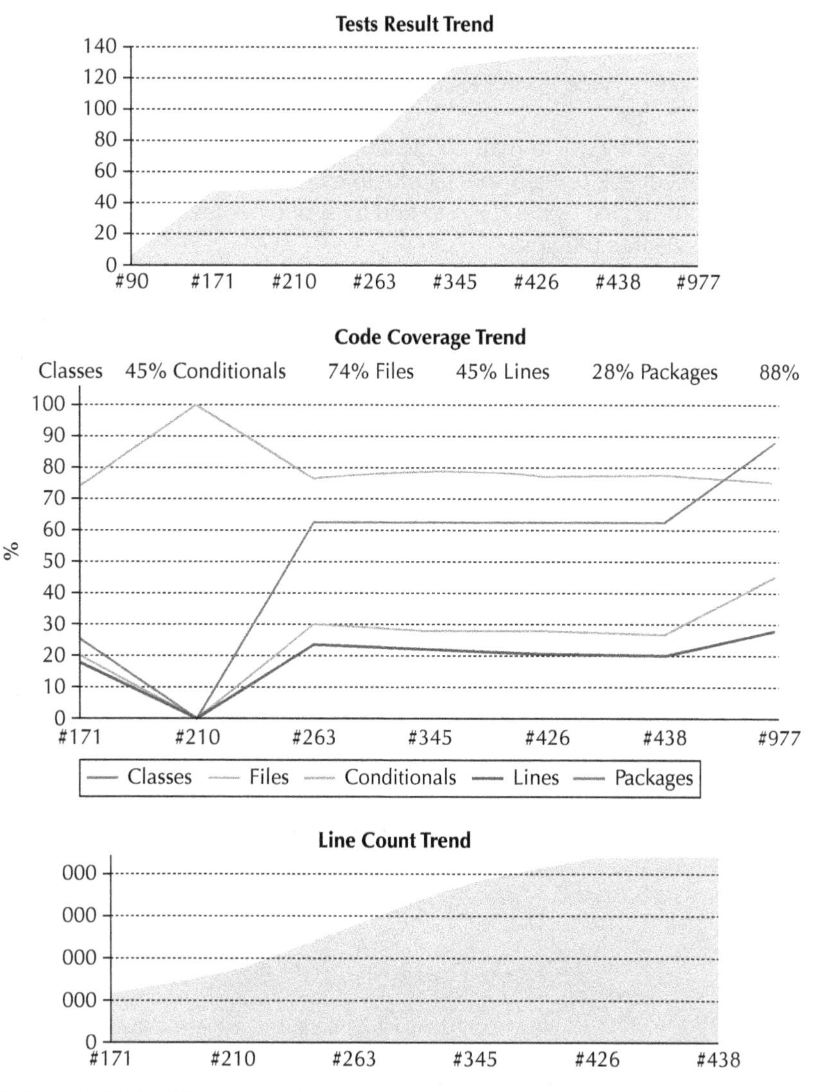

FIGURE 4-19. *Combined unit tests, code coverage, and code metric trends*

Continuous Feedback

One of the main purposes of CI builds is to produce feedback on a commit build. The reason for fast builds and fast build failures is to get quick feedback. Once a commit is done, others need to know as soon as possible if there was a problem with the latest commit. Also, by receiving this information quickly, the developer can immediately fix any problem that arises. Feedback is necessary to take action and to know the current status of the CI build. Hudson has built-in support for feedback via e-mail. There are several free plugins available to support feedback, including Short Message Service (SMS), Really Simple Syndication (RSS), Internet Relay Chat (IRC), and Twitter.

Chapter 3 introduced the basic e-mail notification built into Hudson. Let us see how to set up e-mail feedback using a special plugin called email-ext that enhances the e-mail–based feedback. See Appendix A to find a list of other feedback mechanisms supported by Hudson via free plugins.

Extended E-mail Notification

One of the most widely used plugins for Hudson sending enhanced e-mail is the email-ext plugin. This plugin extends Hudson's built-in e-mail notification functionality and gives the Hudson admin and job owner more control to customize the format and content of the e-mail. Unlike the simple built-in notification mechanism explained in the previous section, extended e-mail notification allows you to select various conditions that trigger an e-mail notification. It also allows customizing the subject and body of the triggered e-mail and specifying who should receive an e-mail for each of the triggered conditions.

Extended E-mail Global Settings

Before using email-ext to send extended e-mail notification from a project, it has to be configured for some global settings. This is done via the Hudson Configuration page under the section titled Extended E-mail Notification, as shown in Figure 4-20.

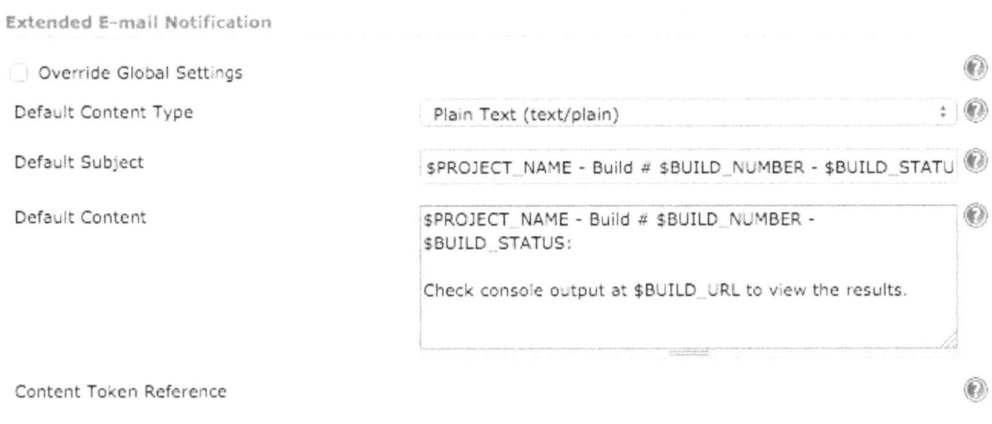

Extended E-mail Notification

Override Global Settings

Default Content Type — Plain Text (text/plain)

Default Subject — $PROJECT_NAME - Build # $BUILD_NUMBER - $BUILD_STATU

Default Content — $PROJECT_NAME - Build # $BUILD_NUMBER - $BUILD_STATUS:

Check console output at $BUILD_URL to view the results.

Content Token Reference

FIGURE 4-20. *Global settings for the extended e-mail notification*

It has a section to override the global mail server settings, but this section is often not used. The configuration allows specifying the default setting for sending e-mail as plain text or as HTML. You can also specify the Default Subject line and the Default Content of the e-mail notification. You can use e-mail tokens (more about the token later in the chapter) in the subject line and in the body content, which will be expanded before the message is sent.

Configuring the Job to Send Extended E-mail Notification

For a job to send extended e-mail notification, it must be enabled in the Job Configurations page by selecting the check box labeled Editable Email Notification in the Post-build Actions section, as shown in Figure 4-21. The configuration has two settings sections: Basic and Advanced.

There are four basic settings for configuring the extended e-mail:

- **Global Recipient List** A comma-separated list of e-mail recipients.
- **Content Type** Either Plain Text or HTML can be selected.
- **Default Subject** Subject line of the e-mail. This setting allows you to use e-mail tokens to easily configure all e-mail Subject lines for the job. This can be overridden for each e-mail trigger type in the Advanced section. The token $DEFAULT_SUBJECT inserts the default subject specified in the global settings.
- **Default Content** The default body content of each of the e-mails sent by various triggers. The token $DEFAULT_CONTENT inserts the default content specified in the global settings. Similar to the Subject line, this can be overridden for each e-mail trigger type in the Advanced section.

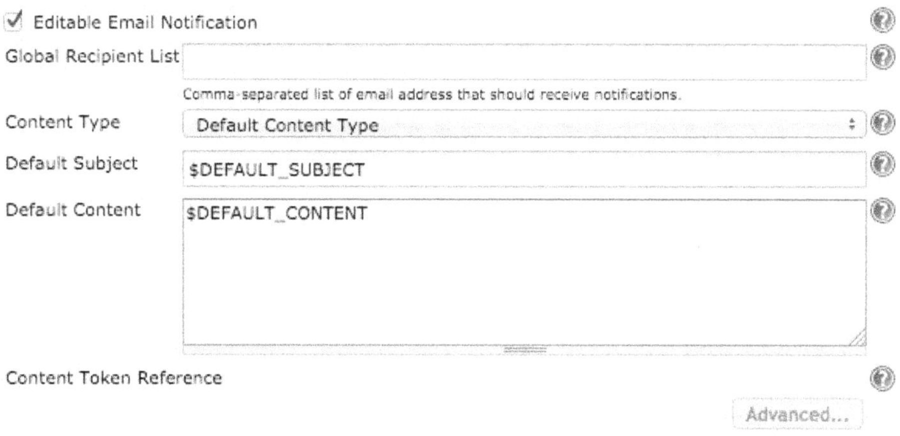

FIGURE 4-21. *Extended e-mail basic settings in a job*

By default, the extended e-mail is configured to trigger e-mails for the Failure condition. E-mail is sent only if the job build fails. However, more conditional triggers can be configured in the Advanced section, as shown in Figure 4-22. E-mail triggers can be configured for the conditions Failure, Success, Fixed, Unstable, Still-Failing, Still-Unstable, and Before-Build. To add more triggers, select one from the drop-down menu and it will be added to the list. By default, e-mails are sent to recipients specified in the basic settings. It is possible to send e-mail to different recipients using More Configuration for each of the triggers, as shown in Figure 4-22. Select the Send to Committers check box to send the e-mail to anyone who checked in code for the last build.

Extended E-mail Tokens

The Extended E-mail plugin uses tokens for dynamic insertion of data into an e-mail subject line or body content. A token is a string that starts with a dollar sign ($) and is terminated by a whitespace, for example: $PROJECT_NAME, which is replaced with the name of the job that triggered the e-mail. Also, the value of a token can contain other tokens; they too will be replaced by actual content. For instance, the

Trigger	Send To Recipient List	Send To Committers	Include Culprits	More Configuration	Remove
Failure	✓	✓		(expand)	Delete
Success		✓		(expand)	Delete
Fixed	✓	✓		(collapse)	Delete

Recipient List

Subject $PROJECT_DEFAULT_SUBJECT

Content $PROJECT_DEFAULT_CONTENT

Add a Trigger: select

select
Unstable
Still-Failing
Still-Unstable
Before-Build

Save

Page generated: Jan 31, 2013 5:42:12 PM Hudson ver. 3.0.0

FIGURE 4-22. *Extended e-mail advanced settings in a job*

$DEFAULT_SUBJECT token is replaced by the text (and other tokens) that are in the Default Subject field of the Extended E-mail global settings. When an e-mail is triggered, all tokens in the subject or content fields will be replaced. To see a list of all available e-mail tokens and what they display, click the help button next to Content Token Reference.

Continuous Delivery or Deployment

The terms Continuous Delivery and Continuous Deployment are often used interchangeably and get confused with one another. Several attempts have been made to clarify the terms. Here is the one by Jez Humble and David Farley:

> Continuous Delivery is about keeping your application in a state where it is always able to deploy into production. Continuous Deployment is actually deploying every change into production, every day or more frequently.

Thus, the distinction is roughly internal versus external; Continuous Delivery is delivery of a production-ready application to internal consumers; Continuous Deployment is delivery of the build result to external customers.

Requirements for Continuous Delivery[8] are

- Your software is releasable throughout its lifecycle.
- Your team prioritizes keeping the software releasable over working on new features.
- Anyone can get fast, automated feedback on the production readiness of your systems whenever somebody makes a change to them.

Continuous Integration is the quickest way to detect errors on every commit through automated build and test. However, in today's world of complex applications, practicing just Continuous Integration may not be enough to ensure that the product will be fully production-ready. The only way to truly ensure that your product is always production-ready is to deploy it to an environment similar to a production environment. The practice of automated Continuous Delivery ensures that the latest checked-in code is deployed, running, and accessible to various roles within an organization.

So far, we have seen that Hudson is an excellent tool for Continuous Integration. With plugins, it is also easy to extend Hudson to deliver the build artifacts to various environments and practice Continuous Delivery or Deployment. Whether it is deploying the application to a live test server to facilitate the QA engineers to conduct

[8] See note 4 earlier in the chapter.

additional tests in a production-like environment or to a semiproduction server for early adopters to test the product, it can be achieved through several free plugins available for Hudson. A more comprehensive list of widely used plugins is included in Appendix A, but those most useful to Continuous Delivery are

- **Deploy** Deploys Java applications to various popular Java Application Servers
- **FTP** and **SCP** Transfers build artifacts from build server to another machine
- **SSH** Executes commands on another server using the SSH protocol

Deploying a Java Application to an Applications Server

The Sherwood software team decided to do Continuous Delivery. They wanted the product to be always in a release state, so that other stakeholders such as the Sherwood Library Team could actually view the progress in a staging environment. At the end of a successful build pipeline (Commit Builds, Extended Test Builds, Functional Test Builds, and Acceptance Test Builds), they deployed their REST APIs (sherwood_checkout_rest and sherwood_returns_rest) and Web applications (sherwood_checkout_webapp and sherwood_returns_webapp) to a freely available Tomcat Application Server.

The Tomcat manager application allows remote deployment to an instance of Tomcat. The Tomcat installation needs to be configured to allow access to the manager application through the plain-text interface. This is accomplished by assigning the manager-script role to the credentials that will be performing deployments. Though it is possible to set up sophisticated authentication realms in the Tomcat server, the easiest is to add the role to $CATALINA_BASE/conf/tomcat-users.xml.

```
<tomcat-users>
    <user roles="manager-script" username="admin" password="secret" >
    </user>
</tomcat-users>
```

The next step is to configure the Deploy plugin settings in the Job Configurations page to deploy the war file created by the job to the Tomcat server. When the Deploy plugin is added to Hudson, it adds the Deploy war/ear file to a container check box in the Post-build Actions section of the Job Configurations page. Select this check box to fill in the configurations to deploy any war file created by the build to Tomcat as shown in Figure 4-23. The pattern ****/*.war** denotes that the deployer should search and find any war file created in any folder in the hierarchy and deploy those war files to Tomcat. On success, the application should be deployed and enabled in Tomcat.

☑ Deploy war/ear to a container

WAR/EAR files	**/*.war
Container	Tomcat 6.x
Manager user name	admin
Manager password	••••••••
Tomcat URL	http://localhost:8080/
Deploy on failure	☐

FIGURE 4-23. *Hudson deployment to Tomcat*

NOTE

Although you can make a job that runs the build and tests to automatically deploy the war build artifact directly to Tomcat, often you might want to deploy via a manual build of a job. For example, assume you found out that the latest war file that was deployed failed acceptance tests and you want to roll back to a previous build. This can be achieved by creating a job that does nothing but copy a war file from another job and then just deploys the war file. Copying the war file from a specific build of a job can be done using the Copy Artifact plugin.

Uploading Build Artifacts to Another Machine

The Deploy plugin helps to deploy war or ear files to an applications server. As part of the deployment pipeline, there are often requirements to copy configuration files or database schemas, test scripts, properties files, install scripts, and so on, that are part of a build to another machine to facilitate an additional test run. Hudson has several uploaders to support this. Two of the popular uploaders are the FTP and SCP plugins. Both plugins provide similar settings to copy files from a build workspace to another machine. While the FTP plugin uses the FTP protocol to copy files, the SCP plugin uses the Secured Shell protocol to copy files.

To use the FTP plugin to upload build artifacts, an FTP repository needs to be established. The FTP repository is a known location on the remote machine where the files will be uploaded. You can add any number of FTP repositories to Hudson via the FTP Publisher plugin's Global settings.

1. Go to the Manage Hudson page, open Configure System, and go to the "FTP repository hosts" section.
2. Click the Add button to add FTP repositories and fill in the required fields as shown in Figure 4-24. Note that the Profile Name is the unique identifier for the added FTP repository and will be used in the Job Configurations page to upload the artifacts after the build completes.

The FTP Publisher plugin will try to automatically connect to the FTP site using the username and password to check if a connection is possible. If the connection fails, red error text is displayed below the User Name, as shown in Figure 4-24, to indicate that the connection failed.

Next, configure the job whose build artifacts need to be uploaded to any of the FTP repositories configured earlier.

Go to the Job Configurations page and select "Publish artifacts to FTP" in the Post-build Actions section. As shown in Figure 4-25, you can select one of the FTP repositories from the drop-down list to publish the build artifacts.

Click the Add button to specify the Source and Destination folders.

FTP repository hosts

FTP sites

Profile Name	acceptance-test-machine
hostname	test2-server.mycompany.com
Port	21
TimeOut	30000
Root Repository Path	/home/tester21/acc-tests
User Name	tester21
	test2-server.mycompany.com
Password	••••••••••••••

Delete

FIGURE 4-24. *FTP repository settings*

Publish artifacts to FTP
FTP site acceptance-test-machine
Files to upload
Source target/sql/*.sql
Destination sql
Delete
Source target/properties/*.txt
Destination properties
Delete
Add

FIGURE 4-25. *Publishing artifacts using FTP*

Sources are the list of files from any folder relative to the job workspace. You can include the files using this pattern: *<folder>/*.<file extension>* (for example,, **target/sql/*.sql**). The *Destination* is a folder on the remote FTP repository where the files will be uploaded. It will be created automatically if it does not exist. Clicking the Add button will add multiple Source and Destination folders as shown in Figure 4-25. After each build, the files as specified in Sources will be uploaded to the Destination folder.

Executing Commands on a Remote Machine

As part of automating every step in a deployment pipeline, FTP and SCP plugins are useful to upload the build artifacts to another machine from within a Hudson build environment. Another requirement may be to be able to execute commands on that remote machine, such as executing installer builds or running database tests using the uploaded build artifacts. One of the useful plugins for that purpose is the SSH plugin. This plugin allows running shell commands on a remote machine via SSH from the build machine.

Setting up the SSH plugin is similar to setting up the FTP plugin, as explained in the previous section. First you need to set up one or more remote SSH hosts. Go to the Manage Hudson page, open Configure System, and scroll down to the "SSH remote hosts" section. Click the Add button to specify the remote host's information and the authentication to connect to the server, as shown in Figure 4-26. The SSH plugin allows two modes of authentication. If you can authenticate with the remote

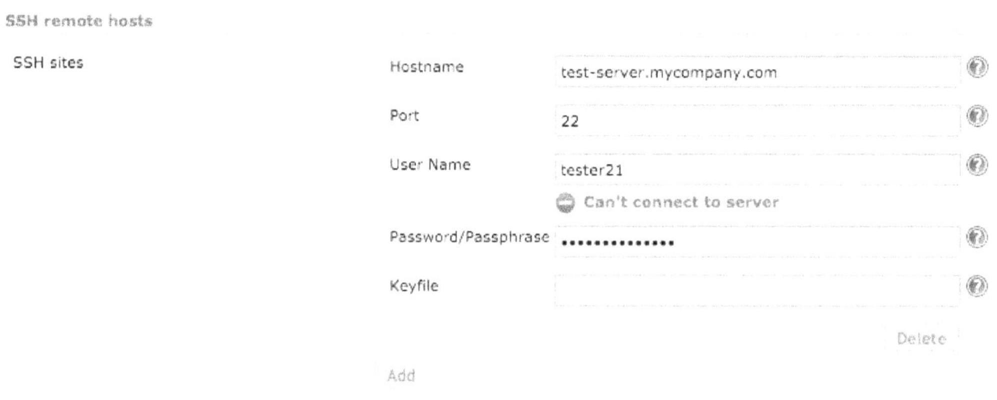

FIGURE 4-26. *SSH remote hosts settings*

machine using a user name and password, then specify them in the corresponding fields. Another way to authenticate with a remote machine is using a private-public key pair. In this case, it is assumed that your public key is already uploaded to the remote machine. You need to specify the file that contains your private key in the Keyfile field (for example, **~/.ssh/ id_rsa**). If your private key is protected by a passphrase, then specify it in the Password/Passphrase field. Just like the FTP plugin, the SSH plugin will try to automatically connect to the server and provide feedback about any connectivity problem, as shown in Figure 4-26. You can add multiple SSH remote hosts using this setting.

Once you successfully set SSH remote hosts, you can issue commands to the remote hosts from any job build. Go to the Job Configurations page and select "Execute shell script on remote host using ssh" in the Build Environment section. You can execute shell scripts before and after the build. Figure 4-27 shows an example to

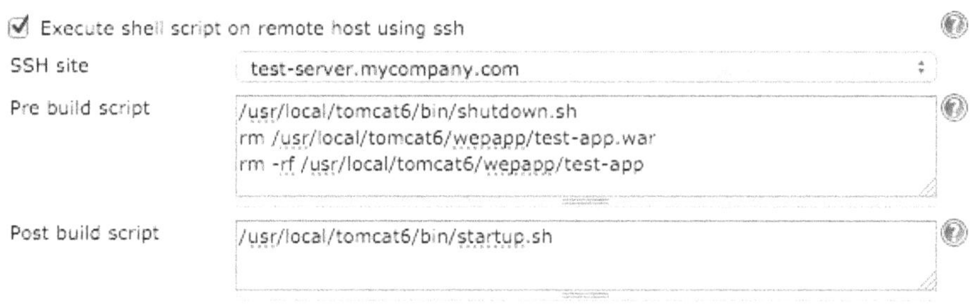

FIGURE 4-27. *Executing remote shell commands*

keep the Tomcat running on the remote host clean for the next deployment of the war created by the current build using the Deploy plugin. The script specified in the pre-build script shuts down the Tomcat server and removes the war file and the corresponding folder where the war content is expanded. After the build completes, a remote command specified via post-build script is executed to start up the Tomcat server. Now, a clean Tomcat instance is ready to deploy the war created by the build.

Summary

A decade ago, Continuous Integration was little known in the software industry. Now, more and more software companies are making CI a central part of their software development process. Hudson is a favorite open source tool for CI. In this chapter, we effectively used Hudson as a CI tool by learning how to:

- Configure the SCM system
- Automate the build
- Automate the testing, code quality, and code coverage analyses
- Speed up the build for faster feedback
- Automate the feedback mechanism
- Practice Continuous Delivery

CHAPTER 5

Hudson and Automated Testing

Continuing on the theme of applying Hudson, this chapter expands on one aspect of the preceding chapter about Continuous Integration: automated testing. Arguably the most significant impact Hudson can have on an enterprise is reducing the cost and increasing the positive impact of automated testing. This chapter is an overview of the theory and practice of automated testing with Hudson.

Containing Code and Code Under Test

Before jumping in, let's define two simple terms. We will use the term "code under test" to mean the code that is being exercised by the testing code. Usually this is the code for which "you" are responsible. This can also be known as "production code" or "main code." If there is a defect in the code under test, the developers need to know about it as quickly as possible, and they need to know the most pertinent information about how to fix the defect. We use the term "containing code" to mean the software in which the code under test runs. In fact, the code under test always has a dependency on the containing code. This fact will be explored later in the chapter when the concept of the lineup is discussed. There are two kinds of containing code: in-house and commercial-off-the-shelf (COTS). In-house containing code is created and maintained within your organization. Examples would be the bespoke billing, purchasing, or invoicing systems with which your code under test runs. COTS containing code could be a servlet container, an application server, an Amazon EC2 instance, or even a Google App Engine app. With respect to automated testing, the focus is on the code under test, but due to the complexity of many testing environments, the containing code is just as important.

TIP
One of the key tenets of Continuous Delivery is to accept the fact that errors in configuration for the containing code can have just as deleterious an effect on software quality as bugs in the code under test.

After defining code under test and containing code, it is clear that one person's containing code is another person's code under test, as Figure 5-1 shows.

TIP
Hudson jobs tend to be encodings of a particular arrangement of code under test and containing code. If possible, make these encodings as clear as possible when designing your jobs.

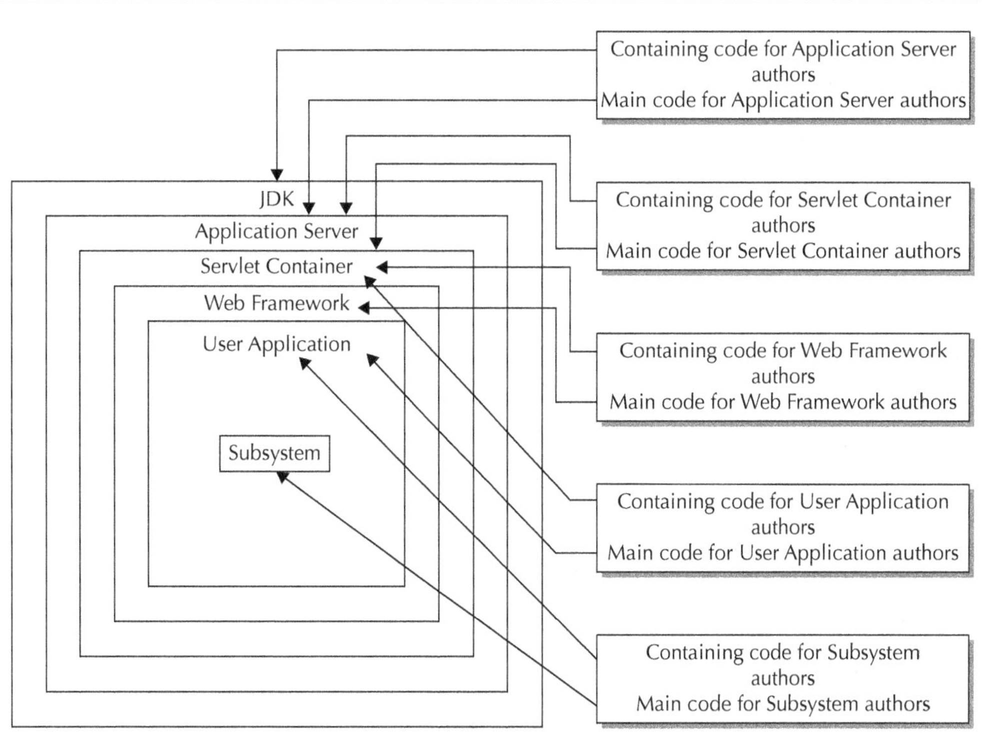

FIGURE 5-1. *Diagram illustrating how one person's code under test is another person's containing code*

Recall the Simple Servlet example from Chapter 3. This section will add a simple automated test to the Maven build, allowing it to be picked up by Hudson in the course of its normal job execution. Because Hudson was simply invoking Maven, up to this point it was sufficient to understand that Maven automatically runs the tests at the right time during the build. For simple unit tests, the "right time" is any time after the test is compiled. When there is containing code to be started before the code under test can be tested, the question of when is the right time to run the tests becomes more complicated. True to the convention-over-configuration nature of Maven, it turns out there is a "build lifecycle" that underpins every Maven execution, and in many cases one need not understand it very deeply. However, in order to understand how to perform automated testing in Maven (via Hudson), it is appropriate to examine the full Maven build lifecycle in more detail.

A Quick Tour of the Maven Build Lifecycle

Previous examples in the book had Hudson invoking Maven with commands such as **mvn clean install**. As we have already seen, much of Maven's action happens behind the scenes, so this seemingly simple invocation actually causes a lot of things to happen. The arguments **clean install** are actually the names of Maven lifecycle phases. The **mvn** command can accept three kinds of arguments on its command line:

- **Options** Such as -DskipTests=true or -PsignArtifacts
- **Lifecycle phases** Such as **clean** or **install**
- **Plugin:goal pairs** Such as **help:effective-pom**, to indicate invoking the maven-help-plugin's effective-pom goal. Plugin goals always imply a specific lifecycle phase.

The first item in the list is used to pass options to **mvn** itself and occasionally to supplement information in the pom.xml. The latter two items in the list interact intimately with the build lifecycle and state the end phase for the build lifecycle for this invocation of **mvn**. Thus, the combination of command-line arguments and the pom.xml are the inputs to **mvn**. What comes out on the other side is hopefully quality software (called "build artifacts" in Maven parlance). The illustration depicts a common vision of how Maven works.

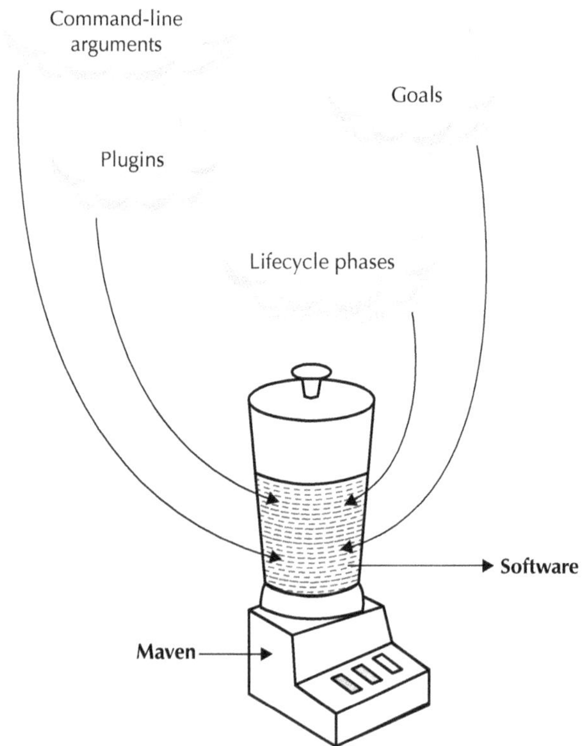

TIP

Maven is an extreme example of the principle of "inversion of control." The key to success with Maven is to work with it, not against it. This is best achieved by avoiding trying to change how Maven does things. Rather, it is best to find out the way Maven intends to do the sort of thing you want and then provide input to that process.

All of the action in Maven happens on top of the backbone of the build lifecycle. All of the work done by Maven during a build is done by plugins executing at specific phases during the build lifecycle. Each specific thing that a plugin does is called a "goal." Plugins typically declare in which lifecycle phases their goals are designed to execute. There are actually three lifecycles that are used in Maven, called *clean*, *default*, and *site*. Every invocation of **mvn** will use at least one of these three lifecycles. When analyzing its command-line arguments, Maven determines which of the three lifecycles to run and the end phase for each one, based on the order in which the arguments are specified. The clean and site lifecycles deal with running the clean and site goals. Clean resets the project to its nonbuilt state, usually just deleting the target directory. Site generates reports, such as code coverage and unit test results. The default lifecycle is the most interesting and is where most of the work is done by Maven and its many plugins. Hudson jobs that invoke Maven will usually have cause to use all of these different lifecycles in one way or another.

Each of the three lifecycles consists of several different phases, each with a name and purpose and executed in sequence by Maven. Maven always executes at least one of the three lifecycles, and when it does, it always executes them from the start phase until the user-specified end phase. You can think of the execution of the lifecycle phases as a journey on a non-express train from the starting station through multiple stations. When traveling on a such a train from the starting station, you can get off at any station, but no stations can be skipped. Figure 5-2 shows the three lifecycles using the non-express train analogy.

Table 5-1 lists the phases of the Maven default lifecycle. Not every build will cause action to take place for every phase, but every phase until the end phase is executed. In other words, the build lifecycle itself is invariant, but the subset of phases to be invoked can vary based on input to Maven.

TIP

*When using Maven from the command line, most of the time **install** is the end phase. When using Hudson for Continuous Delivery, only Hudson should be causing the deploy phase to be executed.*

Phase Name	Purpose
validate	Validate the input and parse the pom.xml.
initialize	Given the kind of <packaging>, create directories and initialize properties.
generate-sources	If using code-generation techniques, allow that code generation to happen.
process-sources	Preprocess sources by expanding Maven variables.
generate-resources	If generating resources, such as CSS or JavaScript files, allow that generation to happen.
process-resources	Copy and process the resources into the destination directory, such as CSS and JavaScript files for a war <packaging> project.
compile	Run any necessary compilers, such as javac, on the source files of the project.
process-classes	Perform any post-processing on the output of the compilation phase.
generate-test-sources	As with source code generation, but for the tests.
process-test-sources	As with main sources, but for the tests.
generate-test-resources	As with main resources, but for the tests.
process-test-resources	As with main resources, but for the tests.
test-compile	Compile the tests.
process-test-classes	Perform any post-processing on the output of test compilation.
test	Run the unit tests.
prepare-package	Gather all the necessary parts together in one directory in preparation for the next phase.
package	Package all the parts from the preceding phase into a distribution unit, such as a jar, war, or ear file.
pre-integration-test	Deploy the package to the containing code.
integration-test	Run the tests that require the containing code from the preceding phase.
post-integration-test	Perform any cleanup action after the running of the containing code and tests.
verify	Perform any verification on the packaged artifact.
install	Install the package into the local repository, usually the $HOME/.m2/ repository.
deploy	Copy the package from the local repository to a remote repository, such as Sonatype Nexus.

TABLE 5-1. *The Maven Default Lifecycle*

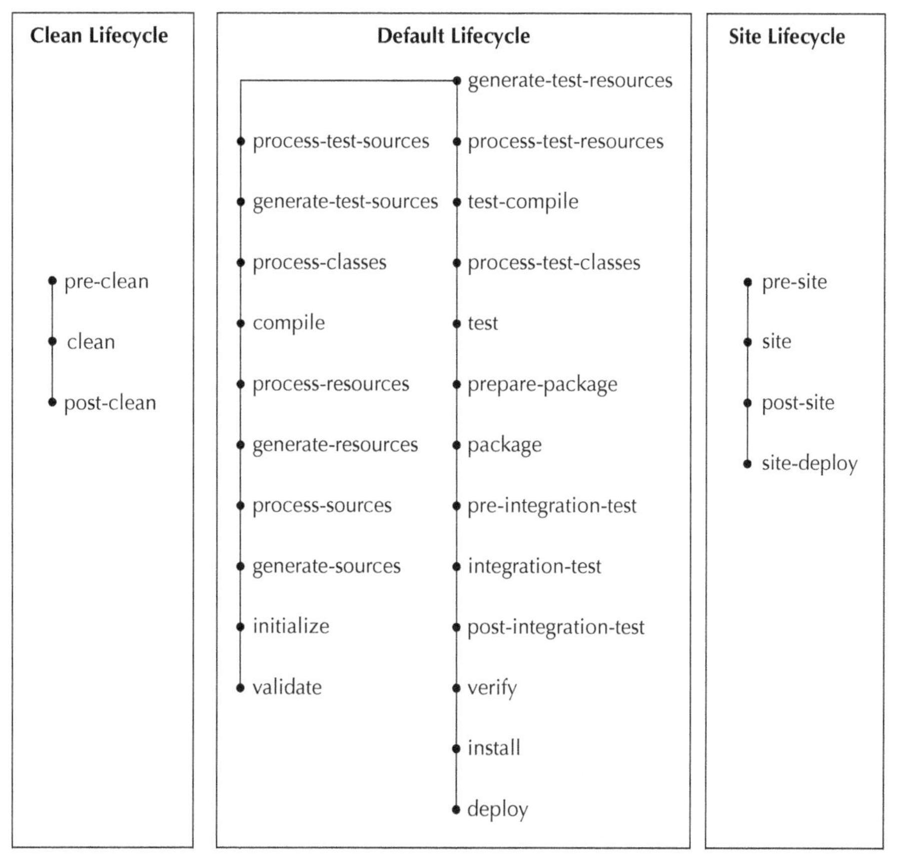

FIGURE 5-2. *Maven lifecycles as non-express trains*

As shown in the preceding examples, all use of Maven involves plugins, and any nontrivial use of Maven involves configuring those plugins in some way. You can think of a plugin as nothing more than a set of goals that the plugin supports. For example, the maven-compiler-plugin supports compile, testCompile, and help.

As mentioned at the start of the section, the **mvn** command line can include options, lifecycle phases, and plugin:goal pairs. The last in this list always takes the form of *plugin-name:goal-name*. By convention, the *plugin-name* is the middle part of the Maven artifactId for the plugin between the words maven- and -plugin. For example, if the maven artifactId is maven-compiler-plugin, the *plugin-name* would be compiler. The way to discover the goals supported by a plugin is to look at the Maven

Web site, by convention at the URL http://maven.apache.org/plugins/maven-*plugin-name*-plugin, or to invoke **mvn** with the *plugin-name*:help goal. For example, here is the help for the compiler plugin:

```
  The Compiler Plugin is used to compile the sources of your project.
This plugin has 3 goals:
compiler:compile
  Compiles application sources
compiler:help
  Display help information on maven-compiler-plugin.
  Call mvn compiler:help -Ddetail=true -Dgoal=<goal-name> to display parameter
  details.
compiler:testCompile
  Compiles application test sources.
```

Plugins are intimately related to the build lifecycle through the concept of goals. The <packaging> specified in the pom.xml is very important because it dictates the set of plugins that will be used, which goals of those plugins will be invoked, and in which order they are invoked. For the purpose of Continuous Delivery, the packaging types supported by Maven are important to understand, because much of Continuous Delivery revolves around the packaging and publishing of many different kinds of artifacts. Table 5-2 lists the bindings between phases in the default lifecycle and the plugin:goal pairs that are used during that phase for the most common kind of packaging.

Now that we have examined the Maven build lifecycle, we can ask some important questions when dealing with containing code versus code under test in Hudson: Who starts the containing code? Who stops the containing code? What happens to the containing code when the test fails?

Default Lifecycle Phase	Plugin:Goal Pairs
process-resources	resources:resources
compile	compiler:compile
process-test-resources	resources:testResources
test-compile	compiler:testCompile
test	surefire:test
package	jar:jar, war:war, par:par, rar:rar, ejb:ejb, ejb3:ejb3
install	install:install
deploy	deploy:deploy

TABLE 5-2. *Default Lifecycle Bindings for jar, war, ejb, par, and rar*

TIP

Dealing with containing code when running automated tests with Hudson is a very environment- and test-specific matter. In general, the most important consideration is responsiveness. You want to choose the finest granularity of starting and stopping the containing code that will meet your requirements for having responsive builds. As mentioned in the preceding chapter, a build should take no more than ten minutes to run from start to finish. If you find that starting and stopping your containing code for every individual test is too slow, consider starting the containing code once, then executing all the tests that need that particular arrangement of containing code, and then shutting it down.

Quick Code Jumpstart: Simple Servlet Testing

Let's revisit the Simple Servlet example from Chapter 3 and add an HtmlUnit test to it. HtmlUnit is a Java library that simulates a Web browser. As such, it is ideal for use by JUnit or TestNG tests that need to interact with containing code that can be accessed from Web browsers. The Library Web application from the preceding chapter would be a fine candidate for testing with HtmlUnit. This example modifies the pom.xml from the Simple Servlet example from Chapter 3 so that it starts up the Jetty server during the pre-integration-test build lifecycle phase, runs an HtmlUnit test case during the integration-test phase, shuts down Jetty during the post-integration-test phase, and verifies that the test was successful during the verify phase. The complete pom.xml is shown next, with the changed areas with respect to the example in Chapter 3 shown in boldface.

```
<?xml version="1.0" encoding="UTF-8"?>
<project xmlns="http://maven.apache.org/POM/4.0.0" xmlns:xsi="http://
www.w3.org/2001/XMLSchema-instance" xsi:schemaLocation="http://maven.
apache.org/POM/4.0.0 http://maven.apache.org/xsd/maven-4.0.0.xsd">
  <modelVersion>4.0.0</modelVersion>

  <groupId>net.hudsonlifestyle</groupId>
  <artifactId>simpleservlet-htmlunit</artifactId>
  <version>1.0</version>
  <packaging>war</packaging>
```

```
<build>
  <plugins>
    <plugin>
      <groupId>org.apache.maven.plugins</groupId>
      <artifactId>maven-war-plugin</artifactId>
      <version>2.3</version>
      <configuration>
        <failOnMissingWebXml>false</failOnMissingWebXml>
      </configuration>
    </plugin>
    <plugin>
      <groupId>org.apache.maven.plugins</groupId>
      <artifactId>maven-compiler-plugin</artifactId>
      <inherited>true</inherited>
      <configuration>
        <source>1.6</source>
        <target>1.6</target>
        <encoding>${project.build.sourceEncoding}</encoding>
      </configuration>
    </plugin>
    <plugin>
      <groupId>org.eclipse.jetty</groupId>
      <artifactId>jetty-maven-plugin</artifactId>
      <version>9.0.1.v20130408</version>
      <configuration>
        <scanIntervalSeconds>10</scanIntervalSeconds>
        <stopKey>foo</stopKey>
        <stopPort>9999</stopPort>
      </configuration>
      <executions>
        <execution>
          <id>start-jetty</id>
          <phase>pre-integration-test</phase>
          <goals>
            <goal>deploy-war</goal>
          </goals>
          <configuration>
            <daemon>true</daemon>
            <reload>manual</reload>
          </configuration>
        </execution>
        <execution>
          <id>stop-jetty</id>
          <phase>post-integration-test</phase>
          <goals>
            <goal>stop</goal>
          </goals>
```

```
          </execution>
        </executions>
      </plugin>

      <plugin>
        <groupId>org.apache.maven.plugins</groupId>
        <artifactId>maven-failsafe-plugin</artifactId>
        <version>2.12.4</version>
        <executions>
          <execution>
            <goals>
              <goal>integration-test</goal>
              <goal>verify</goal>
            </goals>
            <configuration>
              <systemPropertyVariables>
                <integration.base.url>http://${env.HOSTNAME}:${env.
CONTAINER_PORT}</integration.base.url>
              </systemPropertyVariables>
            </configuration>
          </execution>
        </executions>
      </plugin>
    </plugins>
  </build>

  <dependencies>
    <dependency>
      <groupId>javax.servlet</groupId>
      <artifactId>javax.servlet-api</artifactId>
      <version>3.0.1</version>
      <scope>provided</scope>
    </dependency>
    <dependency>
      <groupId>net.sourceforge.htmlunit</groupId>
      <artifactId>htmlunit</artifactId>
      <version>2.9</version>
      <scope>test</scope>
    </dependency>
    <dependency>
      <groupId>junit</groupId>
      <artifactId>junit</artifactId>
      <version>4.10</version>
      <scope>test</scope>
    </dependency>
  </dependencies>
</project>
```

We changed the artifactId to be different from the example in Chapter 3. Two new <plugin> sections were added, one for the containing code and one for the code under test. This will be very typical when using Hudson to run automated tests from Maven.

This example uses Jetty for the containing code. Jetty is a robust and spec-compliant implementation of the Servlet and JSP specifications from the JavaEE stack. The amount of configuration code for Jetty is surprisingly small, but the power it brings is large. First, note the groupId, artifactId, and version.

```
<plugin>
  <groupId>org.eclipse.jetty</groupId>
  <artifactId>jetty-maven-plugin</artifactId>
  <version>9.0.1.v20130408</version>
</plugin>
```

TIP

Always *specify the full groupId, artifactId, and version for all Maven plugins and dependencies. This information must be recorded as part of the lineup, as explained later in the chapter.*

While it's possible to leave the version out, this is *never* a good idea for Continuous Integration because that would put you at the mercy of whenever a new version of the artifact is released. Following is the <configuration> section common to all executions of the jetty-maven-plugin. Most plugins will also have an <executions> section with at least one <execution> section, each of which targets the operation of the plugin in a specific <phase>. In this case, the pre-integration-test phase invokes the deploy-war goal and the post-integration-test invokes the stop-jetty goal. The former has some additional required configuration:

```
<configuration>
  <daemon>true</daemon>
  <reload>manual</reload>
</configuration>
```

The code under test is represented in the pom by the use of the maven-failsafe-plugin.

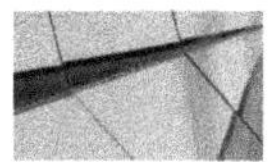

TIP
Previous examples of testing with Maven used the maven-surefire-plugin. In fact, the maven-failsafe-plugin is exactly the same thing as the maven-surefire-plugin, but it does its work in the integration-test phase instead of the test phase. More importantly: a test failure during integration-test will not cause the build to fail, allowing any plugins configured during the post-integration-test phase to continue to do their work regardless of the test outcome. Test failures are instead dealt with in the verify phase. This very important fact allows the containing code to be shut down correctly. This is critically important for Hudson because subsequent builds need to be able to have exclusive access to whatever TCP ports and other resources that must be available before the job starts. Failed tests can leave these resources in a hung and unavailable state unless the cleanup is performed.

The maven-failsafe-plugin is configured to run in the integration-test and verify phases. The <configuration> section passes a system property to the HtmlUnit test integration.base.url. The value of this property in the pom.xml has parameters passed in as environment variables from Hudson.

```
              <systemPropertyVariables>
                <integration.base.url>http://${env.HOSTNAME}:${env.CONTAIN-
ER_PORT}</integration.base.url>
              </systemPropertyVariables>
```

Any string that is of the form ${env.VARNAME} will be replaced with the value of the VARNAME environment variable when the Maven build is executed.

This technique shows the importance of extracting changeable configuration information such as hostnames and port numbers from the build system so they can be passed in from Hudson using the Parameterized Build feature, which will be explained later.

Finally, the additional HtmlUnit and JUnit dependencies are added.

Next, the HtmlUnit test case itself is examined. This test case must reside in the source file src/test/java/net/hudsonlifestyle/SimpleServlet01IT.java.

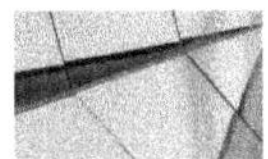

TIP

Any class in any package in src/test/java whose class name starts with IT, or ends with IT or ITCase, is run by the maven-failsafe-plugin.

```
package net.hudsonlifestyle;

import com.gargoylesoftware.htmlunit.WebClient;
import com.gargoylesoftware.htmlunit.html.HtmlPage;
import org.junit.Before;
import org.junit.After;
import org.junit.Test;
import static org.junit.Assert.assertTrue;

public class SimpleServlet01IT {

    private String webUrl;

    private WebClient webClient;

    @Before
    public void setUp() {
        webUrl = System.getProperty("integration.base.url") + "/SimpleServlet01";
        webClient = new WebClient();
    }

    @After
    public void tearDown() {
        webClient.closeAllWindows();
    }

    @Test
    public void testIndexHtml() throws Exception {
        System.out.println("Connecting to: " + webUrl);
        HtmlPage page = webClient.getPage(webUrl);
        assertTrue(page.getBody().asText().indexOf("Servlet SimpleServ-
let01 at") != -1);
    }
}
```

First note the System.getProperty() call. This is the value passed in from the environment variable, via the Hudson parameter. While this particular usage is very simple, the concept could be used for a great variety of complexity in conveying the specifics of the containing code to the code under test. After getting the URL for the servlet to test, an instance of the HtmlUnit WebClient class is created. This class simulates the browser and allows interacting with the Web UI in the same way that a browser would do. This can be seen in the testIndexHtml() method, which uses the webClient to load the URL and assert that the resultant page contains the expected text. The HtmlPage class provides complete access to all the elements of the Web page, such as clicking buttons, setting values in text fields, and even causing

Ajax transactions to happen, just as a real browser would do. This simple example asserts that the text Servlet SimpleServlet01 is present in the Web page. Recall from Chapter 3, that the code under test, SimpleServlet01, contained this code:

```
out.println("<title>Servlet SimpleServlet01</title>");
```

This simple example shows the lengths to which one must go to make assertions about the code under test. Later in the chapter, we examine JBoss Arquillian as a means to reduce the overhead in making assertions about the code under test.

The last piece is to make the Hudson job that executes this test. Clone the 02_mvn job from Chapter 3 as 01_HtmlUnit. Modify the existing Invoke Maven 3 "builder" section, and change the Goals text field to be **clean verify**. Also you must change the POM File text field to be the pom.xml file: **HudsonAndAutomatedTesting/01_HtmlUnit/pom.xml**. The first time this job is run, Maven will download many dependencies related to Jetty, HtmlUnit, and Failsafe. At the top of the Job Configurations page, find the text "This build is parameterized" and click the check box next to it. In the drop-down menu that appears, select String parameter. Fill in **CONTAINER_PORT** as the value of the Name text field, and **8080** as the value of the Default Value text field.

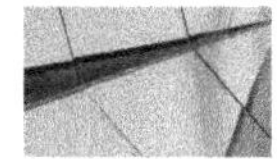

TIP

The usage of 8080 for CONTAINER_PORT here illustrates the reason for using the --httpPort environment variable to instruct Hudson to run on a less commonly used port.

This value must be the same as the default port used by Jetty, because the value is passed in to the HtmlUnit test via the environment variable references in pom.xml. If you wanted to use a different port, you would have to additionally define the environment variable jetty.port with the same value. Note that the environment variable HOSTNAME usually comes via the UNIX shell in which Hudson is running. If your particular environment does not have a HOSTNAME environment variable, one could manually be set as another String parameter. Set the Archive Artifacts path relative to the new folder, **HudsonAndAutomatedTesting/01_HtmlUnit/target/*.war**. Finally, we will tell Hudson where to find the test results. As in Chapter 3, this is accomplished by clicking the check box next to the text "Publish JUnit test result report" and filling in the text field with an expression that finds the TEST-*.xml file, **HudsonAndAutomatedTesting/01_HtmlUnit/target/failsafe-reports/TEST-*.xml**.

This version of the Maven Jetty program must be run with Java 7 or higher, or it will fail with a class version 51 error. If you run the Hudson war directly from the command line, simply make sure the version of Java is 7 or above; otherwise, configure the server to run in Java 7. You do not need to change the Maven compiler settings, as the Java 7 compiler is capable of generating Java 6 class files.

When the build is run, you will be asked if you want to override the default value for the CONTAINER_PORT parameter. Click the Build button to accept the default value. You should see output similar to the following.

```
Started by user anonymous
Checkout:workspace / /var/lib/hudson/jobs/01_HtmlUnit/workspace - hudson.remot-
ing.LocalChannel@8cb09b6
Using strategy: Default
Last Built Revision: Revision ecd3793fe4eb46dca937553b45cd8afacaf70b27 (origin/
master)
Checkout:workspace / /var/lib/hudson/jobs/01_HtmlUnit/workspace - hudson.remot-
ing.LocalChannel@8cb09b6
Fetching changes from the remote Git repository
Fetching upstream changes from https://hudson_in_practice:hudson@bitbucket.org/
hudson_in_practice/hudson_lifestyle.git
Commencing build of Revision ed34271a8d56da176d70e654ed8dab9c5a77ba7a (origin/
master)
Checking out Revision ed34271a8d56da176d70e654ed8dab9c5a77ba7a (origin/master)
[INFO] Using Maven 3 installation: apache-maven-3.0.4
[INFO] Checking Maven 3 installation environment
[workspace] $ /var/lib/hudson/files/apache-maven-3.0.4/bin/mvn --help
[INFO] Checking Maven 3 installation version
[INFO] Detected Maven 3 installation version: 3.0.4
[workspace] $ /var/lib/hudson/files/apache-maven-3.0.4/bin/mvn clean veri-
fy -V -B -DCONTAINER_PORT=8080 -Dmaven.ext.class.path=/var/lib/hudson/maven/
slavebundle/resources:/var/lib/hudson/maven/slavebundle/lib/maven3-eventspy-
3.0.jar:/var/lib/hudson/war/webapp/WEB-INF/lib/hudson-remoting-3.0.0-M2.
jar -Dhudson.eventspy.port=48231 -f HudsonAndAutomatedTesting/01_HtmlUnit/pom.xml
[DEBUG] Waiting for connection on port: 48231
Apache Maven 3.0.4 (r1232337; 2012-01-17 03:44:56-0500)
Maven home: /var/lib/hudson/files/apache-maven-3.0.4
Java version: 1.7.0_07, vendor: Oracle Corporation
Java home: /var/lib/hudson/files/jdk1.7.0_07/jre
Default locale: en_US, platform encoding: UTF-8
OS name: "linux", version: "2.6.39-200.24.1.el6uek.x86_64", arch: "amd64", fam-
ily: "unix"
[DEBUG] Connected to remote
[INFO] Scanning for projects...
[INFO]
[INFO] ------------------------------------------------------------------------
[INFO] Building simpleservlet_htmlunit 1.0
[INFO] ------------------------------------------------------------------------
[INFO]
[INFO] --- maven-clean-plugin:2.4.1:clean (default-clean) @ simpleservlet_html-
unit ---
[INFO] Deleting /var/lib/hudson/jobs/01_HtmlUnit/workspace/HudsonAndAutomated-
Testing/01_HtmlUnit/target
[INFO]
[INFO] --- maven-resources-plugin:2.5:resources (default-resources) @ simpleserv-
let_htmlunit ---
[debug] execute contextualize
[WARNING] Using platform encoding (UTF-8 actually) to copy filtered resourc-
es, i.e. build is platform dependent!
```

```
[INFO] skip non existing resourceDirectory /var/lib/hudson/jobs/01_HtmlUnit/
workspace/HudsonAndAutomatedTesting/01_HtmlUnit/src/main/resources
[INFO]
[INFO] --- maven-compiler-plugin:2.3.2:compile (default-compile) @ simpleservlet_
htmlunit ---
[WARNING] File encoding has not been set, using platform encoding UTF-
8, i.e. build is platform dependent!
[INFO] Compiling 1 source file to /var/lib/hudson/jobs/01_HtmlUnit/workspace/
HudsonAndAutomatedTesting/01_HtmlUnit/target/classes
[INFO]
[INFO] --- maven-resources-plugin:2.5:testResources (default-testResourc-
es) @ simpleservlet_htmlunit ---
[debug] execute contextualize
[WARNING] Using platform encoding (UTF-8 actually) to copy filtered resourc-
es, i.e. build is platform dependent!
[INFO] skip non existing resourceDirectory /var/lib/hudson/jobs/01_HtmlUnit/
workspace/HudsonAndAutomatedTesting/01_HtmlUnit/src/test/resources
[INFO]
[INFO] --- maven-compiler-plugin:2.3.2:testCompile (default-testCompile) @ sim-
pleservlet_htmlunit ---
[WARNING] File encoding has not been set, using platform encoding UTF-
8, i.e. build is platform dependent!
[INFO] Compiling 1 source file to /var/lib/hudson/jobs/01_HtmlUnit/workspace/
HudsonAndAutomatedTesting/01_HtmlUnit/target/test-classes
[INFO]
[INFO] --- maven-surefire-plugin:2.10:test (default-test) @ simpleservlet_html-
unit ---
[INFO] Surefire report directory: /var/lib/hudson/jobs/01_HtmlUnit/workspace/
HudsonAndAutomatedTesting/01_HtmlUnit/target/surefire-reports

-------------------------------------------------------
 T E S T S
-------------------------------------------------------

Results :

Tests run: 0, Failures: 0, Errors: 0, Skipped: 0

[INFO]
[INFO] --- maven-war-plugin:2.3:war (default-war) @ simpleservlet_htmlunit ---
[INFO] Packaging webapp
[INFO] Assembling webapp [simpleservlet_htmlunit] in [/var/lib/hudson/jobs/01_Ht-
mlUnit/workspace/HudsonAndAutomatedTesting/01_HtmlUnit/target/simpleservlet_html-
unit-1.0]
[INFO] Processing war project
[INFO] Webapp assembled in [45 msecs]
[INFO] Building war: /var/lib/hudson/jobs/01_HtmlUnit/workspace/HudsonAndAutomat-
edTesting/01_HtmlUnit/target/simpleservlet_htmlunit-1.0.war
[INFO]
[INFO] >>> jetty-maven-plugin:9.0.1.v20130408:deploy-war (start-jetty) @ simple-
servlet_htmlunit >>>
[INFO]
[INFO] <<< jetty-maven-plugin:9.0.1.v20130408:deploy-war (start-jetty) @ simple-
servlet_htmlunit <<<
[INFO]
```

```
[INFO] --- jetty-maven-plugin:9.0.1.v20130408:deploy-war (start-jetty) @ simple-
servlet_htmlunit ---
[INFO] Configuring Jetty for project: simpleservlet_htmlunit
[INFO] Context path = /
[INFO] Tmp directory = /var/lib/hudson/jobs/01_HtmlUnit/workspace/HudsonAndAuto-
matedTesting/01_HtmlUnit/target/tmp
[INFO] Web defaults = org/eclipse/jetty/webapp/webdefault.xml
[INFO] Web overrides =  none
2013-04-14 01:39:00.777:INFO:oejs.Server:main: jetty-9.0.1.v20130408
2013-04-14 01:39:00.992:INFO:oejpw.PlusConfiguration:main: No Transaction man-
ager found - if your webapp requires one, please configure one.
2013-04-14 01:39:02.113:INFO:oejsh.
ContextHandler:main: started o.e.j.m.p.JettyWebAppContext@84db765{/,file:/var/
lib/hudson/jobs/01_HtmlUnit/workspace/HudsonAndAutomatedTesting/01_HtmlUnit/
target/simpleservlet_htmlunit-1.0/,AVAILABLE}{/var/lib/hudson/jobs/01_HtmlUnit/
workspace/HudsonAndAutomatedTesting/01_HtmlUnit/target/simpleservlet_htmlunit-
1.0.war}
2013-04-14 01:39:02.131:INFO:oejmp.MavenServerConnector:main: Started MavenServer
Connector@65ce0806{HTTP/1.1}{0.0.0.0:8080}
[INFO] Started Jetty Server
[WARNING] scanIntervalSeconds is set to 10 but will be IGNORED due to manual re-
loading
[INFO] Console reloading is ENABLED. Hit ENTER on the console to restart the con-
text.
[INFO]
[INFO] --- maven-failsafe-plugin:2.12.4:integration-test (default) @ simpleserv-
let_htmlunit ---
[INFO] Failsafe report directory: /var/lib/hudson/jobs/01_HtmlUnit/workspace/
HudsonAndAutomatedTesting/01_HtmlUnit/target/failsafe-reports

-------------------------------------------------------
 T E S T S
-------------------------------------------------------
Running net.hudsonlifestyle.SimpleServlet01IT
Connecting to: http://rhombus3:8080/SimpleServlet01
Tests run: 1, Failures: 0, Errors: 0, Skipped: 0, Time elapsed: 2.004 sec

Results :

Tests run: 1, Failures: 0, Errors: 0, Skipped: 0

[WARNING] File encoding has not been set, using platform encoding UTF-
8, i.e. build is platform dependent!
[INFO]
[INFO] --- jetty-maven-plugin:9.0.1.v20130408:stop (stop-jetty) @ simpleservlet_
htmlunit ---
2013-04-14 01:39:04.718:INFO:oejs.Server:ShutdownMonitor: Graceful shutdown org.
eclipse.jetty.maven.plugin.JettyServer@321af6fe by  Sun Apr 14 01:39:34 EDT 2013
[INFO]
[INFO] --- maven-failsafe-plugin:2.12.4:verify (default) @ simpleservlet_html-
unit ---
2013-04-14 01:39:04.721:INFO:oejmp.MavenServerConnector:ShutdownMonit
or: Stopped MavenServerConnector@65ce0806{HTTP/1.1}{0.0.0.0:8080}
[INFO] Failsafe report directory: /var/lib/hudson/jobs/01_HtmlUnit/workspace/
```

```
HudsonAndAutomatedTesting/01_HtmlUnit/target/failsafe-reports
[WARNING] File encoding has not been set, using platform encoding UTF-
8, i.e. build is platform dependent!
[INFO] ------------------------------------------------------------------------
[INFO] BUILD SUCCESS
[INFO] ------------------------------------------------------------------------
[INFO] Total time: 9.635s
[INFO] Finished at: Sun Apr 14 01:39:04 EDT 2013
[INFO] Final Memory: 25M/239M
[INFO] ------------------------------------------------------------------------
[DEBUG] Closing connection to remote
[DEBUG] Waiting for process to finish
[DEBUG] Result: 0
Recording test results
[DEBUG] Skipping watched dependency update; build not configured with trig-
ger: 01_HtmlUnit #6
Finished: SUCCESS
```

Note the boldfaced text in the output. The first test shows that there are no unit tests in this particular build. To avoid this message, the maven-surefire-plugin can be disabled by adding this configuration in the <plugins> section:

```
<plugin>
        <groupId>org.apache.maven.plugins</groupId>
        <artifactId>maven-surefire-plugin</artifactId>
        <configuration>
          <skip>true</skip>
        </configuration>
</plugin>
```

The maven-failsafe-plugin, which has the test, will continue to run.

TIP
This sort of fine tuning of the build is really important, and it must be done regularly to keep builds running fast. Every bit of unnecessary build logic should be eliminated, because all of it adds to the time it takes to complete the build.

Automated Testing: Shields Up!

One of the most striking things about enterprise software development is its potent combination of longevity and complexity. Enterprise software tends to be very complex and it tends to be in operation for a long time. To make matters worse, it tends to get more complex over time as features are added and requirements shift on one side, and the software stack to meet those requirements shifts on the other. These and other threats make it very desirable to have some sort of shield against these incoming threats to the stability of your software. Automated testing is one very effective such shield, and you want your testing shield to be as strong as it can be. Here are some considerations in assessing the strength of your test shield:

- How many tests do you have?
- How susceptible are the tests to spurious errors?
- How many of the tests are ignored or "commented out" from being run by Hudson?
- In which of the potentially many permutations of your stack are the tests run?
- How frequently are the tests run?
- What percentage of the code under test is exercised by the automated tests?

While providing a shield against threats to stability, the tests also need to be useful to the developers, as shown in the following considerations:

- How easy is it to add new tests?
- When a test fails, how easy is it to determine the cause of the failure given the information from the Hudson job?
- How long does it take to run the tests to get a level of assurance that the software is in a known-good state?

Ideally, you have thousands of automated tests, none of them commented out, which cover most of your code under test in all of your supported environments. The tests are run continuously in a cascading manner so that developers only need wait a maximum of ten minutes before being able to conclude with reasonable certainty that the code under test is in a known good state. In practice, many factors can conspire to make the automated testing shield weaker.

The Software Lineup

Reproducibility is the key enabler for Continuous Delivery, and the key enabler for reproducibility is mastery of the software stack on which the code under test runs. This is important not just for the code under test when it is being tested, but also in any other environment in which the code will be run by any of the parties that will be running it, including the production environment. The complete set of software, with version and patch numbers and configuration settings for each, that results in a runnable environment can be thought of as a software lineup. In environments where specific hardware requirements are important as well, the hardware can be considered a part of the lineup. This term is taken from the game of baseball, where it refers to the order in which the players bat. The term is also known as "batting order," but that's much less applicable to Continuous Delivery. In baseball, each of the nine positions in the lineup has a special role, even though they all are essentially doing the same thing: trying to hit the ball. It's the same thing with a software lineup. In baseball, the manager tweaks his lineup specifically for the challenge at hand in each game, carefully filling out the lineup card, which is exchanged with the umpire ceremoniously at the beginning of the game. With software, it's important to keep track of the lineup cards as well, but unfortunately the software tool support for this is not as inclusive as it could be. In the absence of such a tool, the lineup could be kept in a spreadsheet or a database or even on a wiki. The important thing is to have a single source of truth for the known supported lineups and to put that source itself under version control. Table 5-3 shows what could be the software lineup for the production environment of the

Node 1: Library Web Application	
Supported Browsers	Windows: IE 7, 8, 9 Firefox 15 ESR, Firefox 16 ESR Mac: Safari 6.0.3 Firefox 15 ESR GNU/Linux: Firefox 15 ESR
Operating System	Solaris 10 x64, Patch Level Generic_144489-05
JVM	Oracle 1.6.0_31 for Solaris x64 JVM arguments: -Xms512m -Xmx768m -XX:MaxPermSize=786m
Application Server	Two-node cluster of WebLogic Server 12c (and whatever patches and configurations necessary there)
Library Web Application 2.1.7	
Node 2: Database Server	
Operating System	AIX V7
Database	DB2 Version 9.7 Fix Pack (FP) 1
Database Schema version 2.1.7	
Node 3: Checkout and Return System	
Operating System	Red Hat Linux 9.5
JVM	Oracle 1.7_17 JVM arguments: -XX:+UseParallelGC -XX:CMSInitiatingO ccupancyFraction=70
Checkout and Return System 2.1.7	

TABLE 5-3. *Production Lineup Card, Sherwood County Library*

Sherwood County Library. Note that this lineup includes multiple processing nodes as the system is a distributed system.

When comparing similar lineups, even a small difference should be considered sufficient grounds for treating the lineups as not identical. Lineups that are not identical should be treated as entirely different from each other. By keeping firm track of your entire supported lineups, you can quickly fend off any instability caused by running the software with an unsupported lineup element. It is also useful to have several tiers of support. Have at most two "golden stack" lineups for which a high level of support is provided. The second tier may have a few more different lineups, with a correspondingly less urgent level of support.

TIP
If possible, have a little piece of software at the top of your stack that prints out the entire lineup from top to bottom in a way that can be textually compared with another instance of the lineup, say, at a customer site. This makes it easier to troubleshoot problems that arise from unwelcome side effects in the containing code, rather than in the code under test.

How Does Hudson Fit into the Lineup?

Just as there would be a lineup card for every supported lineup in production, there must be similar ones for testing. Ideally it would be a logical subclass of a production lineup card with additional test dependencies. In fact, the version of Hudson itself should be included in the test lineup card. Due to the need to keep Hudson jobs providing results in less than ten minutes, the granularity of the jobs means that Hudson runs inside an already provisioned node in the lineup, rather than having Hudson itself provisioning the lineup as part of its job execution. If there are multiple complete test lineup cards, the Matrix Build feature of Hudson, described in Chapter 7, is very useful for managing the execution of all them.

Who Writes the Tests?

Before revisiting the kinds of tests introduced in the previous chapter, it's important to ask the question, "Who writes the tests?" In the practice of Test Driven Development introduced in the preceding chapter and explained in more detail later in the chapter, the same party who wrote the production code also writes the automated tests for that code. These can be any kind of tests (unit, system, integration, and so on). Any change to the production code must also be accompanied by testing code. While this practice is now widespread, it is important to point out that developer-authored tests are no substitute for the kind of tests written by skilled test engineers who have experience at eliciting bugs that are hard to find but very important to fix. Regardless of who writes the tests, the tests should all be automated and put into integrated Hudson jobs.

TIP

It is tempting to have the developers maintain their own Hudson jobs that run their own tests, while the professional testers maintain their own Hudson jobs that run their tests on the code produced by the developers. Resist this temptation. Such an arrangement is entirely counter to the notion of Continuous Delivery.

Kinds of Tests

The following taxonomy is by no means exhaustive or normative, but it is fairly commonplace and builds on what was introduced in the preceding chapter. The kinds of tests are listed from smallest scope to largest. With respect to Hudson, the only question you need to ask is, "Is it automatable?" If the answer is yes, then the test is a great candidate for Hudson. Also, with respect to the tools used to author these kinds of tests, note that there is no hard coupling between the testing technology and the kind of test. For example, it's perfectly possible to write an integration test using JUnit only, just as it is possible to use Selenium to write a unit test. How the test is written, not the testing APIs used, determines the kind of test.

Unit Tests

The "unit" in unit test is a nod to C programming, where the term "compilation unit" means a single source file with all its #include macros applied by the preprocessor. In a looser sense, a unit test should only exercise code within a single class. An example of a unit test was already provided in the HelloMvn example in Chapter 3. These tests provide super-fast feedback on simple changes. Most importantly, these tests require no containing code. Unfortunately, in most enterprise software, the containing code environment is so complex that unit testing can be challenging. JBoss Arquillian provides a decent answer to this challenge and will be covered in the next section.

Component Tests

The "component" in component test means "software component" or "module." These kinds of tests exercise multiple related classes, but try to stick within the same general area. The Java package concept is one way to define a component in this sense of the word. Testing-wise, these kinds of tests do require containing code such as a servlet container. Tests that use HtmlUnit, such as shown earlier in the chapter, can be component tests.

Functional Tests

Not to be confused with functional programming, which is a style of computer programming for high-end computer science types, the "functional" in functional test means testing the functionality of the code under test. These kinds of tests don't take the structure of the code under test into account. Rather, they are written from the perspective of a user trying to do something practical with the software.

Integration Tests

The scope of such tests is very similar to that of functional tests; however, integration tests *are* aware of the underlying design of the software. They seek to exercise the interfaces between the different software components in the system as a whole. Cargo is a technology often used in automated integration testing.

Load Tests

There are several subcategories of load tests, but all of them try to simulate putting the system under high-demand usage. As such, these tests are usually for multiuser software, but it is conceivable that even a single-user application can have load tests. The Hudson Performance plugin can be used in conjunction with JMeter to establish performance criteria and assert that the build meets that criteria, failing the build if not. This plugin is available in the Others subtab of the Available tab in the Hudson Plugin Manager.

Pretested Commits (Gated Checkins)

Though it is orthogonal to this list of kinds of tests, it is important to mention the concept of pretested commits (also known as gated checkins) because the concept introduces another kind of test: the qualification test. Achieving pretested commits is heavily dependent on the kind of SCM system being used; Git and Mercurial are best suited to the task due to their distributed nature. Code that is ultimately intended to be committed to the main code line is committed to some sort of staging area (such as a Git branch). A Hudson job is configured to merge code from the staging area into a work area local to the Hudson instance, and then run the qualification tests on that work area. There is no restriction on what kind of test can be called a qualification test, except for the proviso that qualification tests should run to completion quickly (certainly in under ten minutes). Only if the tests all pass is the code placed in a queue for a human reviewer to further scrutinize. Tools such as Gerrit or Atlassian Crucible can help make this review process run more smoothly.

Unit and Component Testing with Arquillian in Hudson

The fundamental tenet of unit testing is the absence of containing code. As mentioned earlier, this is challenging to achieve in enterprise software due to its highly integrated place in a larger software environment. One approach to unit testing enterprise software is called "mock objects." In this approach, any time the code under test needs to interact with code outside of its unit, the code under test is handed a "mock object" that has just enough functionality so the test can assert the correctness of the code under test. Several technologies exist to support this style of testing, most notably Mockito and EasyMock, and these technologies work just fine with Hudson. Another approach is to eschew mock objects entirely and make it as easy as possible to just use a real container so the code under test is running in the actual JavaEE environment. This is the approach taken by JBoss Arquillian.

The Arquillian project from JBoss is a good example of that company's commitment to the enterprise Java development community. During a time when their competitors were investing primarily in runtime infrastructure, JBoss introduced a project for the far less lucrative, but far more valuable (from a developer's perspective) testing infrastructure. While it is true that Arquillian does serve to get JBoss (and thus RedHat) technologies into the enterprise software stack, using Arquillian with non-JBoss containers is possible and well supported. This example uses the shortest path to success with Arquillian, which is to stick with their stack wherever possible. First, the Maven pom.xml:

```
<?xml version="1.0" encoding="UTF-8"?>
<project xmlns="http://maven.apache.org/POM/4.0.0" xmlns:xsi="http://www.
w3.org/2001/XMLSchema-instance" xsi:schemaLocation="http://maven.apache.
org/POM/4.0.0 http://maven.apache.org/xsd/maven-4.0.0.xsd">
  <modelVersion>4.0.0</modelVersion>
  <groupId>net.hudsonlifestyle</groupId>
  <artifactId>02_Arquillian</artifactId>
  <version>1.0</version>
  <packaging>jar</packaging>
  <name>02_Arquillian</name>
  <properties>
    <project.build.sourceEncoding>UTF-8</project.build.sourceEncoding>
  </properties>
  <repositories>
    <repository>
      <id>jboss-public-repository-group</id>
      <name>JBoss Public Repository Group</name>
      <url>http://repository.jboss.org/nexus/content/groups/public/</url>
      <layout>default</layout>
      <releases>
```

```
        <enabled>true</enabled>
        <updatePolicy>never</updatePolicy>
      </releases>
      <snapshots>
        <enabled>true</enabled>
        <updatePolicy>never</updatePolicy>
      </snapshots>
    </repository>
  </repositories>
  <dependencyManagement>
    <dependencies>
      <dependency>
        <groupId>org.jboss.arquillian</groupId>
        <artifactId>arquillian-bom</artifactId>
        <version>1.0.3.Final</version>
        <scope>import</scope>
        <type>pom</type>
      </dependency>
    </dependencies>
  </dependencyManagement>
  <build>
    <plugins>
      <plugin>
        <groupId>org.apache.maven.plugins</groupId>
        <artifactId>maven-surefire-plugin</artifactId>
        <version>2.12.4</version>
      </plugin>
      <plugin>
        <groupId>org.apache.maven.plugins</groupId>
        <artifactId>maven-compiler-plugin</artifactId>
        <version>2.3.2</version>
        <configuration>
          <source>1.6</source>
          <target>1.6</target>
        </configuration>
      </plugin>
    </plugins>
  </build>
  <dependencies>
    <dependency>
      <groupId>org.jboss.spec</groupId>
      <artifactId>jboss-javaee-6.0</artifactId>
      <version>1.0.0.Final</version>
      <type>pom</type>
      <scope>provided</scope>
    </dependency>
    <dependency>
      <groupId>junit</groupId>
      <artifactId>junit</artifactId>
      <version>4.10</version>
      <scope>test</scope>
```

```
    </dependency>
    <dependency>
      <groupId>org.jboss.arquillian.junit</groupId>
      <artifactId>arquillian-junit-container</artifactId>
      <version>1.0.3.Final</version>
      <scope>test</scope>
    </dependency>
    <dependency>
      <groupId>org.jboss.arquillian.container</groupId>
      <artifactId>arquillian-weld-ee-embedded-1.1</artifactId>
      <version>1.0.0.CR6</version>
      <scope>test</scope>
    </dependency>
    <dependency>
      <groupId>org.jboss.weld</groupId>
      <artifactId>weld-core</artifactId>
      <version>1.1.9.Final</version>
      <scope>test</scope>
    </dependency>
    <dependency>
      <groupId>org.slf4j</groupId>
      <artifactId>slf4j-simple</artifactId>
      <version>1.6.4</version>
      <scope>test</scope>
    </dependency>
  </dependencies>
</project>
```

This pom introduces two entirely new sections: <repositories> and <dependencyManagement>. <repositories> instructs Maven to first search for artifacts using the stated repository before trying the official Maven central repository, http://repo1.maven.org/maven2/. <dependencyManagement> allows Maven to pull in the right set of subartifacts to expose the Arquillian API to the test we will be writing. This allows us include the following import statements from inside our test.

```
import org.jboss.arquillian.junit.Arquillian;
import org.jboss.shrinkwrap.api.ShrinkWrap;
```

The remaining new content in the pom.xml all relates to satisfying the runtime dependencies that enable Arquillian to provide its unique in-container testing capability. The arquillian-junit-container dependency hooks into JUnit so that the Arquillian infrastructure can be started up and shut down at the right time during the test cycle. The arquillian-weld-ee-embedded-1.1 dependency allows Arquillian to start up weld-core, which is a CDI container. CDI is a Java EE standard programming model. The slf4j-simple dependency is for developers for whom the simple logging provided by JDK 1.4 is not sufficient. With the Maven configuration out of the way, we can move on to the code under test, located at src/main/java/net/hudsonlifestyle/HelloArquillian.java.

```
package net.hudsonlifestyle;

import javax.enterprise.context.ApplicationScoped;
import javax.inject.Named;

@Named
@ApplicationScoped
public class HelloArquillian {

    public void setFirstElement(String [] preAllocated) {
        preAllocated[0] = "" + System.currentTimeMillis();
    }

}
```

This code is an example of a CDI "bean," a term applied to any code whose instantiation lifecycle is managed by the containing code. In this case there is one instance of the HelloArquillian class in the entire container and it is globally scoped. This code has a method that takes a String array and sets its first element to be the current time.

Finally, we can look at the test case itself, located at src/test/java/net/hudsonlifestyle/HelloArquillianTest.java.

```
package net.hudsonlifestyle;

import javax.inject.Inject;
import org.jboss.arquillian.container.test.api.Deployment;
import org.jboss.arquillian.junit.Arquillian;
import org.jboss.shrinkwrap.api.ShrinkWrap;
import org.jboss.shrinkwrap.api.asset.EmptyAsset;
import org.jboss.shrinkwrap.api.spec.JavaArchive;
import org.junit.Test;
import org.junit.runner.RunWith;
import static org.junit.Assert.assertNotNull;

@RunWith(Arquillian.class)
public class HelloArquillianTest {

    @Deployment
    public static JavaArchive createDeployment() {
        return ShrinkWrap.create(JavaArchive.class)
                .addClass(HelloArquillian.class)
                .addAsManifestResource(EmptyAsset.INSTANCE, "beans.xml");
```

```
    }

    @Inject
    HelloArquillian myHello;

    @Test
    public void testPopulateArray() throws Exception {
        String [] oneElement = new String[1];
        myHello.setFirstElement(oneElement);
        assertNotNull(oneElement[0]);

    }
}
```

It turns out that Arquillian makes use of another JBoss API, called ShrinkWrap, which is a way to do at runtime what the maven-jar-plugin does at build time, namely, create jar files. In this case, the createDeployment() method, which could be called anything but *must* be annotated with the Deployment annotation, creates a JavaArchive with a single class, HelloArquillian, and the META-INF/beans.xml file. Note the @RunWith(Arquillian.class). This is how JUnit asks Arquillian to do whatever container startup and shutdown is required. Because Arquillian itself uses CDI, we can cause the test to be given an instance of the @ApplicationScoped bean HelloArquillian using the @Inject HelloArquillian myHello declaration. Finally, the testPopulateArray() method is annotated with the JUnit @Test annotation.

To add this to Hudson, clone the previous job and point to the new pom.xml HudsonAndAutomatedTesting/02_Arquillian/pom.xml. Adjust the Publish JUnit test result report text field to be **HudsonAndAutomatedTesting/02_Arquillian/target/surefire-reports/TEST*.xml**. The artifact of this build is now a jar file at HudsonAndAutomatedTesting/02_Arquillian/target/*.jar.

Running the job should produce the following among the console output.

```
-------------------------------------------------------
 T E S T S
-------------------------------------------------------
Running net.hudsonlifestyle.HelloArquillianTest
31 [main] INFO org.jboss.weld.Version - WELD-000900 1.1.9 (Final)
Tests run: 1, Failures: 0, Errors: 0, Skipped: 0, Time elapsed: 1.581 sec

Results :

Tests run: 1, Failures: 0, Errors: 0, Skipped: 0
```

Hudson Automated Testing Tips

Let's round out the chapter with some assorted tips for automated testing in Hudson.

Environment Parity

One of the most aggravating circumstances in using Hudson is the scenario in which an automated test passes on a developer workstation, but the same test fails when running under Hudson. This is usually due to a lineup difference between the Hudson server and the developer workstation. There is no easy way to avoid this, but one approach to minimize the chances of this happening is to have the Hudson server and the development environment be entirely inside a virtual machine (VM); that way, one can be assured that the development environment and the Hudson server actually are the *same*. One challenge to achieving this in practice is the fact that developers are most productive when they can customize their environment to their preferences, and these will likely not be the same as what would be on a plain vanilla Hudson server.

Eager or Lazy Failure

The strict agile programming methodology states that a single test failure is just as important as a whole host of test failures. When following this methodology, it makes the most sense to have the build fail on the first failed test. There are occasions when you want to allow the build to continue running and then survey the results at the end, perhaps failing the build if a certain percentage of the tests fail. A parameterized build String parameter can be used to pass in an expected passed test count, and this number can be compared to the actual number of passed tests to fail the build if a certain percentage is not met. The following Apache Ant target can be called from a Hudson Ant builder for this purpose.

The <if> and <math> tags are not part of the default Apache Ant installation. Rather they are provided by the ant-contrib project, which can be downloaded from http://ant-contrib.sourceforge.net/.

```
<target name="assert.expected.passed.test.count">
  <if>
    <isset property="expected.passed.test.count" />
    <then>
<echo>perform the assertion</echo>
      <sequential>
        <property name="test.report.dir"
                  value="${impl.dir}/build/test-reports" />
        <loadfile property="report.summary"
                  srcFile="${test.report.dir}/html/overview-summary.html" />
        <propertyregex property="actual.passed.test.count"
```

```
                      input="${report.summary}"
                      regexp="(?s)(.*)(href=.all-tests.html.>)([0-9]{1,6})
(.*)"
                      select="\3"
       />
       <math result="passed.test.count.difference" datatype="int"
             operation="subtract"
             operand1="${actual.passed.test.count}"
             operand2="${expected.passed.test.count}" />
       <propertyregex property="actual.lessthan.expected"
                      input="${passed.test.count.difference}"
                      regexp="^-.*"
                      replace="actual.lessthan.expected" />
       <fail if="actual.lessthan.expected" status="-1"
             message="
--JOB FAILED!-- Fewer than expected tests passed.  Expected: ${expected.
passed.test.count} Actual: ${actual.passed.test.count}"/>
      </sequential>
    </then>
  </if>
</target>
```

This code loads the overview-summary.html file that is generated by the test report and scrapes it for the numeric value of the number of passed tests. It then subtracts the actual from the expected and if the result is negative, it fails the build.

Failure Discoverability

When a test does fail, it is critically important that developers can quickly and easily discover the identity of the failed test and rerun the test on their workstations, seeing the exact same failure in their development environment. When your test suite starts to scale up to thousands of tests, this can be challenging. One remedy is to continually refactor your tests to be well modularized, having a small number of tests in each module.

Adding New Tests

Finally, because testing requires discipline, it is really important to keep the cost of creating new tests as low as possible. Complexity will cause this cost to want to rise over time, but it is important to invest in keeping it low. The Maven archetype feature is a good remedy for this. With this feature you can create easy test jumpstart projects that can reduce the cost of adding a new test to a simple command-line invocation. Of course, you will have to maintain the archetypes and adapt them as your containing code requirements change, but the return is well worth the investment.

Summary

This chapter defines automated testing as it is commonly practiced using Hudson. The Maven build lifecycle is examined in detail, and this knowledge is applied in an example using Servlet technology. The concept of the software lineup is defined with a view toward Continuous Delivery. A lightweight but useful ontology of testing types is introduced, which bridges to a discussion about the merits and drawbacks of using mock objects. The chapter comes down squarely on the side against mock objects and suggests using JBoss Arquillian instead.

The chapter closes with a brief selection of automated testing tips.

CHAPTER 6

Hudson as Part of Your Tool Suite

While much of the work of configuring Hudson involves plugging stuff into Hudson, this chapter is about how to plug Hudson into other stuff. Specifically, this chapter is about how to configure Integrated Development Environments (IDEs), issue trackers, browsers, and operating system desktop environments for Hudson.

IDE Integration

IDEs have become so accepted in the world of enterprise Java development that it is tempting to forget that they actually do integrate many different things into a single development environment. All IDEs integrate at least a code editor and a debugger, but all of them actually allow the integration of many other kinds of development tools. This section examines how NetBeans, Eclipse, IntelliJ IDEA, and JDeveloper support integration with Hudson. For a primer on NetBeans, please see the section "NetBeans" in Chapter 2.

NetBeans has built-in support for Hudson with no additional plugin required. To get started, make sure your Hudson instance is accessible from the workstation that is running NetBeans. We will use a Hudson instance that has been configured for security as shown in Chapter 3. In NetBeans, go to Window | Services and find the Hudson Builders item. Bring up the context menu by right-clicking on the item and fill in a descriptive name and the Hudson URL. The value for Auto Refresh Every can be left with its default value.

TIP

A value of zero (0) for the Auto Refresh Every setting (or unchecking the check box) will cause NetBeans to only synchronize its display of Hudson data when you request to do so by right-clicking on the Hudson builder node and choosing Synchronize.

NetBeans should create a new node under Hudson Builders and quickly populate it with the jobs from the main dashboard. Interaction with the Hudson instance is via a tree control. Each node in the tree control offers a context or right-click menu with features specific to that node. There is a top-level node in the tree for each Hudson instance connected with NetBeans. Figure 6-1 shows NetBeans configured with one Hudson instance.

To give full access to the secured Hudson instance, open the context menu on the newly created Hudson builder, choose Log In, and enter the required credentials. If the Hudson instance has not been configured for security, this step is not necessary.

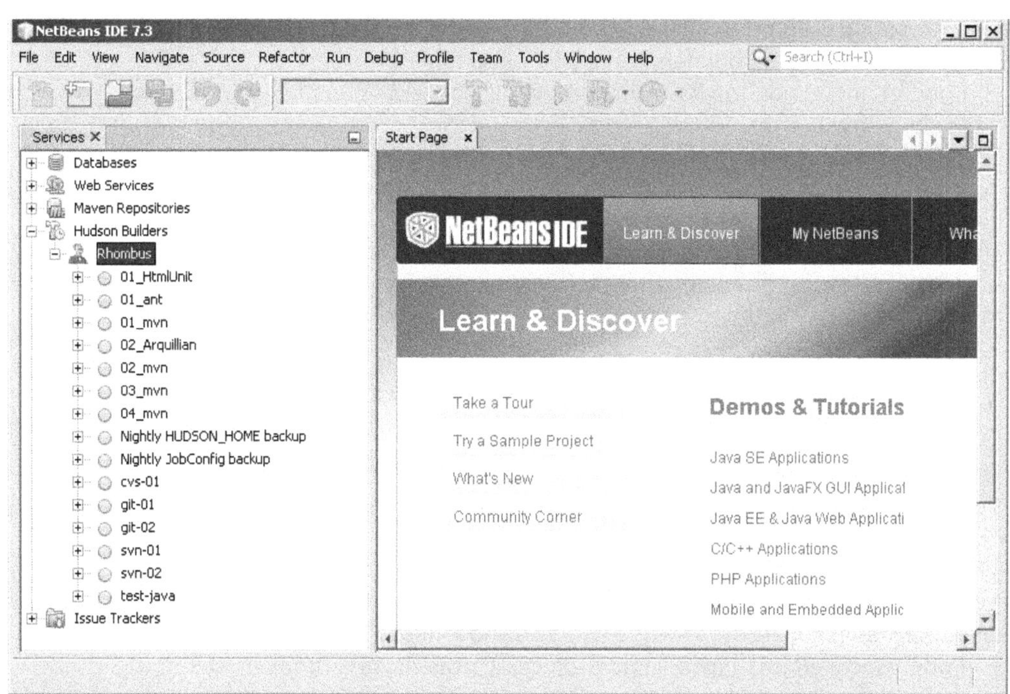

FIGURE 6-1. *NetBeans with Hudson*

The context menu for a Hudson builder will look like this:

If Views have been configured, as described in Chapter 3, the context menu for the builder allows you to only display jobs from a specific view.

New Build is a powerful feature that lets you create a Hudson job from within the IDE, using information gleaned from the IDE project itself. This feature will be explained later in the chapter. Synchronize will manually force NetBeans to poll Hudson and refresh the state of the UI for the builder.

Open in Browser will open the Hudson URL in a browser. Delete will remove the Hudson builder from NetBeans, but no information on the Hudson instance itself will be lost. Deleted builders can easily be re-added.

Properties allows you to view and edit the information you entered when you first added the builder.

Each job in the selected view shows up as a child node under the Hudson builder. The first item in the context menu for a job allows you to start a new build of the job. The Associate With Project button allows you to associate a currently opened NetBeans project with this particular Hudson job. If the project is a Maven project, this will cause text similar to the following to be added to the pom.xml.

```
<ciManagement>
    <system>hudson</system>
    <url>http://rhombus3:7214/job/03_mvn/</url>
</ciManagement>
```

NetBeans will automatically show the Hudson builder for this job when such a project is opened. Other jobs on the same Hudson instance will show up as (not watched). Figure 6-2 shows this arrangement.

The builder will go away when the project is closed. Note that there is the potential for redundancy of Hudson builders in the IDE with this approach because the manually added Hudson instance will also show this job. In general, it is best to use all nonassociated or all associated projects. The associated projects feature is most useful when creating Hudson jobs from projects. Another benefit is the way

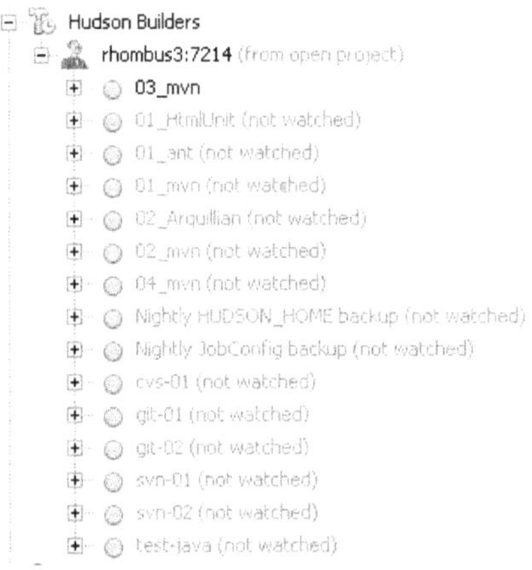

FIGURE 6-2. *Not watched jobs*

output from Hudson static analysis plugins, such as the PMD plugin shown in Chapter 3, is displayed in the Action Items window in NetBeans, as illustrated here.

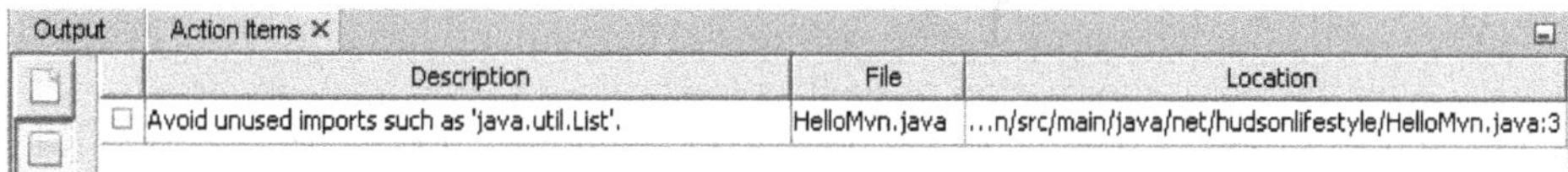

Expanding the node for the job shows nodes for the job's workspace and all of the builds for that job, allowing you to quickly discern the completion status of each. Navigating within the job's workspace from inside NetBeans allows you to open any of the files in the workspace in a read-only mode. If a job has been configured to collect artifacts, these artifacts can be found by drilling down to a specific build within a job, as shown here.

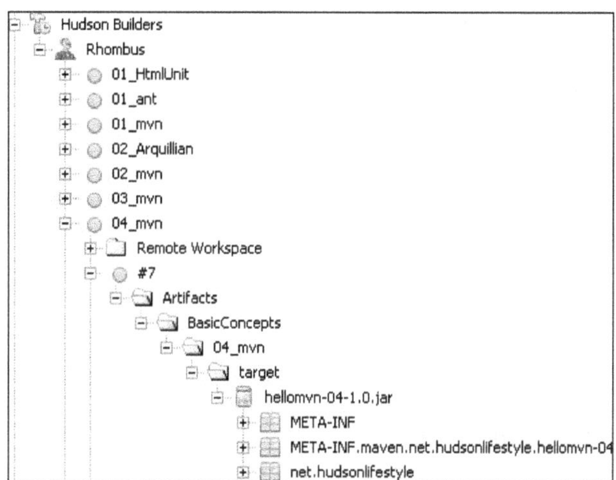

The context menu for each build of a job offers the ability to display the changes and the console log for that build. If the build is currently running, the console output gets updated dynamically as long as that tab is opened. Hudson tracks the former during the SCM interaction of the job by fetching the log messages for each of the revisions to the SCM since the last time the job was run. The latter is the same information you would get from the console output link on the job's dashboard.

Creating a New Hudson Job Directly from a NetBeans Project

If the SCM system of the project is supported by the NetBeans Hudson integration, it is possible to create a new Hudson job directly from the opened project in the IDE. Assuming NetBeans has been connected to a Hudson instance as shown above, choose Team | Create Build Job and select the project in the New Continuous Build dialog that appears. Clicking the Create button will create a new Hudson job and open the browser up to that job's dashboard. Note that you may have to log in again. Opening up the job configuration will reveal that the job has already been populated with the SCM information as well as the builder that invokes the top-level pom.xml. You still must add your own Maven goals. The most useful thing about this feature is that it establishes a clear correlation between what developers do on their workstations and what happens on the Hudson server.

However, New Continuous Build creates a legacy Maven 2/3 project, which is deprecated in Hudson. Build configuration is different than in the free-style jobs you may be used to; in particular, it does not allow multiple build steps. For this reason, you may wish to continue creating free-style jobs in Hudson and connecting NetBeans as described in preceding sections.

Eclipse Hudson Integration

Hudson is integrated with Eclipse via the Mylyn project. This project is the open source offering from Tasktop, which offers Application Lifecycle Management (ALM) products built on top of Eclipse and Mylyn. Tasktop is famous for bringing the so-called "task-focused interface" to the world of enterprise Java development. The key value Mylyn brings to Eclipse is its task-focused workflow, but Mylyn is also the best vehicle for accessing Hudson from within Eclipse. ALM and the task-focused workflow are definitely worth exploring as worthy additions to an enterprise tool suite, but they are beyond the scope of this book. This section will cover how to install and use the Build Server portion of Mylyn, which also supports other CI servers such as Bamboo and Mantis.

Installing Mylyn into Eclipse

Unlike NetBeans, Hudson support is not built into Eclipse; it must be downloaded and installed separately. Start Eclipse and choose the Install New Software item in the Help menu. This will bring up the Install dialog. Click the drop-down menu labeled "Work with." Select the option that includes Mylyn for Eclipse. If it's not present, you can click the Add button and fill in **Mylyn** and **http://download.eclipse.org/mylyn/releases/latest** and click OK. After either selecting the existing Mylyn option, or filling in your own, the middle area of the dialog should populate with the available modules from the site listed in the "Work with" drop-down menu. Use the tree control to expand the Mylyn Integrations item, and check the Mylyn Builds Connector: Hudson/Jenkins check box. Also expand the Mylyn SDKs and Frameworks option and select Mylyn Builds. The other options are useful when using the other features of Mylyn, but they are not pertinent to Hudson integration and will not be discussed here. The dialog should look similar to Figure 6-3.

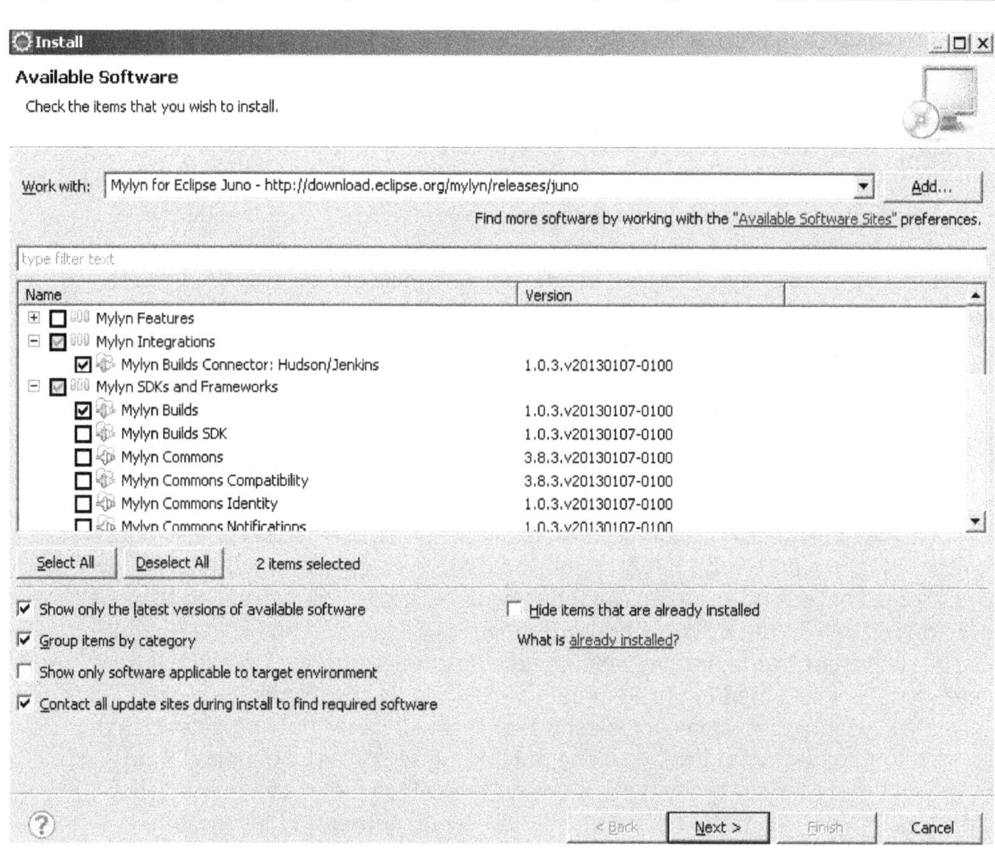

FIGURE 6-3. *Install Available Software dialog*

Click Next and complete the installation process, then click Finish. From the Window menu, choose Show View and then Other. Aside from the first item in the Show View dialog, General, the items are ordered alphabetically. Expand the Mylyn folder and select Builds and click OK. A tab should open that includes the text "No build servers available. Create a build server." Click the link in that text to open the New Repository Select a Wizard dialog. This dialog will take you through the steps of making Eclipse aware of your Hudson instance. Select "Hudson (supports Jenkins)" and click Next. In the Server field enter the URL of your Hudson instance. Enter a descriptive name, such as the Hudson hostname, in the Label field. If the Hudson instance to which you are connecting is secured, uncheck the Anonymous box and fill in the User and Password fields. Click the Validate button in the lower-left corner of the dialog to cause Eclipse to poll the specified Hudson instance. The middle of the dialog should show the list of jobs from the Hudson instance, allowing you to select which ones to monitor. Once configured, the Hudson integration is currently limited to monitoring and starting builds.

IntelliJ IDEA Hudson Integration

IntelliJ IDEA is a popular IDE with the unique distinction that its development has never been controlled or sponsored by a large platform vendor such as Sun (NetBeans), Oracle (JDeveloper), or IBM (Eclipse). As such, it tends to be more inclusive of technologies from across the industry. Unfortunately for Hudson users, due to IntelliJ's focus on its own Continuous Integration product, TeamCity, support for Hudson is limited to build monitoring. This section will describe how to install the Hudson integration into IntelliJ IDEA.

Hudson support is provided via a plugin. IntelliJ plugins come in two styles of distribution: built-in and repository. The former are included with the IDE, but for performance and complexity management reasons it is common to only enable the plugins on an as-needed basis. The latter must be downloaded from a plugin repository. The Hudson Build Monitor is an example of the latter style. To install a repository plugin, start IntelliJ IDEA and observe the Welcome to IntelliJ IDEA dialog. (Some versions may not display the welcome dialog.) The right-hand pane of this dialog is labeled Quick Start. Choose Configure | Plugins to expose the Plugins dialog. If you restart IntelliJ and no welcome dialog appears, choose IntelliJ IDEA | Preferences and select the Plugins item in the list. Click Browse Repositories and change the Category drop-down to select Build. This will cause only plugins related to build technologies to be displayed. The plugins are sorted alphabetically. Find the Hudson Build Monitor entry, right-click and select Download and Install. Click Close. Back in the Plugins dialog, there will now be an entry for Hudson Build Monitor, again in alphabetical order. Make sure the entry is checked and click OK. IntelliJ IDEA must be restarted before the plugin can be used.

Unlike with NetBeans and Eclipse, this plugin operates entirely on a per-project basis; each project may have zero or one Hudson instances associated with it. Therefore, to configure the Hudson Build Monitor, a project must first be opened. Chapter 2 explains how to open Maven projects from IntelliJ IDEA, but any kind of project will do for the purposes of exploring the Hudson Build Monitor plugin. Once a project has been opened, in the File menu, choose Settings, and in the Project Settings area on the left, find the Hudson Build Monitor section. Fill out the values as shown in Figure 6-4. Clicking OK will dismiss the Settings dialog. You should now see a Hudson Jobs icon in the IntelliJ dock on the left side of the IDE. Clicking this icon exposes a tree view where builds can be monitored. Most of the interaction with the jobs is fobbed off to the browser, however.

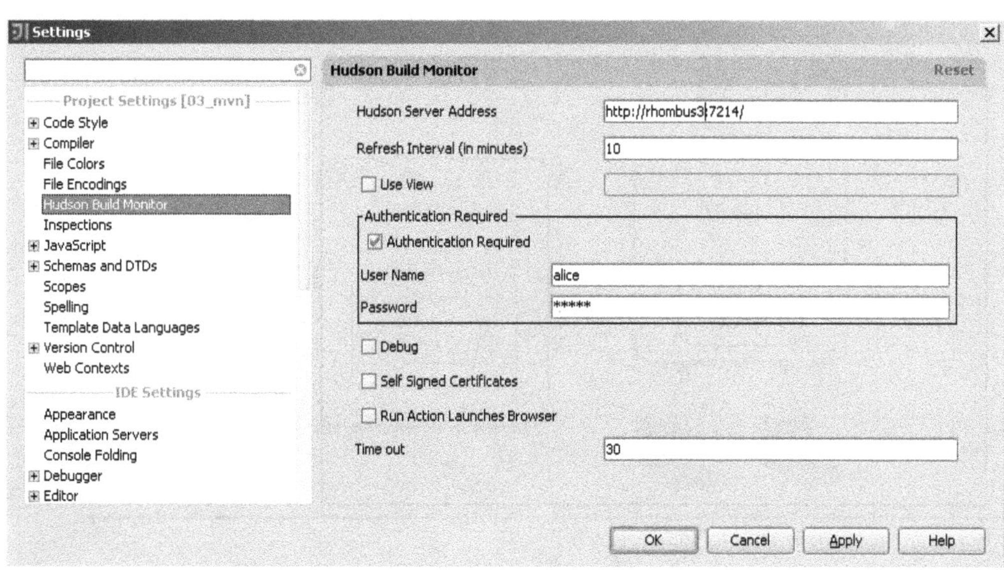

FIGURE 6-4. *IntelliJ IDEA Hudson Build Monitor options*

JDeveloper Hudson Integration

Oracle JDeveloper integrates with Oracle Team Productivity Center (TPC), a full-featured Application Lifecycle Management tool. It is well beyond the scope of this book to cover Team Productivity Center in detail. This section will cover how Hudson integrates with Oracle Team Productivity Center to allow test results to appear in the workflow of JDeveloper. Complete documentation on Team Productivity Center can be reached from the product home page at www.oracle.com/technetwork/developer-tools/tpc/overview/.

Installation Concerns

Team Productivity Center runs as a database-backed Java EE Web application, and as such requires a database and Java EE container. The software is designed to be agnostic to the type of database and EE container, but Oracle XE Database and Oracle WebLogic are guaranteed to work. The installation process for TPC also produces a Hudson plugin, HudsonTpcPlugin.hpi, that allows test results to be collected and delivered to the TPC server, where they are then available to developers using JDeveloper. Figure 6-5 shows a possible arrangement of nodes using TPC with Hudson. TPC has first-class support for software teams, and thus Figure 6-5 shows multiple JDeveloper workstations connecting to the TPC server.

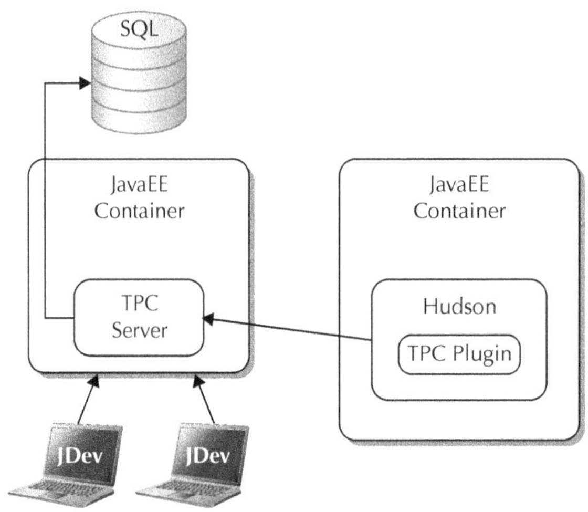

FIGURE 6-5. *System diagram of TPC server*

During the installation process for TPC, you have the option of specifying where the Hudson plugin is written. It is simplest to specify the plugins directory of the Hudson instance. If any other directory was specified, copy the HudsonTpcPlugin.hpi file that was generated by the TPC installation process into the plugins directory of the Hudson instance. Ensure that the TPC server has been installed and is running correctly, and then start or restart Hudson. Configuring the Hudson instance is done on a per-job basis. Visit the configuration page for the job whose test results will be accessible to JDeveloper users and look for the text "Publish test results to Oracle Team Productivity Center." Checking the check box displays a configuration UI where the URL of the Oracle TPC server along with the username and password for publishing results can be provided. The Test Connection button allows verification of the connection. Make sure the check box for Publish JUnit Test Results is checked.

TIP

Even though the check box says JUnit Test Results, more than just JUnit test results can be collected with this technique. Any test technology that conforms to the JUnit test result format can be used, for example HtmlUnit.

The next run of the job will cause the JUnit test results to be captured and sent to JDeveloper.

The final step in the installation of TPC is to connect JDeveloper with the TPC server. In the main JDeveloper UI, open the View menu. Choose Team | Team Navigator and click on the Connect to Team Server icon shown here.

Connect to Team Server

This brings up the Connect to Team Server dialog where you fill in similar values to the ones shown in the Hudson plugin configuration. The only difference might be in the username/password combination. The typical configuration will provision TPC user accounts for each team member on the server, as well as one or more TPC user accounts for Hudson connections. The "Connect when JDeveloper Starts" box can be checked to cause JDeveloper to automatically establish the connection upon startup. This might cause a longer startup time for JDeveloper, so this option should be used with care. Once the connection has been established, the Team Navigator tab appears. The full capabilities of the Team Navigator are covered in the product documentation. The remainder of this section will cover how to explore the JUnit test results collected by the Hudson plugin from within JDeveloper.

Viewing Test Results in JDeveloper

The top of the Team Navigator tab includes two side-by-side drop-down menus. The left one shows the teams available for the current team server connection. The right one offers access to the Build Dashboard tab, which displays the Hudson job test results. This is shown in Figure 6-6. The Branches drop-down menu shows the Hudson jobs for which test results are available. After selecting a job, note the numbers in the left column. These correspond to builds of the currently selected job. Clicking on the

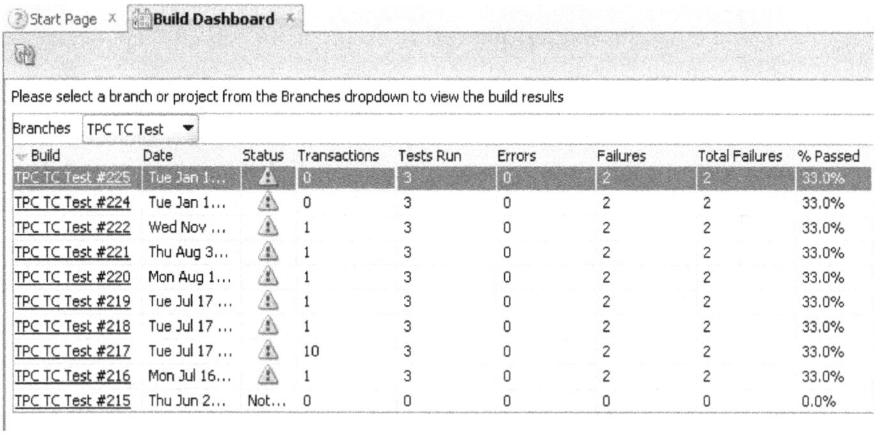

Start Page | Build Dashboard

Please select a branch or project from the Branches dropdown to view the build results

Branches: TPC TC Test

Build	Date	Status	Transactions	Tests Run	Errors	Failures	Total Failures	% Passed
TPC TC Test #225	Tue Jan 1...		0	3	0	2	2	33.0%
TPC TC Test #224	Tue Jan 1...		0	3	0	2	2	33.0%
TPC TC Test #222	Wed Nov ...		1	3	0	2	2	33.0%
TPC TC Test #221	Thu Aug 3...		1	3	0	2	2	33.0%
TPC TC Test #220	Mon Aug 1...		1	3	0	2	2	33.0%
TPC TC Test #219	Tue Jul 17 ...		1	3	0	2	2	33.0%
TPC TC Test #218	Tue Jul 17 ...		1	3	0	2	2	33.0%
TPC TC Test #217	Tue Jul 17 ...		10	3	0	2	2	33.0%
TPC TC Test #216	Mon Jul 16...		1	3	0	2	2	33.0%
TPC TC Test #215	Thu Jun 2...	Not...	0	0	0	0	0	0.0%

FIGURE 6-6 *The JDeveloper TPC Build Dashboard tab*

build number will open a detail tab for that job, which allows you to further interact with the test failure. In a properly configured installation, this dialog can radically decrease the amount of time it takes to find the cause of a test failure, deliver a fix, and verify the correctness of the fix.

Hudson Issue Tracker Integration

In Chapter 3, we saw that the mvn-jxr-plugin–enabled source code files associated with failed tests to be displayed correctly in the Hudson build output. The plugins covered in this section also impact what is shown in the build output. By now it should be clear that a fully productive Hudson instance is one that is configured to be well integrated with all the aspects of your software development lifecycle.

Atlassian JIRA Integration

JIRA is a popular commercial Web-based issue-tracking software. Many open source projects get a gratis license from JIRA because of the liberal marketing policies of its maker, Atlassian. The Hudson JIRA plugin is available from the Recommended subtab of the Available tab of the Hudson Plugin Manager. For an introduction to this key feature of Hudson, see Chapter 3. Once the Hudson JIRA plugin has been installed and Hudson has restarted, visit the Manage Hudson page from the main dashboard, then click Configure System. Find the section labeled JIRA and click the Add button. For the basic level of integration, just fill in the URL of the top-level JIRA instance. If the integration is successful, JIRA issues mentioned in commit log messages will show up as hyperlinks to the issue in JIRA, as shown here.

Changes

1. Test that JAVASERVERFACES-1826 is a link to the java.net JIRA (detail)

A more complete filling out of the configuration, with username and password, will enable Hudson to make comments on issues as a result of the completion status of builds that include a hyperlink to the Hudson job that impacts that issue. This must be configured as a two-step process. First, the username and password must be correctly filled out in the Configure System page. Click the Validate button to test the connection. Second, within each job for which you want this feature activated, find the Post-build Actions section and check the check box next to the text "Updated relevant JIRA issues."

Bugzilla Integration

Bugzilla is another common Web-based issue tracker, which started life alongside the world's first Continuous Integration software, Tinderbox. Both Tinderbox and Bugzilla were pioneering projects in the open source movement from the Mozilla project. Bugzilla–Hudson integration is configured just like the JIRA integration, but the plugin is located in the Others subtab of the Available tab of the Hudson Plugin Manager.

Other Issue Trackers

Hudson also offers integration to Mantis, Trac, and Backlog, all of which have a similar base level of integration with occasionally deeper features as well.

Browser and Desktop Integration

Once Hudson becomes a part of your software development tool suite, it is natural to want to be able to access it from the tools most used by the collaborators in the software development process. IDE integration covers the actual software developers, but there are many other kinds of collaborators in the process of building software, and many of them never use IDEs. For example, designers and technical writers might want to be notified of Hudson status in their Web browsers or via a desktop widget. This section explores some options for browser, desktop, and mobile Hudson integration. All of them take advantage of Hudson's usage of RSS.

TIP

Throughout the Hudson UI are so-called "RSS links." Rich Site Summary (also known as RDF Site Summary or Really Simple Syndication), or RSS for short, is a technology for delivering notifications using a pull-based model. In a pull-based system, the party desiring the notification manually asks to be updated rather than the notification always being pushed to the party whether they want it or not.

Browser Integration

The Web browser is the least-common-denominator UI software, and as such, people tend to spend a lot of time using browsers.

Firefox

Firefox plugins are called "add-ons" because they add functionality on to the base Firefox instance.

There is an add-on for Firefox that monitors Hudson and Jenkins builds. The plugin started out under the name "Hudson Build Monitor" and has since changed its name to "Jenkins Build Monitor," but it still works with Hudson. To install the add-on, visit https://addons.mozilla.org/ from within Firefox and type **Jenkins Build**

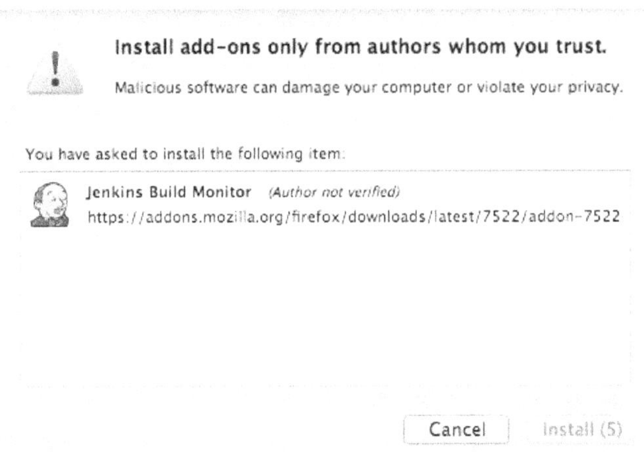

FIGURE 6-7. *Installing the Jenkins add-on*

Monitor into the search box. If more than one match appears, make sure to click the Add to Firefox button next to the one labeled exactly "Jenkins Build Monitor." Clicking the button will cause Firefox to display a dialog similar to the one shown in Figure 6-7.

As with Hudson plugins, Firefox add-ons require restarting the software in/on which you have plugged/added. After doing so, ensure that the Firefox Add-on bar is displayed by selecting Add-on Bar in the View | Toolbars menu. Visit the Hudson instance you wish to monitor in Firefox, and find the job page for the job you wish to monitor. At the bottom of the Build History section are two links labeled "for all" and "for failures."

Open the context menu on the "for all" or "for failures" link. The former is an RSS feed that contains items for all builds of that job, the latter only for failures. If the Firefox Jenkins Build Monitor add-on is installed correctly, the Add Link To Jenkins Build Monitor item should appear. This item is shown in Figure 6-8. Selecting the item causes the build to be placed in the add-on bar. This will give the status of the build. Clicking the build in the add-on bar shows the job history. Clicking each link in the job history creates a new tab with the corresponding job page. The context menu for the build in the add-on bar offers options for starting new builds, and for removing this job from the add-on bar. If the Hudson instance is secured, the Firefox Jenkins Build Monitor may be configured with the credentials by opening the context menu on the Jenkins icon in the add-on bar, selecting Preferences, and visiting the Network tab.

FIGURE 6-8. *The Add Link To Jenkins Build Monitor context menu option*

Chrome

Google Chrome plugins are called "extensions" and they can be obtained by visiting the Chrome Web Store from within the Google Chrome browser. Visit http://chrome.google.com/webstore/ and type **Hudson Monitor** into the search box. If multiple hits are found, the one from Henning Hoefer is the one discussed in this section. Click the + ADD TO CHROME button and click Add in the dialog that appears. Unlike Firefox, this does not require a restart. You should immediately see a Hudson icon appear next to your URL bar. Open the context menu on the Hudson icon and select Options. This opens a very simple panel where you can fill in the URL of the Hudson instance, the polling interval, the credentials, and some options relating to the display of jobs. Clicking on the Hudson icon will pop up a panel with all the jobs, their status, and a link to each job. Clicking a link will simply open a new tab and load that job in the tab. Figure 6-9 shows the Hudson Monitor Chrome Extension from Henning Hoefer.

Desktop Integration

For those who prefer to use the desktop operating system as their notification hub, there are a few options for Windows, Mac, and GNU/Linux platforms.

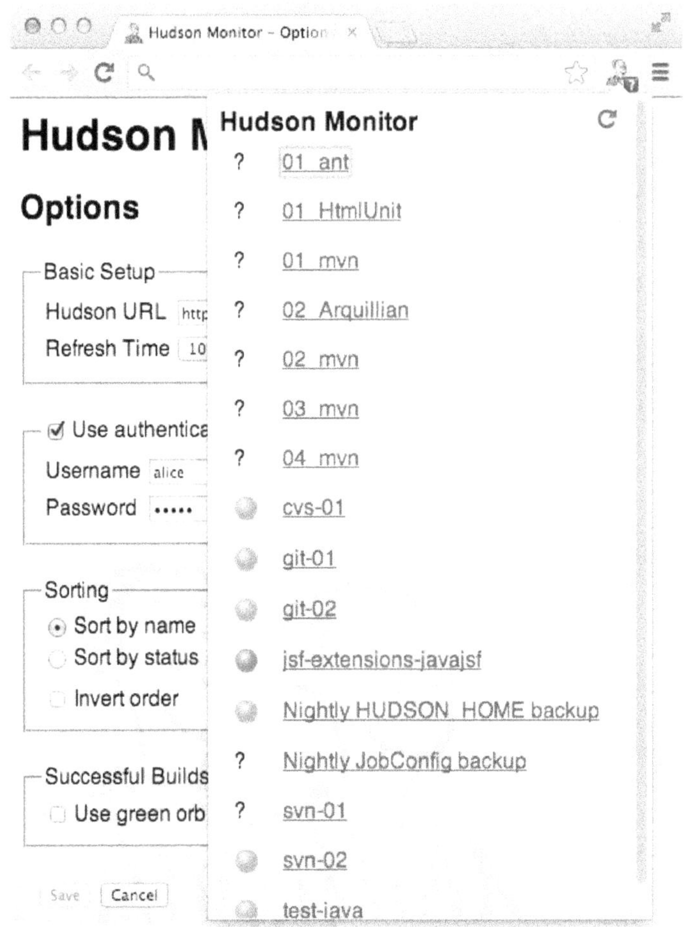

FIGURE 6-9. *Chrome Extension*

Microsoft Windows

The Hudson development community has provided a Windows Sidebar Gadget that can be configured to track an arbitrary number of Hudson jobs. Visit http://code.google.com/p/hudsonmonitor and download the hudson.gadget file. This is an executable file on Windows Vista and later and should automatically install the gadget when double-clicked. Click on the Hudson gadget and then click on the wrench icon to open the settings for the gadget. As of this writing, the authentication feature did not work with Hudson 3.0.1, so this gadget only works with Hudson instances for which security has not been enabled.

Unlike other notification solutions, the hudsonmonitor gadget requires you to manually add each Hudson project you want to show in the gadget one at a time. Only projects added in this way are visible. Fill in the URL to the Hudson instance and click the Get Projects button. This will populate the Projects drop-down with the list of projects on the specified Hudson instance. Select the project you wish to monitor and click Add Project. You can add multiple projects from the same Hudson instance by selecting each project and clicking Add Project for each. Click OK to dismiss the configuration dialog. Repeat this step with all the Hudson projects you wish to monitor, even from those different Hudson instances. Figure 6-10 shows the configuration dialog for hudsonmonitor.

Mac OS X, GNU/Linux

An alternative to hudsonmonitor is the Java-based hudsonTracker. This cross-platform solution is distributed as a Mac OS X .dmg file, a Microsoft Windows .exe file, and a shell script for GNU/Linux. The software may be downloaded from http://hudsontracker.sourceforge.net/. Once the software has been installed and started, an icon with the characters "hT" should appear in your system tray (on Windows) or menu bar (on Mac

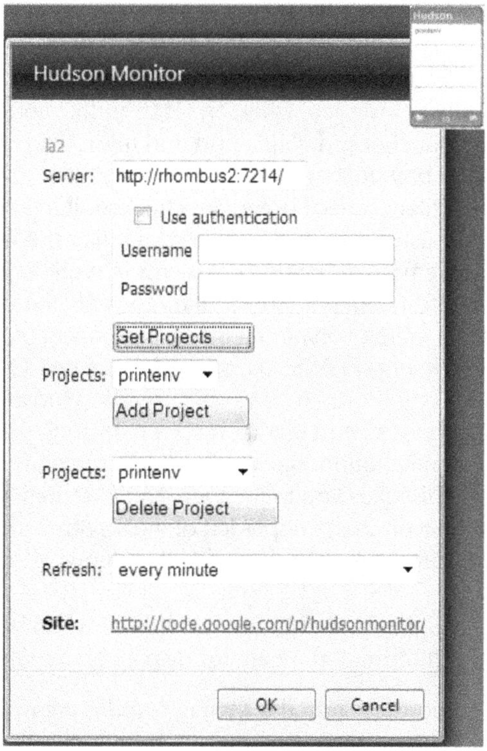

FIGURE 6-10. *Hudsonmonitor Windows gadget*

OS X and GNU/Linux). Click on the hT icon and select Configure to see the panel where the Hudson URL can be filled in. The URL can be any Hudson RSS URL. Unfortunately, hudsonTracker doesn't seem to work with Hudson 3.0.1 authentication, so, as with hudson.gadget. it's necessary to use it with only unauthenticated Hudson instances. Once hudsonTracker has been configured, clicking the hT icon shows a list of all the jobs from that Hudson RSS URL.

Mobile Integration

No treatment of Hudson notification schemes would be complete without covering how to use Hudson from Android and iOS smart phones.

The Google Play Store and iTunes AppStore contain several apps for Hudson, but the one this section covers is called JenkinsMobi. As the name suggests, it can access multiple Jenkins and Hudson instances. This full-featured app offers very extensive coverage of what you can do with an existing Hudson instance once it has been configured as desired. Install the app from the Play Store or iTunes App Store and open the app. The app comes preconfigured with access to a Hudson instance associated with the development of the app itself. Click the Settings button in the lower-left hand corner of the screen to bring up the Configuration Instances pane. Click the plus icon to enter the information for a new Hudson instance. Because it is common to use the app to track multiple Hudson instances, fill in a useful description as the first field. The value entered here will show up on the first page in the app. Fill in the remainder of the fields appropriate to each Hudson instance to be monitored. Click on Host and fill in the hostname of your Hudson instance. Click on "Path suffix" and remove the existing value. Leave HTTP/S unchecked. Click port and fill in the port value. For Hudson 3.0.1, leave the XPath box unchecked. Make sure both the Override Hudson URL and "Use XSLT for xml artifact" check boxes are checked. If the Hudson instance has authentication, fill in the username and password. Unlike the browser and desktop-based notification schemes, authentication seems to work with Hudson Mobi and Hudson 3.0.1. Click the "Test configuration" button to verify the configuration is correct. If so, you should see a dialog containing the text "Connection test PASSED, Login test PASSED, Retrieve view test PASSED," on Android. On iOS, this text is "Connection: SUCCEEDED, Login: OK, Hudson version: OK, Hudson view: OK." Click Back or click Done to leave the configuration screen, making sure to say yes when prompted to save the configuration. Back on the main screen for JenkinsMobi, select one Hudson instance. This takes you to the View Detail screen for the selected Hudson instance. Click on the icon in the upper left of the screen with the nine boxes to see what the app offers. At press time, this included the following options.

- **Views** Shows the same information one would see when browsing the Hudson Views tab, but formatted nicely for display on a mobile device.
- **Nodes** Shows the information in the Manage Nodes area of Hudson.
- **Queue** Shows the jobs currently executing on this instance.

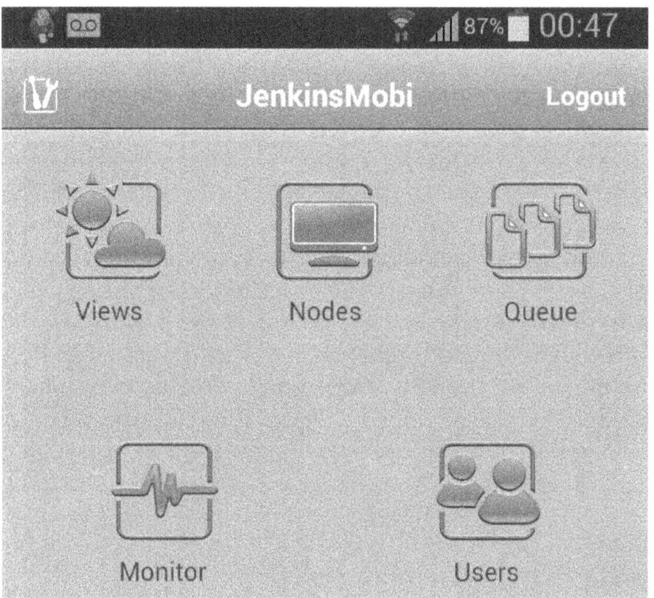

FIGURE 6-11. *Jenkins Mobi Android*

- **Monitor** Allows adding one or more specific jobs to monitor. This essentially gives you the ability to do what a view does with respect to only showing a subset of the jobs available on a Hudson instance, but does not create any view-specific information on the server. This can be useful if you don't have the administrative permissions necessary to create a view.
- **Users** Allows browsing information for the set of user accounts known to the selected Hudson instance.

The main view for the configured Hudson Mobi on Android is shown in Figure 6-11.

Publishing Build Artifacts from Hudson

Another dimension of using Hudson as part of your tool suite is the ability to publish build artifacts directly from Hudson to other tools in the tool suite. Hudson offers plugins that enable publishing build artifacts at several different levels of structure. At the highest level of structure is the ability to publish artifacts to a proper "artifact repository." At the other extreme of structure is the ability to publish artifacts to any FTP server. The choice of which plugin to use depends entirely on the software development environment and the tool suite used therein.

Artifact Repository

The rise of the "artifact repository" as an identifiable single tool in the software development tool suite coincided with the rise of Maven. This is not surprising since artifact management is arguably the most important feature of Maven. The things that a Maven build produces are called "artifacts." Artifacts are stored in an "artifact repository," and with Maven there are two kinds of repository: local and remote. When building software, Maven discovers what other artifacts are needed to build the current project and downloads them from any number of remote repositories to the local repository, from whence other tools such as compilers and linkers can use them. The local repository is really just a special directory on a disk to which Maven downloads artifacts from remote repositories. You can think of it as Maven's version of your browser's Downloads directory. Of course, Maven has a special subdirectory layout that it uses for the local repository. In addition to downloading artifacts from remote repositories, Maven can also upload artifacts. There is a special phase of the Maven build lifecycle dedicated to this process: deploy. You can read more about the Maven build lifecycle in Chapter 5.

Where to Encode the Deployment Logic?

The decision of where to describe, in an executable fashion, the process of deploying to remote repositories is a matter of taste. The most common approach is to encode this description in the build logic that produces the artifact itself, for example in the pom.xml. Another approach, explained here, is to encode the description within a Hudson job. This is another instance of the "centralized versus distributed" choice for configuration information. Putting the artifact deployment logic into the build, such as in a pom.xml, tends toward distributed configuration information, while putting it in the Hudson job tends toward centralized configuration information. In practice, the distributed option gives much greater control because the task of deployment is kept close to the software doing the building (such as Maven) rather than the software that calls the software that does the building (Hudson). One compromise is to use the Maven "parent pom" concept to keep the deployment logic out of the individual leaf nodes of the build, but this level of competency of Maven can be difficult to achieve and maintain.

At this writing, there are three popular artifact repositories: JFrog Artifactory, Sonatype Nexus, and Apache Archiva. All three have gratis downloads and all three are based on open source software in some fashion. The first two also have commercial offerings with paid support. This section describes JFrog Artifactory because it is the only one of the three that offers a Hudson plugin. The other two rely entirely on letting the build system handle the artifact deployment.

First, download and install Artifactory from http://jfrog.org/. Follow the installation instructions for the simple default installation. Artifactory is based on Tomcat. Artifactory configuration is beyond the scope of this book, but the product is well documented and there is sufficient Web search content available to answer most common questions. Make sure Artifactory is running before starting Hudson.

The Artifactory plugin is available in the Recommended subtab of the Available tab in the Hudson Plugin Center. Please see Chapter 3 for instructions on installing plugins. Once the Artifactory plugin has been installed, configuration is done in two phases: Hudson instance level and job level.

Per–Hudson Instance Artifactory Configuration

For the configuration at the Hudson instance level, visit the Manage Hudson page and then the Configure System page. Find the section with the header Artifactory. Click the Add button to display a dialog for adding one or more Artifactory instances. Type into the URL field the same main URL for Artifactory as you would use to access the Artifactory Web interface. When the cursor leaves the field, Hudson will attempt to validate the correctness of the Artifactory installation and should display a message such as "Found Artifactory 3.0.0." If this message is not displayed, or an error message is displayed, please ensure that Artifactory is running and can be accessed from the same host on which Hudson is running.

TIP

Real-world Continuous Deployment environments span many different host computers. It's important to have competence in network administration because the entire configuration of Hudson requires hard-coding hostnames and port numbers. It may be advisable to include DNS configuration as part of your Continuous Deployment software lineup.

Type in the user name and password of the Artifactory default deployer. By default, these are **admin** and **password**, but these values can be changed in the Artifactory configuration. The completed Hudson instance configuration is shown in Figure 6-12.

Because it is perfectly reasonable to have one Hudson instance push to multiple Artifactory servers, it is possible to add additional Artifactory servers using this same method.

Make sure to save the configuration when done.

Per-Job Artifactory Configuration

Now, for each job that is to publish artifacts to Artifactory, additional configuration must be done. In the Configure page for the job, search for the text "Artifactory Integration." There are several check boxes pertaining to Artifactory. Because this

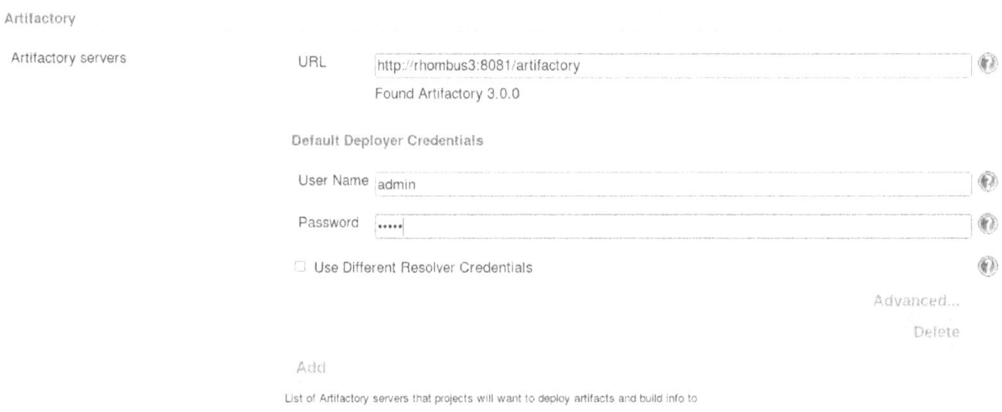

FIGURE 6-12. *Per–Hudson instance Artifactory configuration*

book has focused mainly on Maven, check the one labeled Maven3-Artifactory Integration. This will display the Artifactory Configuration panel. Choose the desired Artifactory server that had been configured in the per–Hudson instance configuration. Leave the "Target releases repository" and "Target snapshots repository" menus with their default values. These values select which of the many repositories within a given Artifactory instance should be used to hold the artifacts. Leave the "Override default deployer credentials" box unchecked. This box allows you to customize the username and password under which the artifacts are deployed. If these boxes are unchecked, the values from the per–Hudson instance configuration are used. For Include Patterns, use the same value as for the "Archive the artifacts" dialog, for any job that publishes build artifacts as downloadable files from Hudson. The remaining values can be left at their defaults. The next time this build runs, the result will be published to Artifactory.

Now, for each job that is to publish artifacts to Artifactory, additional configuration must be done. In the Configure page for the job, search for the text "Artifactory Integration." There are several check boxes pertaining to Artifactory. Check the one labeled Generic-Artifactory Integration. This will display the Artifactory Configuration panel. Choose the desired Artifactory server that had been configured in the per–Hudson instance configuration. Select the Target Repository or leave the default value, for example, **libs-release-local**. These values select which of the many repositories within a given Artifactory instance should be used to hold the artifacts. Leave the "Override default deployer credentials" box unchecked. This box allows you to customize the username and password under which the artifacts are deployed. If unchecked, the values from the per–Hudson instance configuration are used.

For Published Artifacts, use a file path pattern relative to the workspace, for example, **target/*.jar**. The remaining values can be left at their defaults. The next time this build runs, the result will be published to Artifactory. You can verify this by checking the build Console Output. There will be one or more "Deploying artifact" messages. In your Artifactory server, click the Artifacts tab and click the arrow beside the artifact name you configured in Hudson to reveal your deployed artifact.

Deploy to Container

Chapter 5 introduced the distinction between containing code and code under test. The former is the software in which the latter runs during whatever testing is being performed. In Chapter 4, the build system was used to install the code under test into the containing code. The Deploy to Container plugin can accomplish the same thing for those jobs whose build artifacts are JavaEE war or ear files. The plugin supports GlassFish, JBoss, and Tomcat servers. For each server, some administrative action must be taken to ensure that the plugin is able to deploy the artifact. This example covers the necessary action for Tomcat 7.x. In the conf/tomcat-users.xml file, ensure that the following XML is present.

```
<role rolename="manager-script" />
<role rolename="manager-gui" />
<user username="tomcat" password="tomcat" roles="manage-script,manager-gui" />
```

Obviously, a different value for username and password can be used, and the user may have additional roles than manage-script. The manage-script role is necessary for the Deploy to Container plugin to work. The manager-gui role is not necessary for the Deploy to Container plugin to work, but it is useful to be able to use the manager GUI to verify that deployment was successful and to obtain the correct URL for the Hudson plugin configuration. Ensure that Tomcat has started and visit the manager GUI, by default at http://<hostname>:8080/manager/.

Back in Hudson, the plugin is available from the Recommended subtab of the Available tab of the Hudson Plugin Center. Once the plugin has been installed and after Hudson is restarted, visit the configuration page for the job whose artifacts are to be deployed to the running container. Configuration for this plugin is entirely on a per-job basis. There is no per–Hudson instance configuration. Search for the text "Deploy war/ear to a container" and check the check box. In the "WAR/EAR files" box, identify a *single* war or ear file. Even though the box is labeled *files,* the system can only handle one war/ear file because there is only one "Context path" value. In the "Context path" box, fill in the context path at which the war/ear file is to be deployed. Because we have prepared for Tomcat, choose Tomcat 7.x. Fill in the manager user name, manager password, and, most importantly, the URL for the manager GUI corresponding to the Tomcat 7.x instance. The "Deploy on failure" check box controls whether or not a failed build causes the artifact to be deployed. In most cases, this should be left unchecked.

FTP Publisher Plugin

The least structured, but most flexible deployment option is the FTP Publisher Plugin. This plugin relies on the old but reliable File Transfer Protocol. It does not support secure FTP. The plugin is available in the Recommended subtab of the Available tab in the Plugin Center. Once the plugin has been installed and after a Hudson restart, configuration must be done per–Hudson instance and also per job.

Per–Hudson Instance Configuration

The per–Hudson instance configuration defines one or more FTP servers so that each job can deploy artifacts to any of them. In the Configure System page, find the text "FTP repository hosts." Click the Add button and fill in a name in the Profile Name text field. This is the value by which this particular FTP site will be made available in the per-job configuration. Fill in the hostname field with the expected hostname. The port value must be filled in, and the value **21** is used in most cases. A timeout value can be supplied that will cause the build to fail once the value has elapsed without the file transfer completing. The value is specified in milliseconds.

The Root Repository Path value is the directory path relative to the home directory of the FTP server. This directory path must exist on the server; it will not be created automatically. Finally, username and password values must be supplied. Because the entire purpose of this plugin is to upload artifacts, it is highly unusual for anonymous FTP to be used; therefore, no special provision is made for anonymous FTP. The "Flatten Files selected by default" check box provides a default value to a setting that is also configurable in the per-job configuration. Make sure to save the configuration.

Per-Job Configuration

In the job configuration page, find the text "Publish Artifacts to FTP" and check the check box. In the FTP site menu, select the desired site configured in the per–Hudson instance configuration. In the Source text field, fill in a value similar to the one entered in the "Archive the artifacts" text field; however, it is valid for this value to refer to a directory or a file. If it refers to a directory, the directory tree is transferred recursively. The Destination field can be left blank, but can be used if the item to be transferred should be renamed. Note that both source and destination must refer to the same kind of item, either both directory or both file. "Use timestamps" will cause a top-level directory to be created to store the items. The name of the top-level directory will be a timestamp of the form 2013-05-01_18-43-53. This easily allows for the same artifact to be published arbitrarily many times without having to overwrite previous iterations. "Flatten files" will cause any intervening directories in the Source text file to be omitted, putting the resultant file or leaf directory directly in the root as specified in the per–Hudson instance configuration. Finally, the "Skip publishing" check box enables temporarily disabling the publishing step without altering any of the configuration.

Summary

This chapter explains how Hudson can plug into other tools such as IDEs, issue trackers, and user environments such as desktops and mobile devices. The chapter closes with a brief treatment of how to publish Hudson build artifacts to other software systems.

The state of the art of Hudson integration into NetBeans, Eclipse, IntelliJ, and Oracle JDeveloper is surveyed. Atlassian JIRA and Bugzilla are shown to be capable of integrating Hudson. Because most of what Hudson does happens asynchronously, notification of build results is an important feature. Chapter 3 introduced build notifiers for this purpose. This chapter covers another way to accomplish the same thing: having Hudson plug into the software that people sit in front of all day, such as Web browsers, desktops, and mobile devices.

After automated testing, arguably the most important feature of Hudson is what is done with build artifacts. Three techniques are explored to address this: JFrog Artifactory, the Deploy to Container plugin, and the FTP Publisher plugin.

CHAPTER 7

Distributed Building Using Hudson

In the previous chapters, we explored how to install, run, and set up Hudson for CI practice. We also discussed that the best way to achieve build steps from Continuous Integration to Continuous Delivery is properly setting up the building of your software units along with different testing environments in a pipeline of builds. This leads to an increase in number of jobs. Often, the branches in the build pipeline can be executed in a distributed fashion. Hudson supports distributed building of multiple software projects, or buildable units of a single software project maintained by various software teams. In this chapter, we will explore how to set up Hudson for the master-slave mode of operation for distributed building.

Master-Slave Mode

If you are installing Hudson for the first time and have it configured to run jobs, then you are most likely running Hudson in a "master only" mode. In this mode, Hudson builds all of your jobs in the same machine where Hudson is installed. For a small number of jobs that do not require intensive computer power, this arrangement might work. However, often this may not be the case. The machine where Hudson is installed may not scale well to build numerous jobs scheduled based on various Continuous Integration schemes. To alleviate the problem, Hudson offers another more flexible mode of operation called the *master-slave mode* (see the following illustration).

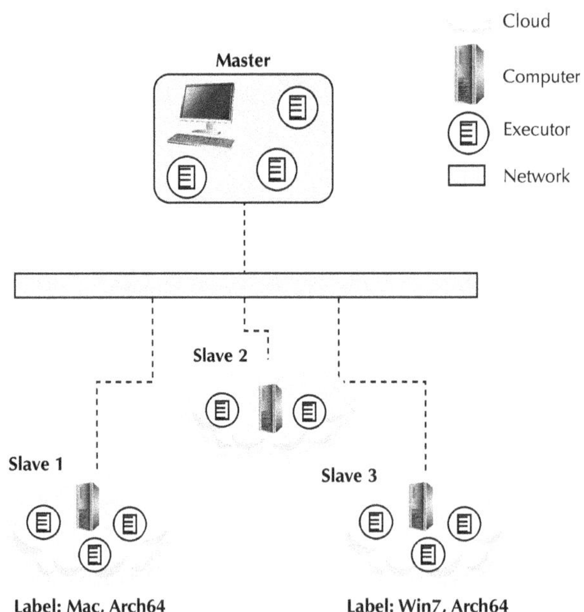

When reading this chapter, you will want to be aware of the following nomenclatures:

- **Master** A full-fledged Hudson server running on a machine. It can do builds of its own or request a slave to do the build. Some of the responsibilities of a master are scheduling job builds, communicating with slaves to execute job builds based on its capabilities, and monitoring the slaves. It is also responsible for providing the UI for user interaction and presenting the build results.
- **Slave Agent** An agent running on a different machine (or on the same machine), which builds on behalf of the master. A slave can live anywhere in the cloud as long as it is accessible to the master via a TCP/IP connection. A slave cannot do anything by itself. Although technically you can install an agent on the same machine as the master, we recommend installing it on a different machine for the sake of better performance of the master.
- **Slave** A machine running the slave agent.
- **Node** A generic term to refer a master or a slave.
- **Executor** A thread that does the actual run of the build. Master or slave can have multiple executors. Each executor can perform a job build in parallel to the execution of a build by another executor. As a rule of thumb, the number of executors is equivalent to the number of CPUs or the number of cores in each CPU of a machine where the master or slave is running. If the value is set to 0, then no job will be executed on that node. This is especially useful if you want to execute all of your jobs only in the slaves and not in the master.
- **Label** A space-separated list of strings provided by a slave to advertise its capabilities, environment, and architecture. It is a powerful mechanism to strategize the build distribution, as explained later in the chapter.
- **Build Grid** A Hudson build system, composed of the master and a "farm" of slaves, set up to do builds of jobs in a grid-like architecture. The build grid is an effective way to share the load across multiple machines or run builds of a single job in different environments, which dramatically improves the capacity of the CI environment.

Hudson Slaves

Slaves are computers (a physical machine or a virtual machine) that are set up to build jobs for a Hudson master. Slave machines run a separate program called slave agent.

The slave agent and Hudson master need to establish a bidirectional byte stream, for example, a TCP/IP socket, to do business together. For security reasons, the origination of the slave agent is always from the Hudson master. In order to start communication between the master and slave, the slave agent requires a key that is unique for every Hudson master. The origination of the slave agent must be from the same Hudson master in order for this key to be correct. When the slave agent is started, it tries to create an HTTP connection to the master by inputting the secret key in the header. The Hudson master responds with a port number. The slave agent then requests a secure socket connection using that port number and the secret key as the credentials. If the connection is accepted, a secure communication channel is established between master and slave.

The slave agent is automatically installed in the slave home directory, although the slave agent can be installed into any directory. The slave agent stores all related data under this directory. While the build steps are being executed in the slave, the slave agent sends all the log messages, test reports, code, and coverage results to the Hudson master on the fly, so you can monitor the build process in real time. After finishing the build, the slave agent sends the build artifacts, such as the installers, jar files, war files, reports, and log files, based on the job configuration, to the Hudson master. These will be available at the master for download.

When slave nodes are added to a master, it automatically starts distributing jobs to slaves. The exact distribution behavior depends on the configuration of each job. The job may be configured to build on a particular slave or a particular type of slave. If not specifically configured, Hudson will pick the next available, suitable slave and build there.

Slave Provisioning

Slave nodes require three levels of provisioning:

- **VM or hardware provisioning** Create a virtual machine, as in cloud provisioning, or bring hardware online. Install the operating system and basic operating software in an OS-dependent manner. Configure the network and provide a unique network address, and so on.
- **Hudson provisioning** Install the software necessary to communicate with the Hudson master. Hudson does this automatically when it connects to a slave node. Hudson can also automatically install certain software tools required by the build in most cases.

- **Tools provisioning** Install the software tools necessary to run Hudson jobs on the slave. Which tools must be installed depends on the jobs. For instance, if a job checks out from the Git repository, Git must be installed on the slave. If a job builds with Maven, Maven must be installed. This kind of provisioning must be done from the slave. It is easy to discover when it is necessary; try to run a job on the slave. If the slave is not adequately provisioned, the job will fail with an error message suggesting the problem. For example, "Error performing command: /usr/local/git/bin/git…" indicates that Hudson did not find Git where it expected. Either Git is not installed on the slave, or it was installed by a tool such as apt-get that did not create the path /usr/local/git/bin/git.

As a counterpart to provisioning, jobs must be configured so that they will run in the slave environment. For example, build steps cannot run UNIX commands on Windows slaves, or vice versa. If a slave is behind a firewall, the job must be configured with correct proxy information to allow HTTP communications with SCM or archive server software, and so on. Matching jobs to slave characteristics is a complex, multidimensional problem. This is one reason Labels (discussed later in this chapter) are so important; they provide a simple way to restrict jobs to slaves they are able to run on.

Types of Slaves

There are three types of slaves based on how the slave agent is started and managed. A particular type of slave is used depending on the availability of hardware and the environment. For example, on a Windows machine, if Hudson does have an opportunity to manage the slave using SSH, then the slave can be provisioned as an unmanaged slave and later can be set up to start with the OS via Windows service technology as explained later in the section.

Managed Slaves

The slave agent of the managed slaves is always under the control of the Hudson master. The master is responsible for copying the slave agent to the slave machine and starting it. If the slave agent dies by any chance, Hudson restarts it when its services are required. Most of the managed slaves are available via plugins such SSH Slaves and Windows Slaves, to name a few. Later in this chapter, we will explore the installation and building of a job using SSH-based managed slaves.

Unmanaged Slaves

In the case of unmanaged slaves, the slave agent must be started and managed by the Hudson administrator. Since the Hudson master does not manage it, if it dies, the administrator must manually restart it. A typical example of unmanaged slaves is the slave agent launched via JNLP, which we will explore later in this chapter.

Cloud Slaves

By default, Hudson allows you to create regular slaves. Since these regular slaves are created on passive machines, the slaves are not created in a cloud-like, active environment. As the name suggests, the slave agent of a cloud slave does live in the cloud environment, and the cloud slaves are provisioned on demand. These can also be deleted and provisioned again based on the build demand. The Hudson master can automatically provision the cloud slaves, similar to the managed slaves. EC2, VMware, and VirtualBox slaves are all examples of cloud slaves. Hudson can provision slaves in several cloud software stacks, like Amazon EC2, GoGrid, Ninefold, vCloud, OpenStack, and Azure through the JCloud API.[1]

Adding a Slave Node to Hudson

To add any type of slave to Hudson, you must first create a slave node, then configure it to specify how the slave will be managed. To create a slave node, go to the Manage Hudson page, and click the Manage Nodes link. This brings up the Nodes Status page as shown in Figure 7-1.

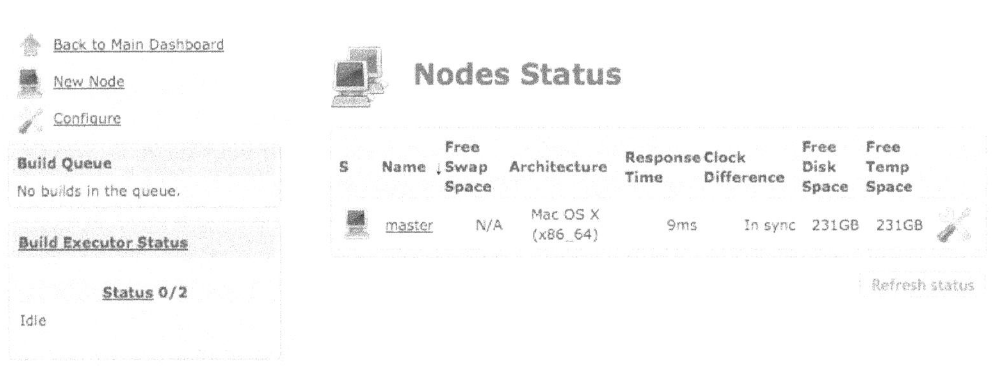

FIGURE 7-1. *Nodes Status page*

[1] JCloud. http://www.jclouds.org/

New Node
Node name
fedora-17-func-test-slave
Regular Slave
Adds a plain, regular slave to Hudson. This is called "regular" because Hudson does not provide higher level of integration with these slaves, such as dynamic provisioning. Select this type if no other slave types apply — for example such as when you are adding a physical computer, virtual machines managed outside Hudson, etc.
OK

FIGURE 7-2. *Create New Slave Node*

Click the New Node link on the left-hand side of this page, which opens a new page that allows you to create a slave node, as shown in Figure 7-2. As mentioned previously, by default, Hudson allows you to create regular passive slaves. Select the Regular Slave option to create the regular slave and give it a unique name in the "Node name" field, for example **fedora-17-func-test-slave**. Click the OK button to create the slave node.

Upon creating the slave node, Hudson will automatically open the Node Configurations page, where it can be configured to use JNLP, SSH, or Shell script to copy and start the slave agent as shown in Figure 7-3.

From here, you can set the following configurations:

- **Name** A unique name to identify the slave within the Hudson instance. Though any string can be used to identify the slave, we recommend using a meaningful name, which reflects the machine hosting the slave and the purpose of the slave; for example **fedora-17-func-test-slave**. By providing each slave with a unique and meaningful name, you will be able to better identify it later in the drop-down box, while selecting it to tie jobs to as explained later in the chapter.
- **Description** A human-readable description of the slave that will be displayed on the job configuration screen. This is useful to specify its purpose and capabilities.
- **# of Executors** A number telling Hudson how many concurrent builds the slave can perform. The number is typically equivalent to the number of CPUs or the number of cores in each CPU of the slave machine.

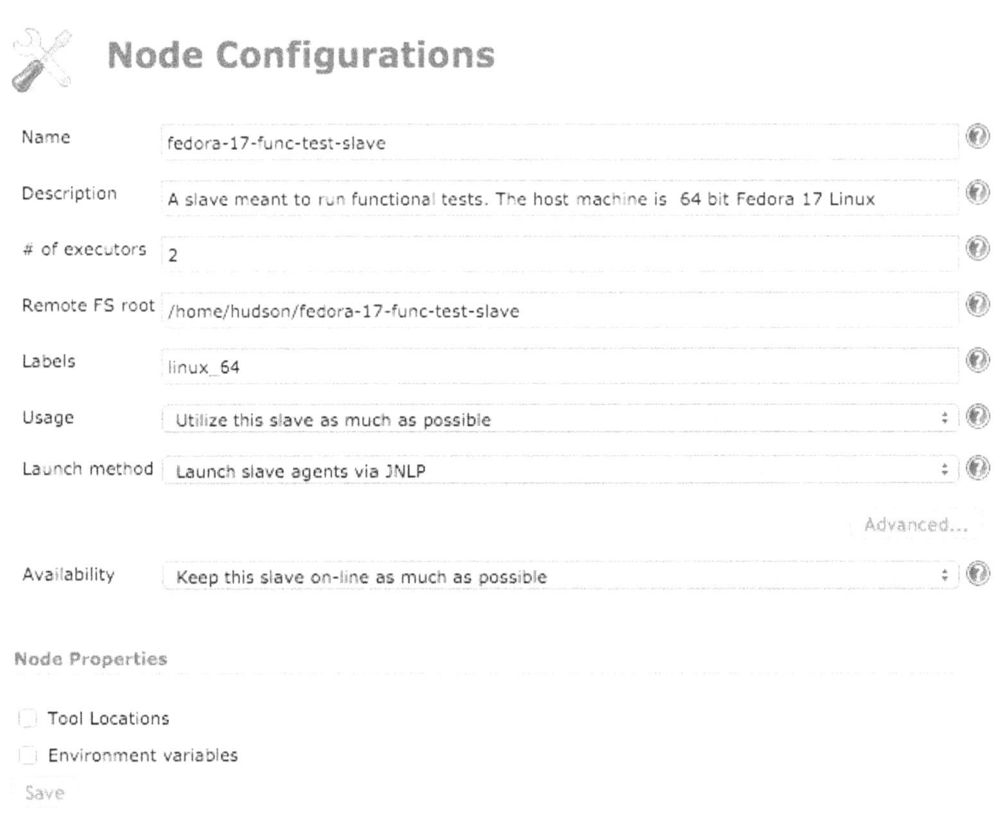

FIGURE 7-3. *Node Configurations page*

- **Remote FS root** A dedicated folder used by this slave specified as an absolute path in the machine hosting the slave, such as /home/hudson/fedora-17-func-test-slave on a UNIX machine or c:\hudson\fedora-17-func-test-slave on a Windows machine. This folder mainly stores the workspaces that contain the sources and resources corresponding to the jobs built on this slave. All other build information is sent back to the master. In general, it is not necessary to back up this folder.
- **Labels** A space-separated list of labels. A label is a unique string used to advertise the capability of the slave. More on labels later in the chapter.

- **Usage** A drop-down list allowing configuration for how intensively Hudson can schedule a job to this slave. The default value, "Utilize this slave as much as possible," tells Hudson to use this slave freely and schedule jobs whenever it has an executor available to do the build. The value "Leave this machine for tied jobs only" tells Hudson not to use this slave freely, but schedule only jobs tied to this slave. We will discuss tying jobs to a slave in more detail later in this chapter.
- **Launch method** A drop-down list allowing you to specify how the slave will launch. Here, you can specify if the slave will be managed by Hudson or manually managed by you. Without any additional plugins installed to add capabilities for Hudson to launch and manage slaves, there are two options for launching unmanaged slaves:
    - **Launch slave agents via JNLP** Starts a slave by launching an agent program through Java Web Start.[2]
    - **Launch slave via execution of command on the Master** Starts a slave by having Hudson execute a command from the master. Use this when the master is capable of remotely executing a process on a slave, such as through ssh/rsh. This command attempts to use the tool javaw. If a headless version of Java (Java runtime only) is installed on the slave, javaw will not be available and this option won't work.

  If you install additional plugins like SSH-slave plugin, then you would see additional options such as

    - **Launch slave agents on Unix machines via SSH** Starts a managed slave with an SSH command.

Save the configuration to add the slave node to Hudson. After adding the slave node, it will appear in the Nodes Status page as shown in Figure 7-4. In the next section, we will set up the unmanaged slave using the JNLP launcher.

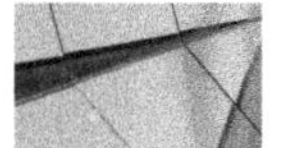

NOTE

If the slave node is unable to launch the slave agent, then the computer icon will be badged with a red mark to indicate the slave is offline and jobs cannot be scheduled to that slave. In such a case, go to the slave node configuration page and make sure the slave is launched correctly and connected successfully with Hudson.

---

[2] Java Web Start. http://en.wikipedia.org/wiki/Java_Web_Start

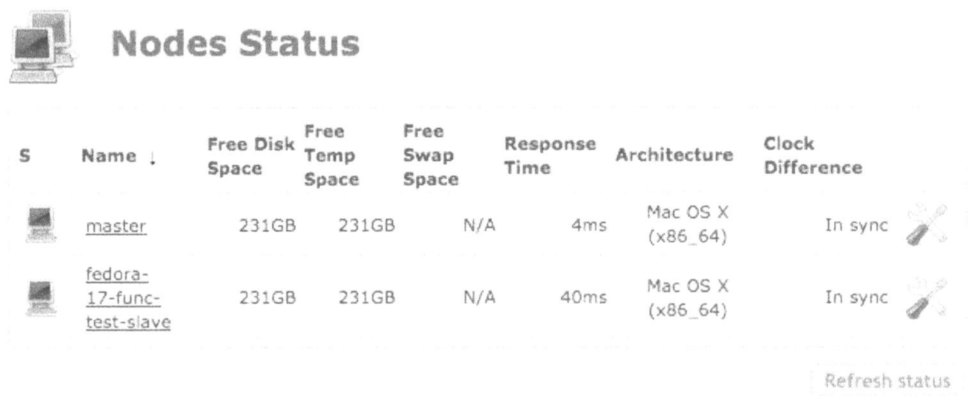

Nodes Status

S	Name ↓	Free Disk Space	Free Temp Space	Free Swap Space	Response Time	Architecture	Clock Difference
	master	231GB	231GB	N/A	4ms	Mac OS X (x86_64)	In sync
	fedora-17-func-test-slave	231GB	231GB	N/A	40ms	Mac OS X (x86_64)	In sync

Refresh status

FIGURE 7-4. *Nodes Status page showing newly added slave node*

Adding an Unmanaged Slave via JNLP Launcher

The Java Network Launch Protocol (JNLP) is used by the Java Web Start technology. It enables a Java application to launch on a remote machine by using resources hosted on a remote Web server. Java plugin software in the browser and Java Web Start software (part of the JDK, so it must be installed in the slave host machine) are considered JNLP clients because they can launch remotely hosted Java applications on a remote machine. The slave agent (slave.jar) is the remotely hosted Java application, and the remote host in the Hudson master.

In the previous section, we saw how to add a slave node to Hudson. To successfully create a JNLP slave, first log on to the machine that will host the slave agent. Then, launch a browser and go to the Hudson Web pages. Next, create a new slave node, **fedora-17-jnlp-slave**, as explained in the previous section, and go to the configuration page. The configuration page provides the option to specify the Launch method. Select the option "Launch slave agents via JNLP" to launch the slave agent using JNLP as shown in Figure 7-5. Save the configuration page, and add the node to the Nodes Status page. The red badge in the computer icon indicates the slave agent is not started, and will need to be manually started.

Launch method: Launch slave agents via JNLP

- Launch slave agents via JNLP
- Launch slave via execution of command on the Master
- Launch slave agents on Unix machines via SSH

FIGURE 7-5. *Configuration option to launch slave agent using JNLP*

The next step is starting the slave agent so it can successfully communicate with Hudson and make itself available for Hudson to distribute builds. Click on the slave name, fedora-17-jnlp-slave, which takes you to the slave information page. This page explains how to start the slave agent using the Java Web Start technology. The two main ways to manually start the slave agent on the slave machine are shown in Figure 7-6. One way is to click the Launch button to automatically install slave.jar on the slave host and the other is to start using one of the command-line suggestions provided by Hudson as shown in Figure 7-6. Whichever method you use, it must be done on the machine that will host the slave agent.

NOTE
To correctly install the slave agent, you must first log in to the machine that will be hosting your slave agent. If you proceeded without doing so, you have installed the slave agent on the wrong machine. Before installing, always make sure you have logged on to the correct slave machine.

When you use Java Web Start to install the slave agent on the slave machine, a security warning dialog pops up to warn you about the applications being installed,

Mark this node temporarily offline

Slave fedora-17-jnlp-slave

(A slave meant to run functional tests. The host machine is 64 bit Fedora 17 Linux)

Connect slave to Hudson one of these ways:

- Launch | Launch agent from browser on slave
- Run from slave command line:

```
javaws http://localhost:8080/computer/fedora-17-jnlp-slave/slave-agent.jnlp
```

- Or if the slave is headless:

```
java -jar slave.jar -jnlpUrl http://localhost:8080/computer/fedora-17-jnlp-
slave/slave-agent.jnlp
```

Labels: linux_64

FIGURE 7-6. *Suggestions provided by Hudson to launch the slave agent using JNLP*

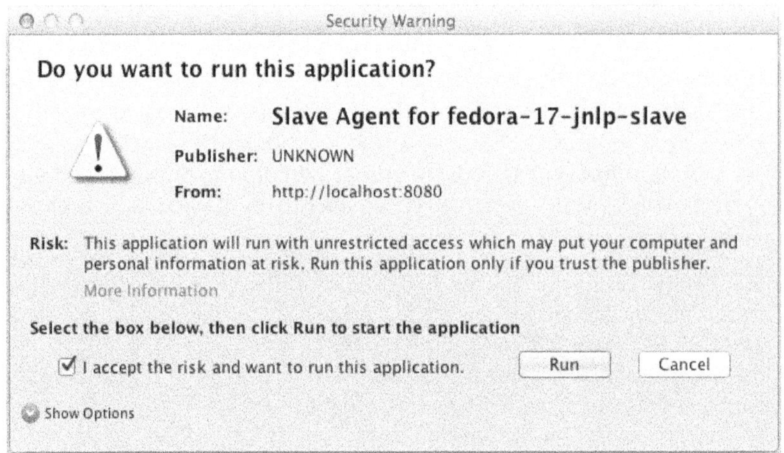

FIGURE 7-7. *Security warning dialog from Java Web Start*

as shown in Figure 7-7. Since this application, slave.jar, is originating from the trusted Hudson master instance, click on the "I accept the risk and want to run this application" check box and click the Run button to install the slave agent. Java Web Start will download the slave.jar file from the Hudson master instance and install it on the slave machine.

NOTE
Java Web Start is included in the Java Runtime Environment (JRE). The JNLP client from this part of Java Web Start is installed in browsers as a browser plugin. So, only with JRE, you can click the Launch button to launch the JNLP slave. However, the command-line JNLP client (javaws) is not available in JRE alone. You must install the full JDK and its bin folder to the PATH environment variable of the OS to access the tool javaws.

The JNLP file (slave-agent.jnlp) used by the Java Web Start has the instruction to start the slave agent. After the slave agent is successfully launched, a dialog appears with the status of the connection. It must display the word "Connected," as shown in Figure 7-8, to indicate that the connection between the Hudson master and slave has been successfully established. If the connection between the master and slave failed, the word "Terminated" will be displayed in this dialog. Do not close this dialog, or the slave agent will terminate.

FIGURE 7-8. *Slave UI indicating connection has been established*

In order to make sure the Hudson master is also connected to the slave and ready to distribute builds to this job, go to the slave dashboard in Hudson and look at the status after refreshing the page. Now the instruction to set up the slave agent using JNLP disappears, and the status is displayed as "Connected via JNLP agent" as shown in Figure 7-9. Also, the red badge in the computer icon in the Nodes Status page disappears to indicate the slave is now alive for doing business.

Installing JNLP Slave as a Windows Service

If you have set up the unmanaged JNLP slave on a Windows machine and it is up and running, you then can set it as a Windows Service. This helps to restart it automatically each time the Windows machine is rebooted. Creating a Windows Service for the JNLP slave is very easy. Go to the slave agent dialog (see Figure 7-8). You should see a File menu at the top bar of the dialog. Click on it and select the Install as Windows Service menu option. This will install the slave agent as a Windows Service, and it will start automatically every time your Windows machine is rebooted.

FIGURE 7-9. *Slave dashboard displaying the connected status of the slave*

Adding an SSH-Based Managed Slave

If you are working in a UNIX-like environment (for example, Linux, Solaris, or Mac), then the preferred method to allow Hudson to manage your slave is using SSH, because most of the UNIX-like environments support SSH out-of-the-box and Hudson has built-in support to communicate with machines that support the SSH protocol. In order to create a new managed SSH slave node, you must first install the ssh-slaves plugin. If the ssh-slaves plugin is not already installed, go to the Hudson Plugin Manager page and install it from the Featured section of the "Available plugins to install" tab. This adds the capability to Hudson to manage the slave agent via SSH. Next, create a new slave node, **fedora-17-ssh-slave**, as explained earlier in this chapter and go to the configuration page. You should see the option "Launch slave agent on Unix machines via SSH" in the "Launch method" drop-down, as shown in Figure 7-10.

In its simplest form, the slave configuration needs the Host address, either a fully qualified domain name or the IP address, of the slave machine as shown in Figure 7-11. In this form, Hudson assumes the user who started the Hudson master can log in from the master machine to the slave machine via passwordless public-private key-based authentication. The usernames at both ends of the machines are same.

Setting Up Public-Private Key-Based Authentication

In order to do public-private key-based authentication, first you need to create private and public SSH keys and put them in the proper place with the appropriate

Launch method | Launch slave agents on Unix machines via SSH
Launch slave agents via JNLP
Launch slave via execution of command on the Master
Launch slave agents on Unix machines via SSH

FIGURE 7-10. *Option to launch slave agent on Unix machine using SSH*

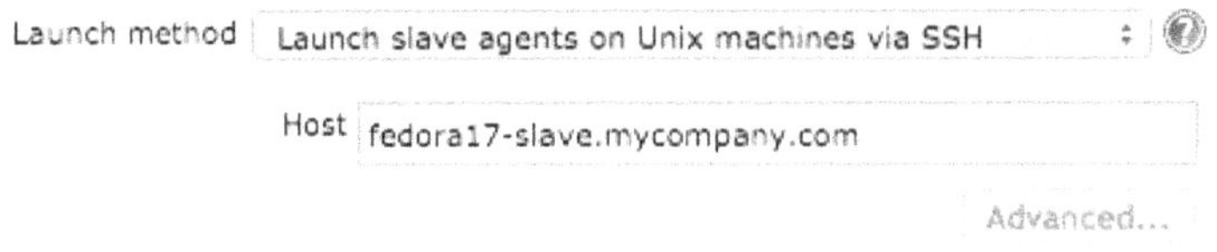

Launch method | Launch slave agents on Unix machines via SSH
Host | fedora17-slave.mycompany.com
Advanced...

FIGURE 7-11. *Simplest form of SSH connection*

permissions. In the home directory of the user that started the Hudson master (assume hudson), create a folder .ssh, if it does not exist already. Next, create the keys with the command

```
$ ssh-keygen -t rsa
```

The ssh-keygen program will ask for a file name to save the key. Press ENTER to accept the default file name. Next, it will ask for a passphrase to encrypt the private key. Press ENTER or provide a passphrase. (If you choose a passphrase, be sure you will remember it, or else the private key you create will be useless.) This creates the keys id_rsa and id_rsa.pub and puts them in the ~/.ssh folder unless specified elsewhere. For the public-private key authentication to work correctly, the private key id_rsa must be readable only by the user that started the Hudson master. So change the permissions of the folder .ssh with the command

```
$ chmod 700 ~/.ssh
$ chmod 600 ~/.ssh/id_rsa
```

NOTE

If you provide a passphrase while generating the SSH keys, then you cannot use the simple form of SSH slave creation. If the username of the account in the slave machine is not the same as the username in the Hudson master, then authentication using simple form does not work; you must use the Advanced section of the SSH slaves creation as explained later in this section.

Next, copy the ~/.ssh/id_rsa.pub file from the Hudson master computer onto the slave computer. If you have SCP access to the slave machine, you can first copy the file to the home folder of the user who will run the slave agent on the slave machine. Suppose the slave computer is named fedora-17.mycompany.com, and the username of the account there is also hudson, just as in the Hudson master; in that case, to copy the file to the slave machine, use the following command, including the ":"at the end of the command

```
$ scp .~/ssh/id_dsarsa.pub hudson@fedora-17.mycompany.com:
```

When asked, provide the password for the user hudson on the slave machine. The file will be copied to the home directory of the user hudson on the slave machine. The next step is to install the public key on the slave machine. Log in to the slave machine as the user hudson. In the home directory, you should see the copied id_rsa.pub. Create an .ssh folder if it does not already exist in the home directory. Then, append the contents of id_rsa.pub to a file in .ssh with the command

```
$ cat id_rsa.pub >> ~/.ssh/authorized_keys
```

This will create the file authorized_keys in the folder .ssh if it does not exist, or append the contents to the end of existing file. The .ssh folder on the slave computer must have the correct permissions. Set the permission with the command

```
$ chmod -R 700 ~/.ssh
```

Next, check if the passwordless public-private key authentication works. Go back to the Hudson master machine and from there issue the command

```
$ ssh hudson@fedora-17.mycompany.com
```

This should allow a passwordless SSH connection from the master machine to the slave machine. If the SSH connection is successful, then the Hudson master is ready to manage the slave using the SSH protocol. When the connection between master and slave is established, something like the following will show in the connection log page

```
[04/01/13 01:31:53] [SSH] Opening SSH connection to fedora-17.mycompany.com.
[04/01/13 01:31:53] [SSH] Authenticating as hudson with /home/hudson/.ssh/id_rsa.
[04/01/13 01:31:53] [SSH] Authentication successful.
[04/01/13 01:50:00] [SSH] Starting slave process: cd '/home/hudson/hudson-ssh-slave'
&& java  -jar slave.jar
<===[HUDSON REMOTING CAPACITY]===>channel started
Slave.jar version: ?
This is a Unix slave
Installing: maven3-slavebundle.zip
done
Slave successfully connected and online
```

Advanced Settings

In the previous section, we used a simple form of an SSH-managed slave, using passwordless public-private key authentication. We also mentioned that the usernames at both the master and slave ends must be the same. However, in real use cases, either the username may be different or setting up passwordless authentication may be impractical. In that case, you must use the Advanced section of the SSH slave connection configuration as shown in Figure 7-12.

Using the Advanced settings, you can specify the following additional configurations:

- **Username** Username of the account in the slave machine. If left blank, the username of the account running the Hudson master will be used.

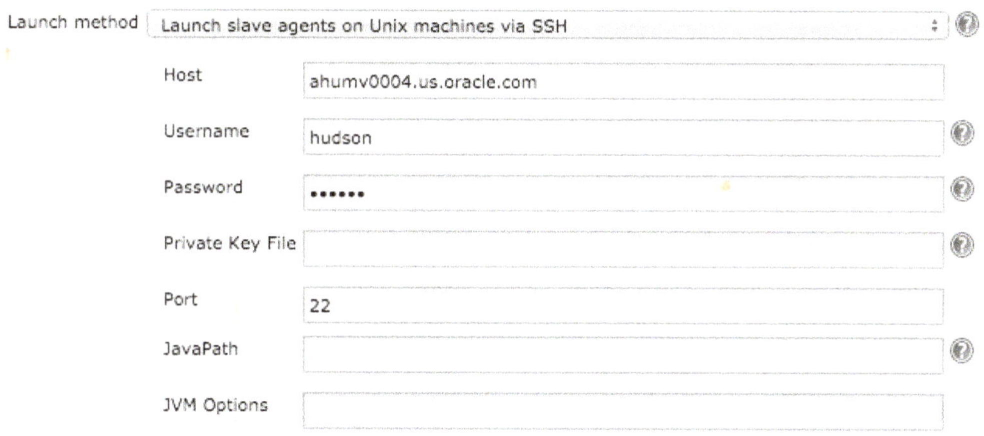

Launch method Launch slave agents on Unix machines via SSH

Host ahumv0004.us.oracle.com

Username hudson

Password ••••••

Private Key File

Port 22

JavaPath

JVM Options

FIGURE 7-12. *SSH slaves connection Advanced settings*

- **Password** Password of the account in the slave machine. This is useful only if you don't want to use passwordless public-private key-based authentication. However, if you are using passwordless public-private key-based authentication and the private key is encrypted with a passphrase, then you must use the password text field to specify it.
- **Private Key File** An absolute path to the private key file on the Hudson master machine to use for the passwordless public-private key-based authentication. By default, Hudson would look for the private key (either id_rsa or id_dsa.) in the .ssh folder in the home directory. However, if the private key does not exist in the default location, then it can be specified here.
- **Port** The port number to use for the SSH connection. The default value is 22. Use this field only if the SSH daemon in the slave machine is running in a different port.
- **JavaPath** The path of the Java binary to invoke the slave agent. This is useful if you want to use a specific version of JDK rather than the default Java installed in the slave machine.
- **JVM Options** The JVM options such as memory settings (-Xmx 256m) that should be passed to the JVM while invoking the slave agent.

Managing the Availability

Finally, for managed SSH slaves there is another useful advanced configuration: Availability. It is a drop-down list of options to specify the control Hudson can have to start and stop this slave. The options are

- **Keep this slave on-line as much as possible** The default mode. Hudson will try to keep the managed slave online always. It will periodically attempt to restart the slave if it is not responding. Hudson will never try to take this slave offline.
- **Take this slave on-line and off-line at specific times** A mode in which Hudson will try to keep the managed slave online according to the configured schedule. It will periodically attempt to start the slave if it is unavailable during the online window. The slave will be taken offline during an offline window, if there are no active jobs running on the slave.
- **Take this slave on-line when in demand and off-line when idle** A mode that instructs Hudson to launch the managed slave based on demand. It will periodically attempt to launch the slave when there are unexecuted jobs that meet the following criteria: the jobs are in the queue for the specified startup demand period and they can be executed on this slave. The slave will be taken offline if no active jobs are running on the slave and the slave has been idle for the specified period of time.

Troubleshooting the SSH Connection

There are a few common errors that can occur while Hudson tries to copy the slave agent and invoke it with an SSH connection.

- **There was a problem while connecting to <Slave Host>** This error may occur if SSH is not enabled in the slave machine. Make sure **sshd** is enabled in the slave machine and can accept SSH connection requests from other machines.
- **hudson.AbortException: Authentication failed** Make sure that SSH is installed on the slave, the **sshd** daemon is running, and the authentication you provided is correct. Again, from a shell, make sure the user that started the Hudson master is able to log in from the master machine to the slave machine using SSH.
- **hudson.util.IOException2: Could not copy slave.jar to slave** This error occurs if the user at the slave machine does not have sufficient permissions to perform the operation. Make sure the folder specified in the Remote FS root field has sufficient permission. It should have read-write permission. Use the command **chmod 755 <remote-fs-root-folder>** to set the correct permission.

Distributing the Builds

In the previous sections, we have set up both managed and unmanaged slaves. Once the slaves are connected, then Hudson is ready to distribute builds of the jobs to the connected slaves. The following illustration depicts a simple scenario of how a job will be scheduled. In case of managed slaves, if the slaves are offline, then an attempt will be made to bring it online first.

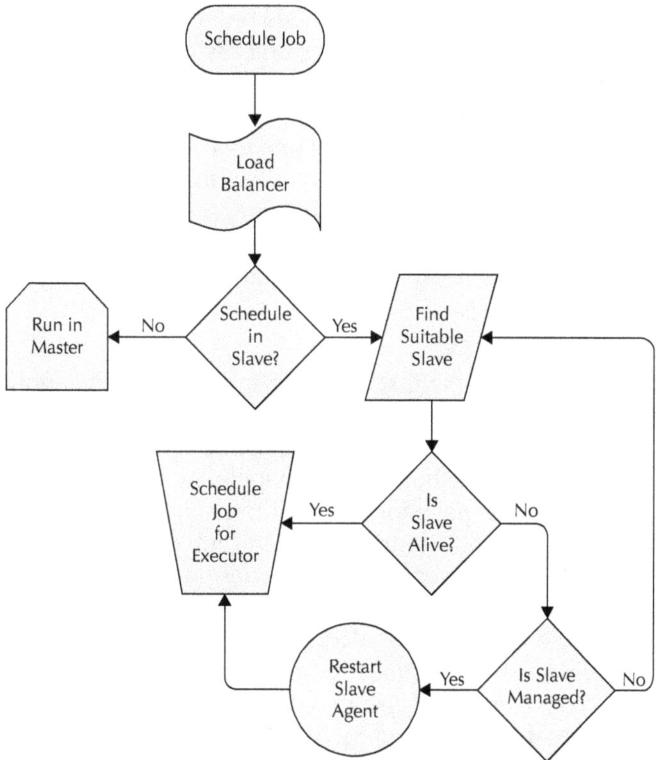

Hudson employs the following scheduling strategy to find a suitable slave for the job.

- If a job is configured to stick to one slave, then it is always honored.
- Hudson tries to build a job on the same slave on which it was previously built.
- Hudson tries to move long builds to slaves, because the amount of network interaction between a master and a slave tends to be logarithmic to the duration of a build. Even if job A takes twice as long to build as job B, it won't require double network transfer, so this strategy reduces the network overhead.

Assigning Labels to Slave

When creating slave nodes, we discussed how to add a label while configuring your slave. A label is a space-separated list of strings provided by a slave to advertise its capabilities and architecture. It is a powerful mechanism used by Hudson to strategize the distribution of builds. It is also a convenient way to specify the characteristics of a slave node such as operating system, target environment, and database type relevant to building a job. A common use case is to label a slave in such a way to identify it to run OS-specific functional tests or label it as a node reserve to execute performance tests. If you are building on slaves that are geographically distributed, then you can use the label to express the location of the slave.

As an example, assume you have set up three slaves. The label of the first one is "Linux," second is "Linux 64bit," and the third one is "Linux 64bit Ubuntu." If a job is configured to build on a slave labeled "Linux," then that job will be scheduled on any of the three slaves. If it is configured to build on a slave labeled "64bit," then it will be scheduled to build only on the last two slaves. If it is configured to build on a slave labeled "Linux Ubuntu," then it will build only on the third slave.

Restricting Build to Slaves

By default, Hudson would pick the first available suitable slave by applying the scheduling strategy discussed earlier. Sometimes a job can only be successfully built on a particular slave or only on the master. In that case, it is possible to restrict in which node or group of nodes the build should happen by specifying the required values in the job configuration page, or tying a job to a node. Go to the job configuration page and select the "Restrict where this job can be run" check box. This opens up the two options for restricting the nodes on which the builds can happen, as shown in Figure 7-13.

The first way of tying a job to a particular node or group of nodes is by using the option "Node and label menu." Selecting this option provides a drop-down list of available nodes based on their name, and a combination of possible node name and labels. Hudson generates this convenient list. If you have set up three slaves, as we explained earlier in the section, and are building a job that needs a 64-bit Linux architecture but you do not care to do any OS-specific packaging, then choose the 64bit (group of linux-slave2, linux-slave3) option, as shown in Figure 7-14. However,

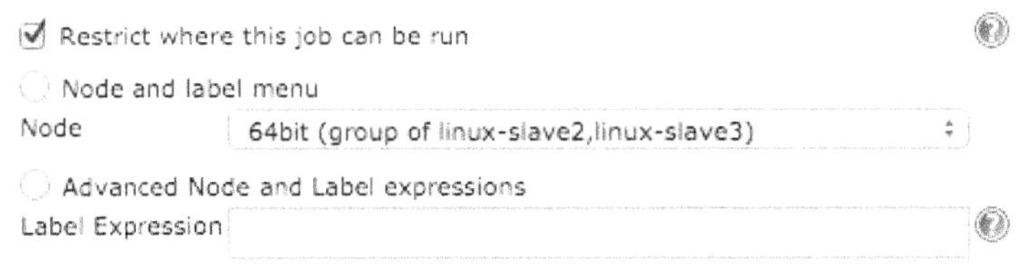

FIGURE 7-13. *Restricting the nodes where the jobs can build*

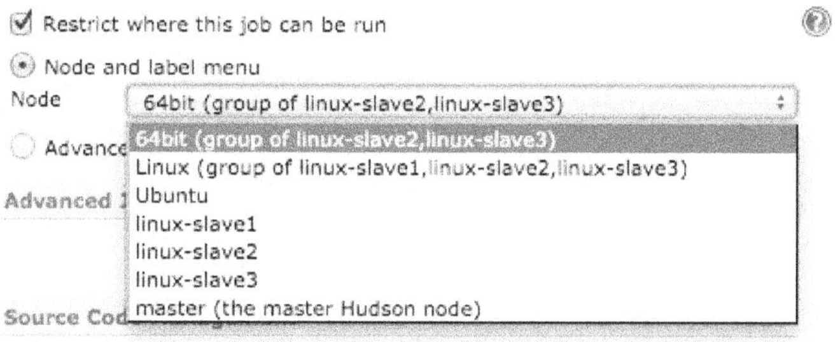

FIGURE 7-14. *Selecting a group of nodes to restrict where a job can be built*

if you want to run a job that builds Ubuntu packages, then you want to tie that job specifically to the label Ubuntu by selecting it from the drop-down list.

For most purposes, Hudson's drop-down list is good enough to find a suitable combination to restrict your jobs; however, in rare cases you might want to write your own expression to tell Hudson how the jobs should be tied to certain slave nodes. You can do so by selecting the second radio button option, labeled "Advanced Node and Label expressions," and inputting the label expression that would be parsed by Hudson to find the slave node group.

If you want to always run this job on a specific slave, just specify its name in this field. However, if you want to tie the job to a cluster of slaves so that Hudson could pick the first available slave from that group, then specify a Boolean expression that filters the slaves into that group based on Boolean operation on slave names or label expression. Label names or slave names can be quoted if they contain unsafe characters. An expression can contain whitespace for better readability; any white space will simply be ignored. The following operators are supported, in the order of precedence, and they are left associative.

`(expr)` parenthesis

`!expr` negation
Example: `!Ubuntu`, any slave except with label Ubuntu

`expr && expr` and
Example: `Linux && 64bit`, must be a Linux and 64bit slave

`expr || expr` or
Example: `Linux-slave1 || Linux-slave2`, either one

`a -> b` "implies"
Example: `Linux->64bit` could be thought of as "if run on a Linux slave, that slave must be 64bit." It still allows Hudson to run this build on Windows slaves if they exist, but it need not be 64bit.

`a <-> b` "if and only if"
Example: `Linux<->64bit` could be thought of as "if run on a Linux slave, that slave must be 64bit, but if not on Linux, it must not be 64bit." Hudson can still run the job on a Windows machine but it must not be 64bit.

So, for example, based on the slave names and labels we used earlier, if we use the Boolean expression, `(Linux && 64bit) || Ubuntu || Linux-slave2`, this expression will add all the slaves that are hosted on 64bit Linux machines and any slave that is hosted on a Ubuntu machine and the slave named Linux-slave2 to the slave group used by Hudson to build that job.

Distributing Build Using Matrix Job

Hudson has a job type called multi-configuration job (or matrix job). This is another powerful feature in Hudson to distribute the builds of a single job. This is particularly useful if you have to build the same job but with a different environment such as a different OS (Linux, Windows, or Mac) or JDK (JDK6 or JDK7). The matrix job is also useful for tests where the application is built by a single build job, but it has to be tested under a wide variety of conditions such as different browsers and databases. Selecting the appropriate option while creating the job, as shown in Figure 7-15, creates the multi-configuration build job.

A multi-configuration build job is very similar to a free-style job, except that it has a section to include multiple build configurations, as shown in Figure 7-16. Each of the new configurations added is called an axis. The same job will be built with each configuration axis defined in this section. By default, Hudson provides two types of axes: Slave axis and User-defined axis. Plugins may provide additional axes.

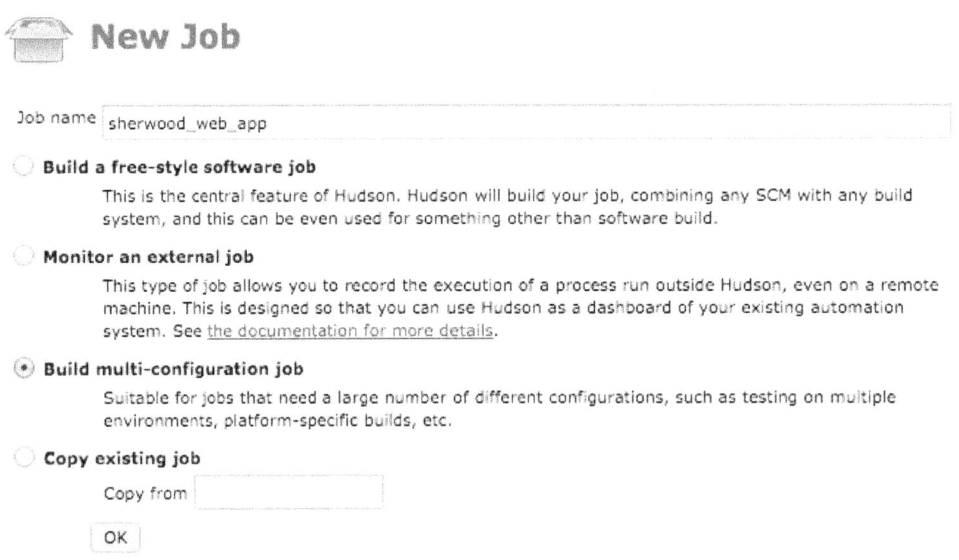

FIGURE 7-15. *Creating a matrix job*

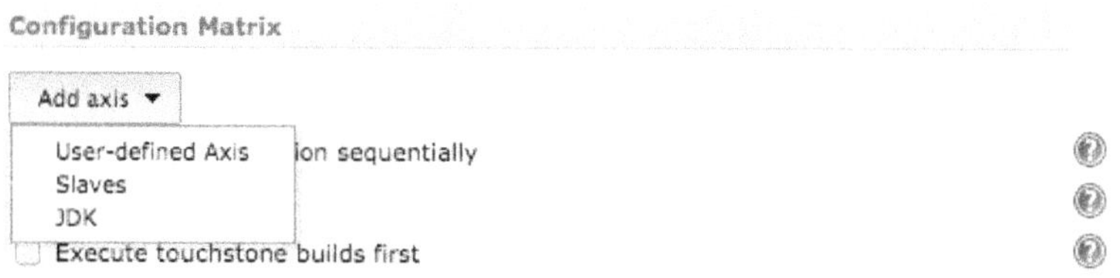

FIGURE 7-16. *Configuration matrix of a multi-configuration build*

Adding a Slave Axis

To add a Slave axis, you select the Slaves option in the "Add axis" drop-down as shown in Figure 7-16. When you select the Slave axis, a UI is provided to select the list of slaves on which this job should be executed. Assume that your job is meant to create executables on a Linux, a Solaris, and a Windows machine; then you would select the slave labeled with the corresponding capabilities, as shown in Figure 7-17. Instead of creating a multi-configuration job, you could create three jobs and tie them to the respective slaves, but a multi-configuration job provides the ability to do the same with a single job.

Hudson would select the slave or group of slaves to build the job based on the following criteria:

- If none is selected, Hudson will choose an available, suitable node to perform a build. This is the same behavior as the free-style job when a job is not tied to a node. This is useful when the job doesn't have a dependency on any particular node, as it allows Hudson to utilize nodes in an optimal fashion.

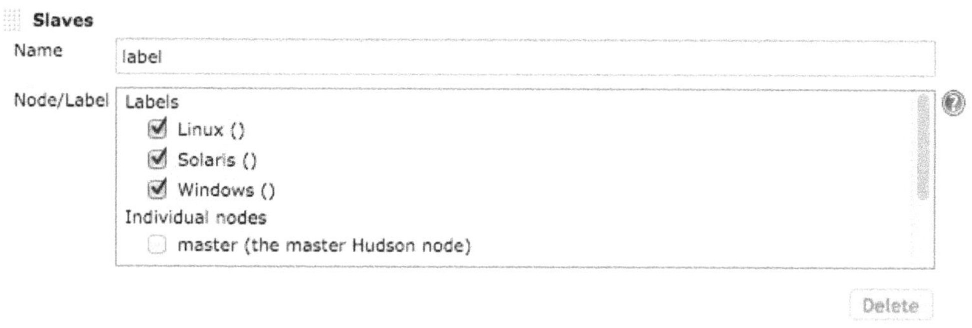

FIGURE 7-17. *Configuring a Slave axis*

- If one is selected, Hudson will always run the build on the specified node. If one is selected from the "Individual nodes" section or one of the nodes that belongs to the label, if the label is selected from the Labels section. This is useful when the build is required to run on a specific machine or a subset of machines.
- If multiple values are selected, the configuration matrix will be expanded to include all of them, and builds will be performed on all of the selected nodes or labels. This is particularly useful if the builds need to run tests on Windows, Linux, and Solaris.

Adding a User-Defined Axis

The second type of axis, User-defined axis, lets you configure the build job based on an arbitrary name-value pair you define. Assume you have to create builds with the following combination:

- Beta version of your product with modes release and debug
- Alpha version of your product with modes release and debug

This combination produces four builds of the same job, but each build should get two environment variables: VERSION=[beta alpha] and MODE=[release debug]. In order to achieve this combination of matrix builds, you use the User-defined axes as shown in Figure 7-18. The values are assigned to the name for each build and exposed as an environment variable. Multiple values are separated by whitespace or newlines.

If both the Slave axis and the User-defined axes are configured for the multi-configuration build job, the combination would create 12 builds, as shown in Table 7-1. The Release and Debug columns indicate the status of the build.

FIGURE 7-18. *User-defined axes*

		Release	Debug
alpha	Linux	success	unstable
	Solaris	success	success
	Windows	failed	success
beta	Linux	success	failed
	Solaris	success	success
	Windows	failed	success

TABLE 7-1. *Builds Resulting from Matrix Configuration*

Advanced Multi-Configuration Build Settings

In general, Hudson builds the job in each of the axes in parallel. However, you can tell Hudson to run each of the axes sequentially by selecting the "Run each configuration sequentially" option. This can be useful if your job builds needs to access a shared resource, such as a database.

By default, Hudson builds all the possible combinations of axes exhaustively, but sometimes this is too many, or may contain combinations that don't make sense. In such a situation, you can make the matrix sparse by filtering out combinations that you don't want through a Groovy expression that returns true or false. For example, let's say you are building on different operating systems for different compilers. Assume that your slave labels are label=[linux, solaris] and you have created an axis as compiler=[gcc, cc]. If you want to filter out cc builds on Linux, then you use the Groovy expression ! (label=="linux") && (compiler=="cc"). When you specify a Groovy expression, only the combinations that result in true will be built. In evaluating the expression, axes are exposed as variables with their values set to the current combination evaluated.

Managing Slaves

In the previous sections we saw how to set up slaves and initiate the communication between Hudson and the slave. Also we looked into the details of how Hudson distributes the builds and how to configure your job to get the build done at the appropriate slave. Hudson also provides a UI to manage the tools you need for your builds and to monitor the status of the slaves.

Managing the Tools Location

Hudson must be told where to find the build tools needed to build jobs on a slave. Some of the common tools include JDK, Maven, Ant, and Gradle. If the build tools

Tool Locations
List of tool locations
Name (Git) Default
Home /opt/hudson/git/bin/git
Delete
Name (JDK) jdk6.0._31
Home /usr/opt/bin/java
Delete
Add

FIGURE 7-19. *Slave tools installation*

are configured to install automatically, no additional configuration is required when setting up the slave; Hudson will download and install the tools as required. However, if the build tools are already installed locally on the slave machine, you must specify their location in the slave configuration so Hudson will know where to find them. To specify the locations of preinstalled tools, select the Tool Locations check box in the slave configuration page and provide the local paths for each of the tools needed for the build jobs as shown in Figure 7-19.

Monitoring the Slaves

The master and the slave nodes are monitored from the Nodes Status page, as shown earlier in Figure 7-2. This page displays several pieces of information:

- **Status of the nodes** If the slaves are offline, then the computer icon is badged with a red mark indicating it is offline. You can click on the name of the slave, go to the slave dashboard to view the reason for being offline, and restart the slave if needed.
- **Node resources details** Few resources and information of the nodes, such as clock difference between the slave and master (which must be in sync for the SCM polling to work correctly), free disk space, free swap space, response time, and the architecture of the machine.
- **Configuration link** This link appears at the sidebar and allows configuring the node.
- **Refresh button** Used to refresh the status of the nodes, reflecting any changes you make.

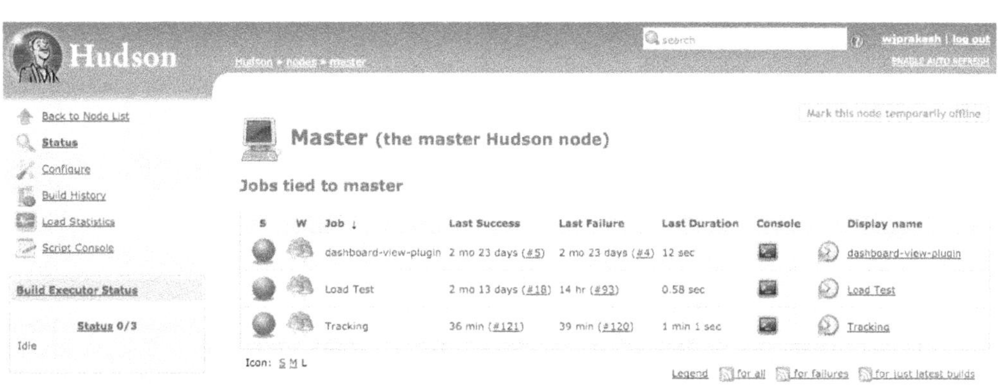

FIGURE 7-20. *Node dashboard showing jobs tied to the node*

Clicking the node name takes you to the node dashboard where you can do configuration and further operations on a particular node, as shown in Figure 7-20. This page displays a table of jobs tied to this node and their build statuses. Further operations that can be performed from this view include:

- Viewing the build history on this node
- Configuring the nodes to specify how the slave agent will be managed and tuning the properties of the slave node
- Load statistics of the node
- Marking the node temporarily offline, so no builds will be scheduled in the node until it comes online again

Summary

In this chapter, we saw how to scale up your Hudson to do builds in a distributed fashion by using slaves. Hudson provides different types of slaves, each available for unique uses and defined based on how Hudson manages their lifecycle. In this chapter, we looked at how to set up each different type of slave. We also discussed that Hudson job builds can be distributed to these slaves by configuring the job. We concluded the chapter with a discussion on managing the slave environment.

CHAPTER 8

Basic Plugin Development

One of the reasons why Hudson is a popular open-source Continuous Integration server is the ability to extend Hudson's functionalities using plugins. Plugins allow developers to do everything from customizing the way builds are done, results are displayed and notified, integration with application life cycle management systems such as SCM, testing, analysis tools, and so on. There is a vibrant community of developers developing plugins for Hudson. More than 400 Hudson plugins supporting various aspects of Continuous Integration are already available for free installation. This chapter covers the basic steps of writing a Hudson plugin.

Requirements

In order to create and build a Hudson plugin, JDK 6 or higher is needed. See Chapter 1 for details on installing JDK 6. The developer must have good Java development experience.

As mentioned in Chapter 2, there are many "builders" Hudson uses to perform the centrally important task of compiling source code into a binary form. The most important of these is Maven, which can be downloaded and installed from the location http://maven.apache.org/download.html. Knowledge of using Maven as a build tool is desirable to write a Hudson plugin.

Writing a HelloWorld Plugin

Let us start by writing a simple "HelloWorld" plugin and install it in Hudson to see it in action. This simple plugin will demonstrate how the plugin project folder needs to be structured to build it using Maven. This exercise also explains how the plugin makes itself visible to the Hudson instance for use in jobs. In this contrived example, the plugin code will hook up with one of the Hudson services called builder. This HelloWorld builder service hook can be chosen as a builder in a Hudson job and executed. Though we write this plugin by hand for the sake of experience, the section HPI Tool in the later part of the chapter covers a tool provided by Hudson to generate sample plugin sources automatically.

Creating the Plugin Project

The first step is to create the plugin project as a Maven project by creating the pom.xml file, which is an XML file that contains information about the project and configuration details used by Maven to build the project. Start by creating a folder named pluginex1 and place the pom.xml at the top level of the folder:

```
pluginex1/
    pom.xml
```

Put the following content into that pom.xml file, which tells Maven that this is a Hudson plugin project and specifies the name of the plugin as PluginEx1:

```
<project>
  <modelVersion>4.0.0</modelVersion>
  <parent>
    <groupId>org.eclipse.hudson.plugins</groupId>
    <artifactId>hudson-plugin-parent</artifactId>
    <version>3.0.00</version>
  </parent>
  <groupId>net.hudsonlifestyle </groupId>
  <artifactId>pluginex1</artifactId>
  <version>1.0-SNAPSHOT</version>
  <packaging>hpi</packaging>
  <name>PluginEx1</name>
</project>
```

For details on the meaning of the elements in pom.xml, please see Chapter 2. For now it is sufficient to know that the parent element tells the locally running Maven instance to go out to the network and fetch another pom.xml file to provide additional project information not listed here.

Creating a Service Hook

The next step is to create a hook that hooks in to a Hudson job as a builder and displays the message "Hello World!" in the console log when we build the job. The hook is created using a simple Java class. Create a file called HelloWorldBuilder .java using the package name net.hudsonlifestyle and place the file under the folder src/main/java/net/hudsonlifestyle:

```
HelloWorldBuilder.java - Java Class
src/main/java - Location where Mavenfinds the Java classes to compile
net/hudsonlifestyle - Java package name path
pluginex1/
  pom.xml
  src/
   main/
    java/
      net/
       hudsonlifestyle/
         HelloWorldBuilder.java
```

Put the following Java code into the HelloWorldBuilder.java file:

```
package net.hudsonlifestyle;
import hudson.Launcher;
import hudson.model.AbstractBuild;
import hudson.model.AbstractProject;
import hudson.model.BuildListener;
import hudson.tasks.Builder;
```

```
import hudson.Extension;
import hudson.tasks.BuildStepDescriptor;
import org.kohsuke.stapler.DataBoundConstructor;
public class HelloWorldBuilder extends Builder {
   @DataBoundConstructor
   public HelloWorldBuilder(){
   }
   @Override
   public boolean perform(AbstractBuild build, Launcher launcher,
                          BuildListener listener) {
        listener.getLogger().println("Hello World!");
        return true;
   }
   @Extension
   public static final class DescriptorImpl extends
                                 BuildStepDescriptor<Builder> {
        @Override
        public boolean isApplicable(Class<? extends
                                    AbstractProject> type) {
             return true;
         }
         @Override
         public String getDisplayName() {
            return "Hello World Builder";
         }
   }
}
```

That is all needed to write our simple HelloWorld plugin. The imports and classes used by this class will be explained in the section Examining the Sample Extension in the later part of the chapter. Now let us build and package the plugin so that it can be installed in Hudson.

Building the Plugin

To build the plugin we use the Maven command line. Open a command-line tool (Command Prompt on Windows or a shell console on any UNIX-flavored OS). Type the Maven build and package command at the top level of the folder pluginex1:

```
pluginex1> mvn package
```

Thanks to the unseen pom.xml file pulled in by the <parent> element, Maven builds the Hudson plugin and creates the plugin package pluginex1.hpi, which can be installed in a Hudson instance. Maven places the package pluginex1.hpi under the folder:

```
pluginex1/
   target/
      pluginex1.hpi
```

NOTE
Maven downloads numerous libraries required by Maven itself to build any Maven project and also libraries required to build the plugin project. As such, a fast and reliable Internet connection is essential to using Maven. It is often necessary to configure Maven to use a proxy when using it behind a corporate firewall. The libraries downloaded by Maven are called "Maven artifacts" and are usually downloaded from a central repository called Maven Central Repository and placed under a folder, usually referred as Local Maven Repository. For subsequent builds, Maven uses the artifacts from this local repository. The default location of this repository is a folder by name .m2 located at your home folder on your operating system.

Testing the Plugin

Open the Manage Plugins page from the Manage Hudson page and go to the Advanced tab. In the Advanced tab, the newly created plugin can be browsed and manually uploaded to be installed in Hudson as shown in Figure 8-1.

Once the plugin is uploaded, Hudson must be restarted for the newly uploaded plugin to take effect. Once Hudson is restarted, the new plugin we just created will be loaded and ready for us to test.

To test the plugin, let us use New Job from the main Hudson page to create a free-style job called PluginTest. If our new plugin is successfully loaded, it should add a new builder called HelloWorldBuilder to the job. Let us configure the job to do a build with our newly installed builder. Open the configuration page of the PluginTest job and scroll down to the Build section of the job. Open the drop-down list of the builders in the Build section. Select Hello World Builder from the drop-down as shown in Figure 8-2.

Upload Plugin

You can upload a .hpi file to install a plugin from outside the central plugin repository.

File: nPluginDevelopment/pluginex1/target/pluginex1.hpi Browse...

Upload

FIGURE 8-1. *Plugin manual upload*

Build

Add build step

Execute Windows batch command
Invoke Maven 2 (Legacy)
Execute shell
Invoke Ant
Hello World Builder
Archive the artifacts

usage

FIGURE 8-2. *Drop-down list of builders*

Click the Save button on the bottom of the Job Configurations page to save this change. Hello World Builder will be added as a builder to the job as shown in Figure 8-3.

Build the job by clicking the Build Now link on the left-hand side of the job dashboard and wait until the job building is completed. Click on the build link in Build History and click the Console Output link to open the console output of the job build to see the result of our build, as shown in Figure 8-4.

The builder provided by our simple plugin has written out a very simple message: "Hello World!". Though our simple plugin is a contrived sample, it demonstrates a very important concept—that you can programmatically extend services provided by Hudson through your own plugin. The rest of the chapter will dive deep into the

Build

Hello World Builder

Delete

Add build step

FIGURE 8-3. *HelloWorldBuilder selected as builder for the job*

```
Started by user anonymous
Hello World!
Finished: SUCCESS
```

FIGURE 8-4. *HelloWorldBuilder console output*

various concepts of the plugin development framework and how you can take advantage of those concepts and implement your plugin to provide a rich user experience to the user.

HPI Tool

Though we wrote our previous sample by hand, the project structure along with some sample code can be generated using a tool provided by the Hudson plugin framework called HPI, which is an abbreviation for Hudson Plugin developer Interface. Since we use Maven for managing and building a Hudson plugin, this tool is written as a Maven plugin. It helps developers to create, build, run, and debug a Hudson plugin.

Maven Plugin and Goals

Like Hudson, Maven is also extended via plugins. Maven plugins are developed and deployed to the Maven Central Repository. Plugins are identified by a groupId, artifactId, and a version. Maven defines the process of building and distributing a particular project in terms of a build lifecycle. The build lifecycle consists of several build *phases*, which are stages executed sequentially in a build lifecycle. The build phases are made up of goals. A *goal* represents a specific task, which contributes to the building and managing of a project. A goal of a plugin is executed using the long form of the **mvn** command:

```
mvn  <plugin-group-id>:<plugin-artifact-id>[:<plugin-
version>]:<goal>
```

or using the short form:

```
mvn <plugin-prefix>:<goal>
```

For the HPI tool, the Maven groupId is com.eclipse.hudson.tools and the artifactId is maven-hpi-plugin. Usually the version number is skipped and Maven downloads and uses the latest version of the plugin from the Maven central repository. The HPI tool defines several goals and participates in various execution phases of the Maven lifecycle. Widely used goals are

- **hpi:create** To create a skeleton plugin project
- **hpi:hpi** To build and package the plugin project as a .hpi archive
- **hpi:run** To install the plugin to a test application server and start the server for testing

To find more details about various goals defined by the HPI tool, run this command:

```
mvn help:describe -Dplugin=org.eclipse.hudson.tools:maven-hpi-plugin -Ddetail
```

The HPI tool is invoked via the command line using the long form:

```
mvn org.eclipse.hudson.tools:maven-hpi-plugin:create
```

where org.eclipse.hudson.tools is the groupId of the tool, maven-hpi-plugin is the artifactId of the tool, and create is the goal. Also it can be invoked using the short form:

```
mvn hpi:create
```

where hpi is the Maven plugin prefix of the HPI tool.

The second form is the easiest and recommended. However, Maven needs to know the groupId it should search to find the prefix of a plugin. The groupId information is specified in a file named settings.xml located in the Local Maven Repository (usually the .m2 folder of your home directory) as shown here:

```
<settings >
  ...
  <pluginGroups>
    <pluginGroup>org.eclipse.hudson.tools</pluginGroup>
  </pluginGroups>
  ...
</settings>
```

Creating a Skeleton Plugin Project

The simple command to create the plugin skeleton project with sample templates is

```
mvn hpi:create
```

This command tells Maven to download all the required libraries to execute the command and prompts for groupId and artifactId for the plugin as:

```
Enter the groupId of your plugin: net.hudsonlifestyle
Enter the artifactId of your plugin: sample-plugin
```

The name of the generated folder depends on the artifactId entered. It will have the following layout:

```
pom.xml - Maven POM file which is used to build your plugin
src/main/java - Java source files of the plugin
src/main/resources - Jelly view files of the plugin
src/main/webapp - Static resources of the plugin, such as images and HTML files.
```

The Java files are generated with the package name the same as that of the groupId entered. In this example it is net.hudsonlifestyle. The complete project structure looks like this:

```
sample-plugin/
  pom.xml
  src/
    main/
      java/
        net/
          hudsonlifestyle/
            HelloWorldBuilder.java
      resources/
        net/
          index.jelly
          hudsonlifestyle/
            HelloWorldBuilder/
              config.jelly
              index.jelly
              help-name.html
      webapp/
        help-globalConfig.html
```

Building and Running the Plugin Project

The skeleton plugin project created is minimal but is a complete Maven project. It can be built and run without any modification using Maven. The plugin project is built with the command

```
mvn package
```

The **package** command tells Maven to build the project and create the HPI package that can be installed directly to a Hudson server.

The skeleton plugin project has a sample extension, which is fully functional. It is possible to run the project and see the result of the extension added by this skeleton Hudson plugin. The plugin project is run with the command

```
mvn hpi:run
```

The command **hpi:run** means automatically install the packaged plugin to a Hudson server and start the Hudson server automatically. Since the plugin project is a Maven project, the configurations needed for the **run** of the project are defined in the pom.xml and its parent POM. The Maven goal hpi:run is responsible for several of the tasks, including starting the Jetty Server, adding Hudson as a Web application to that server, and installing the plugin to Hudson. The "work" subfolder in the plugin project folder is used as Hudson home. The "work/s" folder contains a list of .hpi files corresponding to various bundled plugins. The only notable difference is a

.hpl that corresponds to the currently built plugin project. It is a simple text file, which contains metadata describing all the files (classes, jars, and resources) associated with the currently built Hudson plugin. This file is generated by the HPI tool every time the plugin project is run using **hpi:run**. Hudson knows how to interpret this file and load the entire plugin without packaging the plugin to a .hpi package. This makes it easy to debug during development time.

Once the plugin project runs successfully, and the Jetty Server is fully started, the Hudson main dashboard page can be viewed using a browser and typing the following in the address bar of the browser: **http://localhost:8080**.

Since this is the default URL for Hudson, it is important that no other copy of Hudson is running at the time. The first time you start Hudson with **hpi:run**, you will see the Hudson CI Server Initial Setup page. Simply click the Finish button to proceed to Hudson.

Testing the Skeleton Plugin

Hudson provides a series of extension points that allow developers to extend Hudson's functionality.

As described in the previous section, the **hpi:run** command installs the currently developed plugin to Hudson, which is added to the Jetty Server as a Web application. This plugin

- Adds an extension to the Hudson builder interface. This sample custom builder, called HelloWorldBuilder, does not do anything fancy, but simply prints out the text Hello *<name>* in the build console log.
- Provides a UI to configure the HelloWorldBuilder extension. *<name>* is any name typed in the UI provided to configure the extension.

It is easy to see the HelloWorldBuilder in action by creating a simple Hudson job, say TestJob, and configuring it. Select "Say hello world," the display name of the HelloWorldBuilder, from the drop-down menu. Once it is set as the builder for the project, the Build section displays "Say hello world" as one of the builders. Input a name in the Name field as shown in Figure 8-5 and click Save to save your configuration changes.

Since HelloWorldBuilder is set as the only builder of the TestJob, when a build is started it will be asked to perform its task. The only task of the HelloWorldBuilder is

FIGURE 8-5. *HelloWorldBuilder build step*

```
Started by user anonymous
Hello, winston!
[DEBUG] Skipping watched dependency update; build not configured
with trigger: TestProject #2
Finished: SUCCESS
```

FIGURE 8-6. *TestJob console output*

to print out the message Hello *<name>!* to the console log. Once a build of the TestJob is completed, the result of HelloWorldBuilder can be viewed in the build console output as shown in Figure 8-6.

Understanding the Hudson Plugin Framework

Hudson defines several interfaces or abstract classes that model an aspect of a build system. These model objects are building blocks of the Hudson platform. They hold the data and state of a job. The service objects are model objects that are runnable. The Hudson executor runs these services to complete an execution.

Among various services provided by Hudson, the foremost is building a job. A job, which is a buildable entity, consists of several configurable areas and build steps. Some of the build steps, listed in order of their execution in time, are:

- **SCM checkout** Based on SCM type, source code is checked out.
- **Pre-build** Invoked to indicate that the build is starting.
- **Build wrapper** Prepare an environment for the build.
- **Builder runs** Actual building happens, like calling Ant, Make, and so on.
- **Recording** Record the output from the build, such as test results.
- **Notification** Send out notifications based on the results determined so far.

What Is an Extension Point?

Hudson provides the concept of *extension points* and *extensions* to facilitate contribution of functionalities to the core platform by plugins. Extension points are interfaces that encapsulate entry points to extend certain services or the functionality of a service provided by the core platform.

The extension points define contracts that need to be implemented, and Hudson allows plugins to contribute those implementations. Plugins hook into the model and service objects via extension points. As an example, Hudson provides an SCM extension point. SCM plugins extend this extension point to provide SCM services such as SVN, Git, CVS, and so on. When an SCM plugin is installed in Hudson, the job configuration provides an opportunity to configure the SCM to checkout sources for the job build.

A service advertises itself as an extendable service by implementing the marker interface called ExtensionPoint:

```
Public abstract class HudsonService implements ExtensionPoint{
   abstract void serviceMethod();
}
```

The abstract method, serviceMethod(), needs to be implemented by the Extension provider (namely the plugin).

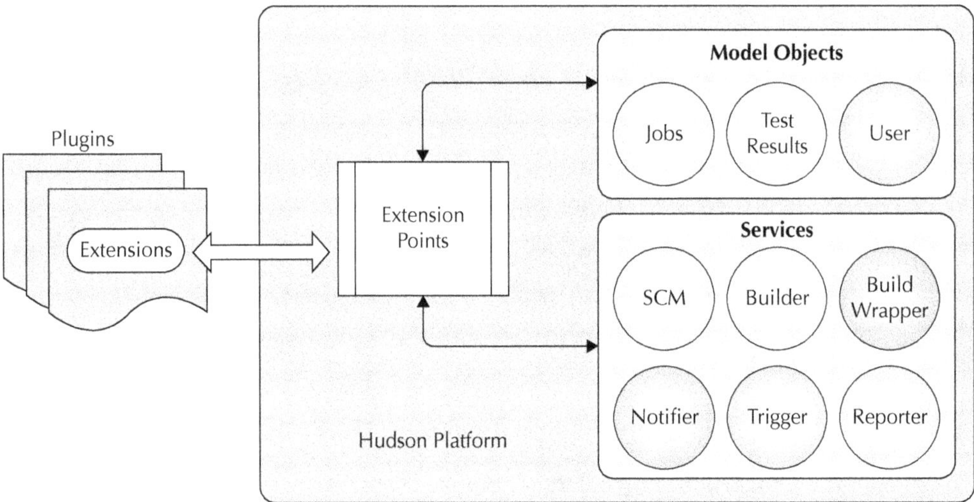

Extending an Extension Point

An extension is an implementation of an interface or abstract classes that marks itself as an extension point, as explained previously. To create an extension component to a service, simply extend the service and annotate your class as an extension:

```
@Extension
public class MyServiceExtension extends HudsonService{
  public void serviceMethod(){
    //Your Implementation goes here
  }
}
```

The annotation @Extension tells Hudson that those annotated classes in the plugin are extension components.

Let us look into some of the code in the sample HelloWorldBuilder.java that extends the Builder extension point to understand

- How to extend an extension point
- How to implement the methods to extend the functionality encapsulated by the extension point

Builders are responsible for building the job. The extension point provided by Hudson to contribute to this builder run step is aptly called Builder. Hudson comes bundled with two of the most popular builders—Ant and Maven. They are in fact extensions to the Builder extension point. So it is possible for any plugin to provide its own builder extension as one of the builders of the job. Several external plugins exist for other popular builders such as Make, Gradle, Rake, and so on. HelloWorldBuilder, our example builder extension, is a contrived example to understand how extensions are built. Far more sophisticated builder extensions are possible using the builder extension point. Let us examine the source to understand how the extension mechanism works.

Examining the Sample Extension

To reiterate, in order for Hudson to understand a class as an extension, it must

- Extend a class that advertises itself as an extension point
- Implement the required abstract methods to extend the functionality
- Tell Hudson that the particular class is an extension

The following illustration shows the UML diagram of the classes the HelloWorldBuilder extends. In this section of the chapter we will examine the model aspect of the extension. The UI part is explained in the next section.

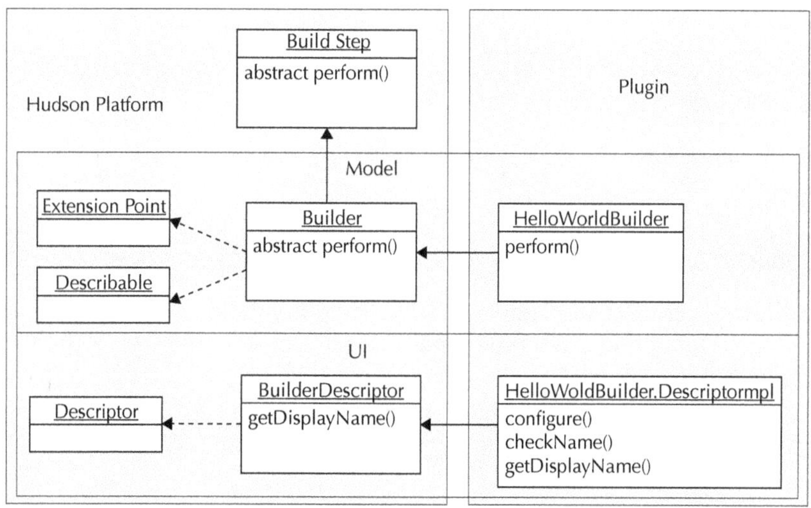

Looking at the source HelloWorldBuilder.java, you'll notice that the class HelloWorldBuilder extends the abstract class Builder, which is the extension point for the builder interface.

```
import hudson.tasks.Builder;
public class HelloWorldBuilder extends Builder {
```

The Builder class itself is a subclass of BuildStep, which defines the abstract method that needs to be implemented by the extensions to contribute to the builder interface. The abstract method needed to be implemented by any builder extension is:

```
import hudson.model.AbstractBuild;
import hudson.model.AbstractProject;
import hudson.model.BuildListener;
public boolean perform(AbstractBuil<?> ab, Launcher launcher,
                 BuildListener bl) throws InterruptedException, IOException;
```

The method BuildStep.perform(..), which is overridden by the HelloWorldBuilder Class, will be invoked by Hudson at runtime to include the build step functionality extended by the HelloWorldBuilder extension.

Finally, to tell Hudson that the class is an extension to some extension point, it must be annotated with the annotation @Extension. The annotation @Extension at the inner class DescriptorImpl tells Hudson that the class is an extension.

```
import hudson.Extension;
import hudson.tasks.BuildStepDescriptor;

@Extension
public static final class DescriptorImpl extends
                                BuildStepDescriptor <Builder>{
```

The overridden BuildStep.perform(..) abstract method gives access to three objects:

- **Build** Object representing the build of the job being performed. The build in turn gives access to important model objects like:
  - Project—The buildable job
  - Workspace—The folder where the build happens
  - Result—Result of the build until this build step
- **Launcher** Launcher that is used to launch the build of this job
- **BuildListener** An interface to communicate the status of the build steps being performed in this builder and send any console message from this build step to Hudson

HelloWorldBuilder uses the BuildListener model object to print the Hello message to the console in the code:

```
HelloWorldBuilder.perform()
@Override
public boolean perform(AbstractBuild build, Launcher launcher, BuildListener
listener) {
 if(getDescriptor().useFrench())
   listener.getLogger().println("Bonjour, "+name+"!");
 else
   listener.getLogger().println("Hello, "+name+"!");
 return true;
}
```

The Build Listener is a holder of an object Logger that is responsible for outputting any message written to it to the job console. The Logger object is obtained via the method listener.getLogger(). The code simply prints the message Hello *<name>!* via the logger.

Modifying the Sample Extension

Hudson provides functionalities via a service called Launcher. As we have seen previously, the BuildStep.perform(..) method gives access to this launcher object. A plugin could

- Use the launcher to execute an external executable
- Send the result of execution to the console

Let us invoke a simple command to list the contents of a folder and send its output to the job console. This is done by adding the following code to the BuildStep.perform(..) method:

```
List<Cause> buildStepCause = new ArrayList();
buildStepCause.add(new Cause() {
  public String getShortDescription() {
    return "Build Step started by Hello Builder";
  }
});
listener.started(buildStepCause);

ArgumentListBuilder args = new ArgumentListBuilder();
if (launcher.isUnix()) {
  args.add("/bin/ls");
  args.add("-la");
} else {
  args.add("dir"); //Windows
}
```

```
String homeDir = System.getProperty("user.home");
args.add(homeDir);
try {
  int r;
  r = launcher.launch().cmds(args).stdout(listener).join();
  if (r != 0) {
    listener.finished(Result.FAILURE);
    return false;
  }
} catch (IOException ioe) {
  ioe.printStackTrace(listener.fatalError("Execution" + args + "failed"));
  listener.finished(Result.FAILURE);
  return false;
} catch (InterruptedException ie) {
  ie.printStackTrace(listener.fatalError("Execution" + args + "failed"));
  listener.finished(Result.FAILURE);
  return false;
}

listener.finished(Result.SUCCESS);
return true;
```

This will require adding the following imports:

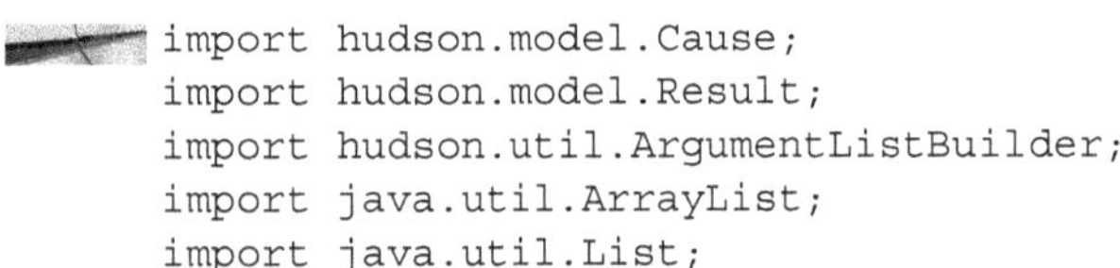

```
import hudson.model.Cause;
import hudson.model.Result;
import hudson.util.ArgumentListBuilder;
import java.util.ArrayList;
import java.util.List;
```

If you are using a Maven-aware IDE like NetBeans or Eclipse, you can simply use the Fix Imports or Organize Imports command after entering the code.

NOTE

If any of the plugin Java code is modified and the plugin is built again, then it is important to shut down the Jetty Server and restart using the ***hpi:run*** *command. However, if a resource file such as CSS, image, or Jelly is changed, then it is not necessary to start the Jetty Server again. Simply refresh your browser window.*

Running the plugin project again shows the console output as:

```
Started by user anonymous
Hello, winston!
Build Step started by Hello Builder
```

```
$ /bin/ls -la /Users/winstonp
total 320
drwxr-xr-x 16 winstonp staff 544 Nov 10 2010 Adobe MAX
drwx------+ 31 winstonp staff 1054 Aug 31 14:54 Desktop
..
Finished: SUCCESS
```

If there is an error, the exception corresponding to the error is displayed in the job console as

```
Started by user anonymous
Hello, winston!
Build Step started by Hello Builder
$ "/bin/ls -la" /Users/winstonp
FATAL: Execution[/bin/ls -la, /Users/winstonp]failed
java.io.IOException: Cannot run program "/bin/ls -la": error=2, No such file or
directory
at java.lang.ProcessBuilder.start(ProcessBuilder.java:460)
at hudson.Proc$LocalProc.<init>(Proc.java:192)
at hudson.Proc$LocalProc.<init>(Proc.java:164)
...
Finished: FAILURE
```

The code added to BuildStep perform(..) is contrived, but explains some of the important concepts. When a build step is started or stopped, let Hudson know about it. This is done via the Job Build Listener interface.

```
listener.started(buildStepCause);
..
..
listener.finished(Result.SUCCESS);
```

This is important for two reasons:

- Hudson heuristically shows the progress of the overall build of the job.
- When a build step fails, Hudson must stop the overall progress of the build and mark the build as FAILED. This is done by sending a message to Hudson about the status of the build via BuildListener.

Use the launcher interface to launch your external executable. Send the console outputs of your execution to Hudson:

```
int r;
r = launcher.launch().cmds(args).stdout(listener).join();
if (r != 0) {
 listener.finished(Result.FAILURE);
 return false;
}
```

Launcher correctly launches the application in the Master or Slave node where the job is running. Always use the return status of the launcher to find out if the execution was successful. The standard output of the launcher is hooked to the listener. This sends the output of the execution to the job build console. This is how the output of the command to list the user directory is displayed in the build console.

Notify Hudson of any failure of the build step using the following code:

```
} catch (IOException ioe) {
 ioe.printStackTrace(listener.fatalError("Execution" + args + "failed"));
 listener.finished(Result.FAILURE);
 return false;
}
```

The stack trace of the exception is sent to the job build console as follows:

```
Exception.printStackTrace(lister.fatalError(..)).
```

Extension UI Configuration

While you're testing the HelloWorldBuilder extension, the Job Configurations page provides a text field to type in some text. Though it is part of the Job Configurations page, the actual UI is provided by the plugin as a configuration for the HelloWorldBuilder extension. There are two ways to configure an extension. One is local to the area of the functionality the plugin extends, typically inside a job configuration page, and the other via the Hudson-wide global configuration page. In this part of the chapter let us see how to configure the extension in the project configuration page and learn

- How to add a UI to get input from user
- How to give feedback to the user on their input
- How to configure the extension with the user input

Hudson has the concept of configurable extension points. Configurable extensions provide a UI for user input. Hudson defines the paradigms Describable and Descriptor to mark an extension as a configurable extension. When an extensible model object is configurable, Hudson marks it with a marker interface called Describable:

```
Public abstract class HudsonService implements Describable, ExtensionPoint {
    abstract void serviceMethod();
}
```

If a plugin extends a Describable object, then it must define a Descriptor object, which is responsible for the interaction between the UI and the model object.

When an extension extends a configurable extension point, it must also implement the corresponding descriptor as an inner class:

```
public class MyServiceExtension extends HudsonService {
  public void serviceMethod(){
   //Your Implementation goes here
  }
  @Extension
  public static class DescriptorImpl extends Descriptor {
    public String getDisplayName() {
      return "Say hello world";
    }
  }
}
```

The methods needed for interaction between the UI and the model object will be defined in the Descriptor inner class. The section Interaction Between UI and Model in the later part of the chapter will cover this concept in detail.

Configuration File Conventions

Hudson uses a UI technology called Jelly. The Jelly UI technology is a server-side technology that uses a rendering engine to convert XML-based Jelly definitions (tags) to client-side code: HTML, JavaScript, and Ajax. Hudson provides a number of Jelly tags for your convenience.

The model objects are bound to these tag attributes via an Expression Language called Jexl.

Expression Language and Jexl

An Expression Language (EL), originally introduced in Java Server Pages (JSP), makes it possible to easily access application data stored in JavaBeans components from pages rendered by server-side UI technology such as Java Server Faces (JSF) and Jelly. Jexl is an extension of EL used by Jelly. For example, the Jexl allows a page author to access a bean using simple syntax such as

```
${extension.method}
```

where extension is the extension model object.

When the tags are rendered into HTML and JavaScript, the rendered code includes information from the model objects to which their attributes are bound. This makes it very powerful to express your view with simple Jelly tags, rather than writing lots of HTML, JavaScript, or Ajax.

The Jelly files you use to render the UI reside in the resources directory of the plugin. Hudson uses a heuristic convention to find these Jelly files. The folder under which these Jelly files must reside should have a path hierarchy similar to the package name of the model class, plus the name of the model class itself.

Hudson uses the same namespace of the Class package as the folder hierarchy plus the model name. In the example plugin, the HelloWorldBuilder model class has the package name net.hudsonlifestyle. So the configuration file must reside under the following folder:

```
src/main/resources/net/hudsonlifestyle/HelloWorldBuilder
```

Hudson uses another convention to tell if the configuration file is meant for local configuration or global configuration. If the configuration is named as config.jelly, it is used as a local configuration file and its content is included in the configuration of the functionality that this extension extends. Since HelloWorldBuilder extends the builder build step of a Hudson job, any Jelly content put in the configuration file

```
src/main/resources/net/hudsonlifestyle/HelloWorldBuilder/config.jelly
```

will be included in the job configuration page to configure the HelloWorldBuilder extension in the builder section of the job configuration.

As explained earlier in the chapter, HelloWorldBuilder extension provides a UI for the user to configure. The UI provided by this extension is a simple TextBox for the user to input their name. The content of the file is very simple. It is a pure XML file with Jelly syntax:

```
<j:jelly xmlns:j="jelly:core" xmlns:st="jelly:stapler"
xmlns:d="jelly:define"
xmlns:l="/lib/layout" xmlns:t="/lib/hudson" xmlns:f="/lib/form">
   <!--
      Creates a text field that shows the value of the "name" property.
      When submitted, it will be passed to the corresponding constructor
      parameter.
   -->
  <f:entry title="Name" field="name">
      <f:textbox />
  </f:entry>
</j:jelly>
```

There are two main tags playing the role of user interaction:

- **entry** Tells Hudson the enclosing tags are considered as user interaction elements and submitted via HTML form
- **textbox** Renders a simple HTML text field whose value will be sent back to the server

Configuration UI Rendering

Let us take a closer look at UI rendering from the Jelly file. If you open the TestJob configuration page and scroll down to the build section and view the Say Hello World builder and its configuration, you will see a Question icon on the right-hand side of the TextField. It displays some help text. Where does this help text come from? If you look at the content of config.jelly, you'll notice there is no such help text. However, Hudson still displays some help. Once again, convention comes into play. In the same folder where your configuration exists, there is a file named help-name.html. Examining the contents of this file, you will see the same help text, which is displayed when you click the help button. How does Hudson know to get the content from this file and display it as help content for the field? The trick is in the name of the file. By convention Hudson looks for a particular file name in the same folder as the config.jelly file. The name of the file should be

```
help-{fieldName}.html
```

In the config.xml file we have

```
<f:entry title="Name" field="name">
      <f:textbox />
</f:entry>
```

field="name" indicates the TextBox should be used as an entry field with the name "name." So based on convention, the help text for that field should exist in a file with name help-name.html.

The content of the file help-name.html is pure HTML. You can include image, text, and hyperlinks in the content to emphasize and enhance your help text. As mentioned in the help text, if you want to use information from Hudson model objects, then you should have Jelly content in the field Help file and the extension of the file name should be .jelly instead of .html. To see this in action, delete the help-name.html file and create the file help-name.jelly. Add the following content to the file:

```
<j:jelly xmlns:j="jelly:core" xmlns:st="jelly:stapler"
xmlns:d="jelly:define">
  <div>
      Welcome to ${app.displayName}. Enter your name in the Field.
  </div>
</j:jelly>
```

Since we have changed only a resource file, the Jetty Server does not need to be restarted again. Simply refresh the Web page. Go to the build section of the page configuration page and click on the Help button on the right side of the text box. You should see in the help text that ${app.displayName} is replaced with "Hudson", which is the name of the application, and the test message is displayed as shown in Figure 8-7.

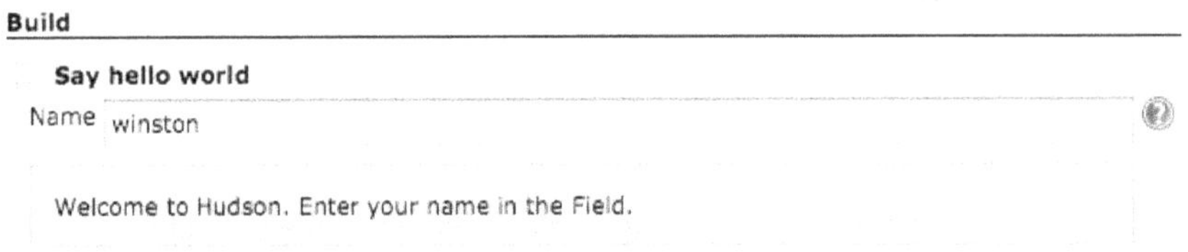

Build

Say hello world

Name winston

Welcome to Hudson. Enter your name in the Field.

FIGURE 8-7. *Help text for an extension UI element*

Interaction Between UI and Model

This part of the chapter will explain how the UI interacts with the Hudson model objects. HelloWorldBuilder is a Hudson model object. It encapsulates data. The UI can interact with this model to get and display its data or get information from the user via fields in the UI and update the model data. Let us examine how this happens.

You created the help file help-name.jelly and included a Jexl expression ${app .displayName} in the content. When the server side of the Hudson application received the request for a job configuration page, it included the HelloWorldBuilder configuration snippet in the job configuration page. Since the help itself is a jelly file, it was given to the Jelly renderer to render it to client-side code. The Jelly renderer is responsible for substituting the corresponding value for the Jexl expression after evaluating it. The first part of the expression evaluates to the model object, then to the method name of the model object.

By default, Hudson registers three identifiers for the model objects to the Jexl expression evaluator:

- **app** The Hudson application itself. For example, ${app.displayName} evaluates to Hudson.getDisplayName().
- **it** The model object to which the Jelly UI belongs. For example, ${it.name} evaluates to HelloWorldBuilder.getName().
- **h** A global utility function (called Functions), which provides static utility methods. For example, ${h.clientLocale} evaluates to Functions .getClientLocale().

Since the expression ${app.displayName} evaluates to "Hudson," the name of the Hudson application, that is what you see in the field help text.

While the UI displays the data of a model, the input of the user in the UI must update the model data when the configuration page is submitted. In this case, the value of the name the user enters in the UI must be updated in the model.

When the UI is submitted, Hudson re-creates the model by passing the corresponding value via the constructor. Hence the constructor of the model object must have a parameter whose name matches the name of the field. In the configuration you have

```
<f:entry title="Name" field="name">
```

So the constructor of your HelloWorldBuilder must have a parameter with name "name." If you look at the constructor of the class HelloWorldBuilder, it does indeed have a parameter "name":

```
import org.kohsuke.stapler.DataBoundConstructor;
@DataBoundConstructor
public HelloWorldBuilder(String name) {
   this.name = name;
}
```

The annotation @DataBoundConstructor hints to Hudson that this extension is bound to a field, and on UI submission it must be reconstructed using the value of the fields submitted.

Also it must have a getter with the name of the field for the config.xml to get the data for the second time around when the project is configured again.

```
public String getName() {
   return name;
}
```

This information is persisted along with the project configuration. Look at the project configuration and note that the value of the Name field is saved as a HelloWorldBuilder configuration.

```
<xml version='1.0' encoding='UTF-8'?>
<project>
  <actions/>
  <description></description>
  <keepDependencies>false</keepDependencies>
  <creationTime>1314407794225</creationTime>
  <properties>
      <watched-dependencies-property/>
  </properties>
  <scm class="hudson.scm.NullSCM"/>
  <advancedAffinityChooser>false</advancedAffinityChooser>
  <canRoam>true</canRoam>
  <disable>false</disabled>
  <blockBuildWhenDownstreamBuilding>false</blockBuildWhenDownstreamBuilding>
  <blockBuildWhenUpstreamBuilding>false</blockBuildWhenUpstreamBuilding>
  <triggers class="vector">
```

```
  <concurrentBuild>false</concurrentBuild>
  <cleanWorkspaceRequired>false</cleanWorkspaceRequired>
  <builders>
     <org.sample.hudson.HelloWorldBuilder>
     <name>Winston</name>
     </org.sample.hudson.HelloWorldBuilder>
  </builders>
  <publishers/>
  <buildWrappers/>;
</project>
```

UI Validation

In the Job Configurations page, go to the Build section | HelloWorldBuilder UI and remove the name in the text field. Then click elsewhere on the page. You will see an error message as shown in Figure 8-8.

CAUTION
Do not press the ENTER or RETURN key. This will submit the configuration page.

Now enter a two-letter word (say "xy") for Name and click somewhere else on the page. You will see an information message as shown in Figure 8-9.

Where does this error message or info come from? If you examine your config.xml or any of the corresponding Field Help files, no such message exists. The magic is in the Jelly file rendering. Some Ajax code is rendered, which contacts the Hudson server behind the scenes and asks what message it should display. You can easily observe these Ajax requests using Firefox and Firebug. When config.jelly was rendered by Hudson, while rendering the jelly tag <f:textbox />, the Ajax

FIGURE 8-8. *UI validation error message*

Build

Say hello world

Name xy

Isn't the name too short?

Delete

FIGURE 8-9. *UI validation information message*

code required to do the checking was also rendered. An Ajax request is sent to the Hudson server as

```
GET /job/TestJob/descriptorByName/org.sample.hudson.HelloWorldBuilder/
checkName?value=xy HTTP/1.1
Host: localhost:8080
User-Agent: Mozilla/5.0 (Macintosh; Intel Mac OS X 10.6; rv:6.0.1)
Gecko/20100101
Firefox/6.0.1
Accept: text/javascript, text/html, application/xml, text/xml, */*
```

NOTE
If you are using the Firefox browser and Firebug add-on to display the Net activity, then you can observe the Ajax request info easily.

Hudson evaluates this request, finds the extension HelloWorldBuilder, then executes the method doCheckName() and returns the result. Again Hudson uses the convention check + {nameOfTheField} as part of the Ajax URL.

NOTE
By default, for every f:textbox tag in the Jelly config file, Hudson will render the Ajax check. However, if your extension class does not include the corresponding method (in this case doCheckName()), then Hudson will silently ignore the check request.

The doCheckName() method is straightforward. The Ajax request specifies the checkName method with the parameter value as {..}/checkName?value="xy". For Hudson to pass the correct value to the parameter value of doCheckName, it must be annotated with @QueryParameter. Also the method must return a FormValidation object, which determines the outcome of the check:

```
public FormValidation doCheckName(@QueryParameter String value)
                                             throws IOException, ServletException {
   if (value.length() == 0) {
      return FormValidation.error("Please set a name");
   }
   if (value.length() < 4) {
      return FormValidation.warning("Isn't the name too short?");
   }
   return FormValidation.ok();
}
```

The doCheckName() method returns FormValidation.error(..) if the parameter value has no text. If the length of the value is less than 4, then the FormValidation .warning() is returned.

Hudson defines a few convenient methods in the FormValidation object:

- **ok** This sends the HTTP code 200.
- **error** The HTML sent back to the browser displays a red text with an error icon.
- **warning** The HTML sent back to the browser displays golden yellow text with a warning icon.

Global UI Configuration

In the previous section you learned how to configure the extension on a per-job basis. You may be able to configure the extension (in this case HelloWorldBuilder) of each job to do different things. However, some of the configuration extension could be global. For example, if you use Git as your SCM system in a project, you might want to configure two different jobs to ask Git to check out from a different repository. So in both the projects, the Git SCM extension must be configured to use two different repository URLs.

If the Git SCM extension needs to know the Git native binaries, then having the UI configure the Git binary location in the job makes little sense, because it doesn't vary job to job. It makes sense to put such a configuration in Hudson's global configuration page.

Our simple HelloWorldBuilder sample extension can be configured to say "hello" either in French or English. The configuration of the language to use is done globally. Once the configuration is set, all the builds of various jobs that use HelloWorldBuilder would either say hello in French or English based on this global configuration.

To configure this global configuration, open the Manage Hudson | Configure System page and scroll down to the HelloWorldBuilder configuration section.

FIGURE 8-10. *Global configuration of HelloWorldBuilder*

Here the global configuration can be set to use French as the language for hello, as shown in Figure 8-10.

For Hudson to include the global configuration of an extension in its global configuration page, it must be placed in a file called global.jelly. The namespace convention for this file is similar to the local configuration file. For the HelloWorldBuilder the global configuration file is

```
net/hudsonlifestyle/HelloWorldBuilder/global.jelly
```

In the HelloWorldBuilder.perform(..) method we have

```
if (getDescriptor().useFrench()) {
  listener.getLogger().println("Bonjour, " + name + "!");
} else {
   listener.getLogger().println("Hello, " + name + "!");
}
```

The global configuration UI of the extension we saw in the Hudson global configuration page is defined in the global.jelly file as

```
<f:section title="Hello World Builder">
   <f:entry title="French" description="Check if we should say hello in French"
        help="/plugin/javaone-sample/help-globalConfig.html">
      <f:checkbox name="hello_world.useFrench" checked="${descriptor.useFrench()}" />
   </f:entry>
</f:section>
```

The decision whether this check box should be checked or not comes from the extension itself. The Jexl expression ${descriptor.useFrench()} would resolve to HelloWorldBuilder.DescriptorImpl.useFrench(), which is defined as

```
public boolean useFrench() {
  return useFrench;
}
```

useFrench is a field in HelloWorldBuilder. This field should be set to true if the user checks the check box. Once the global configuration is submitted, by convention Hudson calls a method called configure() in the descriptor of HelloWorldBuilder and passes a JSON object. The JSON object is constructed as a name-value pair of all the fields in the submitted form of the configuration page. It is up to the extension to find the value of its own fields from its config.xml embedded in the JSON object and use it. HelloWorldBuilder defines this method as

```
@Override
public boolean configure(StaplerRequest req, JSONObject formData) throws
FormException {
  useFrench = formData.getBoolean("useFrench");
  save();
  return super.configure(req, formData);
}
```

The config.xml defined a check box with name "useFrench." So the configure() method needs to find the Boolean value corresponding to the field useFrench and set the value to the field HelloWorldBuilder.useFrench. The next time HelloWorldBuilder.perform() is called during the build of the job, HelloWorldBuilder.useFrench is consulted, and based on its value, the hello message would be either in French or English.

The custom extension is also responsible for persisting and loading the global configuration values. The saving is done by calling the method

```
save();
```

Typically the saving is done in the configure method. Once the form data received as a JSON object is processed, the save() method is called, which in turn persists the values in an XML file in the Hudson home directory.

To load the global configuration, the Descriptor must include a call to the method

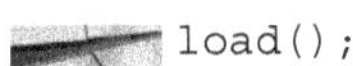

```
load();
```

The best place to have the load() method is in the constructor of the Descriptor. The load() method instructs Hudson to load the saved global configuration and populate the current descriptor when it is constructed.

TIP
For the saving and loading of global properties to work correctly, each property should have proper getter and setter methods.

Summary

Hudson Continuous Integration Server is a popular open source project and recently became a technology project at Eclipse Foundation. It has an ecosystem of plugin developers developing plugins for various aspects of this Continuous Integration system. The Hudson plugin development environment provides a rich set of extension points for plugin developers to develop their custom plugins. This chapter explored the fundamentals of the plugin development framework, explaining various steps involved in developing a simple plugin using the Hudson HPI tool. More advanced topics are covered in Chapter 9.

PART III

The Hudson Lifestyle

CHAPTER 9

Advanced Plugin Development

In Chapter 8, we learned how to develop a simple Hudson plugin. In this chapter we will look into subjects beyond the basic and explore the deeper realm of plugin development. There are several areas plugin developers can extend to participate in the functionalities provided by Hudson. Two major areas that are interesting to many plugin developers are:

- Extending various aspects of Hudson dashboards
- Extending various aspects of Hudson jobs

Once you understand the basic nuances of Hudson plugin development, adding further functionality is more about understanding the Extension Point API and creating the custom extensions and then implementing the appropriate abstract methods.

NOTE
The Hudson Extension Point API is well documented. The JavaDocs for the latest version of the Hudson Extension Point API are available at http://wiki.hudson-ci.org/display/HUDSON/Extension+points.

Extending Various Aspects of Hudson Dashboards

Hudson has three primary dashboards:

- The Main dashboard, which is the primary Hudson portal
- The Job dashboard view, which displays information about the job
- The Build dashboard, which displays information about a particular build of a job

Hudson provides numerous extension points to extend various aspects of these dashboards. Let us look at how we can add some functionality to the main dashboard.

Creating a Custom Rendered Jobs Status View

The main dashboard displays the status of all the jobs. The status of jobs in Hudson is displayed on the Jobs Status page in tabbed sections, and each tab is called a view. By default the job status is displayed as a table in the view from a model class

Jobs Status

Admin | All | Core | Hudson Plugins | Radiator | **Success**

S	W	Job ↓	Last Success	Last Failure	Last Duration
		cvs-plugin_core	4 mo 9 days (#4)	5 mo 4 days (#3)	34 sec
		legacy-maven-plugin_core	4 mo 9 days (#7)	4 mo 9 days (#6)	7 min 38 sec
		maven3-plugin_core	4 mo 9 days (#4)	5 mo 4 days (#3)	6 min 33 sec

FIGURE 9-1. *Default ListView showing only the builds with status success*

named ListView. The model for each table column is a ListViewColumn. The table column displays some status information of a job or some action related to a job. Additional view tabs can be created and configured to display certain jobs filtered by certain criteria. Hudson provides a view configuration page, which can be invoked from the sidebar by clicking the link Edit View to filter jobs based on criteria. Figure 9-1 shows a default view tab that displays only the jobs that have status success.

Though the view created by the default ListView model displays the job status information in table columns, Hudson provides an extension point to create a custom rendered view. In this section let us see how to create a custom rendered view that displays a selected set of jobs based on their build status. This view will display the jobs as a colored graphical representation of the status of the jobs.

Let us start by creating a plugin named sample-view-plugin, place the custom rendered view in that plugin, and call it Sample View. After we finish developing the plugin and install it in Hudson, the Sample View will be available to create a custom rendered view. Here we assume that you have already read Chapter 8 and understand the basic nuances of creating, developing, and deploying a Hudson plugin.

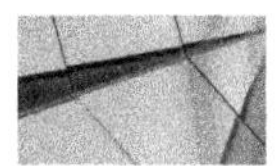

NOTE

You can download the complete sources for the sample plugins in this chapter from www.oraclepressbooks.com.

Custom Rendered View Model

Every UI in Hudson is associated with a model. The model SampleView, for the Sample View UI, is in the file SampleView.java. The SampleView model extends the ListView model (hudson.model.ListView), which in turn implements the extension point View (hudson.model.View).

The model SampleView has a static class, SampleViewDescriptor, which is annotated with @Extension to indicate that it is an Extension class. Since the superclass of SampleView is View, while loading the plugin, Hudson knows to add SampleView as an extension to the extension point View. Thus SampleView will be available to users to create a view with the custom rendering. Also since SampleView is marked as an @Extension via a Descriptor (Hudson.model.Descriptor), Hudson also knows it has an associated UI. The SampleView model delegates the rendering information of the job itself to another model called JobEntry, which provides the rendering information such as the color used by the UI based on status of the job.

Code Listing *SampleView.java*

```
public class SampleView extends ListView {
    private boolean stable, unstable, failed, aborted, running;
    @DataBoundConstructor
    public SampleView(String name) {
        super(name);
    }
    public boolean isStable() {
        return stable;
    }
    public boolean isUnstable() {
        return unstable;
    }
    public boolean isFailed() {
        return failed;
    }
    public boolean isAborted() {
        return aborted;
    }
    public boolean isRunning() {
        return running;
    }
    @Override
    public synchronized List<TopLevelItem> getItems() {
        List<TopLevelItem> base = super.getItems();
        List<TopLevelItem> result = new ArrayList<TopLevelItem>(base.size());
        for (TopLevelItem item : base) {
            if (item instanceof Job) {
                if (running && !((Job) item).isBuilding()) {
                    continue;
                }
                Run lastBuild = ((Job) item).getLastCompletedBuild();
                Result status = lastBuild != null ? lastBuild.getResult() : null;
```

```
                if ((stable && status == Result.SUCCESS)
                        || (unstable && status == Result.UNSTABLE)
                        || (failed && status == Result.FAILURE)
                        || (aborted && status == Result.ABORTED)
                        || (running && status == null) /* Show running job if it has
no completed builds */) {
                    result.add(item);
                }
            }
        }
        return result;
    }
    public synchronized List<JobEntry> getJobs() {
        List<JobEntry> jobs = new ArrayList<JobEntry>();
        for (TopLevelItem item : getItems()) {
            jobs.add(new JobEntry((Job) item));
        }
        return jobs;
    }
    @Override
    protected void submit(StaplerRequest req) throws ServletException, Descriptor.
FormException, IOException {
        stable = req.hasParameter("sample_view.stable");
        unstable = req.hasParameter("sample_view.unstable");
        failed = req.hasParameter("sample_view.failed");
        aborted = req.hasParameter("sample_view.aborted");
        running = req.hasParameter("sample_view.running");
        super.submit(req);
    }
    @Extension
    public static final class SampleViewDescriptor extends ViewDescriptor {
        @Override
        public String getDisplayName() {
            return "Sample View";
        }
    }
}
```

Code Listing *JobEntry.java*

```
public class JobEntry {
    private Job job;
    private String backgroundColor;
    private String color;
    public JobEntry(Job job) {
        this.job = job;
        switch (this.job.getIconColor()) {
            case GREEN:
                this.backgroundColor = "#99FF99";
                this.color = "#339933";
                break;
            case BLUE:
```

```
                    this.backgroundColor = "#99FFCC";
                    this.color = "#339966";
                    break;
                case YELLOW:
                    this.backgroundColor = "#FFC130";
                    this.color = "#AAFFFF";
                    break;
                case RED:
                    this.backgroundColor = "#FF9999";
                    this.color = "#993333";
                    break;
                default:
                    this.backgroundColor = "#AAAAAA";
                    this.color = "555555";
            }
        }
        public String getName() {
            return job.getName();
        }
        public String getUrl() {
            return this.job.getUrl() + "lastBuild";
        }
        public Job getJob() {
            return job;
        }
        public String getBackgroundColor() {
            return backgroundColor;
        }
        public String getColor() {
            return color;
        }
    }
```

Custom Rendered View UI

Figure 9-2 illustrates the model–view relationship. The UI for Sample View has two parts: the UI that displays the view status of the jobs and the UI for configuring the custom view. The Jobs Status view is displayed via the UI definitions in a Jelly file called index.jelly. Hudson knows how to find the Jelly files corresponding to a model based on convention, as discussed in detail in Chapter 4. Thus, the Jelly files for this project will be located in src/main/resources/net/hudsonlifestyle/SampleView/.

The model SampleView can define its own index.jelly. However, in this sample plugin we will not create one, but rather let Hudson use the index.jelly provided by the superclass ListView. This file includes two other Jelly files named main.jelly, which is responsible for rendering a custom view, and noJob.jelly, used for displaying a helpful message when there are no jobs associated with this view.

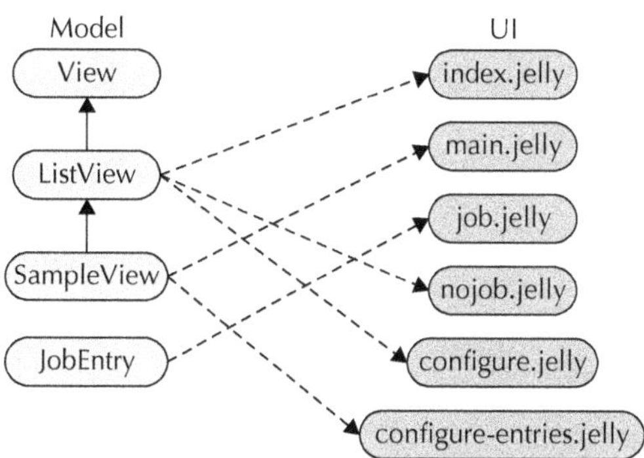

FIGURE 9-2. *Model-View relationship of the custom rendered view*

The job.jelly, which is associated with the model JobEntry, is responsible for rendering the UI for each job status. The jelly file main.jelly uses job.jelly to render the status of all jobs it knows via the model ViewModel.

Code Listing *main.jelly*

```
<j:jelly xmlns:j="jelly:core" xmlns:st="jelly:stapler" xmlns:d="jelly:define"
         xmlns:l="/lib/layout" xmlns:t="/lib/hudson" xmlns:f="/lib/form"
         xmlns:i="jelly:fmt">
    <meta http-equiv="refresh" content="${from.refresh}" />
    <j:choose>
        <j:when test="${empty(items)}">
            <st:include page="noJob.jelly" />
        </j:when>
        <j:otherwise>
            <div style="border-top: 1px solid; border-bottom: 1px solid; padding:
10px;">
                <j:forEach var="job" items="${it.jobs}">
                     <st:include page="job.jelly" />
                </j:forEach>
                <br style="clear:both"/>
            </div>
        </j:otherwise>
    </j:choose>
</j:jelly>
```

Code Listing *job.jelly*

```
<j:jelly xmlns:j="jelly:core" >
    <j:set var="height" value="75px" />
    <j:set var="jobFont" value="40px" />
```

```
    <table align="center" style="margin: 5px; padding: 5px; background-color:${job.
backgroundColor}; border-radius:10px; width:${width}; height:${height}; float: left"
tooltip="${job.name}">
        <tr>
            <td>
                <a
                    style="white-space: nowrap; color: ${job.color}; font-size:
${jobFont};"
                    href="${job.url}">${job.name}
                </a>

            </td>
        </tr>
    </table>
</j:jelly>
```

The job.jelly file tells how to format individual job entries. In this case, it will be a rounded rectangle with job.name, job.backgroundColor, and job.color supplied by the JobEntry object for the job via the methods getName, getBackgroundColor, and getColor, respectively.

A user can configure a view via a configuration UI that provides filtering of jobs and can apply other customizations. The Jelly file for the configuration UI is configure.jelly. The subclasses can provide their own specific customization through another Jelly file, configure-entries.jelly, which will be included by configure.jelly. Since the model SampleView is marked as a describable extension, Hudson would find configure.jelly to display the configuration UI. When the user submits the configurations, Hudson injects the changes back into the SampleView model via the method submit(StaplerRequest req).

Code Listing *configure-entries.jelly*

```
<j:jelly xmlns:j="jelly:core" xmlns:f="/lib/form">
    <f:section title="${%Job Filters}">
        <f:entry title="Build Status" help="/plugin/sample-view-plugin/help-status.
html">
            <f:checkbox name="sample_view.stable" checked="${it.stable}"/> ${%Stable}
            <f:checkbox name="sample_view.unstable" checked="${it.unstable}"/>
${%Unstable}
            <f:checkbox name="sample_view.failed" checked="${it.failed}"/> ${%Failed}
            <f:checkbox name="sample_view.aborted" checked="${it.aborted}"/>
${%Aborted}
        </f:entry>
        <f:entry title="${%Jobs}">
            <j:forEach var="job" items="${app.items}">
                <f:checkbox name="${job.name}" checked="${it.contains(job)}"
title="${job.name}" />
                <br/>
            </j:forEach>
        </f:entry>
    </f:section>
</j:jelly>
```

There is one other jelly file, newViewDetail.jelly. It is a trivial HTML fragment that contains the detail text to be shown in the New View page.

Code Listing *newViewDetail.jelly*

```
<div>
    <i>Sample View</i> to illustrate how to create a custom view in a plugin.
</div>
```

Using the Custom Rendered View

Once the sample-view-plugin is created, compiled, and packaged successfully, the next step is to examine the Sample View we created in the plugin. Run the plugin from the command line using **mvn hpi:run** and then open a browser and view the Hudson main dashboard. If the plugin is successfully loaded, when you're creating a new view by clicking on the "+" sign in the View tab, it should list the Sample View in the selected view types as shown in Figure 9-3. Create a view with the name Sample View – Custom.

Once the Sample View is selected as a custom rendered view for displaying the status of your jobs, Hudson will offer the configuration UI as shown in Figure 9-4. This configuration has settings to filter the jobs it should show in the custom rendered view. It can be customized to show jobs with one or more statuses such as Stable, Unstable, Failed, or Aborted. Also, it lists a check box array of jobs to be displayed in this view.

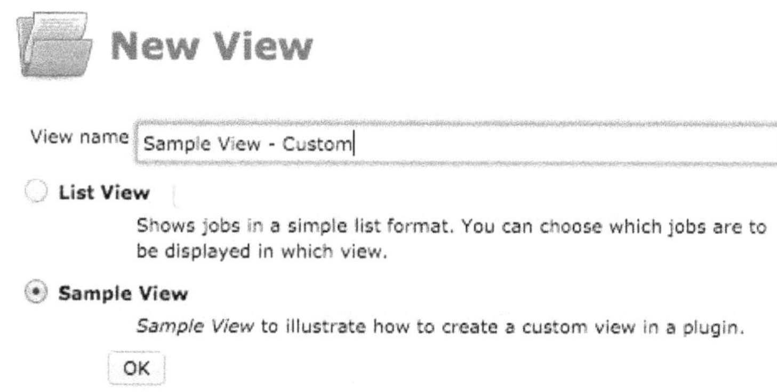

FIGURE 9-3. *Selecting the custom rendered view*

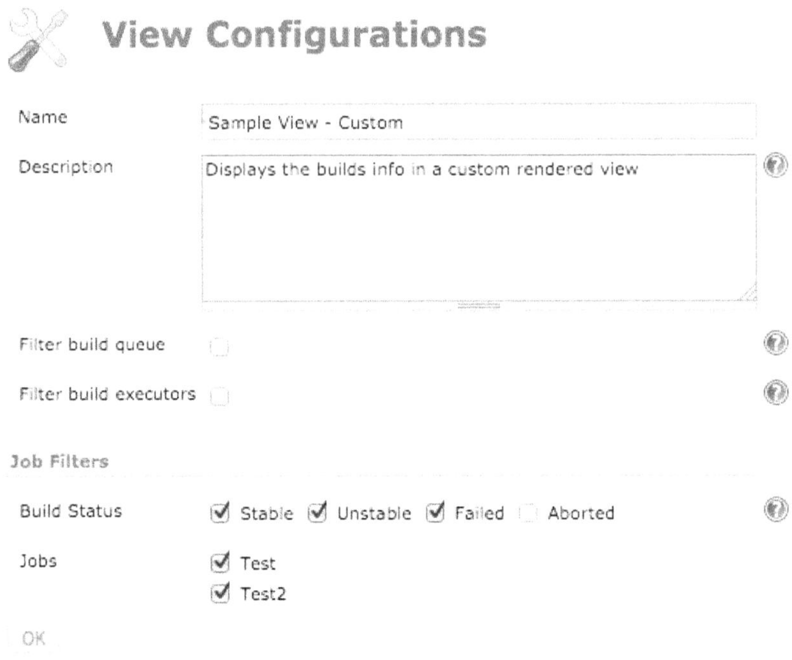

FIGURE 9-4. *Configuring the custom rendered view*

After you've configured and saved the Sample View, it will be ready to display the jobs status based on your filtering. When you go back to the main dashboard, you should see a new tab named Sample View – Custom as shown in Figure 9-5. This tab displays the job status differently than the default model ListView.

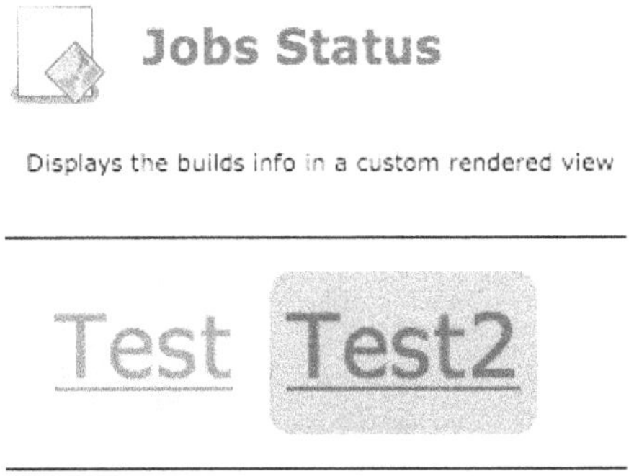

FIGURE 9-5. *Jobs status displayed using a custom rendered view*

The failed builds are displayed as red rectangles and successful builds as green rectangles. The information to display in green or red color is obtained from the model JobEntry. The list of jobs to display in this view is obtained from the model SampleView. Though this is a very simple sample of how a custom rendering of a view could be created, a creative user can create a much more sophisticated view based on the job information available for that custom view.

Adding a Custom Column to the Default View

In the previous section we saw how to add a custom rendered view. Hudson also allows one to add a custom column to the default model ListView. The extension point to use for this purpose is ListViewColumn. In our plugin, sample-column-view-plugin, we create a class called ScmTypeColumn and extend it with ListViewColumn. This class is a describable extension, so we must provide a Descriptor. We have an inner static class, CustomColumnDescriptor, which is annotated as @Extension.

Code Listing *ScmTypeColumn.java*

```
public class ScmTypeColumn extends ListViewColumn {
   public String getScmType(Job job) {
       AbstractProject project = (AbstractProject) job;
       return project.getScm().getDescriptor().getDisplayName();
   }
   @Extension
   public static class CustomColumnDescriptor extends ListViewColumnDescriptor {
       @Override
       public boolean shownByDefault() {
           return true;
       }
       @Override
       public String getDisplayName() {
           return "Custom Column";
       }
       @Override
       public ListViewColumn newInstance(final StaplerRequest request,
               final JSONObject formData) throws FormException {
           return new ScmTypeColumn();
       }
   }
}
```

Custom View Column UI

The UI displayed by the ViewColumn has two sections, the column header and the column data in each of the rows. The column header UI is defined via the jelly file columnHeader.jelly. The column data for each row is defined via the jelly file column.jelly. Hudson passes the job object corresponding to each row in the view to the column.jelly as variable "job". In our sample the SCM information in the jobs

FIGURE 9-6. *Custom SCM type view column*

is extracted from this object and its name is displayed in each of the rows as shown in Figure 9-6.

Note the ${resURL}-relative path in the column.jelly file shown in the next Code Listing. In the project, the image is located at src/main/webapp/icons/scm.png.

Code Listing *column.jelly*

```
<j:jelly xmlns:j="jelly:core">
    <j:set var="job" value="${job}"/>
    <td>
       <img src="${resURL}/plugin/sample-view-column-plugin/icons/scm.png"/>
       ${it.getScmType(job)}
    </td>
</j:jelly>
```

Code Listing *columnHeader.jelly*

```
<j:jelly xmlns:j="jelly:core">
       <th tooltip="Custom Column">
      SCM Type
      </th>
</j:jelly>
```

Adding an Action to the Action Panel of the Main Dashboard

Hudson provides a list of action links on the left-hand side of the main dashboard. This section of the dashboard is called the Action Panel. These action links can be used to display additional information that is currently not displayed in any of the default dashboards. For example, let us say you want to do some auditing of disk space used by various jobs in Hudson. For that you want to add a link to the Action Panel called Show Disk Usage, as shown in Figure 9-7. When you click that link,

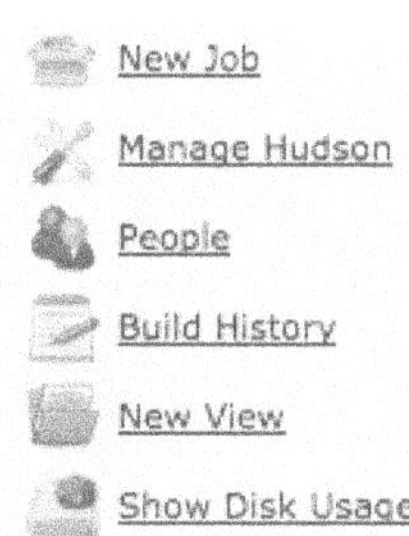

FIGURE 9-7. *Show Disk Usage action link*

you want to display a new page that lists all the jobs in Hudson along with information about the number of builds each job is storing and the total disk space occupied by each job in a table. Let us see how to do this.

RootAction Extension

Hudson provides an extension point, RootAction (hudson.model.RootAction), for this purpose. Let us create a plugin named sample-root-action-plugin and create an extension to extend RootAction and place it in the class DiskUsageAction as shown in the upcoming code listing. This class is annotated with @Extension to let Hudson know that this class should be considered as an extension when the plugin loads. Since this action extends RootAction, Hudson will use the information in this class to create a link and add it to the Action Panel of the main dashboard. As you can see in Figure 9-7, this action needs to specify:

- An icon, which is specified using the method getIconFileName. In this plugin the icons are kept under the folder webapp/icons. In the built plugin, webapp will become the WEB_INF folder, the root of all Web resources, for this plugin. But we need to tell Hudson in which plugin this folder resides. This done by prefixing the icon path with **/plugin/sample-root-action-plugin**.
- A URL to create a link from this action to a page which displays the relevant information. Hudson uses the method getUrlName.

Code Listing *DiskUsageAction.java*

```
@Extension
public class DiskUsageAction implements RootAction {
    public String getIconFileName() {
        return "/plugin/sample-root-action-plugin/icons/diskusage16.png";
    }
```

```
    public String getDisplayName() {
        return "Show Disk Usage";
    }
    public String getUrlName() {
        return Hudson.getInstance().getRootUrl() + "plugin/sample-root-action-plugin/
diskUsage";
    }
}
```

Model Object for the Disk Usage Page

As we have seen in Chapter 8, when Hudson receives a request to serve a URL, it will first try to resolve a model corresponding to the URL path. By default, it will start with the "grandfather" object hudson.model.Hudson and search through the containing tree of objects until an object matches the URL path. However, it is possible to tell Hudson to start with a different grandfather object inside a plugin. By specifying the prefix of the URL name with "plugin/sample-root-action-plugin," we are telling Hudson to find the grandfather object in the plugin sample-root-action-plugin. The grandfather object of a plugin is always a class that extends the interface plugin (hudson.plugin). In our plugins this class is DiskUsagePlugin. It has only one method, getDiskUsage, which returns the object DiskUsage, the model for our disk usage information page. DiskUsage uses a helper model, JobDiskUsage, to display specific information about each job.

Code Listing *DiskUsagePlugin.java*

```
public class DiskUsagePlugin extends Plugin{
    private DiskUsage diskUsage = new DiskUsage();
    public DiskUsage getDiskUsage() {
        return diskUsage;
    }
}
```

Code Listing *DiskUsage.java*

```
public class DiskUsage {
    public List<JobDiskUsage> getJobDiskUsages() throws IOException {
        List<JobDiskUsage> jobDiskUsages = new ArrayList<JobDiskUsage>();
        File hudsonHome = Hudson.getInstance().getRootDir();
        File jobsFolder = new File(hudsonHome, "jobs");
        List<TopLevelItem> items = Hudson.getInstance().getItems();
        for (TopLevelItem item : items) {
            if (item instanceof AbstractProject) {
                AbstractProject job = (AbstractProject) item;
                jobDiskUsages.add(new JobDiskUsage(job, jobsFolder));
```

```
            }
        }
        return jobDiskUsages;
    }
}
```

Code Listing *JobDiskUsage.java*

```
public class JobDiskUsage {
    private String name;
    private long sizeInDisk;
    private int numBuilds;
    public JobDiskUsage(AbstractProject job, File jobsFolder) throws IOException {
        name = job.getName();
        File jobFolder = new File(jobsFolder, name);
        sizeInDisk = getFileSize(jobFolder);
        numBuilds = job.getBuilds().size();
    }
    public String getName() {
        return name;
    }
    public long getSizeInDisk() {
        return sizeInDisk;
    }
    public int getNumBuilds() {
        return numBuilds;
    }
    public long getFileSize(File file) throws IOException {
        long size = 0;
        if (file.isDirectory() && !Util.isSymlink(file)) {
            File[] fileList = file.listFiles();
            if (fileList != null) {
                for (File child : fileList) {
                    size += getFileSize(child);
                }
            }
        }
        return size + file.length();
    }
}
```

Disk Usage Page UI

As we have seen before, if a model object has an associated jelly UI definition page, index.jelly, then Hudson will render that page and send it as an HTTP response. Since our plugin has index.jelly at the correct namespace defined by the Hudson convention, it will be rendered by Hudson to display the disk usage information in a table as shown in Figure 9-8. Though this figure just shows the disk usage table, if you installed the plugin and clicked on the Show Disk Usage link in the Action Panel, the page would show the header and footer as shown in other Hudson

Job name	Number of Builds	DiskUsage
Test	8	34642825
Test2	14	122673

FIGURE 9-8. *Disk usage table entries*

dashboard pages. The correct layout of a dashboard is included in our disk usage page using the jelly tags <l:layout>, <l:side-panel>, and <l:main-panel> as shown in the next code listing. The jelly expression ${it.getJobDiskUsages()} is used to get the PageDiskUsage objects from the model DiskUsage and display the information obtained from it as table columns.

Code Listing *index.jelly*

```
<j:jelly xmlns:j="jelly:core"  xmlns:l="/lib/layout" >
    <l:layout title="${%Disk Usage}" secured="true">
        <l:side-panel>
            <l:tasks>
                <l:task icon="images/24x24/up.gif" href="${rootURL}/" title="${%Back
to Dashboard}" />
            </l:tasks>
        </l:side-panel>
        <l:main-panel>
            <h1>
                <img src="${resURL}/plugin/sample-root-action-plugin/icons/diskus-
age48.png" /> ${%Disk usage}
            </h1>
            <table style="text-align:center" class="sortable pane bigtable">
                <tr>
                    <th>${%Job name}</th>
                    <th>${%Number of Builds}</th>
                    <th>${%DiskUsage}</th>
                </tr>
                <j:forEach var="p" items="${it.getJobDiskUsages()}">
                    <tr>
                        <td>
                            <b>${p.name}</b>
                        </td>
                        <td> ${p.numBuilds}</td>
                        <td>${p.sizeInDisk}</td>
                    </tr>
                </j:forEach>
            </table>
        </l:main-panel>
    </l:layout>
</j:jelly>
```

NOTE
Hudson defines some other actions that can be used similar to RootAction to add links:
***BuildBadgeAction**: This action puts a little icon (or icons) next to the build in the build history.*
***ManagementLink**: This action adds an icon and link to the Hudson management page.*
***ProminentProjectAction**: This action adds a prominent action link with icon at the top of each job page.*
***TransientProjectActionFactory**: Factory to create nonpersisting actions that are displayed in the Action Panel of a job dashboard.*

Custom Decoration of Hudson Pages

In the previous sections we saw how to add some functionality to certain aspects of the Hudson dashboard via a plugin. However, there may be requirements to uniformly change every page. Hudson provides a way to do this using an extension point called PageDecorator. It allows the plugin developer to inject an HTML header element into every page and add additional footer information. By inserting a custom CSS stylesheet header element, you may be able to modify some of the styling of the Hudson pages. A JavaScript header element would allow you to do some client-side execution when the page loads. One good example is adding Google Analytics stats on each page through JavaScript injection.

In this section let us see how to add a footer that displays information about copyright info and administrator contact information. Our sample plugin, sample-page-decorator-plugin, includes a Java class SamplePageDecorator that is an extension for PageDecorator. It is annotated with @Extension to let Hudson know to load it as an extension for PageDecorator when the plugin is loaded. It also acts as a model to hold the name and e-mail address of the system administrator. As you see in the code listing, the name and e-mail address are not hard-coded. This is mainly for the Hudson admin to configure the name and e-mail address at run time.

Code Listing *SamplePageDecorator.java*

```
@Extension
public class SamplePageDecorator extends PageDecorator {
    private String adminName = "";
    private String adminEmail= "";
    public SamplePageDecorator() {
        super(SamplePageDecorator.class);
        load();
    }
```

```
    @Override
    public boolean configure(StaplerRequest req, JSONObject json) throws FormException {
        adminName = json.getString("adminName");
        adminEmail = json.getString("adminEmail");
        save();
        return true;
    }
    public String getAdminName() {
        return adminName;
    }
    public String getAdminEmail() {
        return adminEmail;
    }
}
```

Custom Page Decorator Global Configuration

As mentioned previously, we want to save the name and e-mail address as a global configuration so that it can be changed at run time via a UI as shown in Figure 9-9. As per Hudson convention, any extension that needs global configuration must keep the configuration UI definition in a Jelly file named global.jelly. In our plugin we have the file at the appropriate location as needed by Hudson convention. This file defines two fields: adminName, to get the admin name, and adminEmail, to get the admin e-mail address. This UI becomes part of the global configuration page. Upon submission of the global configuration page, by convention, Hudson will call the method, configure, in our SamplePageDecorator class and pass in a JSON array that would contain the values of adminName and adminEmail. This method is responsible for extracting the values of these fields and saving them for future use.

Code Listing *global.jelly*

```
<j:jelly xmlns:j="jelly:core"  xmlns:f="/lib/form">
    <f:section title="Sample page decorator">
        <f:entry title="Admin Name">
            <f:textbox field="adminName"/>
        </f:entry>
        <f:entry title="Admin E-mail">
            <f:textbox field="adminEmail"/>
        </f:entry>
    </f:section>
</j:jelly>
```

Custom Page Decorator UI

Now that the name and e-mail of the system administrator can be configured via global configuration and available at run time, the next step is to get these values

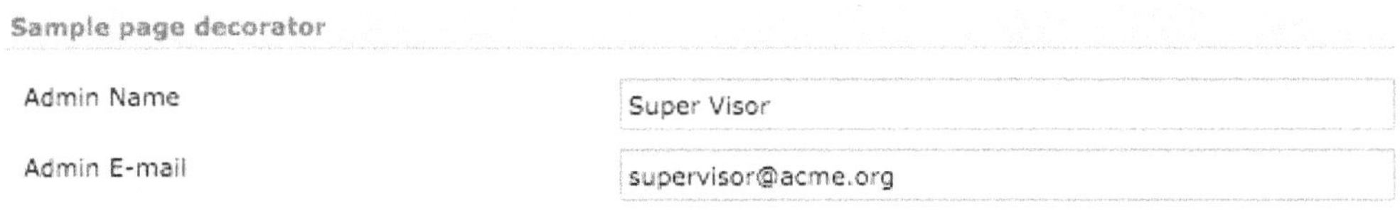

Sample page decorator

Admin Name — Super Visor

Admin E-mail — supervisor@acme.org

FIGURE 9-9. *Custom page decorator global configuration*

and display them in the footer as shown in Figure 9-10. By convention, Hudson expects two jelly files to specify the UI configuration of a PageDecorator. These jelly files are:

- **footer.jelly** The rendered content of this page is added right before the </body> tag of each page. It is a convenient place for adding items such as tracking beacons, copyright info, and so on.
- **header.jelly** The rendered content of this page is added right before the </head> tag of each page. A convenient place for additional CSS stylesheets, JavaScript, <meta> tags, and so on.

Although it's not necessary, for the purpose of understanding how it works, we have both the files in our plugin. The header.jelly simply adds a custom CSS stylesheet to the HTML page header. The footer.jelly has the UI definitions to display the copyright information and the name and e-mail information of the System admin. The mail program might open in the browser and it is not a Hudson page, so we use target="_blank" to ensure that it opens in a new tab or window. The SamplePageDecorator is passed as the "it" object, so that the model values such as adminName and adminEmail can be extracted using a Jelly expression; for example, ${it.adminName}.

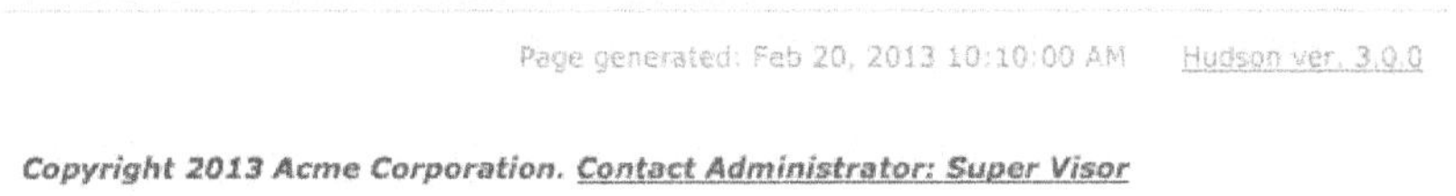

Page generated: Feb 20, 2013 10:10:00 AM Hudson ver. 3.0.0

Copyright 2013 Acme Corporation. Contact Administrator: Super Visor

FIGURE 9-10. *Copyright information added by custom page decorator*

Code Listing *header.jelly*

```
<j:jelly xmlns:j="jelly:core">
     <link href="/plugin/sample-page-decorator-plugin/css/style.css"
type="text/css" rel="stylesheet"/>
</j:jelly>
```

Code Listing *footer.jelly*

```
<j:jelly xmlns:j="jelly:core">
    <h4 class="acmeCopyright">
        Copyright 2013 Acme Corporation.
        <a href=mailto:${it.adminEmail} target="_blank">
            Contact Administrator: ${it.adminName}
        </a>
    </h4>
</j:jelly>
```

Code Listing *style.css*

```
h4.acmeCopyright {
    padding-left:10px;
    color: blue;
    font-style: italic;
}
```

Extending Various Aspects of a Hudson Job

A single Hudson job consists of one or more of the entities listed next. These job entities can be configured (added, deleted, or modified) via the Job Configurations page.

- **Job Properties** Values used by Hudson to take certain actions on the job. Build steps or other services within Hudson can use them.
- **Advanced Options** Similar to job properties, but to be used by advanced users.
- **Triggers** Schedule a build on a certain condition.
- **SCM** Check out sources from a remote repository.
- **Build Wrappers** Performs pre/post-actions for the build process.

- **Build Steps** Hudson invokes these build steps in sequence when the build happens.
  - **Builders** A build step that performs the actual build of the job
  - **Publishers** A build step that runs after the build is completed
    - **Recorders** Special kind of publisher for collecting stats and publishing reports generated by builders; can mark builds as unstable/failure
    - **Notifiers** A kind of publisher that sends the outcome of the builds to other systems and humans

Hudson provides extension points to extend each of the job entities in the preceding list, except the Advanced Options. In this section we will explore how to extend some of these job entities and add our own custom extension via a plugin.

Adding a Custom Notifier to a Job

Build status notification is one of the important aspects of Continuous Integration. There are so many ingenious ways to notify build status such as Lava Lamp, Extreme Feedback Panel, and even starting a siren when the build breaks. Interestingly, Hudson does have plugins to support these types of extreme notifications. In this section let us explore how to write a plugin, sample-notifier-plugin, that would add a custom Notifier to Hudson. For the purpose of this exercise, we have assumed that you have installed a messaging server that is capable of sending SMS messages, sending a message to an IRC channel, or sending the build status message as a tweet to Twitter. In fact, it is very easy to build such a server, given that enough open source libraries are available to achieve this task. Also, we assume the messaging server provides a REST API for our sample Notifier to POST the build status as JSON. Once the messaging server receives the JSON, it would send the build information to any of the devices based on its configuration. Our extension to Notifier is placed in a file called SampleNotifier.java.

Code Listing *SampleNotifier.java*

```
public class SampleNotifier extends Notifier {

    private String msgServerUrl;
    private static ObjectMapper jsonObjectMapper = new ObjectMapper();
    @DataBoundConstructor
    public SampleNotifier(final String url) {
        msgServerUrl = url;
    }
    @Override
    public boolean perform(AbstractBuild<?, ?> build, Launcher launcher, BuildListener
```

```
listener) throws InterruptedException, IOException {
        BuildInfo buildInfo = new BuildInfo();
        buildInfo.setNumber(build.getNumber());
        buildInfo.setUrl(build.getUrl());
        buildInfo.setStatus(build.getResult().toString());
        AbstractProject job = build.getProject();
        JobInfo jobInfo = new JobInfo();
        jobInfo.setBuild(buildInfo);
        jobInfo.setName(job.getName());
        jobInfo.setUrl(job.getUrl());
        Writer writer = new StringWriter();
        jsonObjectMapper.writeValue(writer, jobInfo);
        String jsonString = writer.toString();
        System.out.println(jsonString);
        try {
            WebRequest webRequest = new WebRequest(msgServerUrl);
            webRequest.post(jsonString);
        } catch (URISyntaxException ex) {
            listener.error("Failed to send notification. " +
ex.getLocalizedMessage());
        }
        return true;
    }
    public BuildStepMonitor getRequiredMonitorService() {
        return BuildStepMonitor.BUILD;
    }
    public String getUrl() {
        return msgServerUrl;
    }
    @Extension
    public final static class SampleNotifierDescriptor extends
BuildStepDescriptor<Publisher> {
        @Override
        public boolean isApplicable(Class<? extends AbstractProject> type) {
            return true;
        }
        @Override
        public String getDisplayName() {
            return "Sample Notifier";
        }
        public FormValidation doCheckUrl(@QueryParameter final String value)
                throws IOException, ServletException {
            return new FormValidation.URLCheck() {
                @Override
                protected FormValidation check() throws IOException,
                        ServletException {
                    String msgServerUrl = Util.fixEmpty(value);
                    if (msgServerUrl == null) { // nothing entered yet
                        return FormValidation.ok();
                    }
                    FormValidation result = FormValidation.ok();
                    try {
```

```
                    if (findText(open(new URL(msgServerUrl)), "Messaging Server"))
{
                        result = FormValidation.ok();
                    } else {
                        result = FormValidation.error( //
                                "Could not connect to messaging server");
                    }
                } catch (IOException exc) {
                    result = handleIOException(value, exc);
                }
                return result;
            }
        }.check();
    }
    public FormValidation doTestConnection(@QueryParameter final String url)
throws IOException {
        try {
            WebRequest webRequest = new WebRequest(url);
            WebResponse webResponse = webRequest.post("{\"test\": \"123\"}");
            if (webResponse.getResponseCode() > 201) {
                return FormValidation.error("Connection failed");
            } else {
                return FormValidation.ok("Connection established");
            }
        } catch (Exception exc) {
            return FormValidation.error(exc.getMessage());
        }
    }
  }
}
```

The extension SampleNotifier is a configurable object, so it defines a Descriptor called SampleNotifierDescriptor and annotates it with @Extension to mark it as an extension. When the plugin is loaded, Hudson adds SampleNotifier to the Notifiers list and it becomes available to be added as a Notifier to any job. Hudson uses any Notifier to notify only the status of a build completion or completion of every build step. SampleNotifier specifies its intention to notify only the completion status of the build by returning the object BuildStepMonitor.BUILD via the method getRequiredMonitorService. When Hudson is ready to notify the status of the build through a Notifier, it calls the method perform, which the notifier implements. In our implementation, we obtain the job and the corresponding Build object and retrieve the status information. We use two data models, JobInfo and BuildInfo, to hold the extracted job and build status information. Also, SampleNotifier uses the Jackson Library[1] to convert these models into a JSON string. Finally the JSON is sent as HTML POST to the messaging server REST API. For the sake of brevity we have not listed all the code from the sample-notifier-plugin here. The JSON sent to the messaging server looks similar to the following:

[1] Jackson Java JSON processor. http://jackson.codehaus.org/

Code Listing *Build status JSON*

```
{
   "name":"Test",
   "url":"job/Test/"
   "build":{
        "number":11,
        "status":"SUCCESS",
        "url":"job/Test/11/"
   }
}
```

NOTE
The sample code for this chapter contains a very simple json-server project. After building it with ***mvn clean install****, you can run it with, for example, java -jar target/json-server.jar -port 8081. Then you can use http://localhost:8081 to test the plugin.*

Custom Notifier Configuration UI

All Notifier Extensions are available as selectable check boxes in the Post-build Actions section of the configuration page. The job owner can choose one or more of them. If SampleNotifier is selected as a Notifier, then it must provide a UI for the user to configure the messaging server URL, as shown in Figure 9-11. By Hudson convention, the Jelly definition for the configuration has to be placed in a file called config.jelly. This configuration UI provides two features. The first is automatic validation of the messaging server URL typed in the Message Server field. The second one is a Test Connection button to test if Hudson can connect to the REST API. We have two methods in the SampleNotifier to do the validation and testing. The method SampleNotifierDescriptor.doCheckUrl does the validation of the URL and the SampleNotifierDescriptor.doTestConnection method does the connection testing when the button is clicked.

FIGURE 9-11. *Custom notifier configuration UI*

Code Listing *config.jelly*

```
<j:jelly xmlns:j="jelly:core"  xmlns:f="/lib/form">
    <f:entry title="${%Message Server}" field="url"
             description="${%Messaging server URL must be provided}">
        <f:textbox
checkUrl="'descriptorByName/SampleNotifier/checkUrl?value='+escape(this.value)" />
    </f:entry>
    <f:validateButton
        title="${%Test Connection}" progress="${%Testing...}"
                                    method="testConnection" with="url" />
</j:jelly>
```

The textbox tag in config.jelly defines the value of the attribute checkUrl as 'descriptorByName/SampleNotifier/checkUrl?value='+escape(this.value). This tells Hudson to find the Descriptor SampleNotifierDescriptor and invoke the method doCheckUrl to perform the validation. Similarly, the validateButton tag has the attribute method="testConnection". This tells Hudson to generate JavaScript to call the method SampleNotifierDescriptor.doTestConnection via AJAX to do the connection test. Figure 9-11 shows how the "Connection Established" message appears after clicking the Test Connection button with a valid URL.

Adding a Custom Link to a Job Dashboard

When you create a Hudson job and visit the dashboard, you see a bunch of links such as Workspace and Recent Changes, to name a few, on the left-hand side of the dashboard. These links are useful to display some of the data associated with the job. A need may arise for you to add a custom link to display some data collected by one of the custom publishers you created. In this section we will explore how to add a custom link, Sample Publisher, to the Action Panel of the job dashboard, as shown in Figure 9-12. The same link can be added to the main panel of the job dashboard, as shown in Figure 9-13.

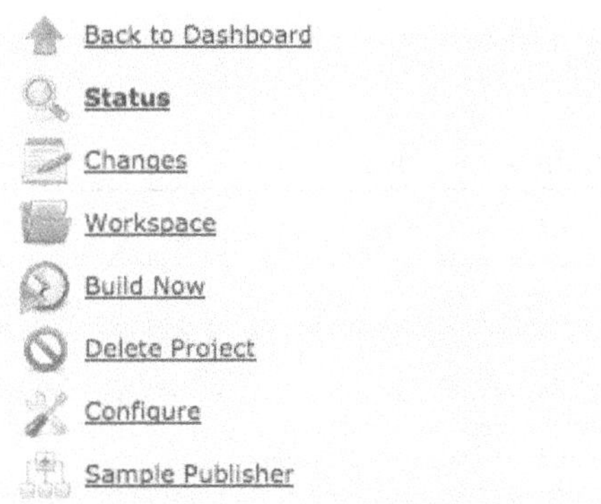

FIGURE 9-12. *Custom link added to the action panel of the job dashboard*

FIGURE 9-13. *Custom link added to the main panel of the job dashboard*

Transient Job Action

The concept of "action" in Hudson has different meanings in different contexts. One purpose of an action, like RootAction, as we saw in the earlier part of the chapter, is to add a link to the job dashboard. Though actions can be used to contribute additional information and behavior to the job, here we are using an action to add the action link UI to the job. By specifying it as a transient action, we are making sure it appears on the job dashboard in a specific context. We are going to associate it with the model SamplePublisher to display some data. So this transient action should appear in the dashboard only if the SamplePublisher is selected in the post-build actions of the job. This is achieved by creating an extension to the TransientProjectActionFactory. In our plugin, sample-job-action-plugin, the extension is SampleJobActionFactory class and marked with the annotation @Extension. The method createFor is used to associate the SampleJobAction with the SamplePublisher. In this example, the SamplePublisher is a dummy one. It does not collect any data in the job build. We will see a real publisher in the next section, which will collect some real data.

Code Listing *SampleJobActionFactory.java*

```
@Extension
public class SampleJobActionFactory extends TransientProjectActionFactory {
    @Override
    public Collection<? extends Action> createFor(final AbstractProject job) {
        assert job!= null;
        Map<Descriptor<Publisher>, Publisher> map = job.getPublishersList().toMap();
        for (Publisher publisher : map.values()) {
            if (publisher instanceof SamplePublisher) {
                return Collections.singleton(new SampleJobAction(job));
```

```
            }
        }
        return Collections.emptySet();
    }
}
```

Code Listing *SampleJobAction.java*

```
public class SampleJobAction implements Action, StaplerProxy{
    private AbstractProject job;
    public SampleJobAction(AbstractProject job){
        this.job = job;
    }
    public String getIconFileName() {
        return "/plugin/sample-job-action-plugin/icons/action.png";
    }
    public String getDisplayName() {
        return "Sample Publisher";
    }
    public String getUrlName() {
        return "samplePublisher";
    }
    public SamplePublisherData getTarget() {
         return new SamplePublisherData(job);
    }
}
```

Every time the job configuration is modified, the SampleJobActionFactory is consulted to see if any transient actions need to be added to the job. Transient actions are not saved to the disk along with other job configurations. The method SampleJobActionFactory.createFor makes sure that the SampleJobAction is added to the job only when the job configuration includes the SamplePublisher as a post-build action. This is important, because the only purpose of the SampleJobAction is to add a link UI to the job dashboard, which when clicked displays the data recorded by SamplePublisher. So if SamplePublisher is not in the job configuration and recording any data, then this link has no meaning in the job dashboard.

Sample Job Action UI

The purpose of SampleJobAction is to add two links. The first link is added to the job dashboard actions panel and the second link is added to the main panel of the job dashboard. The information to create this link is used from the icon, displayName, and urlName properties of the SampleJobAction itself. This is straightforward, but for creating the link in the job dashboard, Hudson uses a somewhat cryptic name for the Jelly definition file called jobMain.jelly.

Code Listing *jobMain.jelly*

```
<j:jelly xmlns:j="jelly:core"  xmlns:f="/lib/form" xmlns:t="/lib/hudson">
    <table style="margin-top: 1em; margin-left:1em;">
        <t:summary icon="/plugin/sample-job-action-plugin/icons/action.png"
href="samplePublisher">
            Sample Publisher Data
        </t:summary>
    </table>
</j:jelly>
```

The purpose of this Jelly file is to provide additional information such as the summary of the data to be displayed in the main panel of the job dashboard. Once the plugin is installed and SamplePublisher is selected in the job configuration, the links should automatically appear in the job dashboard as we saw earlier in Figures 9-12 and 9-13. When the link is clicked, the data collected by the SamplePublisher will be displayed. In this example SamplePublisher does not collect any data, so it simply displays a dummy message as shown in Figure 9-14. In the next section we will create a real Recorder, a kind of publisher that records JUnit test trends and displays the data in a table when the user clicks on the links. We will also see how the link knows to forward to the display page.

Custom Recorder to Display Build Result Trend

The sample plugin, sample-recorder-plugin, is an extension of the plugin we created earlier to add custom links to the job dashboard. In this section let us look at how to make our SampleRecorder record JUnit test result information after each build finishes. Later we add a page that displays the trend of JUnit test results across various builds of a job in a table. The custom link we added to the job in our previous section will forward to this page when clicked. Recorder is very similar to Notifier in terms of implementation. Though both are Publishers, they are meant for two different purposes. A Notifier is meant to notify the results of a build to other systems and humans. But a Recorder collects the data resulted during a build and records them. Later this collected data can be displayed in the Hudson Web page. Notifier is the last step in the build process, but a Recorder is performed before the notification takes place. So a Recorder can mark the build as failed or unstable, whereas the Notifier should not. Our SampleRecorder is an extension and

Sample Publisher Data

Sample Publisher Data is empty
It has nothing to report

FIGURE 9-14. *Sample Publisher dummy message*

implements the Recorder interface as shown in the code listing. Being a describable object, it marks the static inner class SampleRecorderDescriptor with annotation @Extension, so that at plugin load time it can be found and added to the Publisher list.

Code Listing *SampleRecorder.java*

```
public class SampleRecorder extends Recorder {
    private static ObjectMapper jsonObjectMapper = new ObjectMapper();
    @DataBoundConstructor
    public SampleRecorder() {
    }
    @Override
    public boolean perform(AbstractBuild<?, ?> build, Launcher launcher, BuildListener
listener) throws InterruptedException, IOException {
        TestResultAction testResultAction = build.getAction(TestResultAction.class);
        if (testResultAction == null) {
            listener.getLogger().println("There are no test results to import!");
        } else {
            TestResult testResult = testResultAction.getResult();
            if (testResult == null) {
                listener.getLogger().println("There are no test results to import!");
                return true;
            }
            TestResultData testResultData = new TestResultData();
            int failures = testResult.getFailCount();
            int executed = testResult.getTotalCount();
            int skipped = testResult.getSkipCount();
            int passed = testResult.getPassCount();
            int errors = executed - failures - passed - skipped;
            float percentPassed = (executed == 0) ? 0 : (passed + skipped) / executed
* 100;
            testResultData.setBuildNumber(build.getNumber());
            testResultData.setFailed(failures);
            testResultData.setTotal(executed);
            testResultData.setSkipped(skipped);
            testResultData.setPassed(passed);
            testResultData.setErrors(errors);
            testResultData.setPercentPassed(percentPassed);
            Writer writer = new StringWriter();
            jsonObjectMapper.writeValue(writer, testResultData);
            String jsonString = writer.toString();
            File trendFile = new File(build.getProject().getRootDir(), "test-trends.
json");
            PrintWriter out = new PrintWriter(new BufferedWriter(new
FileWriter(trendFile, true)));
            out.println(jsonString);
            out.close();
        }
        return true;
    }
    public BuildStepMonitor getRequiredMonitorService() {
        return BuildStepMonitor.BUILD;
    }
    @Extension
```

```
    public final static class SampleRecorderDescriptor extends
BuildStepDescriptor<Publisher> {
        @Override
        public boolean isApplicable(Class<? extends AbstractProject> type) {
            return true;
        }
        @Override
        public String getDisplayName() {
            return "Sample Recorder";
        }
    }
}
```

During the build process, Hudson fetches all the Recorders configured by the user and invokes the perform method implemented by each of them. In our implementation of the SampleRecorder.perform method, the JUnit TestResult object is fetched and the information regarding total test counts, number of tests passed, number of tests failed, number of errors occurring during test execution, and the percentage of tests passed is extracted and kept in a model called TestResultData. This data model is then persisted to a JSON file using the Jackson library.[2] The file we use to record the data is test-trends.json, and it is persisted in the root directory of the job. During every build, SampleRecorder is called and the JUnit test result information is appended to the JSON file with the following format:

Code Listing *JUnit Test Result trend JSON*

```
{"total":10,"errors":0,"buildNumber":18,"failed":0,"skipped":0,"passed"
:5,"percentPassed":100.0}
{"total":27,"errors":0,"buildNumber":19,"failed":12,"skipped":0,"passed
":15,"percentPassed":55.5}
{"total":27,"errors":0,"buildNumber":20,"failed":5,"skipped":0,"passed"
:22,"percentPassed":81.4}
```

Custom Recorder UI

Our SampleRecorder does not have any configuration UI, because it cleverly uses the JUnit information recorded by the Publish JUnit test result report Recorder. So in order for the SampleRecorder to work, the Publish JUnit test result report Recorder must be selected in the post-build sections, as shown in Figure 9-15. When this is done in a job, during each build of the job, SampleRecorder would record the JUnit info in the test-trends.json file.

After the JUnit information data is saved in the file, the JUnit test result trend must be displayed in a format that can be interpreted easily. For this, our sample plugin provides a UI that displays the trend in a table format. The table rows are

[2] Jackson Java JSON-processor. http://jackson.codehaus.org/

Publish JUnit test result report

Test report XMLs target/surefire-reports/**.xml

Fileset 'includes' setting that specifies the generated raw XML report files, such as 'myproject/target/test-reports/*.xml'. Basedir of the fileset is the workspace root.

Retain long standard output/error

Sample Recorder

FIGURE 9-15. *Sample Recorder and Publish JUnit test result report*

colored to delineate the builds with successful JUnit test results versus builds with failed JUnit tests, as shown in Figure 9-16.

As we know, every UI must be associated with a model to get the data and display it. In our plugin we created a simple model class called SampleRecorderData. It is a container for a collection of TestResultData, the very same model we used earlier to hold and persist the JUnit test result information. Also we use the same Jackson library to read back the JSON data from the storage test-trends.json into this collection. The Jelly UI corresponding to this model is declared in index.jelly. Now that we have a real Recorder to record the JUnit tests information and a UI to display the data collected by the SampleRecorder, clicking the link added by our SampleJobAction, as shown earlier in Figures 9-12 and 9-13, will display the JUnit test results trend as shown in Figure 9-16.

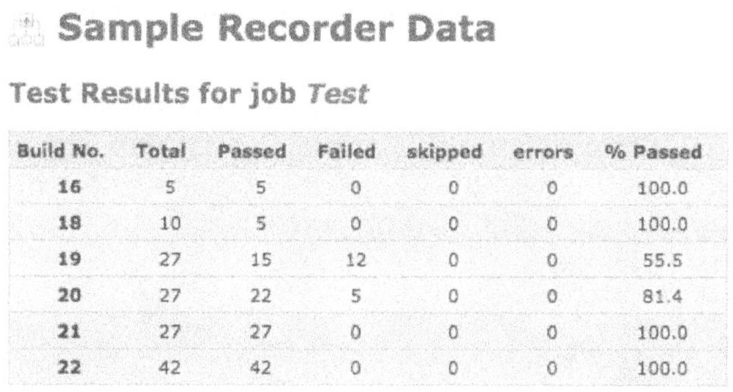

Sample Recorder Data

Test Results for job *Test*

Build No.	Total	Passed	Failed	skipped	errors	% Passed
16	5	5	0	0	0	100.0
18	10	5	0	0	0	100.0
19	27	15	12	0	0	55.5
20	27	22	5	0	0	81.4
21	27	27	0	0	0	100.0
22	42	42	0	0	0	100.0

FIGURE 9-16. *JUnit test result trend*

Code Listing *SampleRecorderData*

```
public class SampleRecorderData {
    private static ObjectMapper jsonObjectMapper = new ObjectMapper();
    private AbstractProject job;
    public SampleRecorderData(AbstractProject job) {
        this.job = job;
    }
    public AbstractProject getJob() {
        return job;
    }
    public List<TestResultData> getData() throws FileNotFoundException, IOException {
        List<TestResultData> testResultDataList = new ArrayList<TestResultData>();
        File trendFile = new File(job.getRootDir(), "test-trends.json");
        BufferedReader in = new BufferedReader(new FileReader(trendFile));
        String jsonString;
        while ((jsonString = in.readLine()) != null) {
            testResultDataList.add(jsonObjectMapper.readValue(jsonString,
TestResultData.class));
        }
        return testResultDataList;
    }
}
```

Code Listing *index.jelly*

```
<j:jelly xmlns:j="jelly:core"  xmlns:l="/lib/layout">
    <l:layout title="${%Sample Publisher Data}" secured="true">
        <l:side-panel>
            <l:tasks>
                <l:task icon="images/24x24/up.gif" href="${rootURL}/job/${it.job.
name}" title="${%Back to Job}" />
            </l:tasks>
        </l:side-panel>
        <l:main-panel>
            <h1>
                <img src="${resURL}/plugin/sample-recorder-plugin/icons/action.png" />
${%Sample Recorder Data}
            </h1>
            <h2>
                Test Results for job <i style="color:green"> ${it.job.name} </i>
            </h2>
            <table style="text-align:center" class="sortable pane bigtable">
                <tr>
                    <th>Build No.</th>
                    <th>Total</th>
                    <th>Passed</th>
                    <th>Failed</th>
                    <th>skipped</th>
                    <th>errors</th>
                    <th>% Passed</th>
                </tr>
                <j:forEach var="testResult" items="${it.data}">
                    <j:if test="${testResult.percentPassed != 100}">
                        <j:set var="style" value="background-color:#ffe4e1"/>
```

```
                    </j:if>
                    <j:if test="${testResult.percentPassed == 100}">
                        <j:set var="style" value="background-color:#DBEADC"/>
                    </j:if>
                     <tr style="${style}">
                        <td>
                            <b>${testResult.buildNumber}</b>
                        </td>
                        <td>${testResult.total}</td>
                        <td>${testResult.passed}</td>
                        <td>${testResult.failed}</td>
                        <td>${testResult.skipped}</td>
                        <td>${testResult.errors}</td>
                        <td>${testResult.percentPassed}</td>
                    </tr>
                </j:forEach>
            </table>
        </l:main-panel>
    </l:layout>
</j:jelly>
```

An attentive reader will have noticed that SampleJobAction provides the link action. However, the UI is associated with the model SampleRecorderData. So where is the connection? This is using another convention; that is, a particular class can proxy a UI to another model. This class must implement the marker class StaplerProxy, in order for Hudson to know it delegates the UI to another model. This marker interface defines a single method, getTarget, which returns the delegated model. SampleJobAction implements the StaplerProxy interface, and in its implementation of the method getTarget, it returns the delegated model SampleRecorderData. That is how the action link of SampleJobAction displays the UI associated with the model SampleRecorderData.

Creating a Custom Build Wrapper

The heart of building a job is the Builder, which does the real building of the job by executing build tools like Ant, Maven, or MSBuild. In Chapter 8, we have seen how to create a custom builder and configure it. There are plenty of free plugins available supporting a variety of build tools. But often, preparing your sources for these build tools to do the build may be very specific for your build system. You might want to do a setup database for your tests or invoke a virtual machine for certain services required by your build. For this purpose, Hudson provides an extension point called BuildWrapper. The main purpose of BuildWrapper is to prepare your build, so it has hooks that are called before the build starts for setup and after the build for cleanup or teardown. Though it is possible to do sophisticated operations during the setup and teardown phase of the BuildWrapper, in our sample plugin, sample-build-wrapper, we are going to do a very simple action.

Our SampleBuildWrapper, which is an extension to BuildWrapper, would set an environment variable that will be used by the builder. Assume that the builder is set to

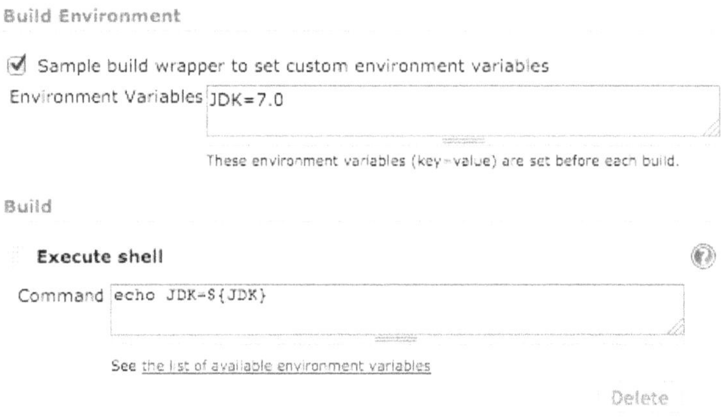

Build Environment

Sample build wrapper to set custom environment variables

Environment Variables JDK=7.0

These environment variables (key=value) are set before each build.

Build

Execute shell

Command echo JDK=${JDK}

See the list of available environment variables

Delete

FIGURE 9-17. *Configuring the custom build wrapper*

build certain sources based on the environment variable JDK. SampleBuildWrapper would provide a configuration UI to set such an environment variable as a key-value pair, for example, JDK=7.0. Since SampleBuildWrapper provides a UI, it has to define a Descriptor and annotate it with @Extension. When our sample-build-wrapper-plugin is loaded, the extension SampleBuildWrapper will be added to the BuildWrapper list, and will subsequently be available in the Build Environment section of the job configuration, as shown in Figure 9-17. The method setup is called during the setup phase of the Build Wrapper. In this method we parse the key-value pair added to this Build Wrapper from the job configuration page, set it to an Environment Object, and return it as a method return value. Hudson makes sure values set to these Environment objects are sent to the Builder object and build variables, which are in turn available to the build tools as system-level environment variables. The Environment object defines a method teardown, which will be called after the build completes. Any build-related cleanup can be done in this method. In our sample, we simply get the job-wide environment variables and search and make sure the environment variable set by us is one of them. This is very contrived, but effectively explains the concept.

Code Listing *SampleBuildWrapper.java*

```
public class SampleBuildWrapper extends BuildWrapper {
    private String customEnvVariables;
    @DataBoundConstructor
    public SampleBuildWrapper(String customEnvVariables) {
        this.customEnvVariables = customEnvVariables;
```

```
    }
    public String getCustomEnvVariables() {
        return customEnvVariables;
    }
    @Override
    public Environment setUp(AbstractBuild build, final Launcher launcher, final
BuildListener listener) {
        final Map<String, String> customEnvMap = new HashMap<String, String>();
        StringTokenizer tokenizer = new StringTokenizer(customEnvVariables);
        while (tokenizer.hasMoreTokens()) {
            String envVar = tokenizer.nextToken();
            if (envVar.contains("=")) {
                String keyValue[] = envVar.split("=");
                customEnvMap.put(keyValue[0], keyValue[1]);
            }
        }
        return new Environment() {
            @Override
            public void buildEnvVars(Map<String, String> env) {
                env.putAll(customEnvMap);
            }

            @Override
            public boolean tearDown(AbstractBuild build, BuildListener listener)
throws IOException, InterruptedException {
                listener.getLogger().println("\nSearching build environment ...");
                Map<String, String> buildEnvs = build.getEnvironment(listener);
                for (String key : buildEnvs.keySet()) {
                    if (customEnvMap.containsKey(key)) {
                        listener.getLogger().println("\nCustom key " + key + " = " +
buildEnvs.get(key) + " found.\n");
                    }
                }
                return true;
            }
        };
    }
    @Extension
    public static final class SampleBuildWrapperDescriptor extends BuildWrapperDe-
scriptor {
        @Override
        public boolean isApplicable(AbstractProject<?, ?> ap) {
            return true;
        }
        @Override
        public String getDisplayName() {
            return "Sample build wrapper to set custom environment variables";
        }
    }
}
```

Custom Build Wrapper UI

As mentioned previously, the SampleBuildWrapper needs to provide a UI for the user to set the environment variable as a key-value pair. As per Hudson convention, the UI definition Jelly file needs to be config.jelly. In this UI, we define a single text area in which the user can set multiple environment values as whitespace-separated key-value pairs. Upon submitting the job configuration page, Hudson would get the value from the text area with name customEnvVariables and set it to our CustomBuildWrapper via the constructor that is annotated with @DataBoundConstructor. After installing the plugin to Hudson, the job configuration would display a new selectable SampleBuildWrapper in the build environment. Upon selecting it, a text area will be presented to the user to enter the environment variable as a key-value pair as shown. Making sure the key-value pair the user enters is available as an environment variable to the builders is easy. As shown in Figure 9-17, add a simple builder that executes a shell command. In the command text area, type **echo JDK=${JDK}**, do a build, and examine the console output. The output would be similar to Figure 9-18, if you set the value of the environment variable JDK as 7.0.

Code Listing *config.jelly*

```
<j:jelly xmlns:j="jelly:core"  xmlns:f="/lib/form" xmlns:t="/lib/hudson">
    <f:entry title="${%Environment Variables}"
             description="These environment variables (key=value) are set before each
build.">
        <f:textarea name="customEnvVariables"
                value="${instance.getCustomEnvVariables()}" />
    </f:entry>
</j:jelly>
```

```
Started by user anonymous
Building on master
[workspace] $ /bin/sh -xe /var/folders/8_/kqhwjkcn0dj8g8g9t3z6ttlw0000gn
/T/hudson1830391537572337793.sh
+ echo JDK=7.0
JDK=7.0

Searching build environment ...

Custom key JDK = 7.0 found.

Finished: SUCCESS
```

FIGURE 9-18. *Job with custom build wrapper console output*

Summary

In this chapter we have seen how to extend Hudson by writing custom extensions to various extension points. Hudson provides several well-documented extension points to extend various parts of Hudson. There are two areas in Hudson that are commonly extended by plugin developers. One of them is to customize the dashboard that displays the job status information. The other common extensions are for customizing the job and its build. In this chapter we have provided a few examples to show how to extend these areas in Hudson. We believe this chapter provides enough knowledge for you to read the documentation of the rest of the extension points and build your own plugin.

CHAPTER 10

Hudson Best Practices

In the previous chapters, we have seen how to set up and effectively use Hudson for your day-to-day work. However, it is important to keep Hudson running smoothly in your environment for better Continuous Integration experience. Based on our real-world experience, we have gathered a few best practices, which we have outlined in this chapter.

Manage the Hudson Resources Effectively

Nothing is infinite, including resources available in your Hudson. So the resources need to be used effectively. In this section let us see how you can monitor and control the usage of those precious resources.

Tune Memory

As per Oracle Java memory-tuning documentation, unless set on the command line, the initial and maximum heap sizes are calculated based on the amount of memory available on the machine. The proportion of memory used for the heap is controlled by the command-line options DefaultInitialRAMFlraction and DefaultMaxRAMFraction. Table 10-1 shows the formula to calculate the heap size and the default value.

If the machine has less than 4GB, then the maximum heap size of the Hudson installation will be less than 1GB of system memory; if more than 4GB, then the maximum heap size will be 1GB. While this memory setting may be good enough to start with, it may not be high enough when the jobs in Hudson grow or if the builds are larger. If the applications built are memory-intensive, you will probably start seeing the build failures with Hudson complaining about heap space and printing the following dreaded exception on the log file:

```
FATAL: Java heap space
java.lang.OutOfMemoryError: Java heap space
```

Heap Value	Formula	Default
Initial heap size	memory / DefaultInitialRAMFraction	memory / 64
Maximum heap size	MIN(memory / DefaultMaxRAMFraction, 1GB)	MIN(memory / 4, 1GB)

TABLE 10-1. *Java Default Memory Settings*

The default maximum heap size depends on many factors. So it is better to find out how much maximum heap is allocated to your Hudson installation, whether it is a standalone or deployed to a container like Tomcat or JBoss. JDK comes with a neat tool called JConsole to monitor memory. Type the command **jconsole** in the OS command window and start the JConsole UI. It will automatically find all local JVMs running processes and ask you to pick the correct one for Hudson. When you select the process corresponding to your Hudson installation, it will display vital resource information. Click on the VM summary panel to find out about the amount of maximum heap size allocated and memory currently used by Hudson, as shown in Figure 10-1.

If the machine running Hudson has enough memory and you noticed that maximum heap allocated to Hudson is low, you can set the maximum heap size to a higher value when you restart Hudson. Setting the memory heap values depends

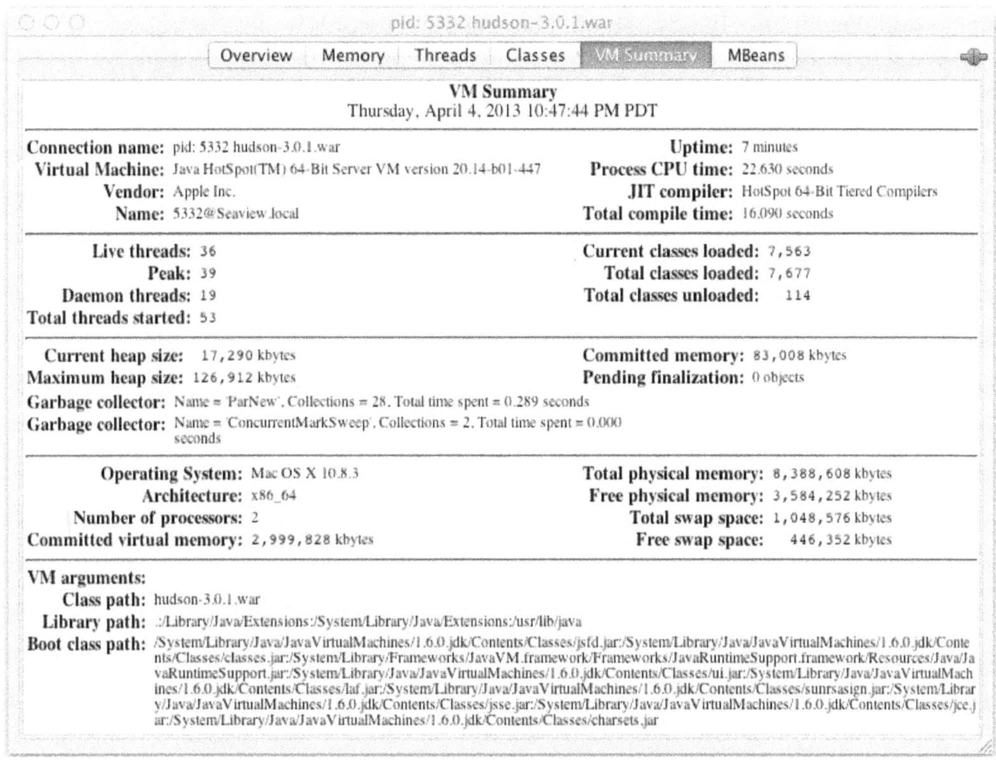

FIGURE 10-1. *JConsole UI showing memory usage by Hudson*

on how you run Hudson. If you are running it as a standalone, then you can set the heap using a command like

```
java -jar hudson.war -Xms64m -Xmx2048m -XX:MaxPermSize=256m
```

If you are running Hudson as a Web application in an application server, then the appropriate configuration file needs to be modified to include the heap settings. For Tomcat, edit the file ${TOMCAT_HOME}/bin/setenv.sh (create it, if does not exist) and add the following:

```
export JAVA_OPTS=" -Xms64m -Xmx2048m -XX:MaxPermSize=256m "
```

On Windows, the file is setenv.bat and the line is

```
set JAVA_OPTS=" -Xms64m -Xmx2048m -XX:MaxPermSize=256m "
```

Restrict Job History Depth

In order to improve Hudson startup time and reduce memory usage, you should limit the stored number of builds per job. Keeping build records under control is the best way to manage the disk usage by jobs. If possible, it's best to discard all unnecessary build records. In the job dashboard on the left-hand side, the build history is displayed as shown in Figure 10-2. By default, Hudson keeps the history of all the builds unless they are explicitly deleted. This may not be desirable if you are

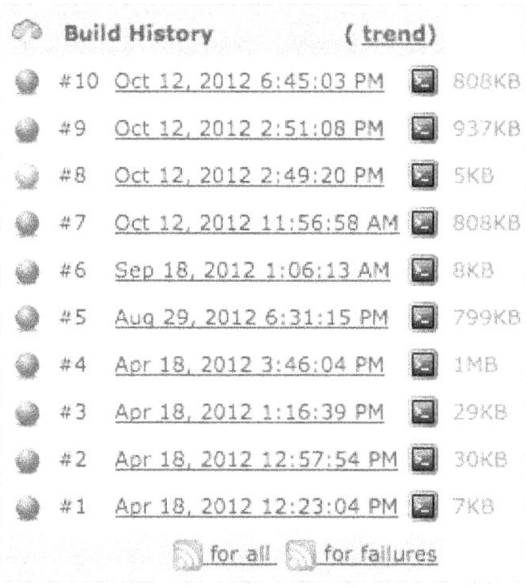

FIGURE 10-2. *Job build history*

practicing Continuous Integration, because builds are scheduled and created on every commit. You should restrict the number of builds to keep per job and discard the old jobs.

To discard the old jobs, in the Job Configurations page select the option Discard Old Builds. This option tells Hudson how long you would like to keep records of the builds such as console output and build artifacts created and stored by Hudson. Hudson offers two criteria as shown in Figure 10-3:

- A criterion based on age. You can instruct Hudson to delete a build if it reaches a certain age.
- A criterion based on just a number. You can instruct Hudson to make sure that it only maintains up to a specified number of build records. If a new build is started after that number is reached, the oldest build record will be removed.

If you click the Advanced button, it allows you to add two more advanced options:

- The option "Days to keep artifacts" allows specifying how many days the artifacts of a build need to be retained before they are deleted. Note that with this option, only the archived artifacts of a build are deleted. Other items such as the logs, history, and reports are still retained.
- The option "Max # of builds to keep with artifacts" is a hint; how many builds are allowed to keep their build artifacts?

While the basic options are for cleaning up the builds, the Advanced option is related to cleaning up the artifacts archived in each build. The number in the

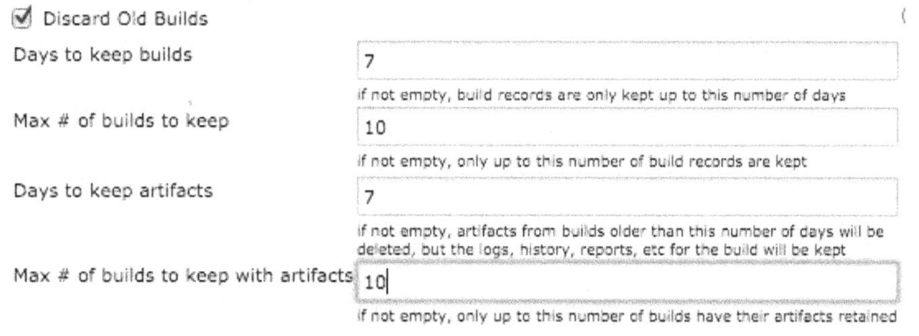

Discard Old Builds
Days to keep builds 7
if not empty, build records are only kept up to this number of days
Max # of builds to keep 10
if not empty, only up to this number of build records are kept
Days to keep artifacts 7
if not empty, artifacts from builds older than this number of days will be deleted, but the logs, history, reports, etc for the build will be kept
Max # of builds to keep with artifacts 10
if not empty, only up to this number of builds have their artifacts retained

FIGURE 10-3. *Criteria set to discard old build*

Advanced section must be lower than the numbers in the basic section to have any meaning.

Assume you have 25 builds and you have set max # to keep as 10 and days to keep as 7. First, the last 10 builds are preserved and the older 15 builds are marked for deletion. However, if any of those 15 builds are built within seven days (days to keep), then it is not deleted. Also, if one of those 15 builds is the last successful build, then also it is not deleted. So if 4 of those builds are within seven days, then net retained builds will be 10 + 4 = 14.

Hudson also allows you to mark an individual build as "Keep this forever," using a button in the Build dashboard to exclude certain important builds from being discarded automatically. The last stable build and the last successful build are always preserved.

Promote Your Good Builds and Discard Bad Builds

If you have a good build of your job, you may want to store it forever and mark it as a "promoted" build so that others in the team can pick it up. The promoted-builds plugin is a good candidate to do this action for you. This plugin introduces a notion called "promotion" to distinguish good builds from bad builds. Assume you have set up a CI build job along with comprehensive test jobs as downstream jobs. After the CI build is successful, the downstream builds will be scheduled. If the CI build and the corresponding tests builds are successful, then the CI build itself can be considered a good build. With this plugin, you can configure the CI job to be marked as "promoted" when all the downstream test jobs have passed successfully, as shown in Figure 10-4. This is a good way to set up the CI build to complete quickly, but have an ability to still distinguish the good builds from bad builds that compiled fine in the CI build but failed long-running extensive tests in the downstream builds.

This plugin also allows multiple levels of promotions. This is useful in case multiple levels of staged testing are required before a build can be promoted as production-ready. Once a build is promoted, it will get a star in the build history view, denoting that other teams can pick it up and use it for another purpose such as deploying to the staging area. Providing an appropriate colored icon (see Figure 10-5), which is used as a promotion star, is very useful. It would give an idea about what stage of promotion the particular software project is in. For example, a blue color star could represent integration test promotion. A purple star could be used for performance test promotion, and a gold star for User Acceptance Test (UAT) test promotion. When the gold star promotion happens, the build can be declared production-ready. Automating this complex scenario leads to an excellent way to practice Continuous Delivery.

Though the automated software project builds have reached a gold level of promotion, often it may be required that someone go to the Hudson Web UI and click the "Approve promotion" button. This is useful when the promotion process requires a human "sign-off" within the build, something like a QA hand-off to

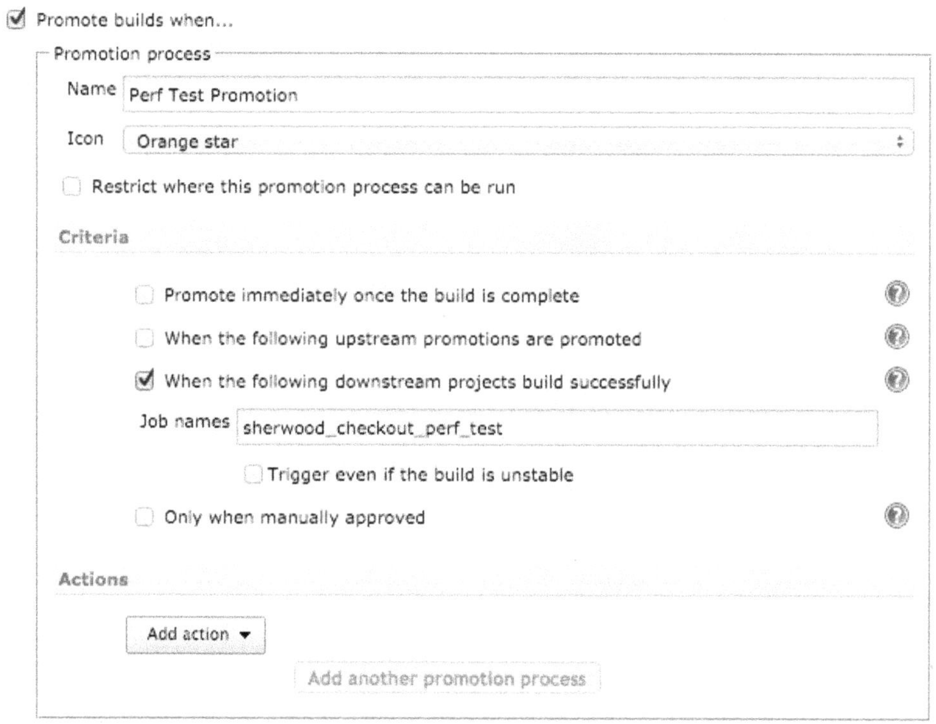

Promote builds when...
Promotion process
Name Perf Test Promotion
Icon Orange star
Restrict where this promotion process can be run
Criteria
Promote immediately once the build is complete
When the following upstream promotions are promoted
When the following downstream projects build successfully
Job names sherwood_checkout_perf_test
Trigger even if the build is unstable
Only when manually approved
Actions
Add action
Add another promotion process

FIGURE 10-4. *Build promotion when downstream jobs are successful*

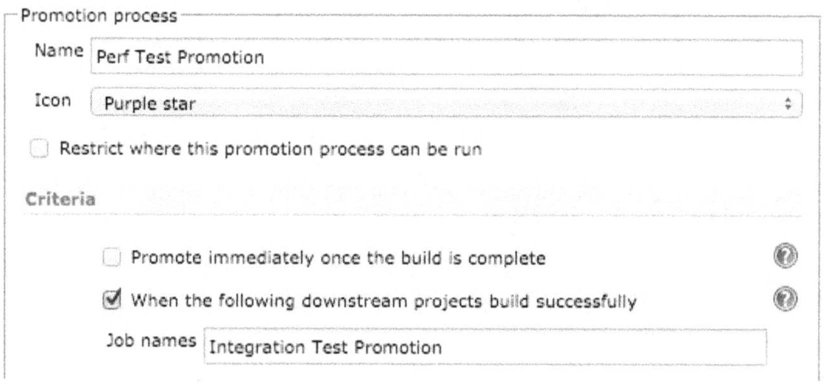

Promotion process
Name Perf Test Promotion
Icon Purple star
Restrict where this promotion process can be run
Criteria
Promote immediately once the build is complete
When the following downstream projects build successfully
Job names Integration Test Promotion

FIGURE 10-5. *Multiple levels of promotion*

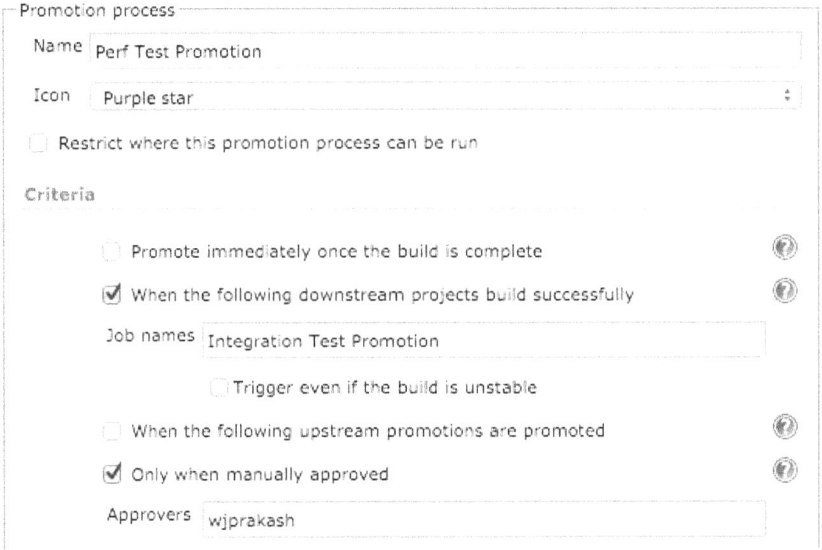

Promotion process
Name Perf Test Promotion
Icon Purple star
Restrict where this promotion process can be run
Criteria
Promote immediately once the build is complete
When the following downstream projects build successfully
Job names Integration Test Promotion
Trigger even if the build is unstable
When the following upstream promotions are promoted
Only when manually approved
Approvers wjprakash

FIGURE 10-6. *Manual promotion*

production. This is possible by adding the criterion "Only when manually approved" as shown in Figure 10-6. In this field you can list user names or groups that are allowed to approve the promotion. The approvers go to the Build dashboard and click the Promotion Status link in the left panel to go to the promotion status page to do the approval.

Finally, as part of reducing disk space usage, you can use the promoted-builds plugin to do artifact storage effectively. Usually the artifacts of a build are stored on each build. It may be desirable to store the artifacts only when a good build happens. With build promotions, you can push only when an artifact meets certain criteria. For example, you might want to push it only after an integration promotion happened in an upstream job. Select the criteria you want to use for the promotion to happen and then add a post-build action, "Archive the artifacts," as shown in Figure 10-7. The post-build action will be executed only if all of the selected criteria are met.

Monitor the Disk Space

In a CI environment, builds are done continuously on every commit. Each build takes up space in the disk. Depending on the size of each build, the disk may soon fill up and Hudson will stop building. It is advisable to reduce the number of builds

Criteria

Promote immediately once the build is complete

When the following upstream promotions are promoted

Promotion names Intergration Test Promoton

When the following downstream projects build successfully

Only when manually approved

Actions

Archive the artifacts

Files to archive **/*.war

Validate

FIGURE 10-7. *Archiving artifacts when given criteria are met*

stored by each job, as we discussed earlier. It is equally advisable for the Hudson admin to monitor the disk space and raise a red flag when a particular job consumes too much space. The Hudson disk-usage plugin is very handy for this job.

After installing this plugin, a new entry appears on the left-hand side panel called Disk Usage. When you click it, it takes you to a page where jobs along with the disk space used by each job are displayed, as shown in Figure 10-8. Identifying the jobs consuming an unreasonable amount of disk space and warning the job

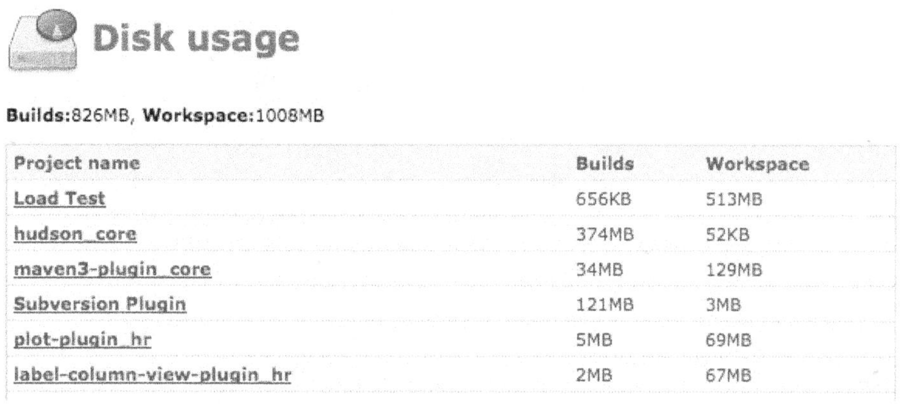

Disk usage

Builds:826MB, **Workspace:**1008MB

Project name	Builds	Workspace
Load Test	656KB	513MB
hudson_core	374MB	52KB
maven3-plugin_core	34MB	129MB
Subversion Plugin	121MB	3MB
plot-plugin_hr	5MB	69MB
label-column-view-plugin_hr	2MB	67MB

FIGURE 10-8. *Disk usage by jobs*

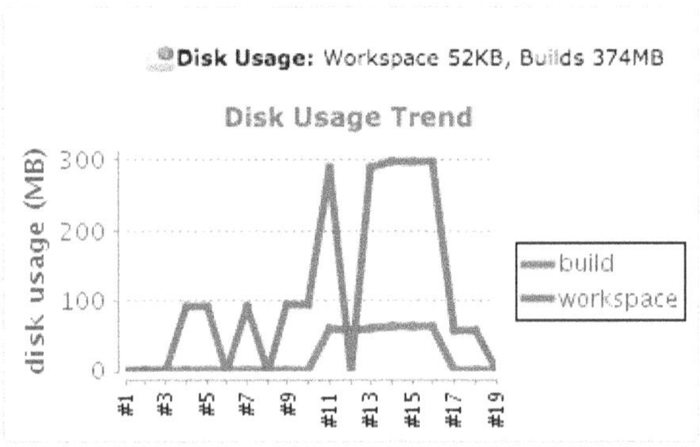

FIGURE 10-9. *Disk usage trend per job*

owner to clean up the unwanted builds is a good practice. The disk-usage plugin scans the jobs in the Hudson Home folder every 60 minutes to calculate the disk usage. You can click the Record Disk Usage button on the page to force a scan.

As a job owner, it is your responsibility to monitor the disk space used by the builds of your job and delete the unwanted builds stored. By default, the disk-usage plugin only shows the total disk usage on the Job page. If the "Show disk usage trend graph on the project page" option is checked in the System Configurations page, the disk-usage plugin adds a disk usage trend graph on the right-hand side of the job dashboard, as shown in Figure 10-9. The disk-usage plugin also displays the disk usage for each build in the Build History. Use that information to identify builds occupying lots of space and delete them if not required.

Put Your Hudson Behind a Web Proxy

In general, HTTP or Web servers are configured to run on port 80. On UNIX machines, generally the Apache Server is installed and used. On Windows, one can install and use the freely available Nginx Server. URLs that access HTTP servers on port 80 need not explicitly specify the port number. The URL http://myserver.mycompany.com/ is equivalent to http://myserver.mycompany.com:80/. By default, when you run Hudson in a standalone mode, the port used is 8080. In order to access the Hudson server, you need to specify the URL as http://myserver.mycompany.com:8080/. Even if you deploy Hudson to an application server like Tomcat or JBoss, with context "hudson," these application servers still may be using a port other than 80 and must be accessed using a fully qualified URL, something like http://myserver.mycompany.com:8081/hudson. Often you may want to completely hide the Hudson server (standalone or deployed to an application server) behind the HTTP server (shown in the following illustration) for a few reasons:

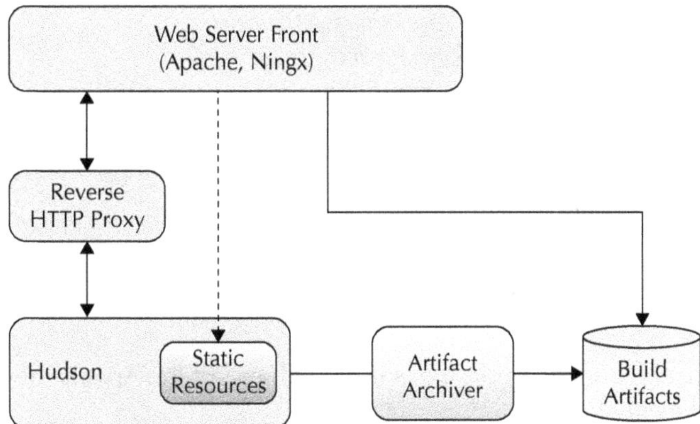

- Ability to access Hudson with a more readable URL, such as http://myserver.mycompany.com/hudson
- Only port 80 may be open in the machine where Hudson is installed
- For maximum performance, stability, and scalability
- Make static contents available through HTTP server

In order to front the standalone Hudson with the Apache Server, first Hudson must be run with a proper context path, say **hudson**. For that, use the following command line to run Hudson:

```
$ java -jar hudson.war --prefix=hudson
```

Similarly, when Hudson is deployed as a Web application to Tomcat, make sure it has the correct context path, say **hudson**. The context path is used when you modify the Apache Server configuration to do the proxy pass.

Next, modify the Apache Server configuration file to do the proxy pass. The place where the Apache Server configuration file is stored depends on the OS. On most Linux and Mac UNIX machines, it is /etc/apache2/httpd.conf. You can edit this file and include the appropriate configuration.

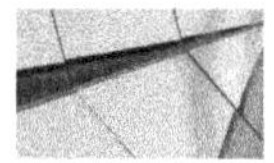

NOTE
On some recent UNIX versions, another method is supported rather than editing the httpd.conf file. Any .conf file created in the folder /etc/apache2/other will be included in the master configuration httpd .conf. For example, if you create /etc/apache2/other/ proxy.conf and put the proxy information there, at run time it will be included in the httpd.conf.

With the context path set up as shown, include the following content in the configuration file.

```
ProxyRequests Off
ProxyPass /hudson http://localhost:8081/hudson
ProxyPassReverse /hudson http://localhost:8081/hudson
```

Once the Apache configuration file is modified, restart the Apache Server for the proxy pass to take effect.

```
$ sudo /etc/init.d/httpd -k restart
Stopping httpd: [ OK ]
Starting httpd: [ OK ]
```

Now Hudson can be accessed with the simpler URL http://myserver.mycompany.com/hudson.

The specific paths in the preceding examples may vary depending on platform and installer. Variables include the location and name of the Apache Server binary, the location of the httpd.conf file, and the location of additional .conf files included by the httpd.conf file. Consult your platform-specific Apache documentation for details.

Do Not Use Your Hudson as a File Server

It is true that Hudson acts as a file server. The build artifacts and source files checked out at the job workspace can be downloaded from Hudson. However, for better performance and stability, it is better to keep Hudson executing the builds rather than serving build artifacts. We have come across issues where Hudson has dropped to its knees and crawled while someone in the team decided to download several large files (as large as 2GB) that were stored as build artifacts. The whole CI setup would work great if those huge files were served through far superior content servers such as Apache Server rather than Hudson.

To use Apache HTTP Server to serve the files, first copy the files from Hudson builds to the desired location on the machine where the server is located, say /var/hudson/artifacts. Several free plugins are available to do the copying or uploading:

- If both Hudson and Apache Server are on the same machine, then use the copyarchiver plugin. This plugin allows aggregating archived artifacts from several jobs into a shared location. Only the archived artifacts of the last successful build will be copied.
- If Apache HTTP Server is not in the same machine as Hudson Server, then the ftppublisher plugin can be used (refer to the section "Uploading Build Artifacts to Another Machine" in Chapter 4), which allows copying files from a particular build to another machine via the FTP protocol. Similarly, if you have SSH access between the two machines, then the SCP plugin can be used.

Once the files are available in the machine where Apache HTTP Server is running, then it is easy to configure it to serve the files. Let's say you want the users to download the build artifacts from http://myserver.mycompany.com/hudson-files; then modify the Apache configuration file and include the following:

```
Alias /hudson-files /var/hudson/artifacts
<Directory "/var/hudson/artifacts">
  Options Indexes FollowSymLinks
  Order allow,deny
  Allow from all
</Directory>
```

As long as the /var/hudson/artifacts folder doesn't contain any Web pages, it will be displayed as a list of files that can be downloaded and folders that can be navigated. You can also use a .htaccess file to control how the directory is displayed.

Periodically Back Up Your Hudson Contents

Hudson configuration files, job configurations, and some build artifacts should be periodically backed up. Since the workspace is a transitional item, it may not be required to back up its contents. There are a few plugins in Hudson to do backup and restore. Two plugins that are useful are

- **Backup** This plugin allows you to back up the Hudson home. Since it backs up the entire Hudson home along with all contents, the backup is triggered manually via UI in the Hudson dashboard.
- **ThinBackup** This plugin is slightly different than the Backup plugin; it backs up only the vital configuration files. It can be scheduled to do periodic backup.

The Backup plugin provides a Backup Manager, which is responsible for performing the backup operations. The Backup Manager is started from the Manage

FIGURE 10-10. *Backup manager page*

Hudson page by clicking the link "Backup manager." The Backup manager page, as shown in Figure 10-10, contains links to

- Configure backup settings (using the Setup link)
- Back up Hudson's configuration (using the "Backup Hudson configuration" link)
- Restore Hudson's configuration from a previous backup (using the "Restore Hudson configuration" link)

The Setup link opens the configuration page of settings used by the backup manager when it performs the backup, as shown in Figure 10-11. The main properties that can be configured in this page are

- Backup directory (the directory where the backup files should be kept).
- Whether to back up only the XML configuration files.
- Format of the backup, such as zip, tar.gz, or tar.bz2.
- Template for the backup file name. The default is backup_@date@ .@extension@. The token @date@ is replaced by the date and time using YYYYDDMM_hhmm format. The @extension@ token is replaced by the chosen compression format.
- Contents to back up such as workspace, builds history, Maven artifacts, and fingerprints.

Backup config files

Backup configuration

Hudson root directory /Users/wjprakash/Hudson/Eclipse-Hudson/org.eclipse.hudson.core/hudson-war/work

Backup directory /Users/wjprakash/Hudson/backup

Format tar.gz

File name template backup_@date@.@extension@

Custom exclusions war

Verbose mode

Configuration files (.xml) only

No shutdown

Backup content

Backup job workspace

Backup builds history

Backup maven artifacts archives

Backup fingerprints

Save

FIGURE 10-11. *Backup manager setup*

The Backup plugin allows backing up the contents manually. You have to go to the Backup manager page and click on the "Backup Hudson configuration" link to start the backup. When backup starts, the Backup manager tries to send a shutdown signal and wait for all jobs to finish building. But it does not actually shut down Hudson; it just keeps it in a quiet mode, so no jobs will run during the backup period. This is done mainly to make sure no files are written to the folder being backed up when the backup happens. This behavior can be changed by checking "No shutdown" in Backup Setup to not send the shutdown signal and start the backup immediately even though some jobs may be building. This is not recommended. The log output of the backup looks something like the following:

```
[ INFO] Backup started at [04/03/13 20:31:30]
[ INFO] Setting hudson in shutdown mode to avoid files corruptions.
```

```
[ INFO] Waiting all jobs end...
[ INFO] Number of running jobs detected : 0
[ INFO] All jobs finished.
[ INFO] Full backup file name : /Users/wjprakash/Hudson/backup/backup_20130403_2031.tar.gz
[ INFO] Saved files : 1286
[ INFO] Number of errors : 0
[ INFO] Cancel hudson shutdown mode
[ INFO] Backup end at [04/03/13 20:32:31]
[ INFO] [60.994s]
```

To restore from the backup, go to the Backup manager page and click on the "Restore Hudson configuration" link. This brings up the Backup Manager Restore page and lists the available backups available as shown in Figure 10-12. Select the backup you want to restore and click the Launch Restore button to start the restore. All the files will be extracted to the restore folder, which can be used to replace the contents at Hudson Home. The log output would look something like the following:

```
[ INFO] Restore started at [04/03/13 20:48:54]
[ INFO] Working into /Users/wjprakash/Hudson_Home/Hudson_Home_restore directory
[ INFO] Uncompressing archive file...
[ INFO] Copying temporary directory to the hudson home...
[ INFO] ****************************************
[ INFO] Reloading hudson configuration from disk.
[ INFO] ****************************************
[ INFO] Backup end at [04/03/13 20:49:26]
[ INFO] [32.598s]
```

Setting up the thinBackup plugin is very similar to Backup. Unlike the Backup plugin, it can perform backup on a scheduled time. It is also possible to set up a differential backup between full backups. The thinBackup manager also has a page with links to do setup (Settings), manual full backup (Backup Now), and restore from

FIGURE 10-12. *Backup Manager Restore page*

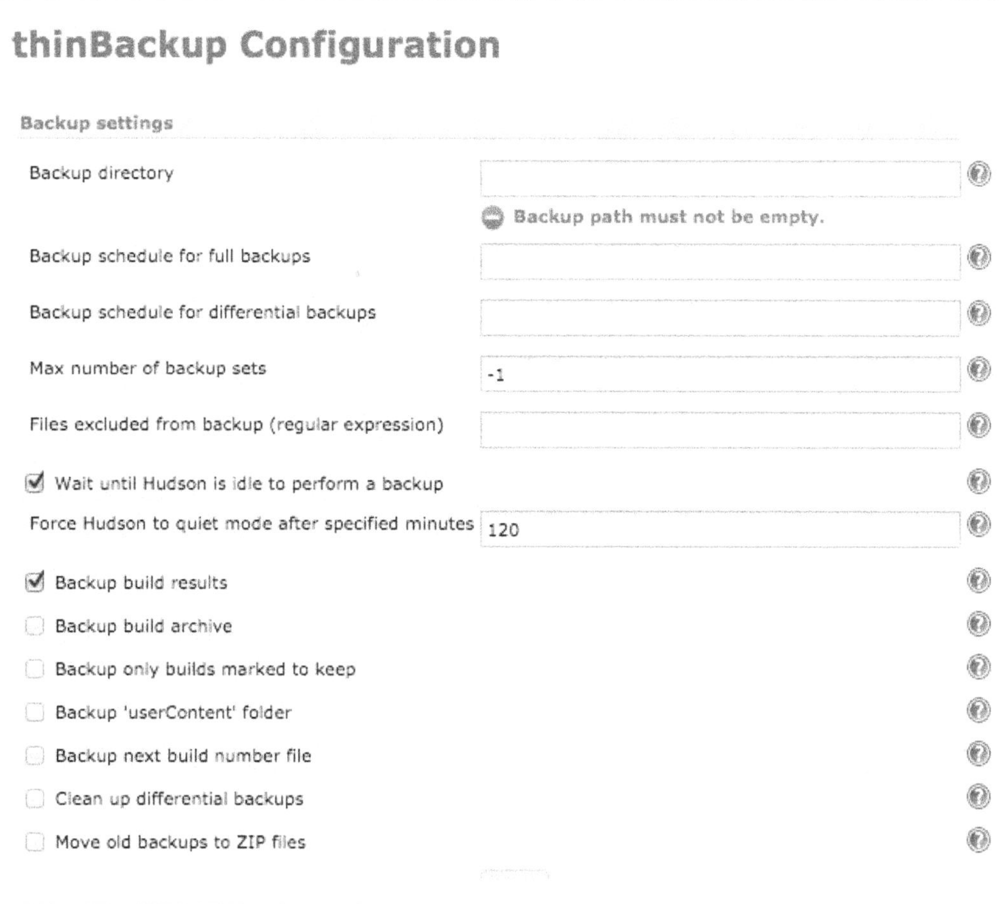

FIGURE 10-13. *ThinBackup settings*

backup (Restore). The thinBackup Configuration page has a few additional settings (see Figure 10-13):

- Backup schedule for full backups – to specify the execution schedule in a cron-like notation when a full backup should be done. (For example: The value `0 12 * * 1-5` executes at 12:00 noon every weekday; Monday to Friday).
- Backup schedule for differential backups – the schedule is specified the same as full backup. A differential backup stores only complete files whose modification is done after the last full backup. For a differential backup to happen, there should be at least one full backup. So a full backup always happens first.

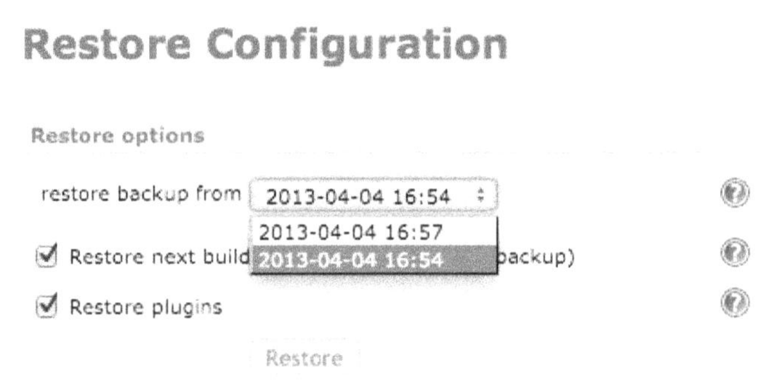

FIGURE 10-14. *ThinBackup restore operation*

- To save disk space you can specify the maximum number of backup sets to keep. A backup set is defined as a full backup together with its referencing differential backups.
- An option to clean up the differential backup when full backup happens.
- Options to specify contents to include in the backup such as build results, build archives, builds marked to keep, "userContent" folder, and next build number file.

A restore operation is slightly different in the thinBackup plugin compared to the Backup plugin. The thinBackup restore operation provides the date and time of the backup rather than the actual backup filename. Also it provides an option to restore the plugins and the next build number file, as shown in Figure 10-14. ThinBackup automatically restores the contents directly into the Hudson home folder. For safe restoration of files, the thinBackup manager sends the shutdown signal to keep Hudson from scheduling any job while a restore happens.

Set Up a Fail-Safe Mode for Your Hudson

Assume that you have set up Hudson to do Continuous Integration and Continuous Delivery, and it is mission critical to keep it online all the time. This is often the case with large enterprises where multiple teams and hundreds of developers depend on the smooth running of Hudson. To meet this need, set up Hudson in a fail-safe mode.

The schematic shown in the following illustration is based on our experience in setting up a fail-safe Hudson at our organization.

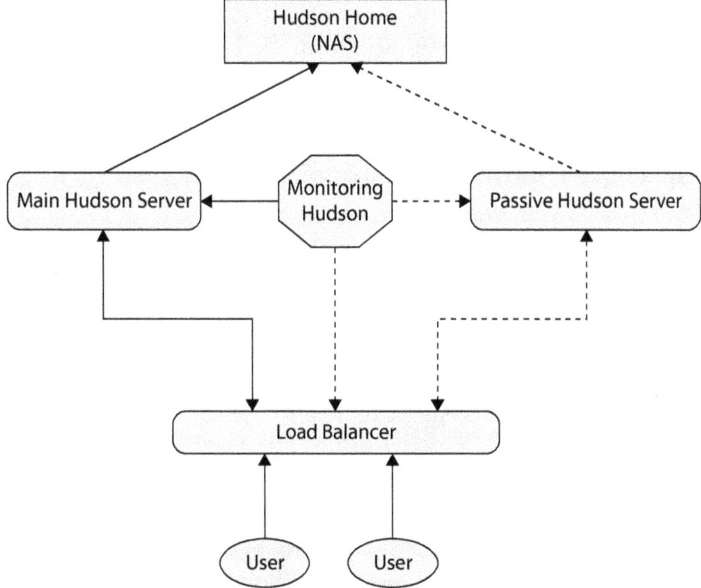

Redundant Hudson Server Setup

The basic idea behind this setup is that there are three Hudson instances available. The first two act as the main master and its redundant server, which is in a Passive mode (not running, but can be invoked at a moment's notice). The third is used for monitoring the main master. If the master stops working for some reason, the redundant server will be booted up to take over the tasks of master until the master's issues are fixed and it can be brought back online. In order to set up this fail-safe mode, some important points need to be considered.

The first important point is that the Hudson home needs to be network-accessible to both the master and redundant Hudson instances. When the master fails, the redundant server boots using the same Hudson home and loads the exact same configuration as the main master. There may be an issue with jobs that were executing at the time of failure. They might not have completed and may need to be manually restarted again. Though Hudson by itself is not smart enough to start those interrupted jobs, there are free plugins available to check and restart interrupted jobs after a fresh reboot.

Another point to consider is that all three Hudson instances should run on separate machines. Here we are taking into consideration two forms of failure: OS-level failure (including hardware-related) and Hudson software-level failure. If both the master and redundant Hudson servers are running on the same machine, and if the failure is only due to no response from the Hudson master because of Hudson software failure, then the redundant server can be easily booted up. On the other hand, if there is an OS-level failure on the machine where the two servers are running, then the redundant server also will be unreachable. The most fail-safe configuration is to have all three Hudson instances running on three different servers.

Monitoring Hudson Setup

The sole task of the Monitoring Hudson is just to make sure the master Hudson is up and running. It runs periodically and checks if the main Hudson server is alive. If not, boot up the redundant Hudson server and notify the operation team about the failure. Setting up such a job is easy. Create a job, add the builder Execute shell, and add the command

```
curl http://hudson-master.mycompany.com/rest/status
```

In order for this command to work correctly, the REST plugin must be installed in the master Hudson. The command returns the following XML:

```
<ns2:status>
   <url>hudson-master.mycompany.com</url>
   <version>3.0.1</version>
   <initLevel>COMPLETED</initLevel>
  <quietingDown>false</quietingDown>
  <terminating>false</terminating>
    ...
</ns2:status>
```

The next setup adds a build trigger to schedule job execution periodically. Select the build trigger "Build periodically" and provide a value. The value provided needs to follow the UNIX-style cron syntax; for example, **@hourly** to run it every hour or ***/15** * * * * to run it every 15 minutes. When the job is able to successfully fetch the XML, then we know the master is responding. But this response does not mean the master is working flawlessly and able to execute all the jobs. In the monitoring job, it is possible to do much more than the simple curl call we explained previously. In our setup we have developed a much more sophisticated way of querying Hudson using Hudson's REST API and reacting to the results we obtain.

When the monitoring job is unable to communicate with the Hudson master, we know something is wrong with the master. The first thing the monitoring job does is to notify the operation team via e-mail. In our setup, we have used the email-ext plugin to send advanced messages rather than the default one supported by the built-in Hudson e-mail mechanism.

Server Switch on Failure

The next step is to set up the Monitoring Hudson to boot the redundant server when the master fails. This is done through another job. This job uses the SSH plugin to run the command on the remote server. To know how to configure the SSH plugin to do remote execution, refer to the section "Executing Commands on Remote Machine" in Chapter 4. When the SSH plugin is added to Hudson, it adds a builder called "Execute shell script on remote host using ssh." This builder is used to run the command to boot the redundant Hudson server, as shown in Figure 10-15.

For this setup to work correctly, the user running the Monitoring Hudson must have SSH access to the machine running the redundant server. In our setup we have configured password-less SSH access as explained in the section "Setting Up Public-Private Key-Based Authentication" in Chapter 7.

Once the job for booting the redundant server is ready, it must be set up to execute when the job to monitor the Hudson master fails. This can be accomplished by using the parameterized-trigger plugin. This versatile plugin allows triggering another build of another job from the build of the current job under various conditions. One of the conditions is only when the current build fails. This is very handy to trigger the build of the job booting the redundant server from the job monitoring the master Hudson when it fails, as shown in Figure 10-16.

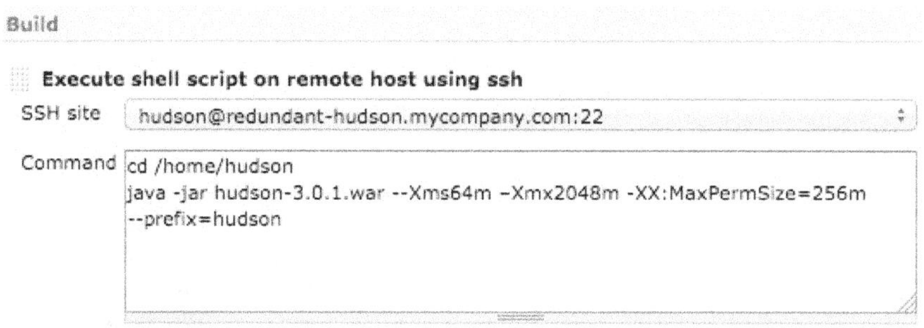

Build

Execute shell script on remote host using ssh

SSH site: hudson@redundant-hudson.mycompany.com:22

Command:

```
cd /home/hudson
java -jar hudson-3.0.1.war --Xms64m -Xmx2048m -XX:MaxPermSize=256m
--prefix=hudson
```

FIGURE 10-15. *SSH command to boot redundant server*

FIGURE 10-16. *Triggering job to boot redundant server from monitoring job*

Redirecting HTTP Traffic to a Redundant Server

The final step is redirecting the HTTP traffic going to the Hudson master to the redundant Hudson server. In our setup we have a load-balancer that directs the traffic to the Hudson master. So it is easy to redirect the traffic to the redundant server in the load balancer. If you don't have a load balancer, there is an easier way to accomplish this. For this, the Apache HTTP server must front your Hudson, as we explained in the section "Put Your Hudson Behind a Web Proxy." Also you should have proper access to start and stop the Apache Server via SSH. Create two proxy configuration files; say proxy.conf.redundant, in the same folder as proxy.conf.master. Their contents are:

```
proxy.conf.master
ProxyRequests Off
ProxyPass /hudson http://hudson-master.mycompany.com:8080/hudson
ProxyPassReverse /hudson http://hudson-master.mycompany.com:8080/hudson
```

```
proxy.conf.redundant
ProxyRequests Off
ProxyPass /hudson http://hudson-redundant.mycompany.com:8080/hudson
ProxyPassReverse /hudson http://hudson-redundant.mycompany.com:8080/hudson
```

Originally when the Hudson master is up and running, the contents of proxy.conf.master will be copied to /etc/apache2/conf/other/proxy.conf. When the redundant server is booted by the job via SSH, the same job could restart the Apache HTTP server after copying the content of proxy.conf.redundant to /etc/apache2/conf/other/proxy.conf. This will make sure the behind-the-scenes switching of Hudson master and redundant server is transparent to the end user.

One additional thing that can be set up is letting the Monitoring Hudson continue to monitor the main Hudson server when it is down. When the master is successfully booted, the second job could shut down the redundant server and route the traffic back to the Hudson master server, by copying the file proxy.conf.master to /etc/apache2/conf/other/proxy.conf and restarting the Apache Server.

The preceding path is just an example. The folder of other .conf files Apache will include when it starts up may be different depending on platform, installer, Apache version, and so on. If you can't find one, you can always create one and add an Include other/*.conf directive to the main .conf file.

Scale Up the Security of Your Hudson

In order to support multiple teams in a single Hudson instance, it must be properly secured so that the privileges to various functionalities can be restricted to certain members of the team. Out of the box, Hudson is open. In Chapter 3, we discussed how to secure your Hudson with simple authentication based on Hudson's own user database mechanism. Also we discussed how to set up authorization using the matrix-based security mechanism. In this chapter let us see how to restrict job configuration access to certain users in Hudson and how to restrict the authorizations based on roles.

Restrict Job Access to Certain Users

The Matrix Authorization Strategy we saw in Chapter 3 either allows certain access (like create, delete, configure, or read) to all jobs or denies the access to all jobs. However, if different teams share Hudson, then you want to give job access only to certain users. In order to restrict user access to certain jobs, you must enable the Job-based Matrix Authorization Strategy by using the Configure Security link in the Manage Hudson page. This mode is an extension to matrix-based security. Specifying the global authorizations is exactly same as the regular Matrix Authorization Strategy we saw in Chapter 3. However, with job-based matrix authorization enabled, the job configuration page gets a new authorization entry, as shown in Figure 10-17. This is where you restrict the access to that job.

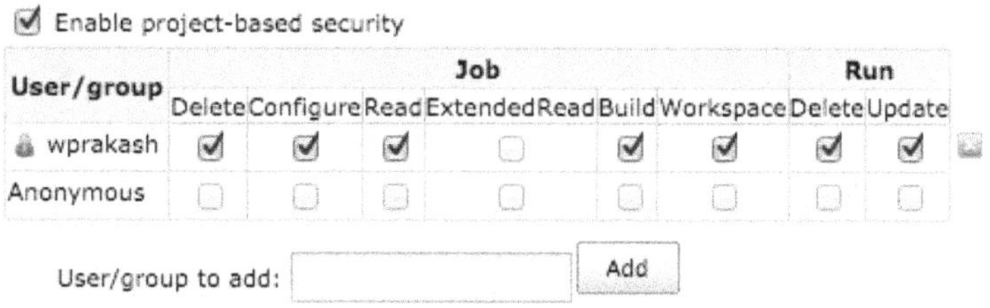

☑ Enable project-based security

User/group	Job						Run	
	Delete	Configure	Read	ExtendedRead	Build	Workspace	Delete	Update
wprakash	☑	☑	☑	☐	☑	☑	☑	☑
Anonymous	☐	☐	☐	☐	☐	☐	☐	☐

User/group to add: [ ] Add

FIGURE 10-17. *Restricting job access authorization*

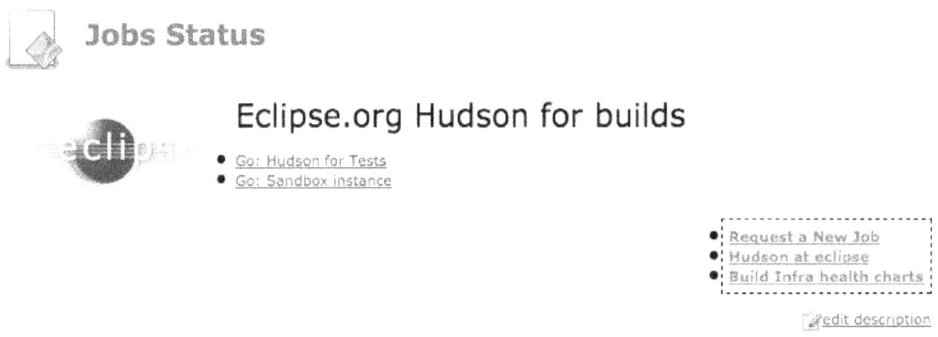

FIGURE 10-18. *Request to create a job at the Eclipse Hudson instance*

In order for this to work properly, you should set the global authorizations for anonymous as overall read permission and jobs read permission. Only the admin users have all the permissions, including creating the job. Now you want to have a way for users to request the creation of jobs. Figure 10-18 shows an example of how the end user of Hudson can request a job using the Hudson instance.

This screenshot is from an Eclipse Hudson instance. Adding HTML to the System Messages field in the Configure System page adds the links shown in Figure 10-18. On the right-hand side, there is a link Request a New Job. Clicking this link takes you to a wiki page that explains how to request a new job. Basically any Eclipse committer who is active in a project can request a new job. As explained in the wiki page, the new job request is done by creating a new bug in the Eclipse Bugzilla, under the component Community and subcomponent Hudson. This Bugzilla component is actively monitored by the Hudson admins. Once they create the new job, the bug is closed and the committer gets notification about the creation. Only the requesting committer gets access to configure the job. This is because, when the job is created, the admin sets the authorization in the job configuration page, as shown earlier in Figure 10-17.

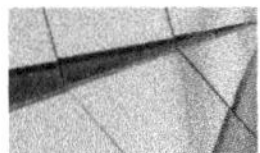

NOTE
Since the user has configure access to the newly created job, the user has permission to add other users or groups to access the job by adding them to the job authorization matrix. If by mistake the users who have job configuration permission click the red button and delete themselves from the job authorization matrix, they lose the access to the job and they have to rely on the Hudson admin or other users who still have configuration access to the job to add them back in the authorization matrix.

Add Roles to the Authorization Matrix

By default, Hudson does not have the concept of Roles. Either an individual user or group of users can be added to the authorization matrix. The Role-based Authorization Strategy plugin fills this gap. The basic concepts of this plugin are creating roles, setting authorizations for these roles, and then assigning roles to users or groups of users.

In order to use role-based authorization, you must go to the Configure Security page and select Role-based Strategy in the Authorization section. Once this setting has been saved, a new link called Manage and Assign Roles appears in the Manage Hudson page. Clicking the link takes you to the corresponding page where you see two links for Manage Roles and Assign Roles. The creation of roles and setting authorizations is done in the Manage and Assign Roles page, as shown in Figure 10-19.

In this page, you can create your own roles and assign authorizations to roles. There are two types of roles:

- Global roles, such as admin, job-admin, job-creator, and so on, that are allowed to authorize Overall, Slave, Job, Run, View, and SCM authorizations on a global basis.
- Job roles for assigning certain Job-, Run-, and SCM-level authorizations only to certain jobs. The set of jobs to which this role applies is specified in the pattern field as a regular expression. For example, if you set the field to **sherwood-.***, then the role will match all jobs names that start with **sherwood-**. Note that the pattern is case-sensitive. To perform a case-insensitive match, use (?i) notation, for example, upper, **Sherwood-.*** versus lower, **sherwood-.*** versus case-insensitive, **(?i)sherwood-.***.

Manage and Assign Roles

Global roles

Role	Overall		Slave		Job						Run		View			SCM
	Administer	Read	Configure	Delete	Create	Delete	Configure	Read	Build	Workspace	Delete	Update	Create	Delete	Configure	Tag
admin	✓	✓	✓	✓	✓	✓	✓	✓	✓	✓	✓	✓	✓	✓	✓	✓
anonymous		✓						✓								
job-admin		✓			✓	✓	✓	✓	✓	✓						
job-creator		✓			✓		✓	✓								

Role to add

Add

Project roles

Role	Pattern	Job					Run		SCM
		Delete	Configure	Read	Build	Workspace	Delete	Update	Tag
sherwood-job-admin	sherwood-	✓	✓	✓	✓	✓	✓	✓	✓
sherwood-job-builder	sherwood-				✓				

Role to add

Pattern

Add

Save

FIGURE 10-19. *Creating roles and assigning authorizations*

Once the roles are created, the next step is assigning roles to users or a group of users. The users and group of users must exist in the Security Realm as explained in Chapter 3. Clicking the Assign Roles link in the Manage and Assign Roles page takes you to the page where a single user or group of users can be assigned roles created as explained earlier, as shown in Figure 10-20. As you can see, the newly created roles appear in the roles assignment matrix. Once the roles are assigned to a user or group of users, when the particular user logs in, the user will only have authorizations assigned to that role.

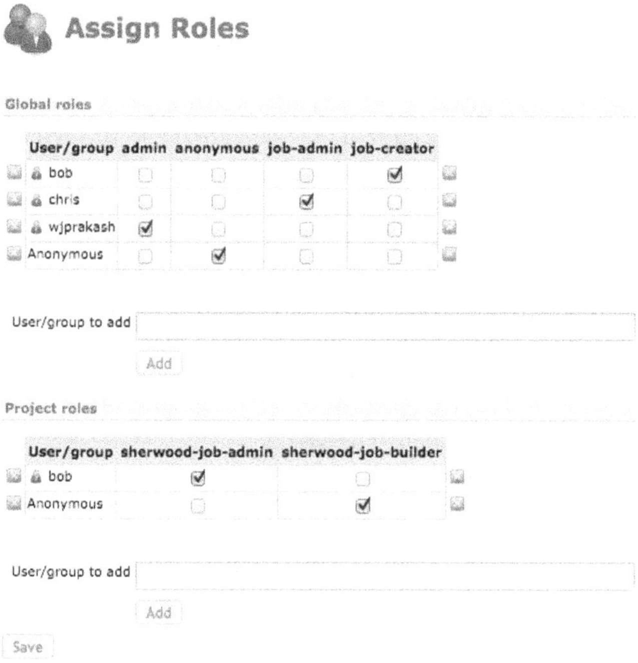

FIGURE 10-20. *Assigning roles to a user or group of users*

Upgrade Your Hudson Diligently

Upgrading Hudson is always a matter of discussion. We have often heard the story: my Hudson is broken after upgrading to the latest version. As with upgrading any enterprise software, it is of the utmost importance to take every precaution while upgrading Hudson. Sure, it is very easy to upgrade Hudson. If you are using standalone Hudson, it is just a matter of downloading the new war, shutting down the older version, replacing it with the newer version, and running the latter with the command as explained in Chapter 1. If Hudson is deployed as a Web application, then it is as simple as undeploying the older version and deploying the newer version. However, it is your responsibility to make sure the upgraded Hudson works well with the existing Hudson home and its content.

The Hudson team works hard to make sure backward compatibility is maintained. However, each Hudson installation is different and the configurations and build artifacts differ vastly from one installation to another, making it impossible to predict whether every Hudson upgrade will be 100 percent successful and backward compatible. So, it is up to the Hudson admin to make sure that upgrading to a newer version does not break the current build environment. This section discusses some basic principles to follow while upgrading Hudson and its plugins.

Understand the Hudson Versioning Scheme

First and foremost, it is important to understand the Hudson versioning scheme and the release schedule for the core component. From version 2.0 onward, the Hudson team has adopted the sequence-based software versioning scheme. Each release is assigned a unique identifier that consists of one or more sequences of numbers or letters: major.minor.maintenance. For example: 3.0.0 is a major release, 3.1.0 is a minor release, and 3.0.1 is a maintenance release.

When upgrading your Hudson to a maintenance release, you can usually let your guard down and upgrade without much fuss. If the version of your current Hudson is 3.0.0 and if a newer version, 3.0.1, is available, then it may be okay to upgrade without exhaustive testing of the new version. We recommend upgrading to this maintenance version as soon as it is available. The Hudson team releases such maintenance versions periodically, usually every month after a major release. A maintenance release includes only bug fixes and is guaranteed not to include any new feature or API changes.

New features are always in demand. The Hudson team implements such features based on popular demand. When new features are added to Hudson, it is released as a minor release. Minor releases usually happen every three to four months. If a newer version of the minor release, 3.1.0, is available, then you should upgrade with some caution. With the minor release, some of the bundled external libraries and plugins may get upgraded to support the new feature. There is a minor risk of core platform changes associated with new feature implementation. A new UI may be added, but it is guaranteed that there will not be any API changes. Still, there is a minor risk of breaking some plugins.

Finally, a major release of Hudson provides no guarantee of backward compatibility of bundled external libraries and may include API changes. Major releases are a next step in Hudson development. To take this bold step, the Hudson team may have to sacrifice backward compatibility for better future operation. There is a major risk involved in upgrading to a major release. You must take every caution when upgrading to this release. Even in a major release, the Hudson team tries hard to keep backward compatibility. If backward compatibility is broken, then they take care to document the changes and to provide an upgrade path to migrate existing configuration and build artifacts to the next major version.

Upgrade in a Sandbox First

This principle is highly recommended when upgrading your Hudson to a major release, and we also recommend following it for minor and maintenance releases. It is seldom wise to directly upgrade your production Hudson; never if it is a major release. To upgrade safely, we recommend creating a sandbox instance of your Hudson installation. A sandbox instance is nothing but another instance of Hudson that is set up to use a different Hudson home and different port (if running on the same machine) than the production Hudson. You could even run it on a different machine than the production Hudson. Some important points to remember while setting up the sandbox Hudson:

- Before upgrading, plugins in both production and sandbox must have the exact same versions.
- The sandbox should have a good representation of jobs (preferably all jobs) that exist in the production version.
- The configuration of jobs in the sandbox must be exactly same as that of the jobs in the production version.
- The sandbox Hudson should also be set up to build on the same slave machines that are used by the production Hudson. However, be careful not to use the same Slave home used by the production slaves.
- If the production Hudson is behind an HTTP proxy server, also put the sandbox Hudson behind the proxy server, giving meaningful URLs. For example, the Eclipse Foundation uses http://hudson.eclipse.org/hudson for the production Hudson and http://hudson.eclipse.org/sandbox for the sandbox Hudson.
- If the production server exports artifacts to a production repository or an external location meant for the production use, make sure to redirect the artifacts produced in the sandbox instance to a nonproduction repository or location.

Keep this sandbox Hudson always ready for future upgrades. When upgrading, first upgrade Hudson in this sandbox. Let it run for several days, even weeks, to make sure builds happen fine in the sandbox environment. If you are upgrading and find any issues, work with the Hudson team via the Eclipse Hudson forum and Eclipse Bugzilla to resolve the problems. Make sure all the plugins work properly, and upgrade to newer versions if necessary. If you file bug reports about any issues you found while upgrading to a major release, wait until the next maintenance release and upgrade the sandbox to the maintenance release to make sure the bugs have been fixed. When you are fully satisfied with the results in the sandbox, go ahead and upgrade your production environment. After upgrading the production environment, be careful to keep the sandbox environment identical. At this point your sandbox environment will be ready for the next upgrade.

Upgrading plugins also must be considered similar to upgrading the core Hudson. Unless you are sure from the release notes of the plugin, you should first use the sandbox Hudson to make sure the plugin upgrade will not break your production environment. Though plugins can be easily installed and rolled back if broken, it is a best practice to use the sandbox instance to verify the upgrade first in order to maintain a stable production environment.

Summary

In this chapter we have seen some best practices one can follow to keep a Hudson installation running smoothly. We saw that fine-tuning the memory used by Hudson, cleaning up unwanted builds, and monitoring the disk space used by builds is the best way to manage the finite resources available to Hudson. Putting Hudson behind a Web proxy and not using Hudson as a file server are the best ways to ensure a better-performing Hudson. We also saw how to create a fail-safe mode for Hudson. Notwithstanding all these precautions, a low percentage possibility of Hudson failing can never be eliminated. So we saw that it is always advisable to back up build data using a backup manager. We discussed how to augment Hudson security using job-based and role-based authorization. We finished by explaining the principles one must follow to upgrade Hudson smoothly.

PART IV

Appendixes

APPENDIX A

Widely Used Hudson Plugins

As we have seen in Chapter 4, the three main concepts of Continuous Integration, Test-Driven Development, and Continuous Delivery or Deployment are the solid supporting pillars of a successful agile team. Hudson CI Server is one of the best tools to practice the three concepts successfully. The plain stock Hudson Server may not be fully suitable to achieve these goals. It has to be augmented with some of the hundreds of freely available plugins, based on the specific needs. However, choosing the right plugin is a tedious task. To help in choosing the right kind of plugin, in this appendix we have listed the popular plugins by category, based on wide usage by Hudson users.

The popularity of the plugins is determined by two criteria. The first is the number of installs. If configured to send Usage Stats, Hudson sends the stats to the Hudson Community infrastructure. The Hudson team analyzes these statistics and determines the most widely used plugins. The second is the community activity around the plugins in terms of forum postings or issues or enhancement requests using Eclipse Bugzilla.

We have grouped the plugins based on some of the CI guidelines we discussed in Chapter 4, as listed here:

- Maintain a single-source repository
- Automate the build
- Every commit should build the mainline on an integration machine
- Make your build self-testing
- Make it easy for everyone to get the latest executable
- Everyone can see what is happening
- Test in a clone of the production environment
- Automate deployment

Maintain a Single-Source Repository

This guideline encourages the project team to use a centralized SCM system to maintain their source code. Hudson supports various SCM systems via plugins. The popularly used SCM plugins are listed here. Hudson additionally supports 20 more SCM vendors.

Plugin	Description	Documentation URL
Git	Provides support to use Git, a free and open-source distributed version control system in Hudson.	http://wiki.hudson-ci.org/display/HUDSON/Git+Plugin

Plugin	Description	Documentation URL
CVS	This plugin integrates Hudson with the Concurrent Versioning System (CVS) SCM.	http://wiki.hudson-ci.org/display/HUDSON/Cvs+Plugin
SVN	This plugin adds support for the Subversion SCM, an open source project at Apache Foundation.	http://wiki.hudson-ci.org/display/HUDSON/Subversion+Plugin
Perforce	With this plugin you can use a Perforce Client spec that will synchronize files to the Hudson workspace.	http://wiki.hudson-ci.org/display/HUDSON/Perforce+Plugin
ClearCase	With this plugin you can use either base ClearCase or UCM ClearCase as the SCM for Hudson projects.	http://wiki.hudson-ci.org/display/HUDSON/ClearCase+Plugin
Mercurial	With this plugin, you can use a Mercurial repository as SCM. Every build will run **hg pull -u** to bring the tip of the branch repository.	http://wiki.hudson-ci.org/display/HUDSON/Mercurial+Plugin

Automate the Build

Automating the build using a single command is an important principle of a CI build. Hudson supports various build tools via plugins, and popular ones are listed next. Hudson additionally supports more than 40 build tools.

Plugin	Description	Documentation URL
Ant	Ant support is integrated into the Hudson platform.	http://wiki.eclipse.org/Using_Hudson
Maven	This plugin adds the Maven 3 build step to a Hudson free-style job.	http://wiki.hudson-ci.org/display/HUDSON/Maven+3+Build+Plugin
Gradle	This plugin makes it possible to invoke a Gradle build script as the main build step.	http://wiki.hudson-ci.org/display/HUDSON/Gradle+Plugin
MsBuild	This plugin allows you to use MSBuild to build .NET projects.	http://wiki.hudson-ci.org/display/HUDSON/MSBuild+Plugin

Plugin	Description	Documentation URL
Nant	This plugin allows for the execution of a Nant build as a Hudson build step.	http://wiki.hudson-ci.org/display/HUDSON/NAnt+Plugin
Rake	This plugin allows Hudson to invoke Rake tasks as build steps.	http://wiki.hudson-ci.org/display/HUDSON/Rake+plugin

Before the build starts, it must be prepared for proper build. Hudson supports various build wrappers by using plugins. They can be used to preprocess the build environment. Build wrappers are usually very specific to the software project. The following are widely used, and Hudson supports an additional 25 build wrappers.

Plugin	Description	Documentation URL
Locks & Latches	This plugin allows controlling the parallel execution of jobs.	http://wiki.hudson-ci.org/display/HUDSON/Locks+and+Latches+plugin
Setenv	This plugin sets up environment variables for a project to be referenced during build steps.	http://wiki.hudson-ci.org/display/HUDSON/Setenv+Plugin
Copy Artifact	Adds a build step to copy artifacts from another project.	http://wiki.hudson-ci.org/display/HUDSON/Copy+Artifact+Plugin
SSH	This plugin can be used to run shell commands on a remote machine via SSH, before or after a build.	http://wiki.hudson-ci.org/display/HUDSON/SSH+plugin

Every Commit Should Build the Mainline on an Integration Machine

Automating the build based on user commit is part of CI. Hudson supports various build triggers via plugins. Apart from the following popular plugins, Hudson additionally supports more than 15 other build triggers.

Plugin	Description	Documentation URL
SCM Trigger	This support is integrated into the Hudson platform and implemented by all SCM plugins.	http://wiki.eclipse.org/Using_Hudson

Plugin	Description	Documentation URL
Gerrit Trigger	This plugin integrates Hudson to Gerrit code review for triggering builds when a "patch set" is created.	http://wiki.hudson-ci.org/display/HUDSON/Gerrit+Trigger
Parameterized Trigger	This plugin allows triggering new builds when a build completes, with various ways of specifying parameters for the new build.	http://wiki.hudson-ci.org/display/HUDSON/Parameterized+Trigger+Plugin
URL Change Trigger	The URL Change Trigger plugin allows you to trigger a Hudson build when the content of a URL changes.	http://wiki.hudson-ci.org/display/HUDSON/URL+Change+Trigger
Downstream Ext Trigger	This plugin supports extended configuration for triggering downstream builds.	http://wiki.hudson-ci.org/display/HUDSON/Downstream-Ext+Plugin

Make Your Build Self-Testing

CI build is not just about catching compilation errors but also catching bugs more quickly and efficiently. Hudson supports various unit-testing frameworks via plugins, and the following are popularly used. Hudson supports more than 10 additional unit-testing frameworks via plugins.

Plugin	Description	Documentation URL
JUnit	The support for JUnit is integrated into the Hudson platform.	http://wiki.eclipse.org/Using_Hudson
NUnit	This plugin makes it possible to import NUnit reports from each build into Hudson and display the results.	http://wiki.hudson-ci.org/display/HUDSON/NUnit+Plugin
Selenium	This plugin turns your Hudson cluster into a Selenium cluster to carry out Selenium tests.	http://wiki.hudson-ci.org/display/HUDSON/Selenium+Plugin
CppUnit	This plugin enables you to publish CppUnit test results in Hudson.	http://wiki.hudson-ci.org/display/HUDSON/CppUnit+Plugin
TestNg	This plugin allows you to import TestNg results into Hudson and display the results.	http://wiki.hudson-ci.org/display/HUDSON/testng-plugin

Plugin	Description	Documentation URL
xUnit	This plugin allows Hudson to transform test result reports produced by different testing tools into JUnit test results.	http://wiki.hudson-ci.org/display/HUDSON/xUnit+Plugin

Self-testing is best achieved if there is uniform code coverage. Hudson supports various code coverage tools via plugins. The following are popular plugins.

Plugin	Description	Documentation URL
Clover	This plugin allows you to capture code coverage reports from Clover.	http://wiki.hudson-ci.org/display/HUDSON/Clover+Plugin
Cobertura	This plugin allows you to capture code coverage reports from Cobertura.	http://wiki.hudson-ci.org/display/HUDSON/Cobertura+Plugin
Emma	This plugin allows you to capture code coverage reports from Emma.	http://wiki.hudson-ci.org/display/HUDSON/Emma+Plugin
Serenity	This plugin adds support to publish results of Serenity, a Java code coverage, and complexity and dependency analysis tool.	http://wiki.hudson-ci.org/display/HUDSON/Serenity+Plugin
Sonar	This plugin adds support for Sonar, an open-source Code Quality Management platform.	http://wiki.hudson-ci.org/display/HUDSON/Sonar+plugin
NCover	Archive and publish .NET code coverage HTML reports from NCover.	http://wiki.hudson-ci.org/display/HUDSON/NCover+Plugin

Static Analysis improves the confidence of self-testing. Hudson supports various Static Code Analysis tools via plugins, and the popular ones are listed in the following table.

Plugin	Description	Documentation URL
Checkstyle	This plugin scans for checkstyle-result.xml files in the build workspace and reports the number of warnings found.	http://wiki.hudson-ci.org/display/HUDSON/Checkstyle+Plugin

Plugin	Description	Documentation URL
PMD	This plugin scans for pmd.xml files in the build workspace and reports the number of warnings found.	http://wiki.hudson-ci.org/display/HUDSON/PMD+Plugin
Dry	This plugin shows the results of duplicate code checker tools.	http://wiki.hudson-ci.org/display/HUDSON/DRY+Plugin
Findbugs	This plugin scans for findbugs.xml files in the build workspace and reports the number of warnings found.	http://wiki.hudson-ci.org/display/HUDSON/FindBugs+Plugin
Crap4J	This plugin reads the "crappy methods" report from Crap4J and displays the results in Hudson.	http://wiki.hudson-ci.org//display/HUDSON/Crap4J+Plugin
Warnings	This plugin generates the trend report for compiler warnings in the console log or in log files.	http://wiki.hudson-ci.org/display/HUDSON/Warnings+Plugin
CCM	This plugin generates reports on cyclomatic complexity for .NET code.	http://wiki.hudson-ci.org/display/HUDSON/CCM+Plugin
Violations	This plugin generates reports for static code violation detectors such as checkstyle, pmd, cpd, findbugs, fxcop, stylecop, and simian.	http://wiki.hudson-ci.org/display/HUDSON/Violations

Make It Easy for Everyone to Get the Latest Executable

Making the build artifacts available to stakeholders is important in CI. Hudson supports various artifact uploaders via plugins. Some popular plugins are listed here. Hudson supports more than 10 additional artifact uploaders.

Plugin	Description	Documentation URL
Maven Release	This plugin allows you to perform a Maven release from a Hudson build.	http://wiki.hudson-ci.org/display/HUDSON/M2+Release+Plugin
SCP Publisher	This plugin uploads build artifacts to repository sites using the SCP (SSH) protocol.	http://wiki.hudson-ci.org/display/HUDSON/SCP+plugin

Plugin	Description	Documentation URL
FTP Publisher	This plugin can be used to upload project artifacts and whole directories to an FTP server.	http://wiki.hudson-ci.org/display/HUDSON/FTP-Publisher+Plugin
Artifactory	This plugin helps Hudson job builds to deploy artifacts automatically to the Artifactory server.	http://wiki.hudson-ci.org/display/HUDSON/Artifactory+Plugin

Everyone Can See What Is Happening

Communicate the state of the build, especially if it is broken. Hudson supports various build notifiers via plugins. Popular ones are listed here, but Hudson supports 20 more such plugins.

Plugin	Description	Documentation URL
Email	E-mail support is part of the Hudson core platform.	http://wiki.eclipse.org/Using_Hudson
Email-ext	This plugin allows you to customize when an e-mail is sent, who should receive it, what the e-mail says, and so on.	http://wiki.hudson-ci.org/display/HUDSON/Email-ext+plugin
IRC	This plugin installs a Hudson IRC bot for your choice of IRC channels.	http://wiki.hudson-ci.org/display/HUDSON/IRC+Plugin
Jabber	This plugin integrates Hudson with the Jabber instant messaging protocol.	http://wiki.hudson-ci.org/display/HUDSON/Jabber+Plugin

Test in a Clone of the Production Environment

The build must happen in various slaves that clone the production environment. Hudson supports various kinds of slave management via plugins so builds can happen in clones of the production environment. The popular ones are listed in the following table.

Plugin	Description	Documentation URL
SSH Slaves	This plugin allows you to manage slaves running on UNIX machines over SSH.	http://wiki.hudson-ci.org/display/HUDSON/SSH+Slaves+plugin

Plugin	Description	Documentation URL
Windows Slaves	This supports installing a Hudson plugin as a Windows service.	http://wiki.hudson-ci.org/display/HUDSON/Installing+Hudson+as+a+Windows+service
Slave Status	This plugin is for monitoring a slave's running status and its resources.	http://wiki.hudson-ci.org/display/HUDSON/slave-status
EC2	This plugin allows Hudson to start slaves on EC2 or Ubuntu Enterprise Cloud (Eucalyptus) on demand.	http://wiki.hudson-ci.org/display/HUDSON/Amazon+EC2+Plugin
VirtualBox	This plugin integrates Hudson with VirtualBox virtual machine.	http://wiki.hudson-ci.org/display/HUDSON/VirtualBox+Plugin
JClouds	This plugin provides an option to launch Hudson slaves on any cloud provider supported by JClouds.	http://wiki.hudson-ci.org/display/HUDSON/JClouds+Plugin
Build Pipeline Plugin	This plugin creates a pipeline of Hudson jobs and gives a view so that you can visualize it from integration to deployment.	http://wiki.hudson-ci.org/display/HUDSON/Build+Pipeline+Plugin

Automate Deployment

One of the CI best practices is to automate the deployment if possible. Hudson supports various type of deployment or external tool integration via plugins.

Plugin	Description	Documentation URL
Deploy	This plugin provides support to deploy to popular open-source application servers such as Tomcat, JBoss, Glassfish, and so on.	http://wiki.hudson-ci.org/display/HUDSON/Deploy+Plugin
WebLogic	This plugin deploys artifacts built on Hudson to a WebLogic-managed server or cluster.	http://wiki.hudson-ci.org/display/HUDSON/WebLogic+Deployer+Plugin

Plugin	Description	Documentation URL
WebSphere	This plugin takes a war/ear file and deploys that to a running remote WebSphere Application Server at the end of a build.	http://wiki.hudson-ci.org/display/HUDSON/Deploy+WebSphere+Plugin
Promoted Builds	This plugin allows you to distinguish good builds from bad builds by introducing the notion of "promotion."	http://wiki.hudson-ci.org/display/HUDSON/Promoted+Builds+Plugin

Hudson UI Configuration

Finally, there are plenty of plugins available to configure various parts of the Hudson UI. Popular ones are listed here, but there are 50 more plugins that can be used.

Plugin	Description	Documentation URL
Disk Usage	This plugin records the disk usage by various jobs both in the master and in the slaves.	http://wiki.hudson-ci.org/display/HUDSON/Disk+Usage+Plugin
Plot	This plugin provides generic plotting (or graphing) capabilities in Hudson.	http://wiki.hudson-ci.org/display/HUDSON/Plot+Plugin
Radiator View	Provides a job view displaying project status in a highly visible manner.	http://wiki.hudson-ci.org/display/HUDSON/Radiator+View+Plugin
eXtreme Feedback Panel	This plugin provides an eXtreme Feedback Panel that can be used to expose the status of a selected number of jobs.	http://wiki.hudson-ci.org/display/HUDSON/eXtreme+Feedback+Panel+Plugin
Nested View	This plugin adds a view type to allow grouping job views into multiple levels instead of one big list of tabs.	http://wiki.hudson-ci.org/display/HUDSON/Nested+View+Plugin

Plugin	Description	Documentation URL
Downstream Build View	This plugin allows you to view the full status of all the downstream builds so that one can graphically see that everything for this build has been completed successfully.	http://wiki.hudson-ci.org/display/HUDSON/Downstream+buildview+plugin
Dashboard View	This plugin contributes a new view implementation that provides a dashboard/portal-like view for your Hudson.	http://wiki.hudson-ci.org/display/HUDSON/Dashboard+View

APPENDIX B

Personal Hudson Instance

Every other chapter in this book assumes that the Hudson instance is running on a dedicated host in a special-purpose user account and that the jobs executed by that Hudson instance provide benefit to a team rather than to just one individual. This appendix explores some of the ways to benefit from running a personal Hudson instance on an individual workstation. This Hudson instance runs with the user's personal credentials and executes jobs entirely for the benefit of that individual user. If the usage of Hudson covered elsewhere in the book puts Hudson in the role of a butler overseeing an entire domestic staff, this chapter puts Hudson in the role of a valet.

Hudson-as-Valet

According to the blog Jane Austen's World (http://janeaustensworld.wordpress.com/), a valet (rhymes with pallet) is "a personal manservant who tends to his master's every need, from a clean room to seeing to his clothes, to making sure that his entire day goes smoothly from the moment he rises to the time he goes to bed." There is no reason why Hudson cannot serve as the software developer's equivalent, with the obvious difference that Hudson must be taught everything whereas a valet is supposed to anticipate the needs of his man before he knows he has them.

This usage of Hudson, called Hudson-as-valet for discussion, is actually one of the initial inspirations for its initial creation. In a 2008 interview for the book *Secrets of the Rockstar Programmers*, Kohsuke Kawaguchi, the initial creator of Hudson, had this to say about optimizing your work environment:

> *It's a good thing to keep investing some of your time to attack your repetitive work. Because when you remove one problem, you see another that you didn't realize, so this laziness is infinite. You see other things that you didn't realize. The keyboard macro might be one example. If you write keyboard macros enough, at a certain point it occurs to you that writing keyboard macros is a waste of time, and you find another way to meta-automate some of it. That's been true with me, I guess. There is no way to jump to this higher state; you have to explore it step by step.*

Kohsuke created Hudson as a way to make it easier for developers to jump to this higher state. In this higher state, using Hudson to get things done becomes a habit, not just something that runs the Continuous Integration jobs.

There are many other ways to achieve the same result as a Hudson-as-valet setup, such as Apple Automator or Windows AutoHotKey. Getting into the habit of baking your optimizations into a Hudson-as-valet instance has a few advantages over these approaches:

- It is cross-platform. The same kind of setup can be deployed regardless of the host OS.
- It is self-contained. The setup can be migrated from workstation to workstation easily.
- It is easy to back up, as described in Chapters 1 and 3.

But the approach also has some downsides:

- The automation cannot manipulate GUI elements in the desktop, as is possible with Apple Automator and Windows AutoHotKey.
- Care must be taken to minimize the performance impact the Hudson-as-valet instance has on the development workstation.
- As with any piece of complexity, it must be maintained to ensure it doesn't grow unwieldy over time.

Optimal Hudson-as-Valet Setup

Chapter 1 includes instructions for causing Hudson to start when a workstation starts up or the user logs in. This technique is well suited to Hudson-as-valet usage. The startup instructions in Chapter 1 use the built-in server instance inside the Hudson war, or the lightweight Apache Tomcat server. With Hudson-as-valet, resource consumption needs to be minimized so that the Hudson instance doesn't get in the way of the productivity of the workstation on which it is running. For this reason, using a full-fledged application server or a multinode Hudson setup is not appropriate for Hudson-as-valet usage.

TIP

One way to get around this problem is to have a spare old computer running alongside the primary workstation to run Hudson-as-valet. This need not be a high-performance computer because many of the Hudson-as-valet type jobs can be scheduled to run a few hours before the workday starts. It works well to have the hard disks of the primary workstation exported so they can be mounted by the Hudson-as-valet machine. Make sure to have exactly the same user permissions on the Hudson-as-valet machine as on the primary workstation, so that when Hudson creates files, they are created with exactly the same permissions as if you had created them manually yourself. For energy savings, the OS facilities for scheduled automatic startup can be used on both the main workstation and on the Hudson-as-valet machine. This should be done so that the main workstation starts ten minutes before the Hudson-as-valet machine. This allows the Hudson-as-valet machine to mount the file systems from the main workstation and start to execute jobs that write to that file system. For added portability, the Hudson-as-valet instance can be installed in a VM running on the spare old computer.

Another important point is to ensure Hudson-as-valet is running on an uncommon port. The port 7214 used in Chapter 1 is such a port. Finally, make Hudson aware of all the development tools on the workstation, or if the Hudson-as-valet is running on a different machine, make sure to install exactly the same versions of development tools. This means basically all the tools in the Configure System page of Hudson: JDK, Git, Ant, and Maven.

Hudson for Work Area Maintenance

By this point in the book it has become clear that the practice of maintaining a software project that builds cleanly and reliably, correctly resolving dependencies, and running tests is challenging over time. As the software project evolves, dependencies and requirements can change, and this causes continual maintenance over time. If you've ever tried to check out and build an open source project for which such maintenance has long since ceased, you'll know the importance of this maintenance to the vitality of a software project. Such an effort often leads to a lot of hacking, manually downloading back-level dependencies, as well as probably a few shell scripts to fill in the gaps of the build process that simply no longer works. Hudson can help prevent getting into this situation in the first place by always ensuring that the software of interest is kept in a buildable, and therefore easily maintained, state.

The Open-Source Liaison Role

Let's take the case of tracking development of open source software. With the rising and ever-increasing importance of open source software (OSS) in enterprise development, it's not uncommon for projects that rely on open source software to need to keep close tabs on its development so they may quickly incorporate new releases, while ensuring that changes to the stack do not disrupt existing functionality. A workflow could be described in which one member of the team might be responsible for keeping tabs on the OSS projects on which the wider team depends. This team member could be thought of as the OSS liaison, and in this capacity they would stay current on the mailing lists for the OSS projects of interest and be able to check out and build the code, producing customized builds incorporating local fixes if necessary. Hudson can be an essential part of making this easier. This section gives a few tips for using Hudson in this way. There is an enormous amount of OSS out there, and much of it is written in Java. This is the sort that is easiest to build with Hudson and what will be covered in this section. However, the authors acknowledge that when measuring by lines of code available, more OSS is *not* written in Java than is. Even though Hudson is written in Java, it is perfectly capable of building software written for any other programming platform. Doing so is left as an exercise for the reader. This section will walk through the steps of building Apache Tomcat and Google Guava with a view toward filling the open-source liaison role on those projects.

Apache Tomcat

Many of the examples in this book use Apache Tomcat, but this section shows how to set up your Hudson-as-valet to build it from source. The process is surprisingly simple considering how widely used Tomcat is. Create a new job on your Hudson-as-valet instance that reflects the project and the source code line for that project, such as tomcat-trunk. When using Hudson-as-valet, one must decide where to store the jobs. As mentioned earlier, it's very convenient to have the Hudson instance write its files directly into your main workstation's work area. This approach requires clicking the Advanced button in the Advanced Job Options section, then clicking the "Use a custom workspace" check box, and filling in the fully qualified directory for Hudson to use as its workspace. This must be done for each job on the Hudson-as-valet instance. Another approach is to simply use the default and get comfortable using the change directory (**cd**) command to get to the Hudson workspace from outside of Hudson. We will bootstrap the tomcat-trunk job using Hudson itself. First, create the job with just the svn URL http://svn.apache.org/repos/asf/tomcat/trunk. If you will be checking out a specific branch of Tomcat, use that svn URL instead, but use a different job name to reflect the different source code line. For example, the Hudson job tomcat-55x could be using the svn URL http://svn.apache.org/repos/asf/tomcat/archive/tc5.5.x/trunk/. Run the job once to cause the source code to be checked out.

TIP

One thing to watch out for with this approach is the impact of using different versions of the same SCM system inside and outside of Hudson. If the Hudson instance is using a newer version of the same SCM system than you are using from the command line in the course of normal development, a situation could arise where Hudson effectively corrupts the work space due to incompatibilities between the versions of SCM. For example, Subversion 1.6 and 1.7 introduced some incompatibilities between the local workspace representation. Another way to get around this is to use an Execute shell builder at the top of the job that manually invokes the SCM commands to update the workspace, for example, **svn checkout** *URL. With this technique, you can guarantee that the exact same SCM executable is used by the Hudson job and by the developer outside of Hudson. One downside of this approach is that Hudson loses the ability to poll SCM to trigger jobs or view changes since last build.*

Once the job has successfully checked out the source code, change the directory to the place where the source was checked out and find the top-level directory containing the main build.xml file. Tomcat still uses Ant as its build system, and has a home-grown dependency management solution that must be told where to put downloaded dependencies. This is done by placing a build.properties file in the same directory as the build.xml file. This pattern was commonplace before the emergence of Maven and can be used to customize many aspects of Ant-based builds. In this case the only customization is to indicate where dependencies must be stored and fetched. This is done by including the following line in build.properties for UNIX-based systems:

```
base.path=/fully/qualified/path/to/a/writable/empty/directory
```

Windows-based systems must use something like this:

```
base.path=c:\\DOCUME~1\\username\\path\\to\\a\\writable\\empty\\directory
```

Note that backslashes must be escaped and that directory names containing spaces must be avoided. To find the space-free name for a directory with spaces in Windows, use the command **dir /x** in the parent directory of the directory with spaces.

Now that the source has been checked out and the work area has been configured with instructions on where to put downloaded dependencies, return to the Hudson job configuration, change your **svn checkout** command to **svn update**, and add an Invoke Ant build step. Fill in **deploy** in the Targets field. If the build.xml file is not at the top level of the workspace, click Advanced and specify the location of the Build File, for example, **trunk/build.xml**. The version of Ant used when writing this text was 1.9.0 on JDK 1.7.0_21. If Java 7 is not the default on your system, click "This build is parameterized" and add a String property with the name JAVA_HOME and the value of the full path to a JDK 7 instance on your system. Set the job to run with the desired frequency by checking the "Build periodically" box in the Build Triggers section. In the open-source liaison role, it is important to use Hudson-as-valet to stay current on the projects you track. Therefore, it is best to set some kind of periodic build policy for tracked projects so that you can quickly become aware of any build failures that may be introduced as the project evolves.

Google Guava

Google Guava is a popular set of Java utilities that happened to appear at Google not long after Joshua Bloch joined Google from Sun. Guava is hosted in Google code under Git and uses Maven to build. The Git repository URL is https://code.google.com/p/guava-libraries/. The same iterative process as with Tomcat can be used here. Create the guava-trunk job and use Git as the SCM, using the preceding URL. Run the build once to check out the code, then change the directory to the workspace to perform an additional modification. Let's assume that we ran into trouble building Guava from source: the guava-gwt module doesn't build correctly. Perhaps the problem is due to the headless nature of the host on which Hudson is running. In any case, this illustrates a technique that can be useful when fulfilling the role of open source liaison: applying local changes to the open source project when building for internal use.

Let's assume that our usage of Guava does not include its GWT integration, and therefore we can disregard any changes in that part of the software. A brute-force, but effective, way to ensure that changes in this part of the software do not interfere with our work is to simply comment out the build from traversing into the guava-gwt module. Open the top-level pom.xml in a text editor, find the line <module>guava-gwt</module>, and comment it out, as follows.

```
<!-- Not interested in guava-gwt integration, and the build failed there anyway
<module>guava-gwt</module>
-->
```

After saving this edit, execute this **git** command to cause the local changes to be stored in the Git "stash":

```
git stash
```

The stash is an anonymous branch that stores changes that can subsequently be applied with other Git commands. This is necessary because Hudson will overwrite any local changes when it updates the workspace using Git. The checkout strategy can be configured to not clean up the workspace if local modifications are made. This is not necessary when the SCM is Subversion. Back in the job configuration, an additional build step must be added, *before the Maven 3 build step*, that applies the stash before building the code. In the Build section, click the "Add build step" drop-down and choose "Execute shell." In the text area that appears, type:

```
git stash apply --list
```

This will apply the changes from the stash on top of the freshly checked-out branch, in this case, commenting out the guava-gwt module.

Click the "Add build step" button once again and choose Invoke Maven 3. The goals should be **clean install** and in the properties section, add **maven.test.skip=true**. Ideally, this step should not be needed, but in practice, with many open source projects, the tests are not always maintained in a 100 percent runnable state. If you are not making any substantive changes to the project locally anyway, it may not be necessary to run the tests. If you want to make sure the tests run cleanly, simply omit adding this property. This will cause the build to fail if the unit tests fail, which may be the desired behavior after all. If desired, add a "Build periodically" Build Trigger as with Tomcat in the preceding section, obviously choosing a different time. Alternatively, you could configure all your OSS builds to happen one after the other using interjob dependencies, as mentioned in Chapter 3.

There is a lot more to filling the open-source liaison role than just building the software, but as far as Hudson is concerned, this section has shown the basics.

The Committer Role

In the open-source liaison role described in the preceding section, the person filling the role may or may not have commit access to the OSS projects he or she is tracking. Usually such a role is not a full-time job, and the same individual will be a committer on one or more other projects.

TIP
In projects using Git, this task is made considerably easier thanks to the strong support in that SCM for branching and merging.

This section covers a potential Hudson-as-valet use case for the committer role. In many organizations, each developer is only working on a small handful of different projects at any given time, perhaps even only one. Within the scope of that handful of projects, it is common to be working on several kinds of programming tasks on any given day. For example, part of the day could be spent on developing new features, while another part of the day could be spent fixing bugs, reviewing code, or writing documentation. In such an arrangement, one would need to have several copies of the workspace for that project checked out on their workstation, each with its own set of changes in progress. Because other team members are also likely working on the same project, it becomes necessary to maintain several copies of the workspace so that any changes made by other developers are cleanly merged in. This helps to avoid a potentially difficult merge in the case when a developer must go for a longer period of time between commits, as is sometimes inevitably necessary.

Let's take an analogy from the real world. Imagine an automotive garage with several service bays as shown here:

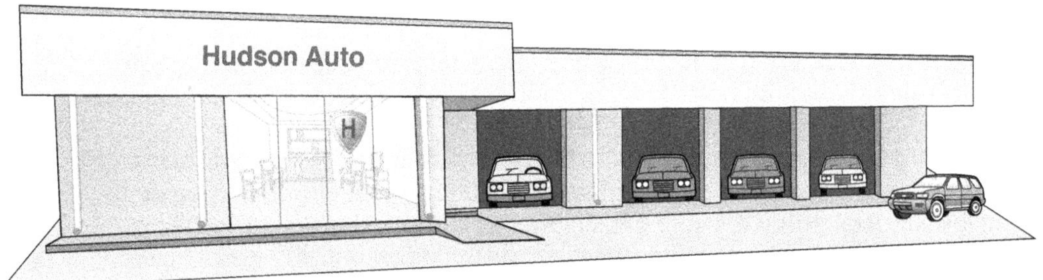

Each service bay can have at most one car at a time. The length of time each service bay is occupied with a car depends on the difficulty of the fix. During the length of time a car is in a service bay being fixed, tools are being used and placed aside, the car is in a state of partial disassembly, and things can get in a state of general messiness unless care is taken during the fix to keep things organized.

The service bays in the automotive garage can be likened to the several copies of the same workspace on a developer's workstation. Hudson-as-valet can be employed to keep each workspace organized and easy to work in, using the same techniques as described in the open source liaison role. A simple expansion of the naming convention for Hudson jobs can be employed to keep things organized. Let's say the project in question is called payroll and you have four copies of the workspace locally, each with its own fix-in-progress. The payroll project has two source lines: 1.0 and trunk. A potential arrangement of work spaces could be:

- payroll-1-trunk
- payroll-2-trunk
- payroll-1-1_0
- payroll-2-1_0

The first two work on fixes going into the trunk code line, and the second two into the 1.0 branch. The Hudson-as-valet instance would be sure to check out, build, and run the tests on each of these local workspaces so that any local changes that are not yet ready for commit can be kept up to date as other changes to the source code are made. Agile best practices recommend committing early and often, so it is best to avoid having changes sit out in such workspaces outside of SCM for any longer than necessary.

TIP

On UNIX systems, filesystem soft links can be used to indicate the issue number being worked on in each workspace, for example: **ln -s payroll-1-trunk issue-2817**. *This makes it easy to keep straight which fixes correspond to which workspace. Note that Application Lifecycle Management tools such as Eclipse Mylyn and JDeveloper Team Productivity Center may have better ways to organize such a workflow, but this lightweight approach can be handy in less formal environments.*

Hudson as General-Purpose Scheduler

In another insight from Kohsuke Kawaguchi's interview in *Secrets of the Rockstar Programmers*, he mentions that the first version of Hudson was really just a wrapper around the UNIX cron(8) command. In general, once you have Hudson, you have no more need for cron. Therefore, if you were using cron for sysadmin work, stop doing so and move those cron jobs into Hudson.

Hudson Plot Plugin

The Hudson Plot plugin can be downloaded from the Others subtab of the Available tab of the Hudson Plugin Center. The Plot plugin is designed to capture one or more single value data points each time a job is executed. Each data point contributes to a data series such that over time, with enough data points, a meaningful plot graph can be produced, providing a graphical representation of arbitrary data. For example, a Hudson job could execute a script that polls the hosts in a server farm to quantify the number of servers that are up at the time the job executes. This data could be captured to a CSV file located in the top level of the workspace for the job. Note that only a single point can be plotted per job execution.

Once the plugin is installed and Hudson restarted, configuration is done on a per-job basis. Find the text "Plot build data" in the Post-build Actions section and check the corresponding check box. Each plot can have an arbitrary number of data series, but keep in mind that each data series can have only one value per job execution. If you have a data file that has multiple values, there is no way to have them all displayed by this plugin in one go. Figure B-1 shows the configuration section for the "Available Hosts" example.

The plugin supports .properties, .csv, and .xml file formats, but because only one data value is plotted per job execution, .csv is the easiest. The data.csv file, which would be written out by the script that does the polling, is shown here:

```
"Available Hosts"
12
```

Now when the job executes, a Plots button appears on the job dashboard. Figure B-2 shows the output of the Available Hosts plot.

Even though the "one value per job execution" limitation may seem daunting, if you keep in mind that the purpose of this plugin is to allow displaying of data sampled over time, there are many potential uses, particularly for the creative sysadmin.

✓ Plot build data

Delete Plot

Plot group: Available Hosts

Plot title: Available Hosts

Number of builds to include

Plot y-axis label: Number of Hosts Online

Plot style: Line

Build Descriptions as labels

Data series file: data.csv

Load data from properties file

Load data from csv file

Include all columns	Include columns by name	Exclude columns by name	Include columns by index	Exclude columns by index
⦿	○	○	○	○

CSV Exclusion values

URL

Display original csv above plot

Load data from xml file using xpath

Delete Data Series

Add

A new data series definition

FIGURE B-1. *Plot Plugin configuration*

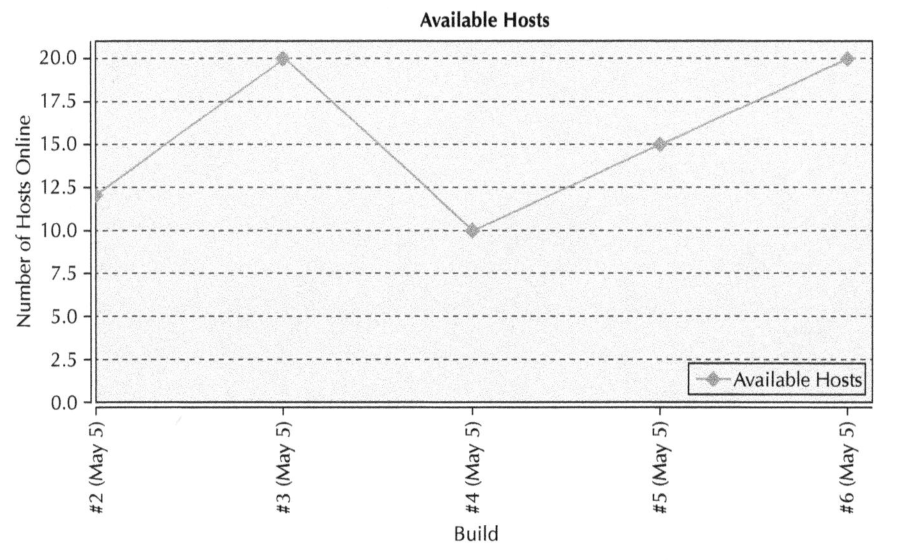

FIGURE B-2. *Available Hosts plot*

Summary

This appendix explores how to get back to Hudson's roots as a personal assistant, rather than just as a team enabling tool. Because this usage of Hudson is wide open and limited only by a user's own intentions, only two techniques are explored with a view toward how other usages may be accomplished in a similar fashion:

- Hudson for Work Area Maintenance
- Hudson as General-Purpose Scheduler

APPENDIX C

Hudson for Windows Developers

While the bulk of developers using Hudson are doing so to develop software for the Java platform, there is nothing inherent in the design of Hudson to prevent its being used to develop software for non-Java platforms. This chapter surveys a few of the non-Java platforms where Hudson is used in practice. Before taking some concrete examples, let's examine the usage at a higher level.

Key Enablers for Using Hudson on Non-Java Platforms

Let's review the basic Hudson workflow, shown in Figure C-1.

The Build and Collect Results boxes are the places with the most sensitivity to the target software platform. Let's take a look at the non-Java aspects for each of those steps.

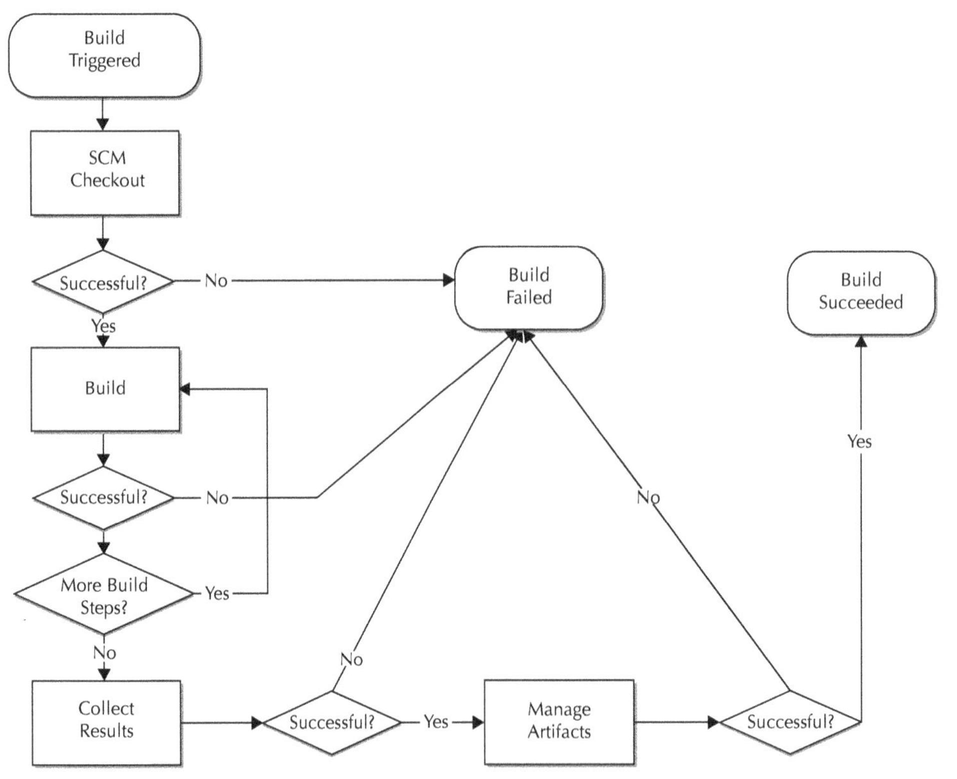

FIGURE C-1. *Hudson workflow*

Build Step

The Hudson concept of builder is defined in Chapter 2. A builder is anything Hudson can call to perform the action of the Build box in Figure C-1. A job can have zero or more builders, and each one can either fail or succeed. Usually a failure means there was an issue with the build, but the system can be configured to proceed in spite of a failed builder. It is helpful to think of builders as falling into one of two categories: integrated with Hudson and separate from Hudson.

Builders that are integrated with Hudson are known by Hudson and have more complete access to the rest of the Hudson build lifecycle. Hudson "knows" about integrated builders. Hudson comes pre-configured with plugins that provide builders with first-class support for Maven and Ant. There are also a wide variety of plugins available, but most of them are for developing for the Java software platform. Later in this appendix three non-Java builders will be covered, for the Microsoft .NET platform, for the Ruby platform, and for the PHP platform.

There is only one builder in the "separate from Hudson" category, and it is represented by the Execute Shell builder. On all platforms where Hudson can run, the Execute Shell build step is a very serviceable fallback to call into whatever native build system is appropriate for the target software platform. In practice, the biggest drawback to using Execute Shell instead of a integrated builder is brittleness. When invoking the shell, the only way Hudson knows if the build step succeeded or failed is the return code from the shell. Such return codes can be error prone to maintain in a cross-platform environment.

Collect Results Step

Hudson performs this step by means of one or more post-build actions. As shown in Chapter 5, the set of available post-build actions depends on what plugins are installed.

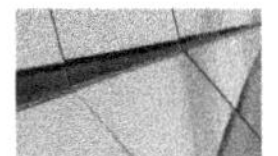

TIP

While Hudson allows for an ordered flow of zero or more builders, the post-build actions are not organized that way. Once a decision has been made to make use of an Execute Shell build step, the distinction of what is "build" and what is "post-build" can become arbitrary. This can lead to using Hudson to simply trigger builds that are collections of Execute Shell builders, some of which build software and others of which collect results. This is certainly an acceptable use of Hudson because the build triggering and artifact distribution features (as described in Chapter 6) of Hudson can be used without regard to the target software platform.

There is no analogous distinction between integrated and separate collect results steps as there is with builders. As such, the non-Java platform offerings for this step are limited to what plugins are available for the specific non-Java software platform in question. These plugins are all in the Others subtab of the Available tab of the Hudson Plugin Center. As such, they are not officially supported by the Hudson Project, so their quality is not guaranteed. The following table lists some details of selected plugins that perform the Collect Results step for non-Java software platforms.

Plugin Name: CCCC	
Description	A SourceForge project created by someone for their master's degree. The project is a code counter for C and C++. Its most recent update was on 22 April 2013.
Version Reported in Plugin Center	0.6
Release Date Reported on Plugin Homepage	24 November 2011
Plugin Name: CCM	
Description	Calls out to the CCM tool for analyzing cyclomatic code complexity in C, C++, C#, JavaScript, and TypeScript. Last updated in October 2012.
Version Reported in Plugin Center	2.5
Release Date Reported on Plugin Homepage	21 December 2010.
Plugin Name: cppcheck	
Description	Another SourceForge project to perform static analysis of C and C++ code. Last updated on 30 April 2013.
Version Reported in Plugin Center	1.14-h-1
Release Date Reported on Plugin Homepage	29 January 2013
Plugin Name: cppncss	
Description	A SourceForge project to perform static analysis of C++ code. Last updated on 3 August 2007.

Version Reported in Plugin Center	1.0
Release Date Reported on Plugin Homepage	3 June 2010
Plugin Name: MSTest	
Description	Runs the MSTest tool distributed with Microsoft Visual Studio to run automated tests on that platform. Converts the test results into JUnit XML format.
Version Reported in Plugin Center	0.6
Release Date Reported on Plugin Homepage	11 February 2010
Plugin Name: Ruby Metrics	
Description	Use the Rcov tool to collect metrics from Ruby code and collect the results for display on a Hudson trend graph. Last updated May 2012.
Version Reported in Plugin Center	1.4.6
Release Date Reported on Plugin Homepage	27 November 2010

Hudson and the Windows Software Platform

The MSBuild plugin, available in the Others subtab of the Available tab of the Hudson Plugin Center, is a solid and simple builder to invoke the MSBuild.exe executable that comes with Microsoft Visual Studio. Once the plugin has been installed and Hudson has been restarted, visit the Configure System page of the Manage Hudson page and find the text "MSBuild installations." One or more MSBuild installations can be identified in this section. The rationale for allowing multiple distinct MSBuild installations is the same as for allowing multiple versions of other types of builders, such as Ant or Maven: the version lineup is explained in Chapter 5.

Figure C-2 shows the completed values for Microsoft Visual Studio Express 2012 for Windows Desktop. The key value is the fully qualified path to the MSBuild.exe file. Note that backslash characters need not be escaped. Save the configuration after filling in the values.

MSBuild

MSBuild installations

MSBuild
Name msbuild
Path to MSBuild C:\Windows\Microsoft.NET\Framework\v4.0.30319\MSBuild.exe
Default parameters
Install automatically
Delete MSBuild
Add MSBuild
List of MSBuild installations on this system

FIGURE C-2. *Visual Studio MSBuild installation*

After identifying the MSBuild installation to the Hudson system, a new type of entry shows up in the "Add build" step: Build a Visual Studio project or solution using MSBuild. The MSBuild plugin relies on the fact that MSBuild is capable of building a .sln or .proj project file previously produced by Visual Studio. The build output produced by such a file is entirely determined by the individual composition of the Visual Studio project file. As with any Hudson builder, there can be as many build steps as necessary; and the post-build artifact collection is also identical, as with any other Hudson job.

TIP
Some versions of Microsoft Windows have a relatively small limit for the maximum allowable path length: 260 characters.

Figure C-3 shows a filled-in MSBuild build step. The command-line arguments to MSBuild provide considerable flexibility in building the project from the command line. In particular the /target: attribute (abbreviated /t:) takes a semicolon-separated

Build

Build a Visual Studio project or solution using MSBuild
MSBuild Version msbuild
MSBuild Build File HudsonForNonJavaDevelopers\01_msbuild\ConsoleApplication1\ConsoleApplication1.sln
Command Line Arguments
Pass build variables as properties
Continue Job on build Failure
Delete
Add build step

FIGURE C-3. *MSBuild Build step*

list of build targets. As with Ant and Maven builders, the decision to use multiple MSBuild build steps versus one MSBuild build step with multiple targets is a matter of taste.

Once configured, the build will run as a regular Hudson build. The following build output illustrates a successful invocation of MSBuild.

```
Started by user anonymous
Checkout:workspace / C:\HUDSON_HOME\jobs\01_msbuild\workspace - hudson.
remoting.LocalChannel@5c4ec4c4
Using strategy: Default
Last Built Revision: Revision e746b965f50d4f9aeb8300f6f-
4b79ccca936f43b (origin/master)
Checkout:workspace / C:\HUDSON_HOME\jobs\01_msbuild\workspace - hudson.
remoting.LocalChannel@5c4ec4c4
Fetching changes from the remote Git repository
Fetching upstream changes from https://hudson_in_practice@bitbucket.
org/hudson_in_practice/hudson_lifestyle.git
Commencing build of Revision e746b965f50d4f9aeb8300f6f-
4b79ccca936f43b (origin/master)
Checking out Revision e746b965f50d4f9aeb8300f6f4b79ccca936f43b (origin/
master)
Path To MSBuild.exe: C:\Windows\Microsoft.NET\Framework\v4.0.30319\MS-
Build.exe
Executing the command cmd.exe /C C:\Windows\Microsoft.NET\Framework\
v4.0.30319\MSBuild.exe HudsonForNonJavaDevelopers\\01_msbuild\\Console-
Application1\\ConsoleApplication1.sln && exit %%ERRORLEVEL%% from C:\
HUDSON_HOME\jobs\01_msbuild\workspace
[workspace] $ cmd.exe /C C:\Windows\Microsoft.NET\Framework\v4.0.30319\
MSBuild.exe HudsonForNonJavaDevelopers\\01_msbuild\\ConsoleApplica-
tion1\\ConsoleApplication1.sln && exit %%ERRORLEVEL%%
Microsoft (R) Build Engine version 4.0.30319.17929
[Microsoft .NET Framework, version 4.0.30319.17929]
Copyright (C) Microsoft Corporation. All rights reserved.

Building the projects in this solution one at a time. To enable paral-
lel build, please add the "/m" switch.
Build started 5/13/2013 10:57:01 PM.
Project "C:\HUDSON_HOME\jobs\01_msbuild\workspace\HudsonForNonJa-
vaDevelopers\01_msbuild\ConsoleApplication1\ConsoleApplication1.
sln" on node 1 (default targets).
ValidateSolutionConfiguration:
  Building solution configuration "Debug|Any CPU".
Project "C:\HUDSON_HOME\jobs\01_msbuild\workspace\HudsonForNonJa-
vaDevelopers\01_msbuild\ConsoleApplication1\ConsoleApplication1.
sln" (1) is building "C:\HUDSON_HOME\jobs\01_msbuild\workspace\Hudson-
ForNonJavaDevelopers\01_msbuild\ConsoleApplication1\ConsoleApplica-
tion1\ConsoleApplication1.csproj" (2) on node 1 (default targets).
```

```
GenerateTargetFrameworkMonikerAttribute:
Skipping target "GenerateTargetFrameworkMonikerAttribute" be-
cause all output files are up-to-date with respect to the input files.
CoreCompile:
  Copying file from "obj\Debug\ConsoleApplication1.exe" to "bin\Debug\
ConsoleApplication1.exe".
  ConsoleApplication1 -> C:\HUDSON_HOME\jobs\01_msbuild\workspace\Hud-
sonForNonJavaDevelopers\01_msbuild\ConsoleApplication1\ConsoleApplica-
tion1\bin\Debug\ConsoleApplication1.exe
  Copying file from "obj\Debug\ConsoleApplication1.pdb" to "bin\Debug\
ConsoleApplication1.pdb".
Done Building Project "C:\HUDSON_HOME\jobs\01_msbuild\workspace\Hud-
sonForNonJavaDevelopers\01_msbuild\ConsoleApplication1\ConsoleApplica-
tion1\ConsoleApplication1.csproj" (default targets).
Done Building Project "C:\HUDSON_HOME\jobs\01_msbuild\workspace\Hud-
sonForNonJavaDevelopers\01_msbuild\ConsoleApplication1\ConsoleApplica-
tion1.sln" (default targets).

Build succeeded.

    0 Warning(s)
    0 Error(s)

Time Elapsed 00:00:01.43
Finished: SUCCESS
```

Hudson and Automated Testing on Windows

As with automated testing on the Java platform, automated testing on the Windows platform is a deep topic. Thankfully, the project file input to MSBuild can be configured to run automated tests. The only trick then is to convert the output into a form more readily understandable by Hudson. Thankfully, the MSTest plugin converts the TRX output format into the JUnit XML format readily understood by Hudson. After installation and restart, a "Publish MSTest test result report" check box appears in the Post-build Actions section. Checking the box allows specifying a workspace relative path to a single TRX file. Multiple TRX files are not currently supported.

Summary

This appendix demonstrates that Hudson is perfectly useful in non-Java-based projects, specifically Windows-based projects. The basic Hudson workflow is reviewed, and two plugins that allow Windows development to proceed along that workflow are explored: MSBuild and MSTest.

Index

A

D

E

F

G

H

I

J

K

L

M

Q

R

S

V

W

X

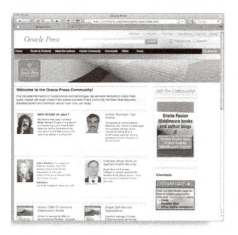

www.ingramcontent.com/pod-product-compliance
Lightning Source LLC
Chambersburg PA
CBHW080148060326
40689CB00018B/3893

* 9 7 8 0 0 7 1 8 0 4 2 8 8 *